Performance Management Systems

Performance management is the process by which organizations set goals, determine standards, assign and evaluate work, and distribute rewards. But when you operate across different countries and continents, performance management strategies cannot be one dimensional. The contrasts between east and west, collectivism against individualism for example, mean that HR managers need systems that can be applied to a range of cultural values – what works in London may cause disruption in Seoul. One size truly does not fit all.

This important and timely text offers a truly global perspective on performance management practices. Split into two parts, it illustrates, first, the key themes: motivation, rater–ratee relationships and merit pay, before outlining a model for a global appraisal process. This model is then screened through the situations in a range of countries, including:

- U.S.A.
- Mexico
- United Kingdom
- France
- Germany
- Turkey
- India
- China
- South Korea
- Japan
- Australia

Using case studies and discussion questions, and written by local experts, *Performance Management Systems: A Global Perspective* outlines the tools to understand and "measure" performance in a range of socioeconomic and cultural contexts. It raises, too, issues surrounding expatriate workers, and, in providing both comparative analysis and in-depth coverage, represents an excellent overview of this key aspect of globalization. This is essential reading for students and practitioners alike working in human resources, international business and international management.

Arup Varma is Indo-U.S. Professor of Management Studies at the Institute of Human Resources and Employment Relations, School of Business, Loyola University, Chicago. His research interests include performance appraisal, and expatriate issues.

Pawan S. Budhwar is a Professor of IHRM and Head of Work and Organisational Psychology Group at Aston Business School, U.K. He is the Director for the Aston India Foundation for Applied Business Research and Aston Centre for HRs.

Angelo DeNisi is Dean of the A.B. Freeman School of Business and Albert Cohen Chair in Business at Tulane University. His research interests include performance appraisal, expatriate management, and work experiences of persons with disabilities.

Routledge Global Human Resource Management Series

Edited by Randall S. Schuler, Susan E. Jackson, Paul Sparrow and Michael Poole

Routledge Global Human Resource Management is an important new series that examines human resources in its global context. The series is organized into three strands: Content and issues in global human resource management (HRM); Specific HR functions in a global context; and comparative HRM. Authored by some of the world's leading authorities on HRM, each book in the series aims to give readers comprehensive, in-depth and accessible texts that combine essential theory and best practice. Topics covered include cross-border alliances, global leadership, global legal systems, HRM in Asia, Africa and the Americas, industrial relations, and global staffing.

Managing Human Resources in Cross-Border Alliances
Randall S. Schuler, Susan E. Jackson and Yadong Luo

Managing Human Resources in Africa
Edited by Ken N. Kamoche, Yaw A. Debrah, Frank M. Horwitz and Gerry Nkombo Muuka

Globalizing Human Resource Management
Paul Sparrow, Chris Brewster and Hilary Harris

Managing Human Resources in Asia-Pacific
Edited by Pawan S. Budhwar

International Human Resource Management, 2nd edition
Dennis R. Briscoe and Randall S. Schuler

Managing Human Resources in Latin America
An agenda for international leaders
Edited by Marta M. Elvira and Anabella Davila

Global Staffing
Edited by Hugh Scullion and David G. Collings

Managing Human Resources in Europe
A thematic approach
Edited by Henrik Holt Larsen and Wolfgang Mayrhofer

Managing Human Resources in the Middle-East
Edited by Pawan S. Budhwar and Kamel Mellahi

Performance Management Systems

A Global Perspective

Edited by Arup Varma, Pawan S. Budhwar and Angelo DeNisi

Routledge
Taylor & Francis Group

LONDON AND NEW YORK

First published 2008
by Routledge
2 Park Square, Milton Park, Abingdon, Oxon OX14 4RN

Simultaneously published in the USA and Canada
by Routledge
270 Madison Ave, New York, NY 10016

Routledge is an imprint of the Taylor & Francis Group, an informa business

© 2008 Arup Varma, Pawan S. Budhwar and Angelo DeNisi

Typeset in Times New Roman by
RefineCatch Limited, Bungay, Suffolk
Printed and bound in Great Britain by
TJ International, Padstow, Cornwall

British Library Cataloguing in Publication Data
A catalogue record for this book is available from the British Library

Library of Congress Cataloging in Publication Data
Performance management systems : a global perspective / edited by Arup Varma,
Pawan S. Budhwar and Angelo DeNisi.
    p. cm.
Includes bibliographical references and index.
1. Performance technology—Management.   2. Performance—
Management.   I. Varma, Arup.   II. Budhwar, Pawan S.   III. DeNisi,
Angelo S.
    HF5549.5.P37P467 2007
    658.4′013—dc22
    2007041951

ISBN10: 0–415–77176–5 (hbk)
ISBN10: 0–415–77177–3 (pbk)

ISBN13: 978–0–415–77176–4 (hbk)
ISBN13: 978–0–415–77177–1 (pbk)

To my mother, Leelawati (AV)

To my mother, Daya Kaur (PSB)

To Adrienne, my partner and support wherever in the world I might go (AD)

Contents

Illustrations

Figures

Tables

Contributors

Zeynep Aycan, Department of Psychology, Koc University, Sariyer, Turkey.

Cordula Barzantny, Groupe ESC, Toulouse Business School, France.

Dennis R. Briscoe, University of San Diego, U.S.A.

Pawan S. Budhwar, Aston Business School, Aston University, Birmingham, U.K.

Lisbeth M. Claus, Atkinson School of Management, Willamette University, U.S.A.

Fang Lee Cooke, Manchester Business School, University of Manchester, Manchester, U.K.

Anabella Davila, Technologica de Monterrey, Garza Garcia, Mexico.

Helen De Cieri, Department of Management, Monash University, Victoria, Australia.

Angelo DeNisi, Dean, A.B. Freeman School of Business, Tulane University, New Orleans, U.S.A.

Deborah DiazGranados, Department of Psychology, University of Central Florida, Orlando, U.S.A.

Marta M. Elvira, Academic Dean, Lexington College, Chicago, U.S.A.

Marion Festing, ESCP-EAP European School of Management, Berlin, Germany.

Barry Gerhart, School of Business, University of Wisconsin-Madison, Madison, U.S.A.

Motohiro Morishima, Hitotsubashi University, Tokyo, Japan.

Rose A. Mueller-Hanson, Personnel Decisions Research Institute, Arlington, U.S.A.

Kevin R. Murphy, Pennsylvania State University, U.S.A.

Ryan S. O'Leary, Auburn University, Arlington, U.S.A.

Ryan Petty, School of Labor and Industrial Relations, Michigan State University, U.S.A.

Shaun M. Pichler, Michigan State University, U.S.A.

Robert D. Pritchard, Department of Psychology, University of Central Florida, Orlando, U.S.A.

Elaine D. Pulakos, Personnel Decisions Research Institute, Arlington, U.S.A.

Chris Rowley, City University, London, U.K.

Tanuja Sharma, Management Development Institute, India.

Cathy Sheehan, Department of Management, Monash University, Victoria, Australia.

Paul Sparrow, Centre for Performance-Led HR, Lancaster University Management School, U.K.

Charlie O. Trevor, School of Business, University of Wisconsin-Madison, Madison, U.S.A.

Arup Varma, Institute of Human Resources and Employment Relations, Loyola University, Chicago, U.S.A.

Hyuckseung Yang, School of Business, Yonsei University, Korea.

Serap Yavuz, Middlesex University Business School, London, U.K.

Foreword

Global HRM is a series of books edited and authored by some of the best and most well-known researchers in the field of global human resource management (HRM). This series is aimed at offering students and practitioners accessible, coordinated and comprehensive books in global HRM. To be used individually or together, these books cover two major perspectives of global HRM: comparative and international human resource management. Taking an expert look at an increasingly important and complex area of global business, this is a groundbreaking new series that answers a real need for serious textbooks on global HRM.

Several books in this series, **Global HRM**, are devoted to HRM policies and practices in multinational enterprises (MNEs). For example, some books focus on specific activities of global HRM policies and practices, such as global compensation, global staffing and global labor relations. Other books address special topics that arise in MNEs across the globe, such as managing human resources in cross-border alliances, developing strategies and structures, and developing the HRM function in MNEs. In addition to books on various HRM activities and topics in MNEs, several other books in the series adopt a comparative, and within region, approach to understanding global HRM. These books on comparative HRM can adopt two major approaches. One approach is to describe the HRM policies and practices found at the local level in selected countries in several regions of the world. The second approach is to describe the HRM issues and topics that are most relevant to the companies in the countries of the region.

This book, *Performance Management Systems: A Global Perspective*, utilizes both the MNE perspective and the comparative HRM perspective. That is, it addresses MNE issues in global PM *and* it provides an understanding of how PM is done in several countries around the globe. In order to provide the most expertise possible in undertaking this book, the authors have taken a co-editorship model. Together, Arup Varma, Pawan Budhwar and Angelo DeNisi have gathered many of the most knowledgeable researchers to produce an outstanding book that provides the reader with an excellent understanding of global performance in MNEs and in 11 major countries around the globe. In addition to writing an excellent Preface and several of the chapters themselves, the co-editors have done a superb job in organizing the contributions of almost 30 contributors from around the globe. Their introductory and concluding chapters are excellent, as are all of the other 15 chapters. This book is extremely well-conceptualized and well-written. No doubt it is a highly valuable book for any global human resource student and scholar or any global human resource professional.

This Routledge series, **Global HRM**, is intended to serve the growing market of global scholars and professionals who are seeking a deeper and broader understanding of the role and importance of HRM in companies as they operate throughout the world. With this in mind, all books in the series provide a thorough review of existing research and numerous examples of companies around the world.

Because a significant number of scholars and professionals throughout the world are involved in researching and practicing the topics examined in this series of books, the authorship of the books and the experiences of companies cited in the books reflect a vast global representation. The authors in the series bring with them exceptional knowledge of the HRM topics they address, and in many cases the authors have been the pioneers for their topics. So we feel fortunate to have the involvement of such a distinguished group of academics in this series.

The publisher and editor also have played a major role in making this series possible. Routledge has provided its global production, marketing and reputation to make this Series feasible and affordable to academics and practitioners throughout the world. In addition, Routledge has provided its own highly qualified professionals to make this series a reality. In particular we want to indicate our deep appreciation for the work of our series editor, Francesca Heslop. She has been very supportive of the series from the very beginning and has been invaluable in providing the needed support and encouragement to us and to the many authors in the series. She, along with her staff including Simon Whitmore, Russell George, Victoria Lincoln, Jacqueline Curthoys, Lindsie Court, Emma Joyes and Vicky Claringbull, has helped make the process of completing this Series an enjoyable one. For everything they have done, we thank them all.

Randall S. Schuler, Rutgers University and GSBA Zurich

Paul Sparrow, Lancaster University

Susan E. Jackson, Rutgers University and GSBA Zurich

Michael Poole, Cardiff University

Preface

Over the past few years, "globalizaton" has become a household word, perhaps due to advances in technology, and the rapid cross-national movement of people and organizations. One obvious outcome of this trend is the need for managers to deal with critical human resource issues in diverse settings, and with individuals from different cultures, with different motivations and expectations. Here, the context-specific nature of HRM makes it critical that managers deal with employees, both country nationals and expatriates, in a manner that is consistent with organizational policies as well as local norms.

Given that the individual employee plays perhaps the most critical role in helping organizations achieve their strategic goals, it is crucial that managers understand how to derive optimum performance from individuals in different countries. Thus, it is important, for example, that managers understand what motivates individuals to work hard in different cultures, and in different contexts. In a country where the manager's concern for the individual's family situation is seen as a major motivator, efforts to motivate through monetary rewards, or other similar means, are likely to fail. Similarly, an understanding of the type of relationship(s) individuals accept and expect from their supervisors is crucial to successful management of performance. For example, in high power-distance cultures, managers are often expected to provide detailed and specific guidelines, and their instructions are not likely to be challenged. On the other hand a laissez-faire or participative manager is likely to be frustrated at the lack of upward feedback and communication.

Undeniably, it is important that managers be aware of such differences and realize that the definition and understanding of performance vary significantly from country to country and that the appropriate management style(s) and strategies are also likely to vary significantly. In addition, the differences in relevant labor/employment laws and availability and use of technology need to be factored into the development and implementation of performance management systems (PMSs) in various nations. Too often, organizations rely on importing established and/or proven systems from the home country/office, without making enough allowances for the realities of the new location.

Clearly, the topic of performance management (PM) deserves close attention, both from academics and practitioners. Indeed, we believe that this is one topic within the broader domain of HRM that provides an automatic bridge between academia and the so-called "real world." From helping define performance to helping develop appropriate tools for measurement of performance, academics can inform practitioners in numerous ways. It is also important for business students to gain an understanding of the different issues relating to PM around the world. In this book, we have made an attempt to present and elaborate upon the key themes of PM, as well as detail how PMSs develop and operate in several leading economies.

Thus, the objective(s) of this volume are two-fold – to provide the reader (i) with an introduction to four key themes of global PM – PM in MNEs, motivation, rater–ratee relationships, and merit pay; and (ii) with an overview of PMSs in 11 countries whose economies have a major impact on global business – U.S., Mexico, U.K., France, Germany, Turkey, India, China, South Korea, Japan, and Australia. Clearly, these lists are not exhaustive, and certain other themes and countries should have been included. However, we are convinced that the inclusion of the key themes, and the coverage of the 11 countries listed above, will provide the reader with more than a flavor of PMSs around the world – indeed, the realization of the practical limitation of including more than a few key economies led to the conscious choice of including a chapter on PM in MNEs.

To achieve our above-stated objective, all country-wise chapters have been written around the core aspects of the framework presented in Chapter 6. This comprehensive framework covers critical pieces of the PM process, including, but not limited to, (i) industry and organizational norms, (ii) frequency and source(s) of appraisal, and (iii) individual and corporate goals. Through the use of this framework, the chapters provide detailed coverage of PMSs in the various countries, while at once allowing for a cross-national comparisons. So, for example, a reader interested in understanding how rater–ratee relationships might affect ratings in different nations will be able to map out the key similarities and differences with relative ease. All the chapters in this volume are original contributions to the field and were specially commissioned for the book.

The genesis of this project lies in the volume editors' interest and work in the area(s) of PM and global HRM. Also, this is a product of long discussions with the series editors and a number of colleagues on the need for such a book. Ironically, even though the issue of managing performance across the globe is of critical importance to MNEs, there isn't a single volume that deals with the critical issues involved. Further, while there are some books and articles dealing with PM issues in a few of the countries included in this volume, this is the first effort to provide information on PM in leading economies, in a single volume, and around a common framework. This book, then, fills a critical gap in the area, and we are confident that the contents will appeal to academics and practitioners, as well as students of business, with interests in PM, HRM, Global HRM and International Management.

We would, of course, be remiss if we did not thank all the people whose help and guidance helped this project to come to fruition. First, our sincere thanks to the series editors for their unwavering encouragement and support as this project evolved from a few hurriedly scribbled notes on coffee-shop-napkins to this final product. Next, we would like to thank the contributors of the various chapters for making time in their schedules to be a part of this effort. Special thanks are also due to the reviewers for providing invaluable comments and suggestions that helped improve the overall quality of this volume. Lastly, we would like to thank Francesca Heslop, Emma Joyes and Simon Whitmore at Routledge for their help and assistance at various stages of the production of this volume.

Arup Varma
Loyola University, Chicago

Pawan S. Budhwar
Aston Business School

Angelo DeNisi
Tulane University

Part I

1 Performance management around the globe: introduction and agenda

ARUP VARMA, PAWAN S. BUDHWAR AND ANGELO DeNISI

The increasing globalization of the world economy has led to the creation of the true multinational enterprise (MNE). While organizations are often able to successfully transfer and implement financial and technical systems to the new location, HR systems present unique challenges. Indeed, the literature on international HR issues has seen a steady stream of articles (e.g. Budhwar and Sparrow, 2002; Schuler, Budhwar and Florkowski, 2002) and books (e.g. Briscoe and Schuler, 2007) addressing the issues faced by MNEs in their people management processes (e.g. expatriate selection, hiring, etc.). However, one topic that has received scant attention is how performance management systems (PMSs) are implemented in different countries around the globe (Milliman, Nason, Gallagher, Huo, Von Glinow and Lowe, 1998). Here, it should be noted that performance management (PM) is the key process by which organizations set goals, determine standards, assign and evaluate work, and distribute rewards (Fletcher, 2001). Further, given that PMSs can help organizations ensure successful implementation of their business strategy (Schuler and Jackson, 1987), we believe this is a subject that deserves close attention.

There is no doubt that the subject of PM "across the globe" defies comprehensive coverage in one book. However, given the speed at which organizations are globalizing and becoming MNEs, along with the rapid rise of emerging markets, both researchers and policy makers are interested in finding out about the kind of HR and PMSs relevant to firms operating in different national contexts. In the absence of reliable literature, this book should prove very useful and timely both for the global corporation, and the global manager. We believe it fills a critical gap in the literature, for both academics and practitioners, by providing a comprehensive coverage of the performance management practices in key countries, with special emphasis on performance appraisal (PA), and some critical themes in PM.

While it is impossible to cover all or even a significant fraction of countries in one book, we have endeavored to provide a rather comprehensive coverage. To do this, we draw upon Ronen and Shenkar's (1985) model clustering countries on attitudinal dimensions, and the Goldman Sachs' report on BRIC countries (Wilson and Purushothaman, 2003). We cover four of the eight clusters from Ronen and Shenkar, and two of the four countries (India, China) from the BRIC report. This was indeed a difficult choice, as we would have liked to include all countries proposed by these two papers. However, this would have made the proposed volume extremely unwieldy. Perhaps the remaining countries can be included in a subsequent volume. The detailed information on PMSs in these countries, with special emphasis on PA, will allow the reader to become familiar with the unique nature of PM and PA systems in these countries. Furthermore, by presenting individual country information based on a single comprehensive model (presented in Chapter 6), the book will allow readers to compare and contrast the practices and processes in these nations, providing a comprehensive overview of a very critical HR process.

Global performance management

One of the critical issues facing MNEs is the management of their multinational workforce, through developing guidelines on how to staff, evaluate, compensate, and train in the international context. PMSs typically have two purposes: (i) administrative decisions, such as promotions, merit raises, and bonuses, and (ii) developmental goals, such as feedback and training (Murphy and Cleveland, 1995). It would seem that most organizations, especially MNEs, would be able to achieve these goals with ease, by setting up appropriate systems that specify the link between performance and outcomes. Indeed, many MNEs fall into this very trap, by implementing PM systems developed in the home country in host country locations. This is problematic, as most MNEs are based in the U.S., and performance may be difficult to evaluate appropriately outside the U.S. context by adopting U.S.-based models (Murphy and Cleveland, 1995).

Furthermore, the very construct of performance is multi-dimensional (Rao, 2004) and "culture-bound" (Aycan, 2005). As such, it is very likely that managers (and employees) view performance differently in different cultures, thus leading to both inter-cultural and intra-culture differences in definition and interpretation of performance. So, in an individualistic culture, the emphasis would be on individual effort and outcomes, calling for objective and quantifiable performance criteria (Harris and Moran, 1996). On the other hand, collectivist cultures are more likely to reward group loyalty, conformity, and harmonious relationships (Sinha, 1990; Tung, 1984).

Clearly, since performance is viewed differently in different cultures, the mechanisms to evaluate and manage performance must be designed to address the local context. For example, seeking feedback on one's performance may be viewed as appropriate and desirable in individualistic cultures like the U.S., but such behavior would be deemed out of place and highly inappropriate in a collectivist culture such as China (Bailey, Chen and Dou, 1997). Thus, an American manager hoping to foster improvements in his/her Chinese subordinates' performance through feedback, is likely to fail in his/her efforts. In this connection, Hempel (2001) has questioned the very use of Western appraisal methods in China, arguing that Chinese and Western views of performance differ significantly, given the differences in culture and social norms.

Next, it is clear that the goals of PMSs vary widely between locations of firms, thus impacting how individuals view performance. For example, in the U.S., performance appraisals are primarily geared towards determining individual rewards (Cardy and Dobbins, 1994), thus motivating individuals to work harder so they may achieve the desired rewards. On the other hand, in a collectivist culture like Japan, performance appraisals emphasize long-term potential (Pucik, 1984), thus encouraging individuals to develop their skills and competencies. Clearly, PMSs must be context-based, to make allowances for the unique circumstances and cultural norms of the location. While the success of all HR initiatives is context-dependent, effective PM calls for special attention to the national context, as issues of culture and legislation, for example, can have significant impact on the implementation and practice of PMSs. This is all the more critical as evaluations are the primary tool for the organization to assess performance, and thus assess the degree to which the MNE's objectives are being met by individual employees, both host country nationals and expatriates (Dowling and Schuler, 1990; Gregersen, Hite and Black, 1996).

In addition to managing the performance of host country nationals, MNEs must also concern themselves with the PM of expatriates, who increasingly form a significant portion of their workforce. Indeed, there is no clear and/or accepted definition of expatriate performance (Shaffer, Harrison, Gregersen, Black and Ferzandi, 2006), and several different criteria have been used to measure expatriate effectiveness, and even these vary widely from between organizations (Gregersen, Hite and Black, 1996; Shih, Chiang and Kim, 2005). Further, as Yan, Zhu and Hall (2002) argue, the expatriate's own goals should also be incorporated into the evaluation system. Ironically, Shih *et al.* (2005) report that expatriate evaluations are often treated as a mere extension of domestic evaluation systems, and that MNEs often use criteria and measures developed for domestic purposes.

Clearly, expatriate performance evaluations are vital to understand how well strategic objectives are being met, and to assess the expatriate's performance on the assignment. However, as Gregersen *et al.* (1996) noted, little scholarly attention has been paid to the development of performance evaluation systems specifically for expatriate assignments. Rather, it seems that expatriate performance evaluations are based primarily on U.S. appraisal models. Indeed, even non-U.S. MNEs often adopt U.S. appraisal models. Given that each expatriate performs in a unique context (i.e. in international locations), it is critical that expatriate appraisal systems take into consideration the unique environmental factors related to the expatriate's location, such as local laws, technology (Shen, 2005), and cultural norms (Tahvanainen, 2000). Apart from examining performance of expatriates, the importance of the impact of such factors is equally strong and worth considering while evaluating performance of any employees in a given national or local context. A due consideration to such forces will enable researchers to highlight the "context-specific" nature of PMS and provide a valid picture of the scene. The current volume is thus designed to take a global perspective on PM, by looking at input, mediators and moderators, and outcome variables of the same.

Structure of the book

This book is divided into two parts. In Part I, apart from this introductory chapter, we have included a chapter on PM in MNEs, and three chapters on critical themes in PM, namely, motivation, rater–ratee relationships, and merit pay. Chapters 2 to 5 each conclude with a short case study, followed by some thought-provoking questions. The case study and questions are designed to help the reader understand and apply the critical concepts presented. The last chapter in Part I (Chapter 6) presents a model of the appraisal process that has been incorporated into the country-specific chapters in Part II. Part II comprises ten chapters that present a comprehensive synopsis of PM practices in 11 selected nations. The final chapter (Chapter 17) is designed to help bring it all together – by highlighting the key findings and emphasizing key similarities and differences among PMSs in the various countries included in this volume and the avenues for future research.

In Chapter 2, Dennis Briscoe and Lisbeth Claus present a discussion of PM practices and policies in MNEs. They discuss how the increasing globalization has resulted in a proliferation of the MNE, and the unique issues associated with managing employees in MNEs. They also propose a model of performance in MNEs that incorporates both the global and organizational contexts. Under the global context, they discuss critical issues such as language and culture, emphasizing the crucial role that language differences can play in host country and home country individuals' interactions. Within the organizational context, the authors emphasize key factors such as organizational culture, structure, and strategy.

The second part of their chapter deals with the process of PM, starting with questions such as how evaluations should be done, and who should do them. In the international context, these are critical questions since, for example, the functional supervisor of the ratee may be located in the home country, while the administrative supervisor may be located closer to the expatriate, that is, in the host country. They next present a discussion of cognitive processes such as motivation and affect, which are known to moderate the performance-evaluation relationship. Finally, they discuss outcome factors such as rewards and organizational justice issues. They conclude by presenting a series of factors that often hinder the effective implementation of PMSs in the international context. By presenting a comprehensive model of PMSs in MNEs, the authors have provided a frame of reference for understanding PMS practices in the various countries included in Part II of this book.

Chapter 3 deals with the dynamics of motivation, and the impact of motivation levels on performance, and thus performance management. Here, Robert Pritchard and Deborah DiazGranados start by defining motivation (*allocating one's energy to actions or tasks*), and then discuss why it is important that managers understand what motivates individual employees, if they are to draw optimal levels of performance from them. They go on to identify ways in which managers might identify individual motivation levels, especially low levels of motivation. This is followed by a comprehensive discussion of their motivation model, which explores the links between the key components of the motivation process, namely, actions, results, evaluations, outcomes, and need satisfaction.

Next, the authors discuss the impact of culture (and cross-cultural issues) on motivation levels, and remind the reader that while the overall motivational process may cut across cultures, the unique and specific features of various cultures (e.g. diversity levels) make it critical that we recognize and understand the impact of culture on individual motivation. The authors conclude by presenting suggestions for future research on the link between motivation and performance management.

In Chapter 4, Shaun Pichler, Arup Varma, and Ryan Petty explore the impact of rater–ratee relationships on individual performance ratings, and the PM process as a whole. They start by highlighting the importance of the social context of PM, and go on to discuss how the type of relationship that develops between a rater and his/her ratees impacts the ratees' outcomes (e.g. performance ratings). Specifically, they discuss two key constructs (interpersonal affect, and leader–member exchange (LMX)) that have been studied to understand how rater–ratee relationships interact with, and impact, performance appraisal. The authors note that in both cases the literature suggests that ratees, who share a positive (or, good) relationship with the rater, are likely to receive inflated ratings. Thus, a rater who likes (i.e. high interpersonal affect condition) a ratee is likely to ignore the shortcomings of that ratee, and instead pay attention only to the positive aspects of his/her performance.

Furthermore, the authors note that while the literature on affect is somewhat equivocal on whether affect truly acts as a bias in the performance management process, the LMX literature is overwhelmingly consistent in its findings – that a good relationship (high LMX) with the rater helps the ratee receive higher ratings and other rewards than those with relatively poor relationships (low LMX), controlling for performance. The chapter also compares interpersonal affect and LMX, the two constructs that are similar, yet operate differently.

Chapter 5 deals with merit pay as it relates to PM. Here, Barry Gerhart and Charlie Trevor present the reader with a succinct discussion of the relationship between performance and rewards, specifically, merit pay. They start by discussing merit pay in the larger context of pay strategy, and also discuss numerous other pay-for-performance options, such as gain-sharing. This is followed by a discussion of the key policy aspects of merit pay systems, and the challenges often faced by organizations in implementing merit pay. For example, the authors argue that merit pay is often defined too narrowly, and that in order to implement merit pay policies appropriately, both raters and ratees need to understand the impact of performance ratings on individual pay. Through the use of several examples and exhibits, the authors explain the basics of merit pay and the numerous issues that organizations need to consider, if they are to attract, motivate, and retain appropriate talent.

Clearly, merit pay is an important outcome of PMSs. Furthermore, as Gerhart and Trevor point out, there needs to be substantial variance among performance ratings for merit pay to have a meaningful effect. However, in the global context, this may be easier said than done. For example, while variance in ratings may be relatively easier to achieve in individualistic countries (e.g. U.S.A.), this may be more difficult in collectivist countries, such as China. The authors conclude by summarizing a series of critical questions that organizations need to ask if they are to implement merit pay policies appropriately.

In Chapter 6, Kevin Murphy and Angelo DeNisi present a model to examine and highlight the appraisal process in different contexts. Given that the present volume deals with various perspectives on the PM process around the world, this chapter provides a set of unifying themes that can be used for the discussions of these perspectives.

The authors propose a two-part model that focuses on the PMS, with part one focusing on the PA process, while part two focuses on the broader PM issue. In the first part of the model, Murphy and DeNisi cover distal factors such as industry norms and the nation's legislative environment, and proximal factors such as the purpose of the appraisal and how well it is accepted. They propose that distal and proximal factors work through intervening factors, such as rater motivation and rater–ratee relationships to impact PM. Included in the first part of the model are distortion factors such as reward systems, and the consequences of the appraisal.

The second part of the model deals with feedback given to the ratee, and the gap between desired and observed performance levels. Here, PM interventions are introduced with the aim of reducing the gap, so as to help meet organizational and individual goals. Adopting the comprehensive framework proposed in this chapter has enabled authors of the country-specific chapters in this volume to comprehensively describe PMSs in different parts of the world, using a common theme.

In Chapter 7, Elaine Pulakos, Rose Mueller-Hanson and Ryan O'Leary discuss PM practices and policies in the United States. They start by discussing the history of the United States, and the development of its truly individualistic culture, which, in turn, has had a significant impact on the American workplace, in general, and PM in particular. Thus, for example, individual performance, accountability, and rewards are key themes of the PM process in the U.S.

The authors take the reader through a historical journey tracing the evolution of PMSs in the U.S., starting with Taylor's "scientific management," all the way through to competency-based human capital systems that became popular almost a hundred years after Taylor's initial efforts at defining and measuring performance.

The authors also discuss the key factors (results-focus automation, and legislation) that have shaped the way performance management operates in the U.S., and the key challenges that sometimes inhibit effective performance management (e.g. lack of open communication between rater and ratee). While it might seem that the key factors listed here are not unique to the U.S., it is important to note that given its unique history (emphasis on capitalism, world's leading economy, immigration from all over the world, etc.), these factors take on a special meaning in the context of PM. For example, legislation related to PM issues is very clear and specific, and both rater and ratee are almost always aware of the law and its implications. To underscore the importance of the legislative environment, the authors have provided specific guidelines for addressing legal requirements in the U.S., especially as these relate to PM. The authors also provide examples of performance standards, both for communicating expectations to employees, and for evaluating them. They conclude by discussing the role of automation in the PM process, and the importance of providing rater training.

Chapter 8 is devoted to discussing PMS in Mexico. Here, Anabella Davila and Marta Elvira present an overview of PMSs in Mexico, based on in-depth interviews conducted with senior HR professionals. The authors highlight the limited amount of published research on both HR and PM issues relating to Mexico. Davila and Elvira note that the practice of formal PMSs started in Mexico in the 1970s and was mostly adapted from U.S. systems. While Management by Objectives was used for senior management professionals, informal merit systems were often used for clerical and manufacturing workers. As far as unionized workers were concerned, there was very little in the way of PM.

The authors point out that one unintended impact of the introduction of formal PMSs in Mexico has been the over-emphasis on structure and systems, thus leaving little room for flexibility, something that is often required when dealing with individual performance, more so in a culture where issues such as supervisor–subordinate relationships play a major role in PMSs. In this connection, the authors highlight that most supervisors are unwilling to provide feedback as they have often not received any training in management skills or evaluation mechanisms. Overall, the authors note that PMS in Mexico is in its nascent stage, and while most organizations and senior executives agree that it is critical, the implementation leaves a lot to be desired.

In Chapter 9, Paul Sparrow presents a comprehensive discussion of PMS in the United Kingdom. Sparrow starts by discussing the socioeconomic, political, and legal issues that have impacted HRM in the U.K. He then discusses four specific developments that have had a significant impact on PMSs in the U.K., namely (i) emphasis on cost effectiveness, (ii) emphasis on the developmental aspect of PM, (iii) need to define performance clearly, and (iv) potential negative impact of PMS on strategy. Sparrow traces the evolution and implementation of these perspectives through a discussion of how managers and organizations view PMSs.

He then goes on to discuss three recent developments that have again changed the focus of HRM in the U.K., and also impacted the practice of PMSs, namely (i) talent management, (ii) employee segmentation, and (iii) total rewards management. The impact of the emphasis on talent management meant that PMSs were beginning to identify and reward those considered as "highly talented," while the related issue of employee segmentation led to PMSs being used to segment employees into one of five categories, based on their deemed contributions to the bottom-line. The final factor, total rewards management, led to the development of systems that assessed and rewarded individual performance in terms of monetary and non-monetary rewards, such as work–life balance and emotional needs.

Next, Sparrow discusses key factors that impact PMSs in the U.K., such as culture, rater–ratee relationships, and HR strategy. This is followed by a discussion of the key challenges to PMSs in the U.K., such as work–life balance and rater bias, increasing diversity of the workforce, and recent legislation on age discrimination. Overall, he argues that PMSs in the U.K. are rather mature, and able to change and evolve along with changes in socioeconomic, political, legal and strategic focus.

Chapter 10 presents a combined analysis of PMSs in France and Germany, authored by Cordula Barzantny and Marion Festing. It should be noted that the editors requested the authors to combine these two countries into one chapter, based on several concerns: (i) the importance of both countries as major economic players in Europe and the world, (ii) the convergence and divergence phenomenon of the European Union, and (iii) the space limitations of the volume.

The authors start by discussing the European context, which, they note, provides for an interesting study of convergent and divergent economies that are working to be a single unified economic entity while retaining their unique historical, social, and legal environments. They then discuss the European HRM systems, emphasizing the context-specificity of Europe, and reiterating that adapting U.S. models may not be the best solution for European companies' needs. The next section discusses PMSs in France, listing the unique characteristics of these systems, such as the legal requirement to invest in employee training, and the emphasis on individual accountability. This is followed by a discussion of the impact of the legal and cultural environments on PMSs in France, noting, for example, the high individualism and power distance features of French culture.

Next the authors discuss PMSs in Germany and the impact of the legal and cultural environment on PMSs there. Here, the authors emphasize the strict German legal environment, and the social market economy, and discuss how these affect PM. For example, the long-standing German practice of long-term employment relationships calls for PMSs to take the long-term view rather than emphasizing a short-term focus. Throughout the chapter, the authors note the similarities and the differences between the French and German contexts, enabling the reader to understand the convergence–divergence perspective as it relates to PMSs. For example, while both countries are similar when it comes to emphasizing long-term employment, France is rated high on femininity, while Germany is rated high on masculinity.

In Chapter 11, Zeynep Aycan and Serap Yavuz present an analysis of PMSs in Turkey. As Turkey gets ready to become a member of EU, its HR systems deserve a closer look. The authors start by discussing the socioeconomic and political background of the nation, noting some of its unique features, such as Turkey being a democratic, secular state, ruled by a single-party government. The authors also discuss changes in the Turkish economy since World War II, such as the continuing emphasis on economic liberalization and reforms.

Aycan and Yavuz then discuss the evolution of HRM and PMSs in Turkey, noting that PMS is a fairly new concept in Turkish HRM, and that there is very limited research on the subject. They then discuss the findings of two major surveys (Andersen, and Cranfield), which provide an overview of HRM in Turkey. Notable among these findings is the fact that by the year 2000, almost 80 percent of Turkish firms were using some form of PMS, even though only 30 percent reported that the PMS in their organizations met their needs.

Next, the authors discuss the cultural context of PMS in Turkey, noting that the society is slowly moving away from its traditional mores of collectivism, hierarchy, and uncertainty avoidance, although paternalism continues to play a major role in the Turkish workplace.

The passage of the new Labour Law (in 2003) is then detailed, along with several organizational variables that hinder effective implementation of PMS, such as family-owned businesses. The authors conclude by discussing several challenges for PMSs in Turkey, such as managers' unwillingness to rely completely on objective standards for performance, by ensuring that personal relationships do not impact their judgment.

Chapter 12 is devoted to describing and analyzing PMSs in India. Here, Tanuja Sharma, Pawan Budhwar and Arup Varma start by noting the current state of the Indian economy – which has been on "over-drive" since the early 1990s, when the government of India changed its economic policies to emphasize an open, capitalistic model. The authors present the history of PMSs in India, noting that while some organizations were using formal and often sophisticated systems decades ago, many others simply had no systems. The authors then discuss some recent changes in the Indian economy, such as the significant increase in the amount of FDI flowing into India, and the large number of Indian firms going global by acquiring firms in other nations, as well as establishing operations in different parts of the world. As the authors note, the arrival of MNEs in India has forced domestic Indian companies to revisit their HR systems, in general, and PMSs in particular, with many admitting a "new-found respect for PMS."

Next, the authors discuss the impact of economic and cultural factors on PMSs. For example, even though India is often listed as a collectivist nation, there has been a not-so-subtle change in recent times, with employees working toward short-term gains, and often emphasizing individual and immediate rewards. Clearly, PMSs need to be adjusted to account for this evolutionary change in culture. Alongside, the paternalistic nature of the Indian workplace also presents a unique challenge, as shop-floor workers continue to look to their supervisors to take care of them, while professionals, especially in the IT industry, tend to rely more on their skills and marketability for their career progression. Finally, the authors list a number of challenges to implementing PMSs in India, including the significant diversity of Indian organizations, in terms of size, structure, ownership, and strategic orientation.

In Chapter 13, Fang Lee Cooke discusses PMSs in China, and starts by noting that while PM is often talked of as a new western concept introduced to China recently, the truth is that a Chinese version of performance appraisal has been practiced in China for a very long time. The author has based her chapter on two sets of data – the first being a set of interviews she conducted with government officials in China, and the second being studies published in both English-language and Chinese-language journals. Furthermore, throughout the chapter, Cooke has provided excerpts from her interviews.

Cooke starts by providing an overview of HR systems in China, tracing the evolution of HR since the founding of the socialist state in 1949. Next, she discusses the development of PMSs in China. She notes that, from 1949 to the early 1980s, the emphasis in Chinese PM was on factors such as attendance and skills, while the post-1980s market reform era has seen widespread implementation of PMSs, both in the private and the public sectors.

The author then goes on to discuss some key factors that impact PMS, namely, organizational size, structure, and type of business. Next, Cooke discusses how culture influences PMSs, specifically noting unique features of the Chinese culture that have a strong influence on performance appraisal. These include respect for age and seniority, and the emphasis on harmony and "face." The author ends the chapter by discussing the major challenges faced by organizations and managers in implementing PMSs in China. These include (i) a lack of strategic goals at the organizational level, (ii) PA seen as a mere formality, (iii) high levels of subjectivity, and (iv) adoption of the collective peer appraisal method.

Chapter 14 is dedicated to discussing PMSs in South Korea. Here, Hyuckseung Yang and Chris Rowley start by emphasizing the impact of Confucian thought on South Korean society, which has impacted the workplace through emphasis on hierarchical relationships and collectivism. They then discuss two key developments that have transformed HRM systems in South Korea – namely, the establishment of a democratic government in 1987, and the Asian economic crisis of 1997.

While the financial crisis forced organizations to change their HRM practices, such as emphasizing individual performance and merit, the change in the political set-up resulted in an increase in individual freedom, and gave workers the right to organize unions and bargain collectively. All of these changes have impacted PMSs in South Korea, resulting in the adoption of output-based performance evaluations over the traditional seniority-based systems. The authors also discuss some limitations in the implementation of PMSs in South Korea, such as the failure of organizations to provide adequate training to raters, and the unwillingness of raters to provide feedback as a result of cultural influences. Overall, the authors note that while a majority of South Korean organizations have attempted to adopt *Yunbongje* (loosely translated as a meritocracy), strong cultural influences (e.g. collectivism) have often prevented successful implementation of PMSs.

In Chapter 15, Motohiro Morishima traces the evolution of PMSs in Japan. He starts by noting that Japanese HRM practices have moved beyond traditional practices such as lifetime employment and seniority to incorporate knowledge acquisition and new learning as critical factors. The author notes that the use of competency-based evaluations, and extensive in-house training, has helped organizations emphasize learning-centered HR systems. In the section following the introduction, the author discusses traditional Japanese HRM systems in some detail. It is noteworthy that traditional Japanese HRM emphasized the input side of the equation much more than the output, resulting in an often weak link between performance and outcomes.

Morishima then discusses the Japanese practice of life-time employment, followed by a discussion of the historical developments that have guided Japanese HRM, such as the economic growth of Japan in the 1970s. In the next section, he discusses the changes that have recently occurred in Japanese HRM, such as output-based evaluation and the emphasis on individual performance evaluations. He concludes the chapter by a discussion on procedural justice, a topic that is currently garnering a lot of attention in the Japanese workplace.

Chapter 16 covers PMSs in Australia. Here, Helen De Cieri and Cathy Sheehan start by discussing the history of industrialization in Australia, and trace the development of current norms that guide PM practices. They discuss changes in the Australian economy, such as the shift from manufacturing to service, and the increase in female and minority representation in the workforce. They also discuss the challenges posed by an ageing workforce, and the increasing use of contingent labour.

Next, the authors present a succinct discussion of the Australian legal system, elaborating upon six key issues related to PM. These are (i) documentation of appraisals, (ii) failure to punish poor performers, (iii) equal employment opportunity, (iv) employer responsibility in case of poor performers, (v) due process before employee dismissal, and (vi) termination of employment. Finally, they discuss factors such as the level of prevalence and acceptance of appraisal systems, as well as purposes and types of PMSs. A brief mention is also made of intervening factors, such as rater motivation and rater–ratee relationships – the brevity reflecting the lack of published literature on the subject.

The last chapter by Angelo DeNisi, Arup Varma and Pawan Budhwar presents a discussion on what has been learned from the different chapters, and suggests future research directions. In addition, the authors compare and contrast the reports of PM systems in different nations, to highlight the convergence and divergence of PM systems across the globe.

References

Aycan, Z. (2005) The interplay between cultural and institutional/structural contingencies in human resource management practices, *International Journal of Human Resource Management* 16(7): 1083–119.

Bailey, J. R., Chen, C. C. and Dou, S. G. (1997) Conceptions of self and performance-rated feedback in the U.S., Japan, and China, *Journal of International Business Studies*, 3rd quarter: 605–25.

Briscoe, D. R. and Schuler, R. S. (2007) *International Human Resource Management*, London and New York: Routledge.

Budhwar, P. S. and Sparrow, P. R. (2002) An integrative framework for understanding cross-national human resource management practices, *Human Resource Management Review* 12: 377–403.

Cardy, R. and Dobbins, G. (1994) *Performance Appraisal: Alternative Perspectives*, Cincinnati, OH: South-Western.

Dowling, P. J. and Schuler, R. S. (1990) *International Dimensions of Human Resources Management*, Boston, MA: PWS Kent.

Fletcher, C. (2001) Performance appraisal and management: the developing research agenda, *Journal of Occupational and Organizational Psychology* 74: 473–87.

Gregersen, H. B., Hite, J. M. and Black, J. S. (1996) Expatriate performance appraisal in U.S. multinational firms, *Journal of International Business Studies* 27: 711–38.

Harris, P. R. and Moran, R. T. (1996) *Managing Cultural Differences*, Houston, TX: Gulf.

Hempel, P. S. (2001) Differences between Chinese and Western managerial views of performance, *Personnel Review* 30(2): 203–26.

Milliman, J. F., Nason, S., Gallagher, E., Huo, P., Von Glinow, M. A. and Lowe, K. (1998) The impact of national culture on human resource management practices: the case of performance appraisal, in J. Cheng and R. B. Petersen (eds.) *Advances in International Comparative Management*, Greenwich, CT: JAI Press.

Murphy, K. R. and Cleveland, J. N. (1995) *Understanding Performance Appraisal: Social, Organizational, and Goal-based Perspectives*, Thousand Oaks, CA: Sage.

Pucik, V. (1984) White collar human resource management: a comparison of the U.S. and Japanese automobile industries, *Columbia Journal of World Business* 19: 87–94.

Rao, T. V. (2004) *Performance Management and Appraisal Systems: HR Tools for Global Competitiveness*, New Delhi: Sage.

Ronen, S. and Shenkar, S. (1985) Clustering countries on attitudinal dimensions: a review and synthesis, *The Academy of Management Review* 10(3): 435–54.

Schuler, R. S., Budhwar, P. S. and Florkowski, G. W. (2002) International human resource management: review and critique, *International Journal of Management Reviews* 4(1): 41–70.

Schuler, R. S. and Jackson, S. (1987) Linking competitive strategies with human resource management practices, *Academy of Management Executive* 1: 207–19.

Shaffer, M. A., Harrison, D. A., Gregersen, H., Black, J. S. and Ferzandi, L. A. (2006) You can take it with you: individual differences and expatriate effectiveness, *Journal of Applied Psychology* 91: 109–25.

Shen, J. (2005) Effective international performance appraisals: easily said, hard to do, *Compensation & Benefits Review* 37(4): 70–79.

Shih, H. A., Chiang, Y. H. and Kim, I. S. (2005) Expatriate performance management from MNEs of different national origins, *International Journal of Manpower* 26: 157–76.

Sinha, J. B. P. (1990) *Work Culture in the Indian Context*, New Delhi: Sage.

Tahvanainen, M. (2000) Expatriate performance management: the case of Nokia Telecommunications, *Human Resource Management* 37: 267–75.

Tung, R. L. (1984) Human resource planning in Japanese multinationals: a model for U.S. firms? *Journal of International Business Studies* 15(2): 139–49.

Wilson, D. and Purushothaman, R. (2003) Dreaming with BRICs: the path to 2050, *Global Economics Paper No. 99.* Goldman Sachs Global Economics Website. www.gs.com

Yan, A., Zhu, G. and Hall, D. T. (2002) International assignments for career building: a model of agency relationships and psychological contracts, *Academy of Management Review* 27: 373–91.

Zhu, C. J. and Dowling, P. J. (1998) Performance appraisal in China, in J. Selmer (ed.) *International Management in China: Cross-Cultural Issues*, London and New York: Routledge.

2 Employee performance management: policies and practices in multinational enterprises

DENNIS R. BRISCOE AND LISBETH M. CLAUS

Introduction

Employee performance appraisal (PA) and performance management (PM) systems have been extensively studied as a core responsibility of the human resource management (HRM) function, particularly in the United States and, more recently, in the United Kingdom (see, e.g., Arvey and Murphy, 1998; Bernardin *et al.*, 1998; Cascio, 1982; *IPD Training and Development in Britain*, 1999; Lawler, 2003; *Performance Management Survey*, 2000; Redman, 2006). Researchers have studied and described it (for reviews of this literature see any current HRM or industrial/organizational/applied psychology textbook; see also ASTD Training Industry Trends, 1996; Cascio, 1982; Locker and Teel, 1988) and academics, consultants, and practitioners have also prescribed it (see, for example, Armstrong and Baron, 1998; Bacal, 1999; Costello, 1993; Delpo, 2005; Grote, 1996; Long, 1986; Smith and Brouwer, 1977; and Smither, 1998). Indeed, electronic literature searches on the topic show over 20 articles published every month with "performance appraisal" in the title (Redman, 2006).

PM is usually described as the system through which organizations set work goals, determine performance standards, assign and evaluate work, provide performance feedback, determine training and development needs, and distribute rewards. PA, a subset of PM, refers to these activities applied to the individual employee and, traditionally, includes some type of manager–employee feedback session. All of these activities are central to management in general and to HRM in particular. You would expect them to be thoroughly studied. And such is the case – except in the international arena. PM, as it is practiced in the West, relies on an extensive body of management knowledge (derived mainly from psychology, sociology, and management theory). But, the literature on PM as applied in cross-border situations (e.g. in non-Western cultures, for employees of multinational enterprises (MNEs), and for international assignees) is highly anecdotal.

There is some evidence of the adoption of PA schemes in some non-Western countries, such as China (Chow, 1994), Hong Kong (Snape *et al.*, 1998), Japan in the form of *Satei* (Endo, 1994), Africa (Arthur *et al.*, 1995), and India (Lawler *et al.*, 1995). Still, there has been comparatively little focus by researchers or HR practitioners on PM in the international context. The aim of this chapter, therefore, is to address that shortcoming, particularly as it applies to the practice of PM in MNEs.

PMSs and MNEs

The past twenty years or so have seen large-scale organizational change, including major adaptations in PM and PA practices, such as the adoption of competency-based appraisal systems, staff appraisal of managers, team-based appraisals, customer appraisals, 360-degree feedback systems, and balanced scorecards. The Workplace Employee Relations Survey in the U.K. finds that organizations that are recognized as "investing in people" are significantly more likely to have a PA scheme in place (Cully *et al.*, 1999). And research in the U.S. has found that organizations with strong PM systems are 51 percent more likely to outperform their competitors on financial measures and 41 percent more likely to outperform their competitors on non-financial measures such as customer satisfaction, employee retention, and quality of products or services (Bernthal, Rogers and Smith, 2003). Yet, even though some form of PA seems to be used by almost every organization (Armstrong and Baron, 1998; ASTD Training Industry Trends, 1996; *IPD Training and Development in Britain*, 1999; Locker and Teel, 1988; Long, 1986), firms seem reluctant to adopt the advice of researchers (Banks and Murphy, 1985; Maroney and Buckley, 1992).

As globalization has increased, MNEs – organizations with headquarters in one country and operations and subsidiaries in one or more other countries – have become common and pervasive. In the early years of globalization, MNEs were primarily large private firms. But, today, MNEs come in all shapes and sizes, from small to large, present in every industry and sector and in every step of the value chain.

Because of the pervasive presence of MNEs, the issues associated with managing the performance of managers and employees in these global firms take on a special importance (Martin and Bartol, 2003). The numerous concerns related to divergent cultures, varying legal and political systems, different performance criteria, and varying task environments require considerations which go beyond those generally associated with domestic performance management (Briscoe and Schuler, 2004; Davis, 1998; Dowling and Welch, 2005; Oddou and Mendenhall, 2000; and Stroh *et al.*, 2005). For example, in the management of expatriates, these differences present significant challenges, such as the major differences that arise between host national perceptions and those of the home office regarding what was being accomplished and the circumstances under which it was being achieved.

So in this chapter, we propose a model of employee PM that helps provide a framework for understanding the complexity of PM in the MNE. Much of this examination is informed by a recent literature review on PM and PA in the international arena performed by the authors (Claus and Briscoe, 2006, 2008). Finally, we identify some issues related to the difficulties of implementing a PM system in an MNE.

A model of employee PM in the MNE

As has been suggested elsewhere (e.g. Beechler *et al.*, 1993; Sparrow *et al.*, 1994; Stroh and Caligiuri, 1998), the long-run success of MNEs is dependent on their practice of successful global HRM. Sparrow *et al.* (1994) define successful global HRM as

> . . . the possession of the skills and knowledge of formulating and implementing policies and practices that effectively integrate and cohere globally dispersed employees, while at the same time recognizing and appreciating local differences that impact the effective utilization of human resources (p. 44).

One of the key areas of HRM policy and practice necessary to implement this definition of successful global HRM is PM, the HRM sub-system that links corporate goals with rewards, improvement of performance, and employee development through the PA and evaluation process (Sparrow *et al.*, 1994).

Figure 2.1 (A model of employee performance management in an MNE) provides a way to understand the relationships between and among the many factors that are involved in the PM system in an MNE and the contexts that influence and constrain it. In general, the model suggests that the PM process in MNEs (design, implementation, and evaluation) takes place in a global (external) context (primarily national culture and structure) as well as an organizational (internal) context (primarily corporate culture, strategy, and design). Employee PM consists of three phases: design, implementation, and evaluation. The design phase deals with the choices that management of an MNE make with regard to its PM system. These decisions relate to identifying the purpose of PM (why), performance criteria (what), method of evaluation and instrument (how), frequency of evaluation (how often), rater identification (who), and whether a standardized or localized approach will be used. The implementation stage includes moderators of the PM process. This stage includes communicating performance expectations, identifying cognitive processes that affect PA, frame of reference training for the participants in the PM process, and establishing the role of performance feedback. In the implementation phase, cognitive processes related to PA (such as motivation, self-efficacy, affective regard, and the rater(s)–ratee context) play a dominant role. Finally, the evaluation phase consists of identifying outcomes of the PM process. Fit, alignment, fairness, performance outcomes, and rewards play an important role in the evaluation phase. This model provides the framework within which this chapter explains and describes the practice of PM in MNEs.

As Figure 2.1 illustrates, the global context (including national cultures and languages and global business and political infrastructure) influences every aspect of the PM system. There

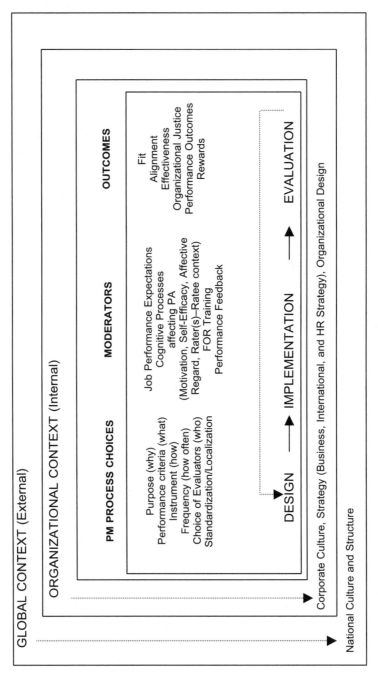

Figure 2.1 A model of employee performance management in an MNE

have been a number of general references that describe this context (Artise, 1995; Black *et al.*, 1999; Briscoe and Schuler, 2004; Dowling and Welch, 2005; Evans *et al.*, 2002; Fernandez, 2005; Logger and Vinke, 1995; Redman, 2006; Sparrow *et al.*, 2004; Stroh *et al.*, 2005; Vance and Paik, 2006) and its impact on PM systems in MNEs.

However, the recent extensive literature review of international PM (refer to Figure 2.2) found only 64 conceptual and research-based articles published in English-language peer-reviewed journals over the period 1985 to 2005 (Claus and Briscoe, 2006, 2008). These articles evidenced no consistent or widely accepted model of critical variables and almost no two articles took the same approach or examined the same factors. Essentially, every research-based article reviewed (refer to Table 2.1) has presented or operated from within a framework or model unique to the individual study.

Global context

The external global context consists of the "culture" and the "structure" of a society in which organizations operate. External cultural elements focus on the values, beliefs, practices, and norms dictated by the national culture. External structure relates to contextual elements such as government regulations, legislation, industry, sector, unionization, and organizational size.

Culture and language are issues that impact all areas of PM (as well as all other areas of HRM). As Figure 2.2 illustrates, aspects of culture were the focus of the single-largest number of studies on PM. Most of the international focus on PM systems has focused on various concerns with culture, for example, can PM/PA from one country be transferred effectively to another and how do various cultural traits influence the practice of PA and PM systems? Of course, in one way or another, culture was involved in every other article, as well (as is true for all research on global business), whether the focus was on country differences or some specific PM concern, such as evidence of convergence versus divergence in the practice of PM across cultures.

As far as could be found in the literature review, no studies were identified that dealt specifically with the impact of language differences on PM and PA. There are potentially many ways in which language differences between parent firm and subsidiary, between raters and ratees, between ratees and colleagues/subordinates and/or customers, can influence understanding, cause a need for translation and localization, and all the potential problems that attend language translation, and lead to significant misunderstandings and thus lack of reliability or validity in PAs and the full PM system.

The external global context also includes structural elements such as size of organization, industry sector, type of ownership, and unionization. These structural elements, studied in the body of knowledge of PM systems, have not really been focused on with regard to how they shape the practice of PM in MNEs.

We can identify the external variables that influence the functioning of the PM system in MNEs, but there is almost no research that helps identify what works when or why.

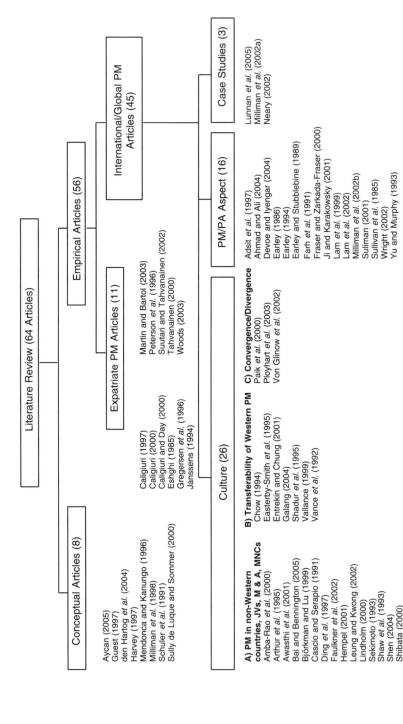

Figure 2.2 Academic research on PM in international/global perspective

Table 2.1 Scope of empirical studies by country and company

Country/Company*	Single Company	Multiple Companies
Multiple countries	Adsit *et al.* (1997)	Arthur *et al.* (1995)
	Caligiuri (1997)	Cascio and Serapio (1991)
	Caligiuri (2000)	Chow (1994)
	Caligiuri and Day (2000)	Earley (1994)
	Devoe and Iyengar (2004)	Earley and Stubblebine (1989)
	Earley (1986)	Easterby-Smith *et al.* (1995)
	Entrekin and Chung (2001)	Faulkner *et al.* (2002)
	Fraser and Zarkada-Fraser (2000)	Galang (2004)
	Lam *et al.* (1999)	Gregersen *et al.* (1996)
	Lam *et al.* (2002)	Hempel (2001)
	Leung and Kwong (2002)	Janssens (1994)
	Lindholm (2000)	Martin and Bartol (2003)
	Lunnan *et al.* (2005)	Milliman *et al.* (2002b)
	Milliman *et al.* (2002a)	Paik *et al.* (2000)
	Neary (2002)	Peterson *et al.* (1996)
	Ployhart *et al.* (2003)	Sullivan *et al.* (1985)
	Tahvanainen (2000)	Suutari and Tahvanainen (2002)
		Vallance (1999)
		Vance *et al.* (1992)
		Woods (2003)
Single country	Ahmad and Ali (2004)	Amba-Rao *et al.* (2000)
	Eshghi (1985)	Bai and Bennington (2005)
	Sekimoto (1993)	Björkman and Lu (1999)
	Shibata (2000)	Ding *et al.* (1997)
		Farh *et al.* (1991)
		Shadur *et al.* (1995)
		Shaw *et al.* (1993)
		Shen (2004)
		Suliman (2001)
		Wright (2002)
		Yu and Murphy (1993)

* Four studies could not be classified.

Organizational context

Inside the constraints and influence of the global context lies the organizational context. The organizational context includes factors such as the organization's culture, its strategy (in all its forms, including its general business strategy, its international strategy, and its HR strategy), and its organizational structure or design. Again, there has been little to no research on these variables and their impact on global PMSs. However, it is clear that these factors do indeed affect the form and practice of PM in the global arena. For example, the organization's culture will determine the importance it places on employee PM; its international and HR strategies will determine the importance placed on the evaluation of performance of foreign operations, at both the individual and organizational levels; and organizational structure will influence global staffing (such as the quantity and relative importance of expatriates and local workforces and their local managers).

Global staffing

One of the factors that make international research and global HRM more complex is the additional types of employees that the MNE must manage. In a simplistic way, in early writing, these types of employees were described as including three distinct groups:

1 those from the parent country (working for the parent company, referred to as Parent Country Nationals – PCNs);
2 those who work in foreign subsidiaries who are from the foreign locale (referred to as Host Country Nationals – HCNs); and
3 those who are hired from another country to work in a foreign subsidiary (referred to as Third Country Nationals – TCNs) (Morgan, 1986).

With each case, there are two levels of employees – managers and non-managers – who are of interest to an understanding of the PM system. In general, managers evaluate the performance of non-managers. But, higher-level managers also evaluate lower-level managers. And, in recent years, we have seen PM systems that incorporate lower-level managers evaluating superiors as well as non-managers evaluating managers. So, combining this with the three types of employees found in the MNE, we have an additional layer of complexity that makes trying to study and draw conclusions about best practice of PM systems in MNEs very problematic. Of course, over time, even this framework has become limiting. For example, Briscoe and Schuler (2004) describe some 20 different types of employees in the global arena expanding the earlier typology of employees in the MNE.

1. Home country employees: managers and non-managers

This is the traditional focus of PM and PA research and not the focus of this chapter. As mentioned earlier, the vast body of knowledge related to PA and PM has been focused primarily on Western domestic firms. With regard to MNEs, there are many things that differentiate an MNE from a purely domestic firm. Variables in both the global and organizational contexts influence the MNE in ways that are not present in the domestic operations. Conducting business within multiple cultures and languages makes everything more difficult and complex.

2. *Host country employees: managers and non-managers*

PM systems and PAs of host country employees of MNEs have not been specifically studied (refer to Claus and Briscoe, 2006). There is a great need for examining the Western body of knowledge related to PM in non-Western societies and companies. There have been a number of studies of PA practices in various countries, some of which have been conducted in MNEs, but no one has yet looked carefully at how management of MNEs deal with PM of their foreign/host country workforces. There have been studies of whether or not foreign PM practices copy those of the parent company. But the kind of studies that would examine the nature of those practices, for example, their reliability and validity, or problems with raters and ratees, such as have been extensively studied within the domestic context, have not been done. Since most of the research on PM systems has been done in Western (primarily North American) MNEs, it is difficult to generalize about the effects of alternative approaches to PM in different countries or about the attitudes of local employees toward these systems.

3. *International assignees*

One of the most important of the staffing complexities is dealing with the PM of international assignees or expatriates. Home (parent or HQ) country employees who go on foreign assignments, and employees who are sent from one subsidiary to work in another, are of special interest to PMs of MNEs. As Table 2.1 indicates, 11 studies specifically focused on expatriate management. This has been the focus of most of the research and prescriptive writing about PAs and PM systems in the global organization. Most of this focus has been on the practice issues of PA: Who does it? What criteria are appraised? When (and how often) are appraisals done? What format is used? What is the context within which such appraisals are performed? (Adler, 2002; Brewster and Harris, 1999; Brewster and Scullion, 1997; Briscoe and Schuler, 2004; Cascio, 2006; Dowling and Welch, 2005; Oddou and Mendenhall, 2000; Stroh *et al.*, 2005).

As central as PM is to IHRM and to organizations, in general, surveys of large MNEs with many overseas assignees and many foreign subsidiaries report that most (83%) do not use PM to measure their IAs' success (Arthur Andersen, 2000); and many (35%) don't use any type of measurement at all (e.g. financial measures). In other studies, 53 percent of firms even self-reported that they are average or below average at effectively assessing the performance of their expatriate managers (Gregersen *et al.*, 1995, 1996). These figures report the result of surveys of large firms (and one would assume firms that are more sophisticated in their HR practices). It is likely that medium-sized to small firms are even less likely to use PM systems in the management of their foreign operations.

An overview of the research on expatriate PM shows that, thus far, no two studies have focused on the same set of variables, which makes the drawing of general conclusions problematic. Even though the approaches described by references such as Briscoe and Schuler (2004), Dowling and Welch (2005), Evans *et al.* (2002), and Stroh *et al.* (2005) are fairly consistent, this evidence is more anecdotal and observational (as reported by HR practitioners) than based on any systematic research (refer to Figure 2.2 and Table 2.1 and Claus and Briscoe, 2006).

Organizational culture

The development of a shared corporate culture is very important for MNEs who operate in different national cultural contexts and have employees from diverse backgrounds. Corporate culture and the various formal and informal linking mechanisms in an organization serve to "glue" the diverse people and organizations together (Evans *et al.*, 2002). A globally integrated PM system (highly standardized but with localized implementation) can be one of those formal linking mechanisms that hold people together in a MNE. In other words, corporate cultures of MNEs can, with regard to PM, mediate the effects of the different national cultures.

International organizational structure

One of the other important variables in the organizational context involves the structure the MNE uses to conduct its international business. The three most-common options used by MNEs are wholly-owned subsidiaries (WOSs), joint ventures, and mergers and acquisitions.

1. Wholly-owned subsidiaries

Our recent literature search was unable to locate any studies that focused on specific PM issues in wholly-owned subsidiaries, other than those which looked at the prevalence of convergence or divergence in PM practices of MNEs (which is addressed later). The primary focus of studies of PM systems applied to WOSs has been on the PM of expatriates – and, to a lesser extent, on the PM of host country managers.

2. International joint ventures (IJVs)

Whenever firms create joint ventures with other firms, many areas of HRM become both complex and, yet, very important to the successful operation of the joint venture. This complexity can be even more difficult when the joint venture is international – which is often the organization structure of choice in the international arena today. In terms of the PM system, the critical issue is whether the PA process will be based on the PM systems operating in one of the parent firms or developed to suit the specific needs of the venture. If the partners try to develop a new PM system specifically for the IJV, input needs to be incorporated from both (all) sides, considering the values and operating preferences of each cultural group in an effort to develop a culturally-sensitive PA format (Cyr, 1995; Schuler *et al.*, 2004).

According to Cyr (1995), the goal of firms with IJVs is to create conditions under which the JV staff can excel in meeting the competitive demands of a global market. PAs are one way to sensitize employees to performance objectives, provide them with performance feedback, and allow managers to gain a better appreciation of employee skills, difficulties, and career aspirations. "Yet despite the possibility of obtaining critical information from the performance appraisal process, managers repeatedly said that employee reviews were a bother, and inconsistently done – if done at all. To some extent, this was a function of time, but in many cases managers seemed to think the reviews were not of essential value" (Cyr, 1995: 137). Of all HRM responsibilities, Cyr (1995) found that even in IJVs, the area of performance reviews generally received the least attention.

In IJVs where one of the partners is from a country where PAs are common practice – but the other country is not used to any PA process – often the country that is familiar with the use of PAs will transfer its practice into the IJV. Sometimes this works to create a new PA culture for the country without the PA experience, at least within the context of the IJV. Sometimes, the country without the common usage of PAs will continue to reject the PM system that uses PAs, and this may lead to malicious compliance and often the dissolving of the IJV.

3. Mergers and acquisitions

International mergers and acquisitions require the integration of two corporate cultures and two national cultures. The post-merger integration of HRM functions will include the integration of PM systems. Which system will prevail will often be determined by the strategy (global integration versus local responsiveness) and organizational structure (centralization versus decentralization) of the newly merged enterprise.

International organizational strategy

All MNEs have to address, in some form, the issue of internationalization strategy which deals with the choice of convergence (global integration) versus divergence (local responsiveness) and the corresponding likely structural dimension (centralization versus decentralization). Stated as a question, the issue is one of: Do we, as a firm, want all of our global operations to follow the same HRM practices we follow at home (in the parent company headquarters and in the parent country)? Or, are we willing to allow – mostly because we think it is necessary or required – HR practices at the "foreign" level to follow local national and cultural practices and laws?

Some research has been conducted on this issue, primarily to try to assess what is happening, that is, is there a discernible pattern of convergence (centralization – following HQs' practice) or divergence (decentralization – allowing local practice) in MNE practice of HRM? This is not the same as trying to determine which practice is best for the organization. Because so much of HR practice is determined by local laws, regulations, culture, and tradition, it would make sense that MNEs have historically allowed HR in foreign subsidiaries to be managed by a local HR manager and to primarily follow local practice (Briscoe and Schuler, 2004; Evans *et al.*, 2002; Sparrow, Brewster and Harris, 2004). But, increasingly, MNE executives seek consistency and centralization of management practices, including HRM functions.

Research on this issue shows clearly that there are a number of different and equally successful ways of organizing economic activities and management in a market economy (Whitley, 1992). These varying patterns of economic organization tend to be a product of the particular institutional environments within the various nation-states and cultures. The development and success of the specific managerial (and HR) practices can only be explained by giving due credit to those various institutional contexts. Because of that, not all management (and HR) methods and practices are transferable. Therefore, the effectiveness of any worldwide conceptualization of HRM will very likely be constrained by the different institutional contexts for national practice. The use of a globally integrated PM system, standard in its concept, yet local in its implementation, is thought to take advantage of both approaches while minimizing the disadvantages common to each.

PM process choices

In the design of their PM systems, MNEs have a number of choices to make and they internalize these choices through formal organizational policies and practices. These choices deal with the purpose of the PM system (why), performance criteria (what), instrument (how), frequency of evaluations (how often), choice of evaluators (who) and whether to use a standardized, localized or integrated approach to PM. Each one of these choices will be heavily influenced by strategy (so that the PM system is internally aligned and externally fit to the competitive environment) and culture.

With regard to what is being evaluated in a PA, national cultural differences impact whether individual versus group performance is considered and whether contextual versus purely task variables are taken into account. With regard to who evaluates (and is being evaluated), research suggests that different sources of performance data (peers, supervisors, subordinates) demonstrate significantly different frames of reference and disagree about the importance of incidents of poor performance (Hauenstein and Foti, 1989). Pertaining to the PM of international assignees, research also suggests that the criteria used to evaluate performance of managers on global assignments are not balanced – in terms of task versus contextual variables. And criteria that do capture the unique work challenges of the foreign assignment are often not used (Brewster, 1991; Gregersen *et al.*, 1996; Lindholm *et al.*, 1999; Stroh *et al.*, 2005; Woods, 2003). Firms tend to use the same criteria as they use at home (Gregersen *et al.*, 1995, 1996), which is not at all realistic, given the challenges of the foreign assignment. Indeed, Gregersen *et al.* (1996) found that only 10 percent of the firms in their survey actively incorporated contextual factors in their international appraisals.

Moderators

Moderators in our model consist mainly of cognitive psychological processes that have been shown to affect PA such as motivation, self-efficacy, affective rewards, and rater–ratee context. It also emphasizes the role of frame-of-reference training to increase the validity and reliability of the process and the importance of feedback.

Motivation

In PM, the motivation of both manager and the employee are considered a moderating factor. Taken into the context of the MNE, the supervisor/manager is crucial in the conduct of PA because it is the manager who ultimately puts PM into practice in the subsidiaries (Harris, 1994; den Hartog et al., 2004). Research has also indicated that there are distinct cultural patterns of managers' perceptions of motivation of their subordinates across borders (Devoe and Iyengar, 2004).

Self-efficacy

A person's estimate of his or her own ability to perform a task is a moderating factor in PM. Two empirical studies (Earley, 1994; Lam et al., 2002) looked at self-efficacy in an international context. Earley (1994) showed that the cultural dimensions of individualism and collectivism were relevant in understanding how training influences efficacy. Lam et al. (2002) extended the concept of efficacy from the individual (self-efficacy) to the group (collective efficacy) and linked the cultural values of individualism and collectivism to individual level orientations that reflect these values (i.e. idiocentrism and allocentrism).

Affective regard

Affective regard, or the supervisor's likings for subordinates, has shown to be associated with higher PA ratings in research in the U.S. context (Lefkowitz, 2000). Only one study was identified that looked at the role of interpersonal affect on performance appraisal (Varma et al., 2005). Using data from supervisors in the U.S. and India, the authors delineated the relationship between interpersonal affect and performance ratings. In both samples, interpersonal affect and performance level were found to have significant effects on performance ratings. Results from the U.S. sample indicated that raters are able to separate their liking for a subordinate from actual performance when assigning performance ratings, suggesting that the interpersonal affect does not operate as a bias in the appraisal process in the U.S. However, results from the Indian sample suggest that supervisors inflate ratings of low performers, suggesting that local cultural norms may be operating as a moderator. The study suggests that affective regard may play an even greater role in non-Western and collectivist societies.

Raters and ratees

The PM body of knowledge focuses on how different types of raters (supervisors, subordinates, peers/colleagues, clients/customers, self) may produce rater biases. Taken in an international context, managers from different cultures judge behavior of subordinates differently (Selmer, 1997; Stening *et al.*, 1981) and subordinates from Asian cultures may rate their own behavior differently due to a possible modesty bias (Farh *et al.*, 1991; Yu and Murphy, 1993). There is also evidence of possible rater bias due to the nationality of raters and ratees (Ji and Karakowsky, 2001).

Within the PM of expatriates, the focus is on the use of home or host country raters, or both. Often local management is expected to play an important role in the evaluation of international assignees as well as of local employees. They are expected to be more familiar with the individual's performance on location compared to the more distant home country manager. But, in practice, they evaluate within their own cultural context, not necessarily focusing on issues or evaluating on the basis of factors that are of importance to the parent organization. As a result, it is important to specify in advance the most important performance areas for the term of the assignment and indicate who will appraise each area (Logger and Vinke, 1995). Research suggests that the criteria for appraisal in today's enterprises include these qualities, in general, for executives: strategic thinking, initiating change, and relationship management (Logger and Vinke, 1995). But additional qualities are required of managers on international assignments, including flexibility, implementing change, interpersonal understanding, empowerment of subordinates, team support, and versatility.

Frame-of-reference training

Frame-of-reference training is commonly used in Western PM to reduce biases in PA for different categories of performance raters (supervisors, subordinates, peers, and self). Logically, such training should be even more important for MNEs operating in diverse cultural contexts because additional biases are likely to occur as a result of cultural differences. This is confirmed by a study that showed that cultural differences (especially individualism and collectivism) were relevant in understanding how training influences efficacy. Although training information provided at either level was always better than no training at all, individualists performed best when exposed to training focused at an individual level, whereas collectivists performed best when exposed to training at the group level (Earley, 1994).

Feedback

Feedback is strongly influenced by cultural dimensions, especially in terms of praise and criticism. PA feedback plays a dual role for subordinates. First, it allows employees to know how they are doing and have a formal, and hopefully meaningful, interaction with their supervisor about their performance. Second, it provides developmental opportunities to employees to focus on the improvement of certain performance dimensions and benefit from planning development opportunities. While feedback is a common feature of PA, the way in which the feedback is delivered differs in individualistic and collectivistic societies (Cascio, 2006). Fair performance evaluations and frequent performance feedback was an important predictor of job satisfaction of host country employees in MNE subsidiaries (Lindholm, 2000).

Outcomes

Outcomes in our model relate to effectiveness of the PM system mainly in terms of reliability and validity, organizational justice, performance outcomes, and rewards. Outcomes of PA and PM systems are directly related to organizational effectiveness and linked to the overall performance of the organization.

Validity and reliability

These are statistical terms (and concepts) that are at the center of most research on various aspects of performance appraisals (see, e. g., Cascio, 2006; Cascio and Aguinis, 2005). They get at the heart of concerns over biases inherent to the PA process. Reducing these biases increases the effectiveness of the PM system and the acceptance of the process by all involved. Especially pertinent to this issue is the earlier discussion related to rater and ratee biases based on nationality and culture, the use of frame-of-reference training to focus on behaviors, and the cultural acceptance of the PM system by all in subsidiaries of the MNE.

Organizational justice

Organizational justice is a component that should be taken into account in the design and implementation of a PM system not only to ensure accuracy and fairness of process, but also to ensure acceptability by the employee. An empirical application of the concept of organizational justice to PM showed that cultures high on self-expression (such as Norway) view the use of standardized PAs as less fair than cultures high on survival (China, Lithuania), indicating that a seemingly universally fair procedure may appear unfair based on the fact that it is standardized (Mercer Traavik and Lunnan, 2005). In expatriate PM, a number of expatriate PA practices (such as a balanced set of raters from home and host countries and more frequent appraisals) relate positively to perceptions of procedural justice by the expatriate, while the use of either a standardized or a customized appraisal form relates negatively to perceived accuracy (Gregersen et al., 1996).

Rewards

If results of the PA are tied to rewards, the review is likely to be more effective because it will be taken more seriously by managers and employees and the organization is likely to spend more resources to ensure that the PM system is used properly (Cascio, 2006). A prerequisite to effective rewards is knowing what motivates employees. In the context of an MNE, research has shown that employees differ as to their preference for intrinsic versus extrinsic rewards and managers differ in their perceptions of employee preference for these rewards based on cultural values (Devoe and Iyengar, 2004).

Conclusions and Recommendations

The management of employee performance in an MNE is very complex. There are many reasons that the international PM system doesn't work very well, including (Briscoe and Schuler, 2004: 354):

- Problems with the choice of evaluator (e.g. local or parent company) and that person's amount of contact with the ratee (expatriate or HCN).
- Host-country management's perceptions of performance. There are often considerable differences between headquarters and foreign locales in what is valued in terms of performance and in terms of perceptions of the actual behavior.
- Difficulties with long-distance communication with headquarters (for example, in the time and the timeliness of the communications and the understanding of the communications, particularly as this relates to performance evaluations, but also as a major component in the expatriate's and foreign manager's job activities).
- Inadequate contact between parent-company rater and subsidiary ratee.
- Inadequate establishment of performance objectives for the foreign operations (i.e. they are unclear or contradictory) and means for recording levels of individual and organizational performance.
- Parent-country ethnocentrism and lack of understanding of the foreign environment and culture.
- Frequent indifference to the foreign experience of the expatriate and to the importance of the international business in general.

A number of recommendations flow from this review. First, and maybe the most important, the study of PM across borders should not necessarily and always start from a U.S. or Western point of view. The inherent Anglo- and U.S.-centric bias in the reviewed literature suggests how important it is to broaden the pool of studies and then broaden the research, itself. This should allow the testing of Western concepts in other contexts, the bringing of non-Western points of view and practice into the discussion, and the facilitation of cross-border learning for better PM in all contexts.

Second, future research on PM across borders and in MNEs should do a better job of linking empirical data to theoretical frameworks that go beyond the examination of purely cultural elements and influences. The various conceptual models that have been proposed each add value to our understanding of PM in MNEs. Yet, there is a need to develop an overall conceptual framework that looks at the different stages of the PM process, rather than just the appraisal of employees. There is a need to look at PM across borders from a strategic HRM perspective using a variety of existing management theories, as suggested by Budhwar and Sparrow (2002), Vance (2006), and Wright and McMahon (1992).

Third, research on PM in MNEs would benefit from the use of a wider variety of designs and methods. Qualitative exploratory research (for which there is still a strong need) derives its strength, not from testing hypotheses, but rather from organizing data, developing propositions, and building theory. Quantitative research derives its strength from testing hypotheses and refining the theoretical models. Both methods (and others) can effectively add value to this underdeveloped research topic.

Fourth, as with much management research in the academic literature, there is a need to translate the results into actionable terms for use by HR practitioners in MNEs (as well as a need for those practitioners to use the research results that are available). For example, in this topic area, researchers can help explore the extent to which a "standardized" global approach to PM can be used effectively in an MNE – and which design, implementation, and evaluation features of the PM process should be localized.

In this chapter, we described a model of employee PM for the MNE, discussed the major issues involved in the design, development, and evaluation of a PM system for the MNE, and illustrated them with related empirical research on the topic. Within HRM, greater attention will need to be paid to employee PM in the MNE as organizations are increasingly operating globally with diverse workforces. Academic researchers in the field of IHRM have only recently taken the Western PM body of knowledge and considered its application in a global context and a systematic approach to the topic is still in its infancy. So far, HR practitioners and managers charged with international employee PM responsibilities must rely on anecdotal (rather than research) evidence of what works and doesn't work when it comes to the PM systems in the MNE. Mostly they seem to rely on using what is familiar, rather than seeking or relying on any systematic or research-based evidence to support their global PM and PA efforts.

Case study

"Open Exchange" at *dmg world media*:

Global Performance Management in Action

dmg world media, a leader in home and consumer exhibitions, is a relatively small yet international company, with fewer than 1,000 employees. Developed mainly through acquisitions of other small companies, *dmg world media* is primarily an intermediary that rents exhibit space and creates exhibits marketed and sold by their teams of employees. Employees are based in the U.K., the U.S., Canada, Dubai, Australia, New Zealand, and Beijing. *dmg world media*'s success is heavily dependent upon high levels of employee performance.

According to Warren Girling, Executive Vice President of HR, "We have a culture of how we manage our people to get that high performance. We select groups of highly motivated and developed people who understand their customers and the business. And, we have an ongoing discussion on how we perform."

The company's previous HR-driven PA system was similar to that of many other firms in that it utilized a rating scale from 1 to 5 that was linked to a percentage merit increase. This traditional system, particularly its reliance on a once-a-year PA, no longer fit the needs of the business or its organizational culture. The merit increase was highly distorted because market forces in this business have a greater impact on performance and resultant salary increases than any judgment of merit based on the appraisal. Additionally, managers considered the system too time consuming and wanted more of a report card type of approach. Moreover, some of the newly acquired companies were often so small that they had no formal experience with performance management (PM).

The new PM system, *Open Exchange*, was developed by a small group within the company, including the three most senior Executive VPs, HR, and selected employees from around the world. The group started with only a blank sheet and a vision that had previously been defined by the company. This vision, or business statement, was developed in the form of a constitution *because constitutions* are the broad foundation documents of modern societies. Yet, much like a standard constitution, not every word of *dmg world media*'s business statement applies to every day-to-day activity. The core elements of *dmg world media*'s constitution are that they are the leaders in their field and they get things done in a very un-bureaucratic and decentralized way by understanding their customers' businesses. Performance is the common purpose behind which the company unites as it reviews every set of results regularly, exhibit by exhibit.

Essential performance dimensions were identified by looking at their high performers and asking, "*If we think about our best/most successful people and customers we love to work with, what are their essential characteristics?*" These essential qualities are sought in the people who join the company, and major features of the new PM system were based on checking performance against these "essentials."

Rather than an annual affair, performance reviews are now done by managers, event by event. As employees work in small teams, they know when someone on the team is not performing and inform the manager. Not only do underperforming people feel peer pressure, but they are required to sit down with the manager, who is held accountable for solving any performance problems. It is *dmg world media*'s strong belief that when someone has a performance problem, the appraisal is not the right place to discuss it. Performance problems cannot wait for a period review.

In the new performance reviews, employee performance is regularly reviewed by the manager and categorized into one of three groups: Employees are either (1) exceptional performers; (2) great but not exceptional performers; or (3) great people but not trainable or right for the job. Exceptional performers are the role models. Great employees may have the essential skills but also some blind spots that can be improved upon. That's where training is an option. The manager completes a grid of training needs analysis and coaches the employee to work on areas needing improvement. Employees who struggle with job know-how and perform poorly on more than one of the essentials, must complete a face-to-face action plan. For those performing below expected levels, training is rarely an option. Most of the time, there are multiple reasons for unacceptable performance: lack of skills, competency, motivation, or simply the wrong person in the wrong job. Sometimes there are bad hires, bad promotions, and bad placements. At *dmg world media*, a very heavy focus is placed on bringing in the right people and putting them in the right jobs.

Managers document performance because the company recognizes that some of the best performers need management confirmation of their accomplishments and stroking. Documentation is the recording of a positive. Negatives are handled outside of the PA process.

Although *dmg world media* does not have a common single workplace and is dispersed throughout different countries, they successfully use a standardized PM system. This is possible because the employees from different national cultures are held together by a single common product (the exhibitor business), common personalities (the type of people that work in the exhibitor business), and a similar organizational culture (their constitution). In addition, they are flexible, adaptable, and willing to be elastic based on these common principles.

Questions

1 How is PM at *dmg world media* different from traditional PMSs at other companies?
2 What was the impetus for developing a different PMS at *dmg world media*?
3 What characteristics of the conduct of this global business and its global talent management (recruiting, developing, and retaining high-performing employees) influence their PM system? How do they impact the PM system?
4 Can a standardized PMS be used effectively with managers and employees from different cultures in an international company?

References

Adler, N. J. (2002) *International Dimensions of Organizational Behavior*, 4th edn., Cincinnati, OH: South-Western College Publishing.

Adsit, D. J., London, M., Crom, S. and Jones, D. (1997) Cross-cultural differences in upward ratings in a multinational company, *International Journal of Human Resource Management* 8: 385–401.

Ahmad, R. and Ali, N. A. (2004) Performance appraisal decision in Malaysian public service, *International Journal of Public Sector Management* 17: 48–64.

Amba-Rao, S. C., Petrick, J. A., Gupta, J. N. D. and Von der Embse, T. J. (2000) Comparative performance appraisal practices and management values among foreign and domestic firms in India, *International Journal of Human Resource Management* 11: 60–89.

Armstrong, M. and Baron, A. (1998) *Performance Management*, London: IPD.

Arthur Andersen Consulting (2000) *Annual Survey of International Assignee Practices*, New York: Author.

Arthur, W., Woehr, D. J., Akande, A. and Strong, M. H. (1995) Human resource management in West Africa: practices and perspectives, *International Journal of Human Resource Management* 6(2): 347–66.

Artise, J. (1995) Selection, coaching, and evaluation of employees in international subsidiaries, in O. Shenkar (ed.) *Global Perspectives of Human Resource Management*, Englewood Cliffs, NJ: Prentice-Hall, pp. 71–111.

Arvey, R. D. and Murphy, K. R. (1998) Performance evaluation in work settings, *Annual Review of Psychology* 49: 141–68.

ASTD Training Industry Trends (1996), *Training and Development*, November: 34–8.

Awasthi, V. N., Chow, C. W. and Wu, A. (2001) Cross-cultural differences in the behavioral consequences of imposing performance evaluation and reward systems: an experimental investigation, *International Journal of Accounting* 36: 291–309.

Aycan, Z. (2005) The interplay between cultural and institutional contingencies in human resource management practices, *International Journal of Human Resource Management* 16: 1083–119.

Bacal, R. (1999) *Performance Management*, New York: McGraw-Hill.

Bai, X. and Bennington, L. (2005) Performance appraisal in the Chinese state-owned coal industry, *International Journal of Business Performance Management* 7: 275–87.

Banks, C. G. and Murphy, K. R. (1985) Toward narrowing the research-practice gap in performance appraisal, *Personnel Psychology* 38: 335–45.

Beechler, S., Bird, A. and Raghuram, S. (1993) Linking business strategy and human resource management practices in multinational corporations: a theoretical framework, *Advances in International Comparative Management* 8: 199–215.

Bernardin, H. J., Hagan, C. M., Kane, J. S. and Villanova, P. (1998) Effective performance management, in J. W. Smither (ed.) *Performance Appraisal: State of the Art in Practice*, San Francisco: Jossey-Bass, pp. 3–48.

Bernthal, P. R., Rogers, R. W. and Smith, A. B. (2003) *Managing Performance: Building Accountability for Organizational Success*, Pittsburgh, PA: Development Dimensions International.

Björkman, I. and Lu, Y. (1999) The management of human resources in Chinese-Western ventures, *Journal of World Business* 34: 306–24.

Black, J. S., Gregersen, H. B., Mendenhall, M. E. and Stroh, L. K. (1999) *Globalizing People Through International Assignments*, Reading, MA: Addison-Wesley.

Brewster, C. (1991) *The Management of Expatriates*, London: Kogan Page.

Brewster, C. and Harris, H. (1999) *International Human Resource Management: Contemporary Issues in Europe*, London: Routledge.

Brewster, C. and Scullion, H. (1997) A review and an agenda for expatriate HRM, *Human Resource Management* 7(3): 32–41.

Briscoe, D. R. and Schuler, R. S. (2004) *International Human Resource Management*, 2nd edition, London/New York: Routledge.

Budhwar, P. S. and Sparrow, P. R. (2002) An integrative framework for understanding cross-national human resource management practices, *Human Resource Management Review* 12: 377–403.

Caligiuri, P. M. (1997) Assessing expatriate success: beyond just being there, *New Approaches to Employee Management* 4: 117–40.

Caligiuri, P. M. (2000) The big five personality characteristics as predictors of expatriate desire to terminate the assignment and supervisor-rated performance, *Personnel Psychology* 53: 67–88.

Caligiuri, P. M. and Day, D. V. (2000) Effects of self-monitoring on technical, contextual, and assignment-specific performance, *Group and Organization Management* 25: 154–75.

Cascio, W. F. (1982) Scientific, legal, and operational imperatives of workable performance appraisal systems, *Public Personnel Management* 11: 367–75.

Cascio, W. F. (2006) Global performance management systems, in G. K. Stahl and I. Björkman (eds.) *Handbook of Research in International Human Resource Management*, Cheltenham, U.K./ Northampton, MA: Edward Elgar Publishing.

Cascio, W. F. and Aguinis, H. (2005) *Applied Psychology in Human Resource Management* (6th edn.), Upper Saddle River, NJ: Prentice-Hall.

Cascio, W. F. and Serapio, Jr., M. G. (1991) Human resource systems in an international alliance: the undoing of a done deal, *Organizational Dynamics* 19: 63–74.

Chow, I. H. S. (1994) An opinion survey of performance appraisal practices in Hong Kong and the People's Republic of China, *Asia Pacific Journal of Human Resource Management* 32: 67–79.

Claus, L. M. and Briscoe, D. R. (2006) What we know and don't know about performance management from an international/global perspective: a review and analysis of empirical research. Paper presented at the annual conference of the Academy of Management, 11–16 August, Atlanta, Georgia.

Claus, L. and Briscoe, D. (2008) Employee performance management across borders: a review of relevant academic literature, *International Journal of Management Reviews* (forthcoming).

Costello, S. J. (1993) *Effective Performance Management*, New York: McGraw-Hill.

Cully, M., Woodland, S., O'Reilly, A. and Dix, G. (1999) *Britain at Work*, London: Routledge.

Cyr, D. J. (1995) *The Human Resource Challenge of International Joint Ventures*, Westport, CT: Quorum Books.

Davis, D. D. (1998) International performance measurement and management, in J. W. Smither (ed.) *Performance Appraisal: State of the Art in Practice*, San Francisco, CA: Jossey-Bass.

Delpo, A. (2005) *The Performance Appraisal Handbook: Legal and Practical Rules for Managers*, Berkeley, CA: Nolo.

Devoe, S. E. and Iyengar, S. S. (2004) Managers' theories of subordinates: a cross-cultural examination of manager perceptions of motivation and appraisal of performance, *Organizational Behavior and Human Decision Processes* 93: 47–61.

Ding, D., Fields, D. and Akhtar, S. (1997) An empirical study of human resource management policies and practice in foreign-invested enterprise in China: the case of Shenzen special economic zone, *International Journal of Human Resource Management* 8: 595–613.

Dowling, P. J. and Welch, D. E. (2005) *International Human Resource Management*, 4th edn., Mason, OH: South-Western.

Earley, P. C. (1986) Trust, perceived importance of praise and criticism, and work performance: an examination of feedback in the United States and England, *Journal of Management* 12: 457–73.

Earley, P. C. (1994) Self or group? Cultural effects of training on self-efficacy and performance, *Administrative Science Quarterly* 39: 89–117.

Earley, P. and Strubblebine, P. (1989) Intercultural assessment of performance feedback, *Group and Organization Studies* 14: 161–81.

Easterby-Smith, M., Malina, D. and Yuan, L. (1995) How culture sensitive is HRM? A comparative analysis of practice in Chinese and U.K. companies, *International Journal of Human Resource Management* 6: 31–59.

Endo, K. (1994) *Satei* (personnel assessment) and interworker competition in Japanese firms, *Industrial Relations* 33(1): 70–82.

Entrekin, L. and Chung, Y. (2001) Attitudes towards different sources of executive appraisal: a comparison of Hong Kong Chinese and American managers in Hong Kong, *International Journal of Human Resource Management* 12: 965–87.

Eshghi, G. (1985) Nationality bias and performance evaluations in multinational corporations, *National Academy of Management Proceedings* 93–7.

Evans, P., Pucik, V. and Barsoux, J.-L. (2002) *The Global Challenge: Frameworks for International Human Resource Management*, New York: McGraw-Hill/Irwin.

Farh, J.-L., Dobbins, G. and Cheng, B. (1991) Cultural relativity in action: a comparison of self ratings made by Chinese and U.S. workers, *Personnel Psychology* 44: 29–47.

Faulkner, D., Pitkethly, R. and Child, J. (2002) International mergers and acquisitions in the U.K. 1985–94: a comparison of national HRM practices, *International Journal of Human Resource Management* 13: 106–22.

Fernandez, F. (2005) *Globalization and Human Resource Management*, New York: HNB Publishing.

Fraser, C. and Zarkada-Fraser, A. (2000) Measuring the performance of retail managers in Singapore and Australia, *International Journal of Retail and Distribution Management* 28: 228–42.

Galang, M. C. (2004) The transferability question: comparing HRM practices in the Philippines with the U.S. and Canada, *International Journal of Human Resource Management* 15: 1207–33.

Gregersen, H. B., Black, J. S. and Hite, J. (1995) Expatriate performance appraisal: principles, practices, and challenges, in J. Selmer (ed.) *Expatriate Management: New Ideas for International Business*, Westport, CT: Quorum Books, pp. 173–96.

Gregersen, H. B., Hite, J. M. and Black J. S. (1996) Expatriate performance appraisal in U.S. multinational firms, *Journal of International Business Studies* 27: 711–38.

Grote, D. (1996) *The Complete Guide to Performance Appraisal*, New York: AMACOM.

Guest, D. E. (1997) Human resource management and performance: a review and research agenda, *International Journal of Human Resource Management* 8: 263–76.

Harris, M. M. (1994) Rater motivation in the performance appraisal context: a theoretical framework, *Journal of Management* 20: 737–56.

den Hartog, D. N., Boselie, P. and Paauwe, J. (2004) Performance management: a model and research agenda, *Applied Psychology: An International Review* 53: 556–69.

Harvey, M. (1997) Focusing the international personnel performance appraisal process, *Human Resource Development Quarterly* 4: 41–62.

Hauenstein, N. M. and Foti, R. J. (1989) From laboratory to practice: neglected issues in implementing frame-of-reference rater training, *Personnel Psychology* 42: 359–78.

Hempel, P. S. (2001) Differences between Chinese and Western managerial views of performance, *Personnel Review* 30: 203–26.

IPD Training and Development in Britain (1999) IPD Survey Report, London: IPD.

Janssens, M. (1994) Evaluating international managers' performance: parent company standards as control mechanisms, *International Journal of Human Resource Management* 5: 853–73.

Ji, L. and Karakowsky, L. (2001) Do we see eye-to-eye? Implications of cultural differences for cross-cultural management research and practices, *Journal of Psychology* 135: 501–18.

Lam, S. S. K., Chen, X. P. and Schaubroeck, J. (2002) Participative decision making and employee performance in different cultures: the moderation effect of allocentrism/ idiocentrism and efficacy, *Academy of Management Journal* 45: 905–14.

Lam, S. S. K., Hui, C. and Law, K. S. (1999) Organizational citizenship behavior: comparing perspectives of supervisors and subordinates across four international samples, *Journal of Applied Psychology* 84: 594–601.

Lawler, E. E., III (2003) Reward practices and performance management system effectiveness, *Organization Dynamics* 32(4): 396–404.

Lawler, J. J., Jain, H. C., Ratnam, C. S. V. and Atmiyanandana, V. (1995) Human resource management in developing economies: a comparison of India and Thailand, *International Journal of Human Resource Management* 6(2): 320–46.

Lefkowitz, J. (2000) The role of interpersonal affective regard in supervisory performance ratings: a literature review and proposed causal model, *Journal of Occupational and Organizational Psychology* 73: 67–85.

Leung, K. and Kwong, J. Y. Y. (2002) Human resource management practices in international joint ventures in mainland China: a justice analysis, *Human Resource Management Review* 13: 85–105.

Lindholm, N. (2000) National culture and performance management in MNC subsidiaries, *International Studies of Management and Organization* 29: 45–66.

Lindholm, N., Tahvanainen, M. and Björkman, I. (1999) Performance appraisal of host country employees: Western MNCs in China, in C. Brewster and H. Harris (eds.) *International HRM: Contemporary Issues in Europe*, London: Routledge, pp. 143–60.

Locker, A. H. and Teel, K. S. (1988) Appraisal trends, *Personnel Journal* 21(2): 139–43.

Logger, E. and Vinke, R. (1995) Compensation and appraisal of international staff, in A.-W. Harzing and J. Van Ruysseveldt (eds.) *International Human Resource Management*, London/Thousand Oaks, CA: Sage Publications in association with the Open University of the Netherlands, pp. 252–70.

Long, P. (1986) *Performance Appraisal Revisited*, London: IPD.

Lunnan, R., Lervik, J. E., Traavik, L., Nilsen, S., Amdam, R. P. and Hennestad, B. (2005) Global transfer of management practices across nations and MNC subcultures, *Academy of Management Executive* 9: 77–80.

Maroney, B. P. and Buckley, P. P. M. (1992) Does research in performance appraisal influence the practice of performance appraisal? Regretfully not, *Public Personnel Management* 21(2): 185–96.

Martin, D. and Bartol, K. (2003) Factors influencing expatriate performance appraisal system success: an organizational perspective, *Journal of International Management* 9: 115–32.

Mendonca, M. and Kanungo, R. N. (1996) Impact of culture on performance, *International Journal of Manpower* 17: 65–9.

Mercer Traavik, L. E. and Lunnan, R. (2005) *Is Standardization of Performance Appraisal Perceived as Fair across Cultures?* Paper Presented at the Academy of Management meeting, Honolulu, HI.

Milliman, J., Taylor, S. and Czaplewski, A. J. (2002a) Cross-cultural performance feedback in multinational enterprises: an opportunity for organizational learning, *Human Resource Planning* 25: 29–43.

Milliman, J., Nason, S., Zhu, C. and De Cieri, H. (2002b) An exploratory assessment of the purposes of performance appraisal in North and Central America and the Pacific Rim, *Human Resource Management* 41: 87–102.

Milliman, J., Nason, S., Gallagher, E., Huo, P., Von Glinow, M. A. and Lowe, K. B. (1998) The impact of national culture on human resource management practices: the case of performance appraisal, *Advances in International Comparative Management* 12: 157–83.

Morgan, P. V. (1986) International human resource management: fact or fiction? *Personnel Administrator* 31(9): 43–7.

Neary, B. (2002) Creating a company-wide, on-line, performance management system: A case study at TRW Inc, *Human Resource Management* 41: 491–8.

Oddou, G. and Mendenhall, M. (2000) Expatriate performance appraisal: problems and solutions, in M. Mendenhall and G. Oddou (eds.) *Readings and Cases in International Human Resource Management*, 3rd edn., Cincinnati, OH: South-Western College Publishing, pp. 213–23.

Paik, Y., Vance, C. and Stage, H. D. (2000) A test of assumed cluster homogeneity for performance appraisal in four Southeast Asian countries, *International Journal of Human Resource Management* 11: 736–50.

Performance Management Survey (2000) Alexandria, VA: Society for Human Resource Management.

Peterson, R. B., Sargent, T., Napier, N. K. and Shim, W. S. (1996) Corporate expatriate HRM policies, internationalization, and performance in the world's largest MNC's, *Management International Review* 36: 215–30.

Ployhart, R. E., Wiechman, D., Schmitt, N., Saccco, J. M. and Rogg, K. (2003) The cross-cultural equivalence of job performance ratings, *Human Performance* 16: 49–79.

Redman, T. (2006) Performance appraisal, in T. Redman and A. Wilkinson (eds.) *Contemporary Human Resource Management*, 2nd edn., Harlow, England: Prentice-Hall Financial Times.

Schuler, R. S., Fulkerson, J. R. and Dowling, P. J. (1991) Strategic performance measurement and management in multinational corporations, *Human Resource Management* 30: 365–92.

Schuler, R. S., Jackson, S. E. and Luo, Y. (2004) *Managing Human Resources in Cross-Border Alliances*, London/New York: Routledge.

Sekimoto, M. (1993) Performance appraisal in Japan: past and future, *The Industrial-Organizational Psychologist* 20: 52–8.

Selmer, J. (1997) Differences in leadership behaviour between expatriate and local bosses as perceived by their host country national subordinates, *Leadership & Organization Development Journal* 18: 13–22.

Shadur, M. A., Rodwell, J. and Bamber, G. J. (1995) The adoption of international best practices in a Western culture: East meets West, *International Journal of Human Resource Management* 6: 735–57.

Shaw, J. B., Tang, S. F. Y., Fisher, C. D. and Kirkbride, P. S. (1993) Organizational and environmental factors related to human resource management practices in Hong Kong: a cross-cultural expanded replication, *International Journal of Human Resource Management* 4: 237–50.

Shen, J. (2004) International performance appraisals: policies, practices and determinants in the case of Chinese multinational companies, *International Journal of Manpower* 25: 547–64.

Shibata, H. (2000) The transformation of the wage and performance appraisal system in a Japanese firm, *International Journal of Human Resource Management* 11: 294–313.

Smith, H. P. and Brouwer, P. J. (1977) *Performance Appraisal and Human Development*, Reading, MA: Addison-Wesley.

Smither, J. W. (ed.) (1998) *Performance Appraisal: State of the Art in Practice*, San Francisco: Jossey-Bass.

Snape, E., Thompson, D., Yan, Ka-Ching, F. and Redman, T. (1998) Performance appraisals and culture: practice and attitudes in Hong Kong and Great Britain, *International Journal of Human Resource Management* 9(5): 841–61.

Sparrow, P. R., Brewster, C. and Harris, H. (2004) *Globalizing Human Resource Management*, London/New York: Routledge.

Sparrow, P. R., Schuler, R. S. and Jackson, S. (1994) Convergence or divergence: human resource practices and policies for competitive advantage worldwide, *International Journal of Human Resource Management* 5(2): 267–99.

Stening, B., Everett, J. and Longton, L. (1981) Mutual perception of managerial performance and style in multinational subsidiaries, *Journal of Occupational Psychology* 54: 255–63.

Stroh, L. K. and Caligiuri, P. M. (1998) Strategic human resources: a new source of competitive advantage in the global arena, *International Journal of Human Resource Management* 9(1): 1–17.

Stroh, L. K., Black, J. S., Mendenhall, M. K. and Gregersen, H. B. (2005) *International Assignments: An Integration of Strategy, Research & Practice*, Mahwah, NJ: Lawrence Erlbaum Associates.

Suliman, A. (2001) Work performance: is it one thing or many things? The multidimensionality of performance in a Middle Eastern context, *International Journal of Human Resource Management* 12: 1049–61.

Sullivan, J., Suzuki, T. and Kondo, Y. (1985) Managerial theories and the performance control process in Japanese and American work groups, *National Academy of Management Proceedings* 98–102.

Sully de Luque, M. F. and Sommer, S. M. (2000) The impact of culture on feedback-seeking behavior: an integrated model and propositions, *Academy of Management Review* 25: 29–49.

Suutari, V. and Tahvanainen, M. (2002) The antecedents of performance management among Finnish expatriates, *International Journal of Human Resource Management* 13: 55–75.

Tahvanainen, M. (2000) Expatriate performance management: the case of Nokia telecommunications, *Human Resource Management* 39: 267–75.

Vallance, S. (1999) Performance appraisal in Singapore, Thailand and the Philippines: a cultural perspective, *Australian Journal of Public Administration* 58: 78–95.

Vance, C. M. (2006) Strategic upstream and downstream considerations for effective global performance management, *International Journal of Cross Cultural Management* 6: 37–56.

Vance, C. M. and Paik, Y. (2006) *Managing a Global Workforce*, Armonk, NY and London: M. E. Sharpe.

Vance, C. M., McClaine, S., Boje, D. M. and Stage, H. D. (1992) An examination of the transferability of traditional performance appraisal principles across cultural boundaries, *Management International Review* 32: 313–26.

Varma, A., Pichler, S. and Srinivas, E. S. (2005) The role of interpersonal affect in performance appraisal: Evidence from two samples – U.S. and India, *International Journal of Human Resource Management*, 16(11): 2029–44.

Von Glinow, M. A., Drost, E. and Teagarden, M. (2002) Convergence of IHRM practices: lessons learned from a globally distributed consortium of theory and practice, *Human Resource Management* 41: 123–41.

Whitley, R. (ed.) (1992) *European Business Systems: Firms and Markets in their National Contexts*, London: Sage.

Woods, P. (2003) Performance management of Australian and Singaporean expatriates, *International Journal of Manpower* 24: 517–34.

Wright, P. M. and McMahon, G. C. (1992) Theoretical perspectives for strategic human resource management, *Journal of Management* 18: 295–320.

Wright, R. P. (2002) Perceptual dimensions of performance management systems in the eyes of different sample categories, *International Journal of Management* 19: 184–93.

Yu, J. and Murphy, K. R. (1993) Modesty bias in self-rating of performance: a test of cultural relativity hypotheses, *Personnel Psychology* 15: 357–63.

3 Motivation and performance management

ROBERT D. PRITCHARD AND DEBORAH DIAZGRANADOS

As is clear from the earlier chapters, performance management (PM) is a key process in any organization. *Performance management* is defined as a range of practices an organization engages in to enhance the performance of a target person or group with the ultimate purpose of improving organizational performance (DeNisi, 2000). PM practices are changes that can be directed at the individual, team, unit, or organizational level of analysis.

There are a variety of PM techniques such as training, feedback in the forms of knowledge-of-results and performance appraisal (PA), goal-setting, and, finally, incentives. There are also more complex practices that combine a number of features of the more basic procedures to PM. Examples of these are: (1) Total Quality Management (TQM) (Ishikawa, 1985; Jablonski, 1991); (2) Empowerment (Conger and Kanungo, 1988; Liden, Wayne and Sparrowe, 2000; Thomas and Velthouse, 1990); (3) Knowledge Management (Bose, 2004; Earl, 2001; Hansen, 2002); (4) Autonomous Work Groups (Cordery, 1996; Wall, Kemp, Jackson and Clegg, 1986); (5) the Balanced Scorecard (Kaplan and Norton, 1996), Six Sigma (Larson, 2003); and (6) the Productivity Measurement and Enhancement System (ProMES) (Pritchard, Holling, Lammers and Clark, 2002).

The aim of this chapter is to introduce the concept of motivation and link it to PM. We define motivation and then introduce a model of motivation. The model of motivation is explained in detail with particular emphasis on the connections between each component of the model. Cross-cultural issues are then mentioned when examining motivation and we conclude this chapter with a case study where the reader can apply the knowledge gained from the chapter.

The importance of motivation in PM

The objective of PM is to maximize employees' contributions to the organization, which means changing employees' behaviors so that they produce this maximum contribution. As soon as we start talking about changing behavior, we are talking about motivation. *Motivation* is the process of allocating one's energy to actions or tasks. Motivation is about the level of effort one imparts to the job, how that effort is allocated across actions or tasks, and the persistence over time of that effort allocation (DeNisi and Pritchard, 2006). So, changing behaviors to make optimal contributions means that we must change motivation (Locke and Latham, 2002). Thus, motivation is important to effective PM (Latham, 2007). Managers can better manage performance if they understand motivation.

Symptoms of low motivation

To know that motivation is very important in PM may be simple, but to diagnose it is another matter entirely. First of all, how do you know whether motivation is high or low? One method of evaluating the level of motivation may be by identifying characteristics of the job that have been linked to low motivation, for example, role ambiguity (Tubre and Collins, 2000). Sometimes whether motivation is high or low is clear from the level of energy people put into the job. However, there are other signs to look for. These signs can be broken down into the effort expended, the direction of that effort, and the persistence of that effort (Bandura, 1986; Kanfer, 1990; Latham, 2007; Mitchell and Daniels, 2003).

Effort represents how hard a person is trying. Some specific examples of low effort can be putting in the least amount of effort possible without being penalized. Unwillingness to take on additional work, working inefficiently but not being willing to change, and avoiding work (being late, leaving early, prolonged breaks or lunches, absenteeism, high turnover when opportunities to leave occur) are also potential examples of exerting low effort. Direction is what tasks the effort is allocated to. People direct effort to some task or goal. Locke (1997: 376) stated that goal directedness is "a cardinal attribute of the actions of all living organisms." Some examples of low motivation levels that show up as direction are when people spend too much time on unimportant tasks or avoid tasks that they do not like. Persistence refers to how long the effort is sustained over time. Persistence problems show up as not putting in the effort to finish the work properly, or giving up on tasks that are difficult.

These concrete examples of how low motivation is represented can make it easier to identify and easier to improve an individual's level of motivation. This is a critical step in the process of PM because you need to know where motivation levels are now to be able to plan steps to make future improvements. In the next section, we briefly touch upon the past approaches to motivation. In the following section, we then introduce a motivation model that suggests how to diagnose and improve motivation.

Approaches to motivation

A great deal of thought has been given to the topic of motivation (see Latham, 2007). Mitchell and Daniels (2003) summarize this literature and point out some important aspects of motivation. First, it should be clear that motivation does vary across individuals and within individuals over time. Additionally, motivation is combined with the ability to produce behavior and, ultimately, performance. Many motivation researchers (e.g. Ford,

1992; Pinder, 1998; Kanfer, 1990) have associated motivation with three general processes. These processes are an arousal component (caused by a need or desire), a directional component, and an intensity component. The coverage of these aspects of motivation in the literature and the development of motivation theories take a variety of approaches. Some approaches focus on goal-setting, rewards and reinforcement, or dispositions and traits, while others may be more cognitive, and still others may be more behavioral (see Mitchell and Daniels, 2003 for a further review).

In order to understand motivation and to use it in PM, you need to know the components of motivation and how they work together. This means you need a model of motivation. This will allow you to understand, diagnose, and, ultimately, to improve motivation with PM techniques.

The motivation model

There are many models of motivation, but the one we will use in this chapter comes from a book by Naylor, Pritchard and Ilgen (1980) and a later elaboration by Pritchard and Ashwood (2007). This model is what is known as an expectancy model because motivation is primarily influenced by the expectancy or anticipation of what will happen in the future. Specifically, it is the expectancy of how applying energy to actions will lead to the future satisfaction of one's needs.

Figure 3.1 shows a graphic representation of the model. The top row of the figure indicates that, at any point in time, people have a certain amount of energy, called the *Energy Pool*. In addition, people also have *Needs* for such things as food, safety, achievement, power, all of which produce forces within the person that must be satisfied. The Energy Pool, which varies across people, as well as across time for any individual, is used to satisfy an individual's needs. The second row of the figure shows this energy pool is used to satisfy needs, and the process by which this is done is motivation. More specifically, the motivation process is a resource allocation process, whereby the resources are a person's time and effort, which come from the Energy Pool. This time and effort are allocated in such a way as to maximize the person's anticipated need satisfaction.

Moreover, the energy can be expended on the job or outside the job. The model focuses not only on the total amount of energy devoted to the job (effort), but also on the allocation of energy across the various tasks or actions on the job (direction) and how this allocation is accomplished over time (persistence). These three components are all important. A person can have problems because they (a) do the wrong tasks (direction), (b) do not put enough energy into a task (effort), or (c) do not continue working on the task long enough (persistence). For instance, we can also talk about someone being "motivated." We might say that someone is highly motivated to finish a report. By this, we mean that the person puts large amounts of time and effort toward some task. Put another way, the person chooses to work on the report (direction), works hard on it (effort), and keeps working on the report until it is finished (persistence).

Components of the motivation model

Boxes

The third row of the figure shows five boxes representing the components of the motivation process: Actions, Results, Evaluations, Outcomes and Need Satisfaction. To explain each of these, consider the example of a manager who has to write a report of their unit's operations over the last month. The manager devotes energy to Actions, such as talking to subordinates, reading reports, analyzing data, and writing the report. These actions lead to a Result, a finished report. The report is then evaluated first by the manager, and then by others that read it, such as the manager's supervisor. These Evaluations essentially place the report on an evaluative continuum from good to bad in the mind of the evaluator. There are often multiple evaluators, including the manager, their supervisor, and possibly the peers, subordinates and higher management as well. Evaluations can be quite formal, such as a regular performance review, or they may be informal, such as a comment from the manager's supervisor about how good the report was. The evaluators then provide Outcomes. Outcomes are the good and bad things that happen to the manager on the job. Some outcomes are extrinsic, such as pay, promotions and working conditions. Others are intrinsic, such as feelings of accomplishment or fatigue. Outcomes get their motivating power because of their ties to Need Satisfaction. We desire outcomes that satisfy needs while we wish to avoid outcomes that produce need dissatisfaction.

As with most expectancy theories, motivation is viewed as a future-oriented concept, in that people anticipate the amount of need satisfaction that will occur when outcomes are received (Arvey, 1972; Campbell and Pritchard, 1976; Heckhousen, 1991; Kanfer, 1990, 1992; Latham, 2007; Mitchell and Daniels, 2003). It is this anticipated satisfaction that determines behavior. As the person makes choices about how much time and effort to devote to which tasks, the ultimate goal in mind is to maximize the total anticipated need satisfaction.

Connections

Between each of the boxes is an arrow, called a connection. These connections are critical parts of the model and are areas where performance management is most likely to have an impact. The first arrow is between Actions and Results and this connection is called the *Actions-to-Results connection*. It is the person's perceived relationship between the amount of effort devoted to an action and the amount of the result that they expect will be produced. A manager who has written the monthly progress report for some time probably sees a high relationship between the amount of effort devoted to preparing the report (the actions) and the amount of the report actually finished (the result). However, effort devoted to a budget projection may have a lower relationship with the amount of the finished budget projection because much of the information needed to complete the report must come from others. So the manager does not have nearly as much control. Sometimes, no

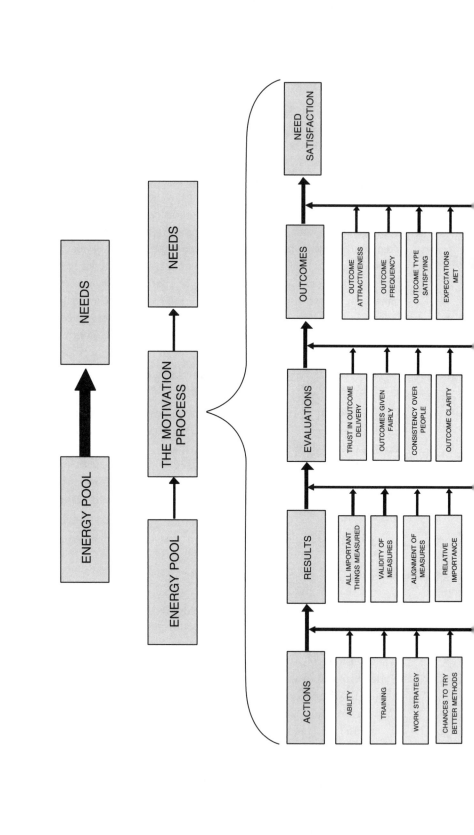

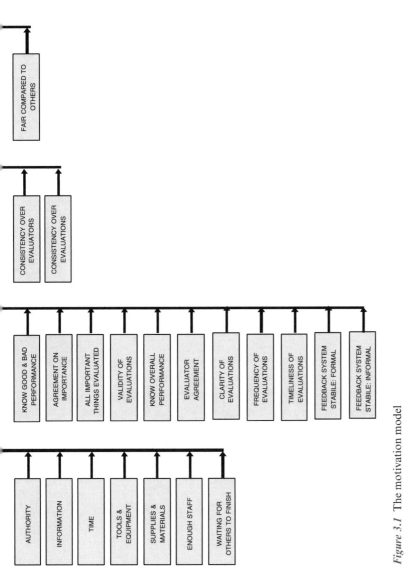

Figure 3.1 The motivation model

matter how much time is devoted to obtaining the required information, it is not provided by others.

The *Results-to-Evaluations* connection reflects the person's perceived relationship between the amount of the result that is produced and the level of the evaluation that is expected to occur. There would be such a connection for each different result and for each person who evaluates the result(s). For example, the manager in the above example may believe that how well the monthly departmental report is written has little effect on their evaluation. This means they see a low results-to-evaluations connection for that report. However, the manager may see a much stronger connection between how well the budget projection is written and their evaluation. The strength of this connection captures how important the result is. In our example, the monthly report is not as important as the budget projection.

Next, the *Evaluations-to-Outcomes* connection defines the perceived relationship between the level of the evaluation and the level of an outcome that will occur based on that evaluation. If pay increases are entirely based on the supervisor's evaluation, the manager would likely see a strong evaluation-to-outcome connection between the evaluation and the size of their pay increase.

The final connection is the *Outcome-to-Need Satisfaction* connection. This connection is the relationship between the outcomes received and the degree of anticipated need satisfaction that will result. If variation in the size of a raise results in large changes in the person's anticipated need satisfaction, the outcome-to-need satisfaction connection is high and this means that pay raises are very important to that person. If there is less variation in the person's anticipated need satisfaction, pay raises are less important to that person.

Motivation as a process

This combination of the motivation components implies that motivation must be viewed as a process and, as such, each stage of the process must function well for motivation (the outcome of the process) to be high. For example, if outcomes with high need satisfaction potential are tied to evaluations and these evaluations are clearly tied to the level of the results, yet people do not believe that they can produce the results, motivation will not be high. This is an extremely important aspect of the model that will be very useful in understanding the effects of the different PM techniques. For motivation and, ultimately, for performance to be high, all the connections in the model must be high.

Implications for motivation

We can use this model to guide the ways in which we design, implement, and maintain PM practices. In simplest terms, to maximize motivation, the connections must be maximized. That is, motivation will be high if all of the following conditions are met:

- People see a strong relationship between how much energy they devote to work actions and the amount of the results they produce.
- People see a strong relationship between the results they produce and the favorableness of the evaluations they get by each major evaluator.
- People see a strong relationship between the level of each major evaluator's evaluations and the level of outcomes they receive.
- The outcomes provided are important to people in that they see a strong relationship between the amount of the outcome and the level of anticipated need satisfaction.

To maximize the connections, we first need to understand which factors influence which connections. These determinants are shown in the bottom part of the figure. They are the boxes that feed into each connection arrow. If we know which ones of these determinants are causing the lack of motivation, we can focus on these specifically to design PMSs that maximize motivation. In particular, we can use the list of determinants to diagnose potential motivation problems. By ascertaining whether there is a problem with any of these determinants, this will help guide us in deciding what must be changed in order to improve motivation.

Action-to-results connections

To have clear and strong action-to-results connections, the determinants indicate that people must have the ability, knowledge, training, and authority in order to do the needed actions. People also need good work strategies (i.e. the way they go about doing the job). A good work strategy maximizes the translation of actions into results. With a poor strategy, it takes more energy to produce the same results, which results in a reduction in the action-to-results connection. In addition to work strategies, another determinant of the action-to-results connection is the opportunity for an employee to try improved methods of doing their job.

The design of the work setting must allow for controlling how effort is applied to different actions. For example, an assembly line manufacturing process decreases the flexibility of how to apply effort to actions. In such a case, an employee may be waiting to start their job because the co-worker ahead of the employee has fallen behind. Another determinant of the action-to-results connection is information. Without the proper information at the right time, it is difficult to produce the needed results and, over time, motivation will be reduced.

Another determinant of the action-to-results connection is time. Insufficient time to produce the needed results reduces the action-to-results connection, thereby affecting an employee's overall motivation. The final determinant here is the availability of resources. Resources can take the form of tools and equipment, supplies and materials, and even staff (i.e. co-workers). Such resources are important for an employee to successfully complete their job. A Human Resources team cannot produce paychecks on time if they do not get the information on the amount of time employees worked.

Results-to-evaluation connections

Developing good results-to-evaluation connections has major implications for feedback systems. The feedback system should not only measure all the important results, but should also evaluate all the important results. The term important refers to results that are essential to evaluators who control valuable outcomes for the person. Feedback on only a subset of the important results means that the results-to-evaluation connections are affected, although not all important results are equally vital. In order to optimize work strategies, the person must know the relative importance of the different results so as to give more attention to those that are more valuable to the organization.

Providing accurate descriptive measures of all the important results is critical for the feedback system and for forming good results-to-evaluation connections. However, the feedback system must also provide evaluative information. For example, knowing that 89 percent of the customers are satisfied is useful; however, knowing that 89 percent is considered rather low is also necessary. In other words, the descriptive feedback is considered the result and the evaluative feedback is the evaluation; thus, they are both necessary. This means the person must be able to translate the amount (how much) of the result into the level of evaluation (how good).

These evaluations and measures of results must not only be valid, they must be perceived to be valid. If the measures used or the ways these measures are translated into evaluations are seen as capricious, unreliable over time, or otherwise inaccurate, the results-to-evaluation connections will suffer because the identical results produce different evaluations. An accurate results-to-evaluation connection is enhanced when feedback on both results and evaluations is given on a regular established schedule and when the feedback is given soon after the performance period.

Other determinants of the results-to-evaluation connections deal with evaluators. The person must know who all the important evaluators are (Ilgen and Hollenbeck, 1991). Clearly, the supervisor and higher levels of management or supervision are evaluators, but peers, internal and/or external customers, people within the organization who must coordinate with that person, and the person themselves, may also be evaluators. One frequent problem with multiple evaluators is that different evaluators do not use the same evaluation system because different evaluators may think different results are important or may give different evaluations for the same level of results (Bobko and Colella, 1994; Motowidlo, 2000; Rotundo and Sackett, 2002). This is essentially an issue of role conflict. To minimize role conflict and maximize the result-to-evaluation connections, all of the important evaluators should agree. Ideally, this means all of the important evaluators need to agree on the evaluation system. This evaluation system delineates which results are important, their differential importance, and how the levels of results are translated into the levels of the evaluations. It is also important that the components of the evaluation system remain stable over time, but if a change is needed, it should be clearly communicated.

It is also important to consider that virtually all jobs produce multiple results. From a motivational perspective, it is valuable for the feedback system to combine the evaluations from these multiple results into an overall evaluation; a single number that reflects overall performance.

Finally, how results are evaluated should be consistent with how much value they create for the organization. If the evaluation system is not aligned with the broader organizational goals, individuals and units will be evaluated in a manner that is not consistent with what is actually valued by the organization as a whole and will develop suboptimal results for the organization (Boswell, 2001; Boswell and Boudreau, 2001; Gratton, Hope-Hailey, Stiles and Truss, 1999; Ramstad, Pritchard and Bly, 2002; Steers and Porter, 1991). If this mismatch occurs, it is likely that, in time, the individuals or organizational units will be told that they are not adding the value to the organization that is needed or expected. This means that the results-to-evaluation connection was wrong, decreasing confidence in the accuracy of the connection, thereby weakening the connection and decreasing motivation.

Evaluation-to-outcomes connections

Evaluation-to-outcomes connections are essentially the formal and informal reward systems in the organization. To have good evaluation-to-outcomes connections, the consequences of good and poor performance must be clear and these consequences must be consistent as well. This consistency will help to facilitate trust in the delivery of these outcomes. For example, it should be clear to a restaurant service employee that good performance, as demonstrated by superior service and accurate customer billing, leads to positive outcomes (i.e. relief from an unpleasant task, or better table assignments), while poor performance, as demonstrated by sub-par service and inaccurate customer billing, leads to negative outcomes (i.e. increased tasks, or remedial service training). The point is that both good and poor performance result in an outcome that is identified and can be expected each time performance is evaluated.

Additionally, in order to maximize motivation, there should be as many intrinsic and extrinsic outcomes as possible that can be linked to evaluations. Outcomes that are associated with evaluations can increase motivation. In addition, the perceived fairness of the reward system is important. Fairness means that the outcomes associated with results (either positive results or negative results) must be consistent across evaluators (i.e. peers, supervisors, and management), across recipients, and over time.

Outcome-to-need satisfaction connections

Good outcome-to-need satisfaction connections are also part of the reward system. The model says that in order to have powerful outcomes that will influence motivation, the outcome-to-need satisfaction connections for the outcomes must be high. This means that the available outcomes must be able to satisfy important needs of the workers, and outcomes should satisfy as many needs as possible.

Other determinants of the outcome-to-need satisfaction connections are outcome attractiveness and outcome frequency. It is essential to understand that not every employee will be attracted to the same outcome. What is attractive to men may be different from what is attractive to women, and what is attractive to a tenured older worker may be quite different from what is attractive to a new and younger employee.

Finally, as with all the connections, the outcome-to-need satisfaction connection is perceived relationships about how well outcomes are *expected* to satisfy needs. Therefore, it is important that these expectations are accurate because inaccurate expectations can lead to over or underestimating the need satisfaction of outcomes once they are actually received.

In summary, all the connections of the motivational process must be high for a person's motivation to be high. If any of the connections are low, this sets an upper limit on the resulting level of motivation. If, for example, the action-to-results, results-to-evaluation, and outcome-to-need satisfaction connections are all very high, but the people doing the work see that evaluations are not tied to outcomes (the evaluation-to-outcomes connection), and this one connection is low, then motivation as a whole will also be low. Additional diagnostic information is provided by evaluating the determinants for each connection, so that you can determine why the connection is weak, and prescribe a solution for the low motivation.

In the following section we introduce cross-cultural issues when understanding motivation. We will introduce some specific examples when applying this model to individuals from other cultures. The important thing to consider is that applying the model that we have introduced can be done across cultures, but it is critical to consider the cultural differences in the determinants for each connection.

Cross-cultural issues

Organizational globalization has made cross-cultural issues very salient in the twenty-first century. Therefore, in understanding motivation, it is important to consider how a model such as this generalizes across cultures. Several influential publications discussing workplace diversity and the impact of different cultures on an organization are available in the extant literature (see, Hofstede, 2001; Triandis, Kurowski and Gelfand, 1994). Some specific differences are individualism and collectivism, uncertainty avoidance, and masculinity and femininity.

Culture may define gender roles. Cultural values and societal norms may perpetuate gender role stereotypes. Such stereotypes may result in the belief that men should be strong and are self sufficient, whereas females should be caring and are needy. These stereotypes vary among different cultures as well as different ethnic groups (Franklin, 1984; Harris, 1994; Landrine, 1985), and can impact an individual's requirement for motivation.

Individualism versus collectivism is the extent to which people act predominantly as an individual or as a member of the group or organization. Hofstede (2001) has identified certain countries that may exhibit differences among this variable. He identified such countries as Argentina, Brazil, Greece, Saudi Arabia, and Japan as collectivistic. On the other hand, such countries as the Netherlands and the United States are rated as individualistic. Those considered being individualistic rate individual goals (i.e. those that may have material outcomes) as higher in priority than collective goals. In addition, individuals that are considered to be individualistic prefer to work alone and do not prefer the collaboration of working with a group of people.

It is important to consider that the differences between cultures, and even within a particular culture, on this continuum may result in varying values being placed upon the components found in the motivation model. A worker in Colombia may evaluate their action-to-results connection as weak because they are not provided with any co-workers to accomplish the task. Whereas a worker in the United States may evaluate their action-to-results connection as weak because they are provided with co-workers over whom they have no real control.

Uncertainty avoidance is defined as a preference for strict laws and regulations rather than ambiguity and risk. Those countries identified as being high on uncertainty avoidance are Belgium, Portugal, and Israel. Countries such as the United States, China, and India are rated low on uncertainty avoidance. To illustrate this point, a worker from Israel may not take as many risks in changing a work strategy that works to improve their productivity. Employees from Israel with a supervisor from China may be evaluated as poor performers because they resist changing their task strategies. Another example is using individual-level performance measures or outcomes in cultures that are collectivistic and prefer group level or team outcomes.

The major point here is that while the overall motivation process is probably quite similar in different cultures, the specific components of the model and people's preference for them can be quite different. A skillful manager needs to be sensitive to these differences and approach the diagnosis and improvement of motivation with care.

Future research

There are several avenues for future research that can be taken in terms of motivation and PM. The most general issue is whether we can diagnose the motivational state of individuals or organizational units and then use this information to make improvements that will improve motivation and performance. Research on the specific model presented here should focus on determining which of the connections in the model are most important in that they influence overall motivation the most. A related issue is the frequency with which each connection is low or high. It would also be important to identify the most effective techniques by which a manager could impact an individual's motivation level. The effect of cultural differences on motivation is an area of needed research. For example, future research could examine the impact that culture and the various cultural differences (e.g. power distance, collectivism, etc.) have on this or other motivation models.

Conclusion

It should be clear from this chapter that motivation is an important part of PM. Accordingly, the motivation model provides a way to understand motivation and how it influences behavior. Understanding the components, especially the connections and their determinants, provides the manager with an opportunity to apply motivational principles to the tasks of designing, implementing, and maintaining PMSs.

A case study

Pat is a financial analyst for a large, successful company. This is his first job out of college and he has been working there for three years. His goal for this job is to gain as much experience as possible, be promoted to manager, and save as much money as he can before moving on to a different company in the next few years.

Pat was raised in a Latin American country and has always enjoyed working with others. He was extremely active while at university in student organizations as well as university social engagements. He also thoroughly enjoys interacting with others and taking initiative and risks.

Pat's job deals with financial services sold to individual customers. He identifies new contacts for the company (40% of his time), sells services to clients (50% of his time), and supports more senior financial analysts when needed (10% of his time). In developing relationships with potential customers, he must follow a clearly defined company script which he cannot change.

Even though Pat has not received any formal evaluations by his supervisor, several peers and co-workers have taken the time to give him informal feedback. He was confused by this feedback because some have praised Pat's work and others have found problems with his work. Pat is looking forward to hearing what his supervisor has to say.

When his supervisor does meet with Pat to review his performance, Pat is looking forward to hearing his supervisor's evaluation. Yet, the supervisor's evaluation was rather vague and general. Nevertheless, the feedback given is positive and, as a result, the supervisor grants Pat several years of tenure to be applied to the required 10 years of vesting for Pat's profit sharing plan.

Questions

1 What is your evaluation of Pat's motivation level?
2 What is your assessment of what Pat received from his supervisor after his review; do you think Pat is happy about what he received?
3 Evaluate the results-to-evaluations, and the outcomes-to-needs satisfaction connections; do you see any improvements that can be made to strengthen these connections for Pat?

4 Using the motivation model, what are some of the changes to be made in order to improve Pat's motivation?

References

Arvey, R. D. (1972) Task performance as a function of perceived effort-performance and performance-reward contingencies, *Organizational Behavior & Human Decision Processes* 8: 423–43.

Bandura, A. (1986) *Social Foundations of Thought and Action: a Social Cognitive Theory*, Englewood Cliffs, NJ: Prentice- Hall.

Bobko, P. and Colella, A. (1994) Employee reactions to performance standards: a review and research propositions, *Personnel Psychology* 47: 1–29.

Bose, R. (2004) Knowledge management metrics, *Industrial Management & Data Systems* 104(6): 457–68.

Boswell, W. R. (2001) Aligning employees with the organization's strategic objectives: out of "line of sight," out of mind. Paper presented at the meeting of the Academy of Management, Human Resource Division, Washington, DC.

Boswell, W. R. and Boudreau, J. W. (2001) How leading companies create, measure, and achieve strategic results through "line of sight," *Management Decision* 39: 851–9.

Campbell, J. P. and Pritchard, R. D. (1976) Motivation theory in industrial and organizational psychology, in M. D. Dunnette (ed.) *Handbook of Industrial and Organizational Psychology*, Chicago, IL: Rand-McNally, pp. 63–130.

Conger, J. and Kanungo, R. (1988) The empowerment process: integrating theory and practice, *Academy of Management Review* 13: 471–82.

Cordery, J. L. (1996) Autonomous work groups and quality circles, in M. A. West (ed.) *Handbook of Work Group Psychology*, Chichester: John Wiley, pp. 225–46.

DeNisi, A. S. (2000) Performance appraisal and performance management: a multilevel analysis, in K. J. Klein and S. W. J. Kozlowski (eds.) *Multilevel Theory, Research, and Methods in Organizations*, San Francisco, CA: Jossey-Bass, pp.121–56.

DeNisi, A. S. and Pritchard, R. D. (2006) Performance appraisal, performance management and improving individual performance: a motivational framework, *Management and Organization Review* 2(2): 253–77.

Earl, M. (2001) Knowledge management strategies: toward a taxonomy, *Journal of Management Information Systems* 18: 215–33.

Ford, M. E. (1992) *Motivating Humans: Goals, Emotions, and Personal Agency Beliefs*, London: Sage.

Franklin, C. M. II (1984) *The Changing Definition of Masculinity*, New York, NY: Plenum.

Gratton, L., Hope-Hailey, V., Stiles, P. and Truss, C. (1999) Linking individual performance to business strategy: the people process model, *Human Resource Management* 38: 17–31.

Hansen, M. T. (2002) Knowledge networks: explaining effective knowledge sharing in multiunit companies, *Organizational Science* 13(3): 232–48.

Harris, A. C. (1994) Ethnicity as a determinant of sex role identity: a replication study of item selection for the Bem Sex Role Inventory, *Sex Roles* 31: 241–73.

Heckhousen, H. (1991) *Motivation and Action*, Berlin, Germany: Springer.

Hofstede, G. (2001) *Culture's Consequences: Comparing Values, Behaviors, Institutions and Organizations across Nations* (2nd edn.), Thousand Oaks: Sage.

Ilgen, D. R. and Hollenbeck, J. R. (1991) The structure of work: job design and roles, in M. D. Dunnette and L. M. Hough (eds.) *Handbook of Industrial and Organizational Psychology*: Vol. 2, Palo Alto, CA: Consulting Psychologists Press, pp. 165–207.

Ishikawa, K. (1985) *What is Total Quality Control? The Japanese Way*, Englewood Cliffs, NJ: Prentice-Hall.

Jablonski, J. R. (1991) *Implementing TQM: An Overview*, San Diego, CA: Pfeiffer.

Kanfer, R. (1990) Motivation theory and industrial/organizational psychology, in M. D. Dunnette and L. Hough (eds.) *Handbook of Industrial and Organizational Psychology: Vol. 1. Theory in Industrial and Organizational Psychology*, Palo Alto, CA: Consulting Psychologists Press, pp. 75–170.

Kanfer, R. (1992) Work motivation: new directions in theory and research, in C. L. Cooper and I. T. Robertson (eds.) *International Review of Industrial and Organizational Psychology*: Vol. 7, London: Wiley, pp.1–53.

Kaplan, R. S. and Norton, D. P. (1996) *Using the Balanced Scorecard as a Strategic Management System*, Boston, MA: Harvard Business School Publications.

Landrine, H. (1985) Race x class stereotypes of women, *Sex Roles* 13: 65–75.

Larson, A. (2003) *Demystifying Six Sigma*, New York, NY: AMACOM Books.

Latham, G. P. (2007) *Work Motivation: History, Theory, Research and Practice*, Thousand Oaks, CA: Sage.

Liden, R., Wayne, S. and Sparrowe, R. (2000) An examination of the mediating role of psychological empowerment on the relations between the job, interpersonal relationships, and work outcomes, *Journal of Applied Psychology* 85: 407–16.

Locke, E. A. (1997) The motivation to work: what we know, in M. L. Maehr and P. R. Pintrich (eds.) *Advances in Motivation and Achievement*, Vol. 10, Greenwich, CT: JAI Press, pp. 375–412.

Locke, E. A. and Latham, G. P. (2002) Building a practically useful theory of goal setting and task motivation: a 35-year odyssey, *American Psychologist* 57: 705–17.

Mitchell, T. R. and Daniels, D. (2003) Motivation, in W. C. Borman, D. R. Ilgen and R. J. Klimoski (eds.) *Handbook of Psychology, vol. 12: Industrial Organizational Psychology*, New York, NY: Wiley, pp. 225–54.

Motowidlo, S. J. (2000) Some basic issues related to contextual performance and organizational citizenship behavior in human resource management, *Human Resource Management Review* 10: 115–26.

Naylor, J. C., Pritchard, R. D. and Ilgen, D. (1980) *A Theory of Behavior in Organizations*, New York, NY: Academic Press.

Pinder, C. C. (1998) *Work Motivation in Organizational Behavior*, Englewood Cliffs, NJ: Prentice-Hall.

Pritchard, R. D. and Ashwood, E. A. (2007) *Managing Motivation*. Unpublished manuscript.

Pritchard, R. D., Holling, H., Lammers, F. and Clark, B. D. (eds.) (2002) *Improving Organizational Performance with the Productivity Measurement and Enhancement System: An International Collaboration*, Huntington, NY: Nova Science.

Ramstad, P. M., Pritchard, R. D. and Bly, P. R. (2002) The economic validity of ProMES components, in R. D. Pritchard, H. Holling, F. Lammers and B. D. Clark (eds) *Improving Organizational Performance with the Productivity Measurement and Enhancement System: An International Collaboration*, Huntington, NY: Nova Science, pp. 167–94.

Rotundo, M. and Sackett, P. R. (2002) The relative importance of task, citizenship, and counter-productive performance to global ratings of performance: a policy-capturing approach, *Journal of Applied Psychology* 87: 66–80.

Steers, R. M. and Porter, L. W. (1991) *Motivation and Work Behavior*, New York, NY: McGraw-Hill.

Thomas, K. and Velthouse, B. (1990) Cognitive elements of empowerment: an interpretative model of intrinsic task motivation, *Academy of Management Review* 15: 666–81.

Triandis, H. C., Kurowski, L. L. and Gelfand, M. J. (1994) Workplace diversity, in H. C. Triandis, M. D. Dunnette and L. M. Hough (eds.) *Handbook of Industrial and Organizational Psychology: Vol. 4.* (2nd edn), Palo Alto, CA: Consulting Psychologists Press, pp. 769–827.

Tubre, T. C. and Collins, J. M. (2000) Jackson and Schuler (1985) revisited: A meta-analysis of the relationships between role ambiguity, role conflict, and job performance, *Journal of Management* 26: 155–69.

Wall, T. D., Kemp, N. J., Jackson, P. R. and Clegg, C. W. (1986) Outcomes of autonomous work groups: a field experiment, *Academy of Management Journal* 29: 280–304.

4 Rater–ratee relationships and performance management

SHAUN M. PICHLER, ARUP VARMA AND RYAN PETTY

Introduction

Performance appraisal (PA) is one of the most heavily researched topics in the industrial-organizational psychology and human resource management (HRM) literatures because of its ubiquity in organizations and its importance for administrative decision-making. Performance ratings are typically used to differentiate employee performance and, on this basis, to make decisions about the allocation of training and development activities, compensation, promotions and other organizational rewards, such as merit pay. Given its link to the allocation of scarce resources, the performance appraisal (PA) process, and the accuracy of the resultant ratings, has received extensive attention in management theory, research and practice.

While researchers have traditionally assumed, based on the psychometric model of PA, that rating accuracy is a function of rating instrument format and rater cognitive processing abilities, attention has shifted in recent years to the affective and interpersonal variables that systematically explain variance in performance ratings. As will be explained below, while mechanisms designed to increase rating accuracy based on the psychometric model have shown some improvement in rating accuracy, interpersonal factors have been found to be particularly important, over and above these efforts, in predicting performance ratings.

The purpose of this chapter, therefore, is to introduce readers to the primary concepts, theoretical frameworks and research literatures that explain how rater–ratee relationships affect the PA process and performance ratings. It is important to note that PA is but one very important aspect of an organization's overall PM process. According to the model developed by DeNisi (2000), the purpose of PA is to accurately diagnose individual and group performance so as to be able to reward good performance and remedy poor performance such that, in the aggregate, organizational performance will be enhanced. If characteristics of interpersonal relationships between raters and ratees systematically distort performance ratings, this would suggest that performance problems will be under-identified and, perhaps, exacerbated; conversely, good performance may go unrewarded. In the aggregate, this could seriously jeopardize the effective use not only of cash and monetary resources, but also the organization's most valuable resource – its human resources. Thus, it is important to examine if and how rater–ratee relationships affect performance ratings; if indeed this systematic variance should be considered a source of bias or inaccuracy; and how this relates to future performance – at both the individual and organizational levels.

The importance of social context

The traditional psychometric model of PA assumes that ratings that are free from halo, leniency and range restriction are accurate (see Saal, Downey and Lahey, 1980), and that training raters to avoid these biases, or developing rating instruments which prevent these biases, will increase rating accuracy. This is because researchers have assumed that rating biases operate at a sub-conscious level (Arvey and Murphy, 1998). One critical inadequacy of this logic is demonstrated through the finding that interpersonal variables explain unique variance in ratings even when ratings are made more accurate through training and instrument development. Researchers have, accordingly, argued that rater motivation, affected in part by interpersonal relations, consciously affects performance ratings (see Murphy and Cleveland, 1995).

In order to understand how to train raters to more accurately observe ratee performance, researchers developed theoretical models based on a cognitive psychology research tradition. Indeed, the PA literature has largely been dominated by cognitive models of the appraisal process (Rynes, Gerhart and Parks, 2005). These models posit that the way in which raters attend to, encode, and retrieve performance-related information in memory affects performance ratings (cf. DeNisi, Cafferty and Meglino, 1984; DeNisi and Williams, 1988). While these models have been helpful to our understanding of the appraisal process, they are limited in that they do not fully account for variance in performance ratings, in part because of their limited attention to the social or interpersonal processes that influence the appraisal process. Performance evaluations naturally involve interpersonal processes, and to ignore this broader social context leads to under-specified, incomplete models of the appraisal process. To be sure, subordinates are typically active participants in the appraisal process, and make efforts to influence this process through impression and information management (Ilgen and Feldman, 1983; Wayne and Ferris, 1990).

In fact, researchers have, for some time, criticized the performance appraisal literature for failing to consider the social context within which the appraisal occurs (e.g. Dipboye, 1985; Guion, 1983; Wexley and Klimoski, 1984), and have advocated studying how social relationships between supervisors and subordinates affect performance ratings (e.g. Cleveland and Murphy, 1992; Murphy and Cleveland, 1995). Research on interpersonal affect, based largely on Byrne's (1971) similarity attraction paradigm, and the leader–member exchange model, based on role theory (Kahn *et al.*, 1964) and social exchange theory (Blau, 1964), have been extremely influential in this respect.

The following section will, accordingly, review the extant literature on how affect and leader–member exchange are related to performance ratings. Since affect is typically viewed as an antecedent to leader–member exchange, we review this literature first, followed by a section which integrates affect and leader–member exchange.

Interpersonal affect and rater–ratee relationships

In an examination of the effects of job-related and interpersonal factors on performance ratings, Borman, White and Dorsey (1995) found that while ability, knowledge and task proficiency were all related to performance ratings as previous research had suggested, the addition of interpersonal variables to a model of supervisor ratings increased model fit and increased the variance explained two-fold. Given that the interpersonal variables they studied (e.g. dependability and lack of obnoxiousness) contributed to the social–psychological context of an organization, the authors argued that they should be interpreted as contextual performance, as opposed to biasing factors. Of course, subsequent research has confirmed that contextual performance is related to performance ratings (Motowidlo and Van Scotter, 1994). The key here is in variable operationalization; the interpersonal variables used in the study by Borman and colleagues measured personal characteristics of ratees – not characteristics of dyadic rater–ratee relationships per se. For example, while the relationship between ratee dependability and performance ratings may not be viewed as a bias, what about interpersonal attraction between a rater and ratee?

Research on interpersonal affect has been somewhat more contentious. Interpersonal affect is defined as the extent to which a rater likes or dislikes a ratee (Murphy and Cleveland, 1991), and is based on an emotional or affective reaction to, and evaluation of, that ratee (Zajonc, 1980). Interpersonal affect is paramount to the study of rater–ratee relationships in the context of performance appraisal in that affect is "the major currency in which social intercourse is transacted" (Zajonc, 1980). In this connection, Tsui and Gutek (1984) defined affect in terms of interpersonal liking, as well as admiration and respect.

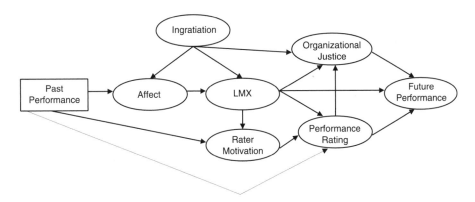

Figure 4.1 Past–future performance model

Thus, their definition of affect, as well as measures and studies based on this definition, emphasize what has been called job-related affect as opposed to purely social likeability (Robbins and DeNisi, 1994). Nevertheless, since the affect construct is typically construed and measured largely as interpersonal liking, scholars have traditionally characterized affect as a source of unconscious bias or inaccuracy in performance ratings (Dipboye, 1985; Landy and Farr, 1980; Latham and Wexley, 1981). Consistent with this research, Tsui and Barry (1986) found that affect was systematically related to rating errors (i.e. halo, leniency and inter-rater agreement), in the predictable direction. So, for example, where a rater had positive (or high) affect toward a ratee, s/he displayed leniency in rating that subordinate's performance. Similarly, Jacobs and Kozlowski (1985) found that halo increased as a function of interpersonal familiarity.

In order to explain these relationships, Feldman and others (Feldman, 1981; Srull and Wyer, 1980) have suggested, based on social-cognitive models of the appraisal process, that information about ratees is stored in memory based on ratee categories or prototypes (i.e. overall impressions of whether a worker is likeable or dislikeable), which lead to systematic under-evaluation and over-evaluation in performance ratings. This is because raters seek performance-related information that reaffirms their impressions of ratees (Feldman, 1981). In a test of this proposition, Robbins and DeNisi (1994) found that raters were more likely to use affect-inconsistent *and* affect-consistent information more than affect-neutral information during the encoding and weighting of performance-related information, which partially supported this hypothesis. However, it was affect-inconsistent information that was given more importance when assigning an actual rating, thus contradicting the above hypothesis. This finding calls into question the assertion that overall impressions of ratees as likeable or dislikeable acts as a source of bias in the appraisal.

In this connection, Robbins and DeNisi (1994) suggested that affect may be difficult to distinguish from past performance in field settings, and that past performance may be a more useful measure in field research since affect tends to suggest bias, especially when it is a result of demographic similarity. However, affect-inconsistency still predicted performance ratings after controlling for past performance; moreover, while past performance was more strongly correlated with job-related affect (.42) than social-related affect (.35), neither of these correlations would suggest that performance and affect are indistinguishable. In both a laboratory and a field study, Wayne and Ferris (1990) found that objective performance and affect explained unique variance in performance ratings, again suggesting that objective performance and affect are separable, mutually important determinants of ratings. Thus, while affect may be highly correlated, and even determined by previous performance, the two constructs seem distinguishable.

As Robbins and DeNisi (1994) highlighted, the ambivalence–amplification hypothesis proposed by Katz and Glass (1979) suggests that high performers and low performers will receive differential ratings based on their level of performance only when the rater is ambivalent. Positive affect and negative affect, on the other hand, are likely to inflate or deflate ratings, respectively, the authors argued. In a test of this theoretical rationale for a biasing mechanism, Varma, Pichler and Srinivas (2005) found differences in the relationship between interpersonal affect and performance ratings across cultures. Performance ratings of low performers in India were systematically inflated when they were liked by their supervisors, whereas this was not the case in their U.S. sample, suggesting that it is important to consider cultural norms in the context of PA. This is consistent with research by Schaubroek and Lam (2002) who found in a cross-national study of U.S. and Hong Kong bank tellers that personality similarity between supervisors and subordinates was a better predictor of promotions in more collectivist work units. This line of research would suggest that cultural demands, such as group cohesiveness, may increase the likelihood of a relationship between affect and performance ratings. But is this a source of bias per se? We will return to this topic later; until then, let us consider how rater–ratee similarity is related to interpersonal affect.

Given that demographic similarity is such a strong predictor of interpersonal liking in general (Byrne, 1971), and since affect predicts performance ratings in work settings, one could hypothesize that liking leads to discriminatory performance ratings as a function of demographic similarity. This general hypothesis has been examined repeatedly. For instance, Varma and Stroh (2001) developed a process model of the relationship between gender and performance ratings which posited that gender similarity influenced likeability, which in turn influenced leader–member exchange, which ultimately influenced ratings of performance. The authors found support for each component part of their model, indicating that supervisors rate subordinates of the same sex higher than those of the opposite sex as a function of the higher quality relationship that is developed among same-sex dyads through interpersonal attraction. Given that more supervisors are men than women in most occupations, this could ultimately result in discrimination claims. That said, the mounting research literature tends to suggest, in total, that the demographic similarity → affect → performance rating chain is tenuous (see Oppler, Campbell, Pulakos and Borman, 1992).

In this connection, deep-level similarity may be more important than these surface-level, demographic factors (Harrison, Price and Bell, 1998). Indeed, Schaubroek and Lam (2002) found that personality similarity predicted promotion decisions; this effect was partially mediated by leader–member exchange and communication with one's supervisor. Demographic similarity, on the other hand, was of limited predictive utility. Liden, Wayne and Stillwell (1993) found that perceived similarity, but not demographic similarity, between supervisors and subordinates predicted leader–member exchange.

Leader–member exchange and performance appraisal

It should be increasingly evident based on the preceding paragraphs that interpersonal affect, or liking, is closely linked to the quality of the rater–ratee relationship. Researchers have consistently suggested that affect determines, in large part, the relationship quality between supervisors and subordinates, and empirical evidence is supportive (see Liden and Mitchell, 1988; Varma, DeNisi and Peters, 1996; Wayne and Ferris, 1990). Early theoretical work posited that mutual liking was one of three primary components of leader–member exchange (Dienesch and Liden, 1986). In fact, Liden, Wayne and Stillwell (1993) found that affect was a more important causal determinant of exchange quality than were demographic similarity and performance ratings.

It is not surprising, accordingly, that leader–member exchange theory has been proposed as the primary lens through which to examine how interpersonal relationships between supervisors and subordinates are related to performance appraisal processes and outcomes (see Klein, Snell and Wexley, 1987). Leader–member exchange theory posits that supervisors (leaders) develop different (i.e. in-group and out-group) relationships with subordinates (members), and that the treatment subordinates receive is based on the quality of their relationship with supervisors (Dansereau, Graen and Haga, 1975; Graen, 1976). In-group members receive higher levels of trust, increased delegation and better rewards as compared to out-group members. The theory assumes that the relationship quality that is built from mutual trust, reciprocity and support (Dansereau *et al.*, 1975) can affect a variety of important outcomes for both supervisors and subordinates, including performance ratings and promotions. Not surprisingly, this theory has received ample empirical support (see Wayne and Ferris, 1990).

One of the reasons supervisors may give lower ratings to out-group subordinates is because they attribute their performance to different factors than those of in-group members. For instance, Heneman, Greenberger and Anonyuo (1989) found that effective performance was attributed to internal factors, that is, ability and effort, for in-group, but not out-group, members, whereas poor performance was attributed to ability and effort for out-group, but not in-group, members. These results indicate that supervisors make judgments about performance based not only on objective performance, but relationship quality as well. This is consistent with theory that argues raters are more likely to recall performance information that is consistent with their overall impressions (i.e. positive or negative) of ratees (e.g. Murphy, Gannett, Herr and Chen, 1986).

In this connection, Judge and Ferris (1993) offered theoretical rationale for the social–contextual significance of rater–ratee relationships in PA. They explained that when raters retrieve performance-related information in memory, they typically envisage interpersonal interactions as opposed to specific performance incidents; thus, to the extent that a rater has a high-quality relationship with a ratee, his or her judgment about that ratee's performance will be influenced by positive affective information. In support of this, Kacmar, Witt, Zivnuska and Gully (2003) found that communication frequency moderated the relationship between leader–member exchange and performance ratings such that frequent communication was related to higher performance ratings for in-group members, whereas frequent communication was related to lower performance ratings for out-group members. The authors speculated that this finding was due to the fact that communication reinforces positive or negative interpersonal relations, and that the information recalled in memory, when assigning a performance rating, is based on these communication patterns and interactions.

In essence, then, communication and leader–member exchange interact to affect the extent to which raters recall positive or negative information about ratees when assigning performance ratings. Since time to observe actual job-related behavior is naturally limited, communication with supervisors about job performance takes on an added importance. What is problematic, then, from a PM perspective is when a high-performing subordinate has difficulty explaining performance-related information to a supervisor simply as a function of their low-quality relationship, since this could potentially result in an artificially low performance rating. In this connection, if the subordinate feels that the rating is unfair, because of poor communication, this discrepancy in perceived performance is not likely to lead to improved future performance.

The situation described immediately above could create a self-fulfilling prophecy such that the subordinate's performance actually worsens after performance feedback. Other negative ramifications such as turnover are also likely. In this connection, Liden, Wayne and Stillwell (1993) found that rater expectations of ratees, several days into relationship formation, predicted leader–member exchange several weeks and several months later. While performance was not measured at later time periods, these results suggest that raters' expectations developed very early – a relationship that predicts subsequent relationship quality between raters and ratees, as well as subsequent role rewards.

Based on the preceding literature, it is clear that the ratees' ability to express job-related information to raters is an important determinant of relationship quality and the perceived fairness of PA – and perhaps future performance. In an investigation of the effects of interpersonal relationships on appraisal content and outcomes, Nathan, Mohrman and Milliman (1991) found that relationship quality between supervisors and subordinates was positively related to three appraisal process variables, namely (i) the extent to which subordinates participated in the process, (ii) behavioral criteria were used, and (iii) career outcomes were discussed. Further, these process variables were related to subsequent changes in job satisfaction and performance, controlling for past performance. Similarly, Elicker, Levy and Hall (2006) developed and tested a comprehensive model of the relationship between supervisor–subordinate relationships and reactions to performance feedback. They found that, controlling for the discrepancy between self and supervisor ratings of performance as well as subordinate liking of supervisors, leader–member exchange affected the extent to which subordinates felt they were treated fairly during their appraisal. This, in turn, affected appraisal outcomes such as the perceived accuracy and utility of the appraisal, as well as motivation to improve performance.

The above research indicates that relationship quality affects ratees' perceptions of the fairness of the appraisal process. Given that results from a survey among Fortune 100 firms indicated that perceived justice is the most important performance appraisal outcome to practitioners (Thomas and Bretz, 1994), it is certainly important to consider the connections between relationship quality and fairness perceptions related to performance appraisal. In fact, Folger, Konovsky and Cropanzano (1992) argued that perceived justice is a primary criterion by which PASs should be judged given inconsistencies between raters in performance judgments. They proposed a due process model of PA which allows ratees a voice in the process and opportunity to react to negative feedback. In this connection, empirical research indicates that ratee reactions to the PA, in terms of perceived fairness and job attitudes, are more likely to be positive under a due process model (Taylor *et al.*, 1995). While a due process model of the PA may indeed increase the perceived fairness of the appraisal process, as well as rating accuracy, we are still left with the question about how ratees can influence the rating process when their organization does not follow a due-process model.

One way ratees influence appraisal ratings in such situations is through ingratiation. Ingratiation is a form of supervisor-focused impression management whereby the ratee attempts to influence relationship quality through liking (cf. Wayne and Ferris, 1990; Wayne and Liden, 1995). Ingratiation has been found to be positively related to interpersonal affect as well as performance ratings (Wayne and Liden, 1995). In this connection, Dulebohn and Ferris (1999) found that supervisor–subordinate relationship quality and supervisor-focused influence tactics were positively related to subordinate perceptions of performance evaluation procedural justice. The authors posited that ingratiation acts as an informal voice mechanism, which was supported by the finding that ingratiation was more strongly related to procedural justice when opportunity for decision control was low, and that ingratiation was important regardless of supervisor–subordinate relationship quality. Similarly, Wayne and Liden (1995) found that ingratiation affects supervisor perceptions of interpersonal similarity, which affected performance ratings.

Conclusion

Results from existing theory and research clearly indicate that it is important to examine how the social context, within which PA occurs, affects performance ratings in terms of their accuracy and perceived fairness. Existing research is still somewhat ambivalent as to whether or not interpersonal affect or relationship quality act as biases in the appraisal process per se (see Lefkowitz, 2000; Robbins and DeNisi, 1998; Varma *et al.*, 1996; Varma *et al.*, 2005). Regardless, practitioners must be aware of how rater–ratee relationships affect performance ratings when designing PA systems, and evaluating their effectiveness. Researchers should model how these relationships unfold over time, and how they are influenced by other contextual features of organizations (Murphy and Cleveland, 1995).

Kossek and Pichler (in press) argue that while due process PA and other HRM strategies are important mechanisms to manage increasing organizational diversity, increase justice, and enhance organizational effectiveness, it is important to acknowledge the broader culture within which these strategies take place. For instance, if due process is limited to the PA process, and organizational culture is such that employees have few voice mechanisms, they may be skeptical about exercising voice in the PA process for fear of negative repercussions. Of course, broader cultural issues at more macro levels of analysis, such as power distance (Hofstede, 1980), should also be considered. The idea here is that future researchers should consider and measure the context within which the appraisal is taking place when conducting this research. In this way, we can better understand how context influences appraisal outcomes directly, as well as through its effects on rater–ratee relationship variables.

From a practitioner perspective, it is critical that HR executives train raters to conduct PA objectively and fairly. Perhaps a first step in this training could be to make raters aware of the potential for them to form in-groups and out-groups, often subconsciously. Such training is likely to lead raters to take the process more seriously, and also make them aware that the organization treats PA as a critical tool in the employee development process.

Further, raters will be more motivated to rate accurately, despite the interpersonal characteristics of the rater–ratee dyad, if they are rewarded for doing so, either extrinsically (e.g. raises, promotions, praise by superiors) or intrinsically (e.g. satisfaction), and value these rewards. Also, raters will be more motivated to rate accurately, again despite the interpersonal characteristics of the rater–ratee dyad, if there are punishments for rating inaccurately (e.g. reprisals from superiors). Finally, raters will be more motivated to rate accurately if there is a high probability that rewards or negative consequences will come to fruition following the occurrence of accurate/inaccurate ratings.

Since researchers have raised concerns that performance appraisal has little impact on actual performance change (Mohrman, Resnick-West and Lawler, 1989), another important extension of this research is to, in fact, measure changes in performance as a result of differential motivation due to performance feedback, and how relationship quality affects perceptions of feedback.

Case study

Susan works in the Product Development department of Pegasus, and reports to Jack, the head of Product Development. She has noticed that Jack spends a lot of time talking with her male colleagues, but rarely spends any time with her. In fact, she believes that Jack gives her most of the routine assignments, like generating reports, and compiling competitor product information. On the other hand, Scott and Tom, her male colleagues, get to work on important and strategic assignments, and often accompany Jack to the divisional meetings. Susan has approached Pat, the head of Human Resources, about this, and has expressed her displeasure at being treated like an outsider. Pat spoke to Jack, who was surprised by Susan's allegations. Jack noted that he felt he treated everyone on his team equally, and gave assignments, etc., based purely on team-member qualifications. When pressed by Pat, Jack admitted that he doesn't spend as much time with Susan as with his male team members, (i) he and Susan don't have much in common ["she hates football!"], and (ii) Susan had not shown much initiative to come and ask him for higher-level assignments.

Questions

1 What are the potential problems with this situation? How is this likely to affect Susan's performance?

2 What is Jack's responsibility in this situation, given he is Susan's supervisor?

3 How can Pat convince Jack that he needs to change his supervisory style?

4 If you were to offer supervisory training to Jack, what specific elements related to this case would you include?

References

Arvey, R. D. and Murphy, K. R. (1998) Performance evaluation in work settings, *Annual Review of Psychology* 49: 141–68.

Blau, P. (1964) *Exchange and Power in Social Life*, New York: Wiley.

Borman, W. C., White, L. A. and Dorsey, D. W. (1995) Effects of ratee task performance and interpersonal factors on supervisor and peer performance ratings, *Journal of Applied Psychology*, 80: 168–77.

Byrne, D. (1971) *The Attraction Paradigm*, New York: Academic Press.

Cleveland, J. N. and Murphy, K. R. (1992) Analyzing performance appraisal as goal-directed behavior, *Research in Personnel and Human Resources Management* 10: 121–85.

Dansereau, F. J., Graen, G. and Haga, W. J. (1975) A vertical dyad linkage approach to leadership within formal organizations: a longitudinal investigation of the role making process, *Organizational Behavior and Human Performance* 13(1): 46–78.

DeNisi, A. S. (2000) Performance appraisal and performance management: a multilevel analysis, in K. J. Klein and S. W. J. Kozlowski (eds.) *Multilevel Theory, Research, and Methods in Organizations*, San Francisco, CA: Jossey-Bass.

DeNisi, A. S., Cafferty, T. P. and Meglino, B. M. (1984) A cognitive view of the performance appraisal process: a model and research propositions, *Organizational Behavior and Human Performance* 33: 360–96.

DeNisi, A. S. and Williams, K. J. (1988) Cognitive approaches to performance appraisal, in G. R. Ferris and K. M. Rowland (eds.) *Research in Personnel and Human Resource Management*, Vol. 6, Greenwich, CT: JAI Press, pp. 109–55.

Dienesch, R. D. and Liden, R. C. (1986) Leader–member exchange model of leadership: a critique and further development, *Academy of Management Review* 11: 618–34.

Dipboye, R. L. (1985) Some neglected variables in research on discrimination in appraisals, *Academy of Management Review* 10: 116–27.

Dulebohn, J. H. and Ferris, G. R. (1999) The role of influence tactics in perceptions of performance evaluations' fairness, *Academy of Management Journal* 42: 288–303.

Elicker, J. D., Levy, P. E. and Hall, R. J. (2006) The role of leader–member exchange in the performance appraisal process, *Journal of Management* 32(4): 531–51.

Feldman, J. M. (1981) Beyond attribution theory: cognitive processes in performance appraisal, *Journal of Applied Psychology* 66: 127–48.

Folger, R., Konovsky, M. A. and Cropanzano, R. (1992) A due process metaphor for performance appraisal, in B. M. Staw and L. L. Cummings (eds.) *Research in Organizational Behavior*, Greenwich, Conn.: JAI Press, pp. 129–77.

Graen, G. (1976) Role making processes within complex organizations, in M. D. Dunnette (ed.) *Handbook of Industrial and Organizational Psychology*, Chicago, IL: Rand McNally, pp. 1201–45.

Guion, R. M. (1983) Comments on Hunter, in F. L. Landy, S. Zedeck and J. Cleveland (eds.) *Performance Measurement and Theory*, Hillsdale, NJ: Lawrence Erlbaum & Associates, pp. 267–75.

Harrison, D. A., Price, K. H. and Bell, M. P. (1998) Beyond relational demography: time and the effects of surface and deep-level diversity on work group cohesion, *Academy of Management Journal* 41: 96–107.

Heneman, R. L., Greenberger, D. B. and Anonyuo, C. (1989) Attributions and exchanges: the effects of interpersonal factors on the diagnosis of employee performance, *Academy of Management Journal* 32(2): 456–76.

Hofstede, G. (1980) *Culture's Consequences*, Beverly Hills, CA: Sage.

Ilgen, D. R. and Feldman, J. M. (1983) Performance appraisal: a process focus, *Research in Organizational Behavior* 5: 141–97.

Jacobs, R. and Kozlowski, S. W. J. (1985) A closer look at halo error in performance ratings, *Academy of Management Journal* 28(1): 201–12.

Judge, T. A. and Ferris, G. R. (1993) Social context of performance evaluation decisions, *Academy of Management Journal* 36(1): 80–105.

Kacmar, K. M., Witt, L. A., Zivnuska, S. and Gully, S. M. (2003) The interactive effect of leader–member exchange and communication frequency on performance ratings, *Journal of Applied Psychology* 88(4): 764–72.

Kahn, R. L, Wolfe, D. M., Quinn, R. P. and Snoek, J. D. (1964) *Organizational Stress: Studies in Role Conflict and Ambiguity*, New York: Wiley.

Katz, I. and Glass, D. C. (1979) An ambivalence-amplification theory of behavior toward the stigmatized, in W. G. Austin and S. Worshel (eds.) *Social Psychology of Intergroup Relations*, Monterey: Brooks-Cole, pp. 55–70.

Klein, H. C., Snell, S. C. and Wexley, K. N. (1987) Systems model of the performance appraisal interview process, *Industrial Relations* 26(3): 267–80.

Kossek, E. E. and Pichler, S. (in press) EEO and the management of diversity, in P. Boxall, J. Purcell and P. Wright (eds.) *The Oxford Handbook of Human Resource Management*, Oxford: Blackwell.

Landy, F. J. and Farr, J. L. (1980) Performance Rating, *Psychological Bulletin* 87: 72–107.

Latham, G. P. and Wexley, K. N. (1981) *Improving Performance Through Effective Performance Appraisal*, Reading, MA: Addison-Wesley.

Lefkowitz, J. (2000) The role of interpersonal affective regard in supervisory performance ratings: a literature review and proposed causal model, *Journal of Occupational and Organizational Psychology* 73: 67–86.

Liden, R. C. and Mitchell, T. R. (1988) Ingratiatory behaviors in organizational settings, *Academy of Management Review* 13: 572–87.

Liden, R. C., Wayne, S. J. and Stillwell, D. (1993) A longitudinal study on the early development of leader–member exchanges, *Journal of Applied Psychology* 78(4): 662–74.

Mohrman, A. M., Resnick-West, S. and Lawler, E. E. (1989) *Designing Performance Appraisal Systems*, San Francisco: Jossey-Bass.

Motowidlo, S. J. and Van Scotter, J. R. (1994) Evidence that task performance should be distinguished from contextual performance, *Journal of Applied Psychology* 79: 475–80.

Murphy, K. and Cleveland, J. (1991) *Performance Appraisal: An Organizational Perspective*, Boston: Allyn and Bacon.

Murphy, K. R. and Cleveland, J. N. (1995) *Understanding Performance Appraisal: Social, Organizational, and Goal-based Perspectives*, Thousand Oaks, CA: Sage.

Murphy, K. R., Gannett, B. M., Herr, M. C. and Chen, E. (1986) Effects of subsequent performance on evaluations of previous performance, *Journal of Applied Psychology* 71: 654–61.

Nathan, B. R., Mohrman, A. M. and Milliman, J. (1991) Interpersonal relations as a context for the effects of appraisal interviews on performance and satisfaction: a longitudinal study, *Academy of Management Journal* 34(2): 352–69.

Oppler, S. H., Campbell, J. H., Pulakos, E. D. and Borman, W. C. (1992) Three approaches to the investigation of subgroup bias in performance measurement: review, results and conclusions, *Journal of Applied Psychology* 77(2): 201–17.

Robbins, T. L. and DeNisi, A. S. (1994) A closer look at interpersonal affect as a distinct influence on cognitive processing in performance evaluations, *Journal of Applied Psychology* 79(3): 341–53.

Robbins, T. L. and DeNisi, A. S. (1998) Mood vs. interpersonal affect: identifying process and rating distortions in performance appraisal, *Journal of Business and Psychology* 12: 313–25.

Rynes, S. L., Gerhart, B. and Parks, L. (2005) Personnel psychology: performance evaluation and pay for performance, *Annual Review of Psychology* 56: 571–600.

Saal, F. E., Downey, R. G. and Lahey, M. A. (1980) Rating the ratings: assessing the psychometric quality of rating data, *Psychological Bulletin* 88: 413–28.

Schaubroek, J. and Lam, S. S. K. (2002) How similarity to peers and supervisor influences organizational advancement in different cultures, *Academy of Management Journal* 45(6): 1120–36.

Srull, T. K. and Wyer, R. S. (1980) Category accessibility and social perception: some implications for the study of person memory and interpersonal judgments, *Journal of Personality and Social Psychology* 38: 841–56.

Taylor, M. S., Tracy, K. B., Renard, M. K., Harrison, J. K. and Carroll, S. J. (1995) Due process in performance appraisal: a quasi-experiment in procedural justice, *Administrative Science Quarterly* 40: 495–523.

Thomas, S. L. and Bretz, R. D. (1994) Research and practice in performance appraisal: evaluating employee performance in America's largest companies, *SAM Advanced Management Journal* 4: 28–34.

Tsui, A. S. and Barry, B. (1986) Interpersonal affect and rating errors, *Academy of Management Journal* 29(3): 586–99.

Tsui, A. S. and Gutek, B. A. (1984) A role set analysis of gender differences in performance, affective relationships, and career success of industrial middle managers, *Academy of Management Journal* 27: 619–36.

Varma, A. and Stroh, L. K. (2001) The impact of same-sex LMX dyads on performance evaluations, *Human Resource Management* 40(4): 309–20.

Varma, A., DeNisi, A. S. and Peters, L. H. (1996) Interpersonal affect and performance appraisal: a field study, *Personnel Psychology* 49: 341–60.

Varma, A., Pichler, S. and Srinivas, E. S. (2005) The role of interpersonal affect in performance appraisal: evidence from two samples – U.S. and India, *International Journal of Human Resource Management* 16(11): 2029–44.

Wayne, S. J. and Ferris, G. R. (1990) Influence tactics, affect and exchange quality in supervisor–subordinate interactions: a laboratory experiment and field study, *Journal of Applied Psychology* 75: 487–99.

Wayne, S. J. and Liden, L. (1995) Effects of impression management on performance ratings: a longitudinal study, *Academy of Management Journal* 38(1): 232–60.

Wexley, K. N. and Klimoski, R. (1984) Performance appraisal: an update, in K. M. Rowland and G. R. Ferris (eds.) *Research in Personnel and Human Resources Management, 2*, Greenwich, CT: JAI Press, pp. 35–79.

Zajonc, R. B. (1980) Feeling and thinking: preferences need no inferences, *American Psychologist* 35: 151–75.

5

Merit pay

BARRY GERHART AND CHARLIE O. TREVOR

One key purpose of performance management (PM) and performance appraisal (PA) systems in most organizations is to recognize and reward performance. By doing so, an organization hopes to motivate its current workforce, as well as influence the composition of its workforce by increasing the probability that high performing employees will choose to join and stay with the organization. Merit pay, as typically defined, refers to a policy where organizations give larger base salary increases to employees receiving higher performance (or merit) ratings than to employees receiving lower ratings.

In this chapter, we begin by placing merit pay in the broader context of pay strategy. We then describe the fundamental policy aspects of a merit pay system, as well as the typical challenges encountered in executing these merit pay policies. We next make the case that merit pay is often defined and studied too narrowly and that a fuller picture (e.g. including the effect of merit ratings on salary via their influence on promotion) is necessary. We close with a summary of key merit pay decisions and a few concluding remarks.

Merit pay and pay strategy

Before addressing merit pay specifically, it is useful to make the general observation that compensation or pay strategies, of which merit pay is a part, differ across organizations (Milkovich, 1988; Gerhart and Milkovich, 1992; Gerhart and Rynes, 2003) in terms of how much they pay (pay level) and how they pay (pay basis). Pay level can be defined in terms of an organization's average cash compensation (including wages, salaries, bonuses, stock-related payouts), or more broadly to also include benefits, which, in the United States, for example, adds roughly another 40 cents on top of every dollar paid in cash. Typically, pay level is chosen in the context of survey information regarding what competitors pay for similar types of employees. An organization must decide whether to pay the same, more, or less relative to the competitor group of companies. If an organization decides that some skills are more critical to business strategy execution, it may have higher pay levels for those jobs than for other jobs that are seen as less central. An organization may also choose different market positions for different components of pay level. For example, an organization may decide to have its base salary at the 40th percentile of competitor companies. However, with strong company performance, profit-sharing, stock options, and so forth, may, on average over time, result in total cash compensation being at the 75th percentile. Benefits levels too come into play with considering how to position total compensation, as in a country like the United States, where, as noted, benefits are a substantial portion of total compensation.

Pay basis refers to how organizations pay. In other words, what criteria are used to decide the amount of pay received by individual employees? For example, does an organization pay for seniority (e.g. in a unionized setting perhaps), does it pay for performance (e.g. using merit pay), or is some combination used? If its focus is on paying for performance, how is performance measured and how strongly is it rewarded? Are there different target market positions for high performers compared to those performing at lower levels? Do low performers have the option of remaining with the organization or does consistently low performance result in their exiting the organization?

In most organizations, especially for managerial and professional employees, one element of pay for performance is merit pay (Cohen, 2006). As noted above, merit pay is typically defined as an increase to base salary (often on an annual basis) that is based on PA ratings. Merit bonuses are similar in that they are based on PA ratings, but different in that the payment (bonus) does not become part of base salary, thus limiting growth in fixed labor costs. Although there appears to be some shift away from merit pay to merit bonuses (White, 2006), at least in the United States, over 90 percent of employees continue to receive base pay increases (Cohen, 2006). In this chapter, our focus is primarily on merit pay, though much of our discussion is also relevant for merit bonus systems.

An important point is that organizations tend to vary less on the pay level dimension than on the pay basis (e.g. merit pay) dimension (Gerhart and Milkovich, 1990). One explanation is that constraints on pay level are stronger. Organizations are constrained from paying too little by labor market pressures (the need to attract and retain quality employees) and from paying too much by product market pressures (the need to control labor costs because they are typically a substantial share of total cost and thus affect the price competitiveness of products/services.)

By contrast, two organizations that have the same pay level targets may differ significantly in the basis for that same pay level. For example, some organizations may pay 10 percent to 20 percent above market pay for all jobs regardless of performance, while other organizations are careful to pay above market only if the organization performs (e.g. profitability) above market. Perhaps in the former case, a higher pay level is deemed important to allow selectivity in hiring and to increase employee retention. In the latter case, there may be more of an incentive focus, thus the effort to align employee pay levels with organization performance. Yet another strategy, in the case of merit pay, is for an organization to only pay high performing employees 10 percent to 20 percent above market pay, while paying average performers at the market rate, and below average performers below the market rate. Such a strategy may provide a direct incentive for high performance, as well as encourage low performers to leave. To the degree that any of the above strategies contribute to higher productivity, it may be that the organization that has a higher pay level per employee may actually have lower unit labor costs (i.e. labor cost per unit of output/revenue) because the higher productivity of its employees more than offsets their higher compensation levels. In other words, it is possible that more revenue can be generated using a smaller number of highly productive and highly paid employees than can be generated using a larger number of less productive, lower paid employees (Gerhart and Milkovich, 1992).

The key point then is that organizations not only have more flexibility (Gerhart and Milkovich, 1990) with respect to pay basis (i.e. how they pay) than pay level (how much they pay), but it is also the case that the pay level and pay basis decisions are (or should be) interrelated and that paying high salaries and wages is not necessarily inconsistent with controlling costs and being efficient (Gerhart and Rynes, 2003).

Another way to put merit pay in context is to consider other pay-for-performance programs. These include profit sharing, stock plans, gainsharing, individual incentives, sales commissions, and, of course, the focus of this chapter, merit pay (Milkovich and Newman, 2008). As Table 5.1 shows, these programs can be classified on two dimensions (Gerhart and Rynes, 2003; Milkovich and Wigdor, 1991): level of measurement of performance (e.g. individual, plant, organization) and type of performance measure (results-oriented or behavior-oriented). As Table 5.1 indicates, merit pay is a pay-for-performance program geared toward recognizing individual performance contributions where performance is measured partly or fully by subjective assessments (i.e. behavior-based measures). It is important to note that, in practice, many employees are covered by what might be called hybrid pay programs. In other words, rather than working under merit pay or under profit sharing, in many cases, employees will be covered by both types of plans and perhaps others as well.

Table 5.1 Pay for performance programs, by level and type of performance measure

Type of Performance Measure	Level of Performance Measure			
	Individual	*Facility/Plant*	*Organization*	*Multiple Levels*
Behavior-based	Merit Pay		Merit Pay for Executives	Hybrid
Results-based	Individual Incentives Sales Commission	Gainsharing	Profit Sharing Stock Plans	Hybrid
Results-based and Behavior-based	Hybrid	Hybrid	Hybrid	Hybrid

Fundamentals

Two basic purposes of merit pay are first, to provide incentives to motivate current employees to perform at a high level by recognizing and rewarding performance over time, and second, to build the best workforce possible by attracting and retaining high performers (Gerhart and Milkovich, 1992). These are also known as incentive and sorting effects, respectively (Gerhart and Rynes, 2003). As shown in Table 5.2, the idea behind merit pay is to pay consistently high performing employees above the average market salary, average performers at the average market salary, and low performers below the average market salary. By doing so, it is hoped that employees will have an incentive to perform at high levels and that high performers will be attracted and retained (or "sorted," Lazear, 1999) by paying them a salary that is above the average for their occupation/skill set. Alternatively, it may be thought of as there being different sub-markets based on performance and that motivation and retention of high performers requires that their pay be consistent with the sub-market rate for high performers (Trevor, Gerhart and Boudreau, 1997). As noted, paying for performance is also expected to help attract applicants with high potential future performance.

A third objective of merit pay is cost effectiveness. What does it cost the organization and what is the organization receiving in return? For example, if cash compensation is at the 70th percentile among product market competitors, is productivity (e.g. sales/employee or better, sales/labor cost) also at or above that level? Are high potential applicants interested in working in the organization and are high performing and/or high potential employees retained in a cost-effective manner? Are there other, more cost-effective ways (e.g. a better benefits package, more opportunities for advancement, work-life flexibility) to achieve the desired goals?

Companies such as Whole Foods, Lincoln Electric, and Nucor Steel have relatively high labor cost per worker, but believe that these higher labor costs are more than offset by higher productivity. Indeed, in these companies, a heavy emphasis on merit pay and pay for performance more broadly ensures that labor cost per worker can be high only when productivity is high. Other companies, such as the SAS Institute, rely less on merit pay, competing instead by offering a benefits package that is unique in its extensiveness and value, by limiting the work week to 35 hours, and by providing an environment where there are many opportunities for learning and self-development.

Table 5.2 Target salary as a percentage of market salary (compa-ratio), by performance rating

Performance Rating	Target Salary as a Percentage of Market Salary
Exceeds Expectations	110 to 125%
Meets Expectations	90 to 110%
Below Expectations	80 to 95%

As noted earlier, the higher target salary levels for higher performing employees under merit pay are based on a pattern of *consistently* high performance (Milkovich and Newman, 2008; Noe, Hollenbeck, Gerhart and Wright, 2006). A standard way of putting this philosophy into practice is to move employees toward the target salary that corresponds with their most recent performance rating, but not to make all-or-nothing adjustments in any single year. If an employee consistently performs at a high level, than based on the targets shown in Table 5.2, the organization will want the employee to earn between 110 percent and 125 percent of the market salary. However, if an employee has performed at an average level in previous years and receives a high performance rating in the most recent year, that employee will not be immediately moved to 110 percent to 125 percent of market salary. Rather, the employee will be moved toward that part of his/her salary range, but will have to perform at the high level consistently over time to actually reach that salary target (Milkovich and Wigdor, 1991; Milkovich and Newman, 2008).

Thus, as shown in Table 5.3, organizations often use a merit increase grid (sometimes also referred to as a merit matrix, salary matrix, salary increase grid). As can be seen, the merit increase when using such a grid depends not only on performance rating, but also current position in range, typically defined as the compa-ratio, the ratio of the employee's current salary to the midpoint of his/her salary range. In turn, the salary midpoint range would be set based to an important degree on external market pay surveys that report what other organizations pay for a particular skill set (Milkovich and Newman, 2008; Noe *et al.*, 2006).

A second and related reason for using position in range or compa-ratio as a factor in assigning merit increases is cost control. If an employee with a high compa-ratio were to continually receive high salary increases in percentage terms, then that employee's salary would soon exceed the market rate for high performers. Consider, for example, the "Rule of 72," which comes to us from the finance and investing community. It says that to estimate the number of years it takes for an investment to double in size, divide the rate of return (or interest rate) into the number 72. Using this rule, an employee receiving a 6 percent salary increase each year would double his/her salary every 12 years. Clearly, labor costs could get out of hand quickly without the cost control aspect of the merit increase grid.

Table 5.3 Merit increase grid. Recommended salary increases by performance rating and Compa-Ratio

	Compa-Ratio[a]		
	80% to 90%	*91% to 110%*	*111% to 120%*
Performance Rating			
Exceeds Expectations	8%	6%	4%
Meets Expectations	6%	4%	3%
Below Expectations	3%	2%	0%

[a] Employee salary/midpoint of their salary range

An example of this cost problem appears to have occurred at Circuit City, a consumer electronics retailer (Leonhardt, 2007). It announced that it would be dismissing about 8 percent of its workforce, not because it was eliminating the positions, but because the workers in the positions had gotten to be too expensive and thus would be replaced by lower paid workers. Apparently, although Circuit City had a policy like that described above under which employees at the top of their pay ranges were not supposed to get anything beyond cost of living adjustments (unless, of coure, they were promoted), managers "found it hard to stick to this policy" and gave raises that pushed employees beyond the maximum of the range. As a result, labor costs got out of hand and Circuit City felt it needed to take the step of dismissing these workers. Presumably, the dismissals could have been avoided if managers had adhered to the merit increase grid policy.

What this cost control mechanism means for an employee is that after some point, the value of their contributions in the same job, as indicated by their salary increases, is limited. To obtain further salary growth, the employee would need to seek to be promoted to a higher salary range. Alternatively, some organizations have gone to broadband systems, which provide a higher maximum salary rate for their salary ranges. These systems are used by organizations that wish to de-emphasize promotion as a path toward salary growth and wish to more strongly emphasize rewarding contributions in the current job. The potential downside, of course, is weaker control of labor costs.

Execution challenges

Most organizations report that they have merit pay policies. However, many organizations also report that an ongoing challenge is to execute their merit pay program so that there really is merit pay. In many organizations, employees are not convinced that high performers receive salaries and salary increases that differ in a meaningful way from what average and lower performing employees receive. In that case, motivation/incentive and attraction/retention objectives are likely to be undermined. The two culprits in employee skepticism are, first, an objective lack of merit pay, and/or second, inadequate communication to employees.

Merit pay can be said to objectively exist when performance ratings validly differentiate employees performing at different levels and these different performance ratings are positively and meaningfully correlated with salary levels and salary increases. Thus, the existence of merit pay is an empirical issue that can be assessed using what is often readily available data. (As noted, whether employees perceive this relationship is a somewhat different question. More on this issue follows below.)

One common problem with performance rating measures is that ratings are often clustered tightly and somewhat lenient. Table 5.4 provides an example of what this distribution might look like. This lack of variance in performance ratings translates directly into a lack of variance in salary increases, thus undermining merit pay. This lack of variance arises due to a number of factors. First, supervisors may be reluctant to give different ratings to members

Table 5.4 Distribution of performance ratings

Performance Rating	Frequency
Exceeds Expectations	40%
Meets Expectations	55%
Below Expectations	5%

of their workgroup because of a concern about its effect on workgroup cooperation and/or because managers may fear demotivating or angering people upon whom they depend for future productivity. Second, in many organizations, supervisors are asked to explain/justify low or high ratings, but not other ratings. Third, the performance rating system may not be well-designed and credible enough to support differentiation between employees. Among the ways this aspect can be improved are by setting specific performance goals in conjunction with employees, having multiple raters so as to reduce favoritism or idiosyncratic ratings, and involving employees in the design of the PA system.

Organizations have other tools at their disposal as well to increase differentiation in merit pay. Some organizations use a forced distribution policy, whereby a certain percentage of employees must fall into each of the performance rating categories. For example, rather than having a distribution that often comes out to be in the neighborhood of 40%–55%–5% or some other distribution that results from individual managers having discretion, a forced distribution policy (see Table 5.4) might require a distribution of 20%–70%–10%. A number of companies have instituted these forced distribution systems. Some (e.g. General Electric, GE) have continued to use them over time, while others have encountered problems (e.g. Pfizer, Ford) having to do with employee morale and/or equal employment opportunity (e.g. age-related) litigation, leading them to discontinue their use of such systems. Even GE, long known for its "vitality curve" (a 20–70–10 distribution), has modified its policy to be more flexible.

One of the stated reasons for going to a more flexible distribution at GE was a concern that the middle performance group, containing 70 percent of its employees, was being targeted in recruitment efforts by competitors. Under the more flexible distribution policy, 30 percent to 40 percent (versus 20% formerly) may now fall into the top performance group and fewer than 10 percent (and possibly even 0%) of employees are now permitted to fall into the lowest performance category. As such, this policy change addresses another issue, which is that under the previous, less flexible system, high-performing units having many high-performing employees would have had employees getting smaller salary increases than deserved and lower-performing units with fewer high-performing employees would have received too much. Under a more flexible system, an organization may decide to allow higher-performing units to give out a larger share of high ratings and require lower-performing units to give out fewer high ratings.

Another potential drawback of a forced distribution system is that cooperation and teamwork may be harmed if the available pool of performance ratings and merit increases is fixed, regardless of the performance of the organization or units within the organization. This effect must be balanced against the hoped-for positive effects on motivation and attraction/retention of top performers. If low performers are not satisfied with the system, that can be a positive, if there is an effective PM mechanism for moving those low performers out of the organization. The threat to teamwork/cooperation is likely to be greatest where there is greater interdependence among employees. The potential for problems is also likely to depend on whether the distribution is flexible and the degree to which competitive aspects are balanced by pay for performance programs (e.g. team, business unit or organization-wide incentives) that provide an incentive for cooperation.

Another potential roadblock to pay for performance is the design of merit guidelines, including the merit increase grid discussed above (see Table 5.3). Obviously, even if performance ratings are differentiated, there will be little pay for performance if the size of merit increases does not differ significantly according to different performance ratings. Also, as discussed above, merit increase grids are typically designed to give smaller merit increases to those already paid above the midpoint (i.e. those with higher compa-ratios) for cost control reasons and because those employees are thought to be already at the appropriate pay level relative to market. However, there is the potential for de-motivation for these employees, especially if opportunities for promotion based on performance are limited. In such cases, broadbands (see above) may be considered. Another possibility is the use of merit-based bonuses, which do not become part of base salary (e.g. Kahn and Sherer, 1990).

These features of merit pay programs can create a situation where employees perceive there to be little in the way of pay for performance (Gerhart and Rynes, 2003). Consider the case of two employees, each earning $50,000 per year. Suppose that the first receives an "excellent" performance rating and a 6 percent merit increase, while the second receives a "very good" rating and a 5 percent increase. On an annual basis, the differential is only 1 percent, or $500. On a weekly basis, the differential is $500/52 = $9.62. With a marginal tax rate of say 40 percent, the after-tax weekly differential is $5.77. Is this performance payoff sufficient to motivate Employee A to maintain the same level of high performance or to motivate Employee B to aspire to higher performance? Many people would say "no." Furthermore, given the imprecision of performance ratings, there is no assurance that better performance by Employee B would actually result in a higher rating and the modestly higher take-home pay.

Thus, it is easy to understand why employees often are skeptical about the real link between pay and performance. Consider, for example, a survey of employees in 335 companies conducted by the HayGroup (2002). Employees were asked whether they agreed with the statement, "If my performance improves, I will receive better compensation." Only 35 percent agreed, whereas 27 percent neither agreed nor disagreed, and 38 percent disagreed with this statement.

Academics too have expressed skepticism regarding the effectiveness of merit pay (e.g. Deming, 1986; Pfeffer, 1998). A review of the arguments and counter-arguments is not possible here. The interested reader is referred to Heneman (1992) for a thorough treatment of merit pay and to Gerhart and Rynes (2003) for a review of merit pay and, more generally, incentive pay. Here, we note that Gerhart and Rynes concluded that "despite considerable skepticism about merit pay, the actual evidence on merit pay is primarily positive" (p. 189). In addition, they argued that "important effects of merit pay have been largely ignored in the research literature" and upon accounting for these, "the evidence is bound to look considerably more positive" (p. 190). We discuss these ignored issues below.

A fuller picture

Without in any way minimizing the challenges discussed above, it can be argued that merit pay is stronger than usually believed for the following reasons. First, small differences in merit pay can accumulate significantly over time. Returning to our scenario above, after 20 years, Employee A is earning $121,024, while Employee B is earning $101,078. Moreover, during that 20-year period, Employee A has earned $148,785 more than Employee B, which is a substantial amount, even if adjusted to its present value ($76,690 using a 5% discount rate). If employees were informed that performing at a level consistently above average during the first half of their careers would yield this amount of extra cash, perhaps their instrumentality perceptions would be stronger and they would react differently to merit pay, even at modest levels. However, this hypothesis remains untested to date.

Second, "merit pay" is often defined too narrowly. Whether Employees A and B in our example receive significantly different pay increases in one year or over time is only part of the story. Rather, one must recognize that merit ratings influence not only annual salary increases (and/or bonuses), but also influence promotions (Gerhart and Milkovich, 1989).

Promotions, in turn, generally have a two-fold effect on career earnings (Gerhart and Milkovich, 1992; Trevor, Gerhart and Boudreau, 1997). First, there is typically a pay increase that goes along with the promotion, which may be considerably larger than the typical annual merit increase. The average pay increase due to promotion is in the range of 8 to 12 percent (Milkovich and Newman, 2008: 363), which is considerably higher than the average within-grade merit increase (roughly 3% in recent years in the United States). Moreover, the pay increase due to promotion is considerably larger at top management levels, often more than 70 percent (Gerhart and Milkovich, 1990).

Second, a promotion usually moves the employee to a new pay grade where he or she will have a lower compa-ratio. As we have seen, merit increase grids typically provide larger percentage increases to those with lower compa-ratios in the interest of moving their pay toward the target level for that position. Thus, the impact of performance on promotions can have significant consequences for the strength of pay-performance relationships, but these will be revealed only by examining the relationship over time.

Finally, sorting effects may also lead us to underestimate the true magnitude of the relationship between pay and performance (Gerhart and Rynes, 2003). For example, in organizations that use selective and valid hiring procedures and that systematically "manage out" those who do not meet performance standards, those hired and those that remain employed will be more likely to perform at acceptable or higher levels (Boudreau and Berger, 1985). While there may be little variance in performance and/or pay within this group, this selected group of employees may have above market pay, consistent with what may be their above market performance. Thus, there are differences in pay based on performance, but it is a between group difference (current employees versus former employees) rather than a within group (current employees) difference. Similarly, on the employee side of the decision, it may be that high performers are more likely to be interested in organizations that pay for performance and less likely to voluntarily exit from such organizations as well. In summary, even when there is little observed variance in performance ratings and/or pay within an organization, it may nevertheless be the case that sorting effects (and promotion can be included under this heading) have resulted in major differences in performance between organizations.

Key decisions

Although we have touched on some key decisions in using merit pay, we now identify and summarize these more systematically. Key decisions include:

1 Dimensions: what areas are included in our measure of merit/performance? A job analysis is necessary to identify the key dimensions of job performance. Anything that is not measured and included in performance assessment risks being ignored.
2 Pay for performance strength or differentiation: how strongly or weakly are pay and performance related? As discussed above, for merit pay to have incentive and sorting effects, the relationship between pay and performance must be meaningful.
3 Criteria type: results or behaviors? Although, by definition, merit pay pertains to behaviors as judged by one or more raters, pay for performance systems more generally can include other types of performance measures. At first blush, the objective nature of results-oriented measures (e.g. physical output, sales, profits) may be seen as a major advantage. While according to agency theory, results-based measures can have superior incentive properties and should require fewer supervisors (a significant source of potential savings), agency theory also says that employees are risk-averse and thus require higher pay levels to accept results-based measures because they carry more inherent risk (e.g. sales may fluctuate due to factors beyond the employee's control, such as changes in product market competition). Behavior-based measures, while subjective, can account for such factors and can also be used to verify that results are obtained in a way that is consistent with the organization's values (Milkovich and Wigdor, 1991).
4 Individual or aggregate performance measures? Although merit pay is typically defined as individual-oriented, as with the results versus behavior issue, it must be recognized that, in practice, pay for performance more broadly may include individual and aggregate measures of performance. As noted under "Dimensions" (No. 1 above) what is not measured and rewarded may be ignored (Milgrom and Roberts, 1992). Thus, organizations may either include dimensions such as teamwork in merit ratings or else

seek to complement individual level programs like merit pay with programs that reward aggregate performance (e.g. profit sharing, stock plans).

5 Sources of performance evaluation: supervisor or supervisor + others? Traditionally, the immediate supervisor has provided the merit rating. However, some organizations now use multi-source systems (e.g. "360" systems that add feedback from subordinates, peers, and/or customers, London and Smither, 1995). To date, most organizations use multisource systems more for employee development and career management than for making pay and promotion decisions (Rynes, Gerhart and Parks, 2005). Nevertheless, merit pay systems can have greater credibility and reliability if multiple raters are used. Most commonly, this would involve adding additional raters at the level of the employee's supervisor or above (rather than peers, subordinates, or customers).

6 Standards: absolute or relative (e.g. ranking, forced distribution)? As discussed earlier, left to their own devices, managers tend to compress their distribution of assigned performance ratings, thus making it difficult to differentiate between employees in the merit pay process. A relative system such as a forced distribution can very efficiently change the distribution to have more variance. The potential drawbacks include: penalizing units that do in fact have many high performers and creating too much competition between employees for the limited number of high ratings, which may harm cooperation and teamwork.

7 Merit salary increases or merit bonuses? Traditionally, most white-collar employees received annual merit increases that became a permanent part of their base salary. From an employer's point of view, these increases become part of long-term fixed labor costs. When sales decline, an employer's only option for reducing labor costs under this system is to reduce employment. Alternatively, variable pay plans seek to have labor costs vary in alignment with variance in sales and/or profits. Such plans provide employees payments in the form of bonuses, which do not become part of base salary. A merit bonus would typically depend on both company performance (e.g. profits) and an individual employee's merit rating. While variable pay plans offer the potential to align labor costs and company performance, the effect on motivation is less clear. Based on agency theory (e.g. see Eisenhardt's 1989 review), the more risk (risk is usually defined in terms of variance) there is in pay, the higher the pay level must be (i.e. a compensating differential for risk). In its absence, employee relations problems and/or employee retention problems may arise. In addition, the cumulative (and thus larger) effect of merit ratings on salary over time would be weakened by the use of merit bonuses, which, by design, do not accumulate.

8 Process: top-down or participative? How to communicate? In any situation where rewards are distributed, employees are likely to evaluate fairness along two dimensions (Folger and Konovsky, 1989): distributive (did they receive the right amount?) and procedural (was the process used to distribute rewards fair?). Involving both those covered (employees) by the merit pay program and those who will implement the program (managers) has the potential to result in better design, understanding, acceptance, and implementation. Communicating the merit pay program effectively (e.g. written or electronic communications, meetings) is also a basic requirement.

Conclusion

Merit pay is a policy that is intended to provide different pay increases to employees performing at different performance levels. Over time, high performing employees are expected to move to higher pay levels in a salary range than low performers. In addition, merit influences promotion, which typically results in still larger differences in pay levels as a function of performance over time. Another important, but often overlooked effect of merit pay is to sort prospective and current employees (Cadsby, Song and Tapon, 2007) such that high performers are more likely to be found at firms having stronger merit pay systems. These effects of merit pay depend on first, a meaningful link being established between merit/performance ratings and pay, and second, employee understanding and a perception that the system is fair and credible. Processes used to develop, implement, and communicate merit pay are important in this respect. Merit pay systems differ significantly across organizations and the eight key decision areas represent the many ways in which design can differ. Finally, it is important to recognize that merit pay systems are often combined with other pay for performance systems.

For researchers, merit pay is an area that has been under-studied, at least in terms of designs that (Rynes et al., 2005) include control groups (or significant variation across units or organizations in merit pay strength), intervening process variables (e.g. perceptions of merit pay strength), and/or careful longitudinal analyses (Rynes et al., 2005). Empirical work is also needed on the costs and benefits of forced distribution systems, on whether the merit pay and employee development aspects of PM and PA should or should not be linked, and on the effects of merit pay when both sorting and incentive effects are examined and when merit pay is defined more fully to include not only merit increases for current performance, but also the effect of merit ratings on promotion and overall pay growth over time (Gerhart and Rynes, 2003; Rynes et al., 2005). Finally, further research is needed that focuses on quantifying the costs and benefits of merit pay decisions (e.g. Sturman, Trevor, Boudreau and Gerhart, 2003).

Short case study

John Smith, President of a small company that provides software to corporate clients, wishes to make sure that his company's pay for performance system supports its strategic goals and their execution. Strategic goals include developing innovative new software applications, customer satisfaction, and customer retention, while keeping costs in check. Currently, salespeople are paid using a commission plan, which determines payments on the basis of quarterly revenues for each salesperson. Software engineers are currently covered by an incentive plan where payments depend on how much software code they write per quarter. Merit ratings are also conducted. Each employee is assigned an overall rating by the immediate supervisor once per year. However, these ratings have little impact on pay because most people receive the same ratings and also, there is a belief that objective measures of performance are better.

Questions

1 Are the incentive systems in place aligned with the company's strategic goals? Is there any role for merit pay to play a greater role in achieving better alignment? Explain.
2 If merit pay is to play a larger role, what sort of changes to the current system may be necessary?
3 In addition to the sales and software engineers mentioned above, what other employee groups would a merit pay plan be likely to cover and what unique issues would be relevant to consider in designing merit pay for these different groups?

References

Boudreau, J. W. and Berger, C. J. (1985) Decision-theoretic utility analysis applied to employee separations and acquisitions (Monograph), *Journal of Applied Psychology* 70: 581–612.

Cadsby, C. B., Song, F. and Tapon, F. (2007) Sorting and incentive effects of pay-for-performance: an experimental investigation, *Academy of Management Journal* 50.

Cohen, K. (2006) The pulse of the profession: 2006–07, *Salary Budget Survey*. *Workspan* (September), 23–26.

Deming, W. E. (1986) *Out of the Crisis*, Cambridge, MA: MIT, Center for Advanced Engineering Study.

Eisenhardt, K. M. (1989) Agency theory: an assessment and review, *Academy of Management Review* 14: 55–74.

Folger, R. and Konovsky, M. A. (1989) Effects of procedural and distributive justice on reactions to pay raise decisions, *Academy of Management Journal* 32: 115–30.

Gerhart, B. and Milkovich, G. T. (1989) Salaries, salary growth, and promotions of men and women in a large, private firm, in R. Michael, H. Hartmann and B. O'Farrell (eds) *Pay Equity: Empirical Inquiries*, Washington, DC: National Academy Press, pp. 23–43.

Gerhart, B. and Milkovich, G. T. (1990) Organizational differences in managerial compensation and financial performance, *Academy of Management Journal* 33: 663–91.

Gerhart, B. and Milkovich, G. T. (1992) Employee compensation: research and practice, in M. D. Dunnette and L. M. Hough (eds) *Handbook of Industrial and Organizational Psychology*, 2nd edn., pp. 481–570, Palo Alto, CA: Consulting Psychologists Press.

Gerhart, B. and Rynes, S. L. (2003) *Compensation: Theory, Evidence, and Strategic Implications*, Thousand Oaks, CA: Sage.

HayGroup (2002) Managing performance: achieving outstanding performance through a "culture of dialogue." Working paper.

Heneman, R. L. (1992) *Merit Pay: Linking Pay Increases to Performance Ratings*, New York: Addison-Wesley.

Kahn, L. M. and Sherer, P. D. (1990) Contingent pay and managerial performance, *Industrial and Labor Relations Review* 43: 107S–120S.

Lazear, E. P. (1999) Personnel economics: past lessons and future directions, *Journal of Labor Economics* 17: 199–236.

Leonhardt, D. (2007) One safety net is disappearing. What will follow? *New York Times*, April 4, Nytimes.com.

London, M. and Smither, J. W. (1995) Can multisource feedback change perceptions of goal accomplishment, self-evaluations, and performance-related outcomes? Theory-based applications and directions for research, *Personnel Psychology* 48: 803–39.

Milgrom, P. and Roberts, J. (1992) *Economics, Organization, and Management*, Englewood Cliffs, NJ: Prentice-Hall.

Milkovich, G. T. (1988) A strategic perspective on compensation management, *Research in Personnel and Human Resources Management* 6: 263–88.

Milkovich, G. T. and Newman, J. M. (2008) *Compensation*, Boston: McGraw-Hill/Irwin, 9th edn.

Milkovich, G. and Wigdor, A. (1991) *Pay for Performance: Evaluating Performance Appraisal and Merit Pay*, Washington, DC: National Academy Press.

Noe, R. A., Hollenbeck, J. R., Gerhart, B. and Wright, P. M. (2006) *Human Resource Management*, New York: McGraw-Hill/Irwin.

Pfeffer, J. (1998) Six dangerous myths about pay, *Harvard Business Review* 76: 108–20.

Rynes, S. L., Gerhart, B. and Parks, L. (2005) *Annual Review of Psychology* 56: 571–600.

Sturman, M. C., Trevor, C. O., Boudreau, J. W. and Gerhart, B. (2003) Is it worth it to win the talent war? Evaluating the utility of performance-based pay, *Personnel Psychology* 56: 997–1035.

Trevor, C. O., Gerhart, B. and Boudreau, J. W. (1997) Voluntary turnover and job performance: curvilinearity and the moderating influences of salary growth and promotions, *Journal of Applied Psychology* 82: 44–61.

White, E. (2006) Employers increasingly favor bonuses to raises, *Wall Street Journal* B3 (August 28).

6

A model of the appraisal process

KEVIN R. MURPHY AND ANGELO DeNISI

Over the years, a number of scholars have proposed models of the performance appraisal (PA) process, primarily as a means of organizing past research and generating propositions for future research. Many of these models have focused on the rater as a decision maker who must acquire and process information in order to make appraisal decisions (e.g. DeCotiis and Petit, 1978; DeNisi, Cafferty and Meglino, 1984; Feldman, 1981); while others have expanded this view to consider organizational and contextual factors influencing appraisals in addition to rater decision-making activities (Landy and Farr, 1980; Murphy and Cleveland, 1995; Wexley and Klimoski, 1984). These models have generated a large amount of research and have generally served the field well in terms of suggesting new ideas for research. We do not mean to endorse or challenge any of these models or the ideas they have generated, but we have drawn upon several of these to propose a model of the appraisal process that has a somewhat different goal.

The present volume deals with various perspectives on the processes of PA and PM, prepared by scholars and managers from all around the world. Our goal, in this chapter, is to provide a set of unifying themes that can be used for the discussions of these perspectives. That is, we do not propose a model to generate new research ideas (although we will discuss some possibilities along these lines later in the chapter), nor do we propose a model that is to replace any of the models already available. Instead, we propose a model that includes contextual factors that we believe influence appraisal decisions at various levels of analysis, as well as cognitive and motivational factors at individual level that are likely to affect appraisals in a wide range of settings. Our goal is to provide a template for the various authors of the chapters in this volume that can be used to discuss the different systems using a set of common issues and topics. In particular, we propose a framework that can be used to compare PA and PMSs across organizations, nations, and cultures.

We believe that all PMSs, wherever they occur, can be analyzed in terms of the factors in our model. For example, in any country, in any setting, cultural norms, the legal system, and technology will play a role in determining how appraisals are done and how they are used. But, since the actual norms, systems, and technology will vary from setting to setting, the particular features of PA and PMSs will almost certainly vary across industries, nations, etc. We believe that analyzing diverse PA and PMSs in terms of the models we present here will help to illustrate the commonalities and explain the differences in systems. While we do not

claim that our framework is comprehensive or universal, we do believe that it provides a
basis for integrating global studies of PA and PMSs.

The proposed model: Part I

The model we will use is presented in two parts, in Figure 6.1 and Figure 6.2. The first model
(Figure 6.1) focuses on the PA process, and ends with an evaluation which becomes part of
the feedback to an individual employee (or team), as part of the PM process aimed at
improving performance at both the individual and the organizational levels. The second

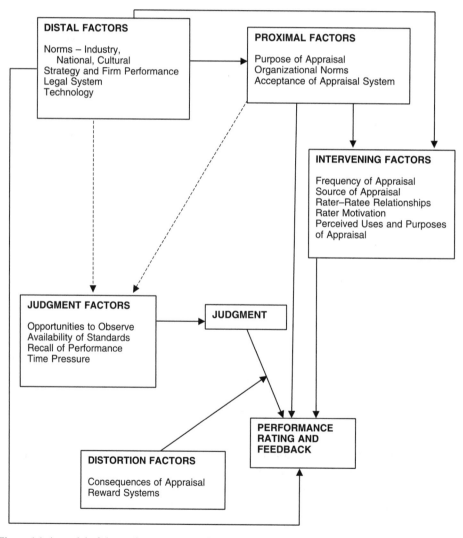

Figure 6.1 A model of the performance appraisal process

model (Figure 6.2) deals with the PM process and begins with the feedback provided in the appraisal process. We will discuss this second model in more detail below, but we focus first on our PA model. As can be seen in the figure, the first model is divided into several distinct segments, and we will describe each in turn.

Distal factors

The model begins by acknowledging the role of distal factors that operate at the level of the nation or region, but which can still influence the appraisal process. We will discuss each of these below, but these factors are things that are fixed, for the most part, as far as the organization is concerned, and so act as constraints or parameters for actions the organization might take. Also included here are organizational factors at the most macro level of analysis, such as firm performance and firm strategy. These factors are somewhat under the control of the organization but, even in cases where the factor can be changed (such as the strategy pursued), they are not likely to be changed simply to make the PM process more effective, and so, these too serve primarily as constraints or parameters within which the PMS must operate.

Norms

Norms for behaviour exist at the level of the country, the industry, and the specific organization. For example, norms differ as to the way appraisals are used in organizations. In some organizations, it is the norm for all compensation decisions to be based on appraisals. This is also more likely to be the case in non-unionized sectors of the economy (e.g. service industries) and in individualistic societies, such as the United States. In these cases, appraisals are likely to be conducted once a year, since that is when permanent pay adjustments are likely to be made. Furthermore, the appraisals would likely occur at some point not far before the pay decisions must be made. On the other hand, in organizations where it was the norm for appraisals to be used for feedback purposes only, appraisals would likely occur more frequently, and at less regular intervals.

Also, in societies where hierarchical relationships are more important (e.g. China), it is more likely that PA will be the sole province of the supervisor. In these societies, the notion that a subordinate might appraise his or her superior would be difficult to accept. Yet, in other societies, where values such as power distance were low, it would be perfectly acceptable to have appraisals done by peers and even subordinates. In fact, in some societies where power distance was low, and collaboration and collectivist views were valued, traditional supervisory PA might be seen as an illegitimate infringement on the rights of the workers or the workgroup, whereas in a culture with higher power distance, such supervisory appraisals would not only seem acceptable, they might be desired.

Thus, norms, whether they exist at the level of the organization, the industry or the nation, can influence the appraisal process. These norms help to determine exactly which practices are acceptable and which are not, and so they serve as constraints on what the organization can realistically do with appraisals.

Strategy and firm performance

The strategy a firm pursues in competing will also affect the appraisal process. This link is actually readily observable, even though strategy is a distal factor in our model. For example, organizations that pursue an aggressive strategy of cost-cutting will probably develop appraisal (and PM) systems that focus on behaviors that save money. Furthermore, one would expect to find PMSs that reward employees or provide cost savings, such as Scanlon Plans (which are group incentive plans where employees are rewarded, financially, for proposals which lead to significant cost savings). Organizations that concentrate on providing stable service in a specialized niche would be likely to appraise things such as customer service and satisfaction, and might even try to hire employees who fit the image of the niche in which the firm competes.

Different PA systems might be expected in an organization that has a long history of success and profitability than in an organization that is struggling to survive in a turbulent environment. In the former case, we would expect to have clear statements of standards and a shared understanding of how individual behavior relates to firm performance. In the latter case, there might be few formal rules and perhaps even the absence of a formal appraisal system. Appraisals might be based more on short-term goals and objectives which would change frequently. But, the nature of the appraisal system might also be affected by where the firm is in the "organizational life cycle." Several scholars (e.g. Whetten, 1987; Whetten and Cameron, 1983) have discussed the stages in an organization's life, as well as its decline, and several others have suggested how this can influence the structure of the firm as well as how performance is defined and measured (see review in Murphy and Cleveland, 1995: 79–81).

Finally, firms that perform well are more likely to employ the latest innovations in appraisal systems, as opposed to less successful firms. In fact, this is related to one of the dilemmas facing scholars who work in the area of Strategic Human Resource Management (Huselid, 1995). Specifically, these scholars have established relationships between firm performance and the presence of certain HR "best practices." But these two variables exist at the same time, and so it is difficult to determine if the adoption of certain HR practices leads to increased firm performance or if firms that perform well do many things well and can simply afford to adopt the best practices available.

Legal system

The legal system operating in a country, or a part of the country, is also likely to influence the way performance information is obtained and used. In the United States, a strong emphasis on litigation and accountability is likely to lead to an appraisal system that emphasizes detailed and specific record-keeping and clear links between the behavior of the ratee and the ratings he or she receives. But, even within the United States, state laws differ to a large enough degree that lawsuits dealing with unfair appraisal practices are more likely to be successful in some states than in others. In states where such suits are more successful, more detailed and well-documented appraisals are more likely to be found.

Legal systems also differ in terms of the kinds of protection they offer employees. For example, in many Western European countries, employees' protection against being terminated is so strong that it makes little sense to try to use appraisals as a basis for termination. Also, in the United States there are specific laws forbidding discrimination on the basis of race, religion or gender. Other nations have similar laws, but still others have laws protecting some groups but not others, and there are still countries in the world where it is legal to discriminate against women in work settings. The greater the protection, and the more far-reaching the protection, the more likely it is that appraisal systems will be carefully designed and well-documented.

Technology

Technology can influence the type of performance information that is collected and how it is used. Computerization and the internet make it possible to appraise employees who cannot be observed directly, such as employees working in a different country. In such cases, it is unlikely that appraisals will focus upon behaviors and more likely that they will focus upon outcomes, since these are readily available at a distance. However, computer monitoring of performance does allow the appraisal of certain types of behaviors – even at a distance. These systems make it possible to monitor when a customer service representative is on the phone with a customer versus doing something else. This technology, then, can drive the content of the appraisals system itself, as well as that of the PMS. For example, if it were easier to tell how many customers a service representative was speaking to, rather than how satisfied each customer was, the appraisal system and the PMS would more likely focus on the number of calls handled or the length of the calls, rather than on the quality of service.

Also, the increasing affordability and ease of web-based information-collection systems make it more likely that some organizations will factor feedback from clients and customers into their normal PAs, simply because it is so easy to collect the information. Such systems also make it easier for feedback to remain anonymous (if that is desirable) and for managers at different levels in the organization to share performance information about employees. Finally, improved technologies make it easier to document performance information, and also make any such documentation easier to retrieve in court cases where there is disagreement over what was said to whom about their performance.

These distal factors, then, are aspects of the situation that are not immediately associated with PAs, but can play an important role in the way appraisals are conducted and in how performance information is used. As noted earlier, these distal factors are not usually under the control of the person conducting PAs, and some cannot easily be changed by anyone in the organization. These factors, therefore, act to set the parameters of what can be done in the area of PA and so function as constraints. But in order to fully understand appraisal systems in a global environment, it is critical that we appreciate the fact that such constraints do exist, and that we try to understand exactly what effect they have on the resulting appraisals systems.

Proximal factors

In addition to more distal factors, there are also a number of more proximal factors that exist at a more localized level and that affect the appraisal process. These factors exist primarily at the level of the organization or unit involved. These also serve as constraints for any PMS, but these are things that are more closely under the control of the organization. They are also, of course, factors that will more directly affect the process and so are somewhat more critical to manage. There are three proximal factors which are likely to be particularly important for understanding PA systems.

Purpose of appraisal

The purpose for which an appraisal is being conducted will likely have a major impact on the appraisal process. First, as noted earlier, the purpose for the appraisal is likely to have an impact on the frequency and timing of appraisals. This is true whether we are talking about norms regarding the use of appraisals or simply the ways in which appraisal information is used in a given firm. Purpose is likely to affect also who conducts the appraisals. Specifically, PAs that are used to make administrative decisions about pay or promotion will probably draw heavily on annual evaluations only from supervisors. On the other hand, appraisals to be used primarily for feedback can (and probably should) come from subordinates and peers as well as supervisors.

The purpose for the appraisals is related also to a rater's motivation to provide accurate evaluations, and in particular, the rater's willingness to give high versus low ratings and to give ratings that discriminate among employees. Specifically, when appraisals are used for administrative decisions such as pay increases, raters might be motivated to give ratings that produce the desired distribution of these outcomes (e.g. similar raises to all members of a workgroup) rather than reflecting the performance levels of ratees. Thus, in this case, the ratings would be less accurate and there would be less willingness to discriminate among members of the work group (Murphy and Cleveland, 1995).

Finally, the purpose of the appraisal can have an effect by changing the nature of the relationship between the rater and the ratee. In the case of appraisals that are to be used primarily for feedback, the rater takes on the role of a "coach" trying to help the subordinate develop. But, in the case of appraisals used for determining raises or promotions, the rater takes on more of the role of "judge" and he or she then hands down a judgment to the ratee. The nature of this relationship can have long-term implications for performance since the rater and ratee will continue to have to work together.

Organizational norms

We discussed norms at the national or cultural levels as being distal factors influencing appraisals, but norms existing at the organizational level can be important as well, and they are more proximal. For example, both authors have encountered organizations where there was a strong norm to suggest that no one is rated "outstanding" or that no one is rated "poor." Other norms might dictate that the highest ratings go to the most senior people regardless of their true performance, or that the true purpose of appraisals is to punish employees who do not follow group work rules. Some of these other purposes for appraisals are discussed in more detail in Cleveland, Murphy and Williams (1989). In each case, these norms would have a direct effect on the nature of the ratings that were given and (probably) on how the ratings were interpreted by higher levels of management.

Acceptance of the appraisal system

Acceptance of the appraisal system by employees (as well as by managers) is also an important factor to be considered. When an employee receives an evaluation suggesting he or she needs to improve, this is done so that the employee will be motivated to change behavior and improve his or her performance. But, if employees do not accept the appraisal system as legitimate, they are less likely to see the ratings as fair (cf. Folger *et al.*, 1992) and, rather than try to improve performance, the employees will resent the low ratings and will instead reduce their efforts at work. The knowledge that employees either accept or do not accept the legitimacy of the appraisal system can also influence raters' willingness to give low ratings. Finally, acceptance of the system by the raters/supervisors can also influence their rating behavior such that they will rely upon other means of changing behavior outside the appraisal process, if they do not see the process as legitimate. In this case, they would likely give all employees relatively positive evaluations regardless of their true levels of performance.

Intervening factors

These are the result of the effects of distal and proximal factors and they can be viewed almost as mediator variables. That is, the factors we have listed as proximal and distal have an effect on the PM process through these factors, as was discussed above. For example, as noted, factors such as culture and norms will affect PM processes through their effects on factors such as the frequency of appraisal and the reward structures in place. These factors will have a very strong and close relationship with the ratings made as part of the PM process.

PA systems ask raters to discriminate among ratees and to give high ratings to good performers and low ratings to poor performers. The rater's willingness to actually make these discriminations and to identify good and poor performance might depend substantially on the norms of the organization (e.g. in many organizations, virtually everyone receives very positive PAs, making it difficult for raters to signal truly good or truly poor performance) and the degree to which both raters and ratees accept the appraisal system as accurate and legitimate.

Judgments versus ratings

In our discussion thus far, we have focused on how distal and proximal factors can affect the appraisal process, but it is important that we make another distinction now, before proceeding further. Following the work of Murphy and Cleveland (1995), we distinguish between judgments and ratings in our model. A *judgment* is viewed here as a relatively private evaluation of a person's performance in some area. Accurate judgments require that raters observe and recall the actual performance of subordinates, and that they compare their observations with appropriate and widely-shared standards. This task is likely to be difficult under the best of circumstances and doubly difficult when raters are carrying out their evaluations under time pressure or under conditions where their attention is likely to be diverted from the task of PA. Nevertheless, a judgment is a cognitive process and it is not really shared with anyone. *Ratings*, on the other hand, are a public statement of that judgment or evaluation which is made for the record. These ratings, then, are shared with others, but it is the central assumption of many models of a motivational processes PA (e.g. Murphy and Cleveland, 1995; Longenecker, Sims and Gioia, 1987) that the ratings individuals receive do not always correspond with the rater's private judgments about the performance levels of individual subordinates. We will discuss the factors that we believe lead to this discrepancy, but it is first necessary to establish the fact that we see these as two different outcomes, with different factors proposed to affect each one.

Judgment factors

These are the factors we suggest affect the private judgments or evaluations raters develop concerning ratees. These judgment factors *may* be influenced by the distal and proximal factors proposed to affect the entire process, but it is more important to think about these as factors which, on their own, affect judgments. Specifically, these are factors which research on cognitive processes involved in the appraisal process (e.g. DeNisi, 1996) has determined to affect those private, cognitive judgments. These are presented in Figure 6.1 and are mostly self-explanatory. For example, if a rater does not have sufficient opportunity to observe a ratee performing all aspects of the job it will be impossible for the rater to form an accurate judgment of the ratee's performance. When an incident of performance *is* observed, the rater needs to have clear standards of performance available so that she or he can decide whether the incident was illustrative of good or poor performance. But performance is ongoing and so the rater must be able to store information (either behavior or judgments) in memory over time, until they are needed to form an overall judgment. Unfortunately, information stored in memory can be forgotten or distorted over time, so that the information available to the rater when a judgment is needed is either limited or distorted (or both). Finally, time pressures operating on the rater, who has additional responsibilities besides evaluating a given employee, will make it more likely that that information is never observed, or is never evaluated correctly, or is simply forgotten. Thus, these judgment factors really make it less likely that the judgment formed by the rater, of the ratee's performance, is accurate (i.e. reflects the ratee's *true* performance). Regardless of the accuracy of this judgment, however, it must still be made public as a rating on a scale. Our model proposes several factors which can distort the translation of a judgment into rating, so that public ratings can be quite different than private judgments.

Distortion factors

There are a number of factors which might lead a rater to make a rating that is somehow different from the judgment he or she has formed. For this discussion, we assume that the underlying judgments are as accurate as they can be. That is, we assume that the extent to which the rater is able to do so, her or his judgments accurately reflect the ratee's performance. Distortion, then, indicates that the ratings provided do not reflect the judgments upon which they should be based. Two factors strike us as particularly important in affecting this distortion: the reward systems of the organization and the consequences of the appraisal. The reward systems here refer to the issue of whether there are rewards for ratings which accurately reflect judgments and/or sanctions that follow ratings which do not reflect judgments. Organizational handbooks and mission statements often describe PAs as critical to the organizations, but raters often reach the conclusion (usually a correct one) that organizations do not always value ratings that reflect accurate judgments.

Instead, there are many systems where there are actually sanctions for providing ratings that reflect accurate judgments, and/or rewards for ratings which do not reflect those judgments. For example, in organizations using forced distribution rating forms (i.e. forms that require certain percentages of ratees to each rating category) raters are "punished" if their ratings reflect judgments that all the ratees are performing well. Instead, they are *rewarded* if they adjust their ratings to fit the required distribution, even though they realize these do not accurately reflect their judgments. Other systems "punish" raters for ratings that accurately reflect their belief that some of their employees are weak performers, while other raters rate all of their employees as "outstanding," even if this does not reflect their judgments about those employees.

Although these rewards and sanctions can be important, in most situations, the motivation to either give accurate ratings (i.e. ratings that reflect judgments), or to distort ratings, is usually driven by the consequences associated with those ratings. For example, in an organization where performance ratings have a strong impact on desired outcomes (e.g. promotions, raises), raters are often strongly tempted to inflate their ratings so that their ratees will not suffer. In some work groups, a rater might distort ratings so that each group member receives the same rating, even if the rater does not believe this to be the case. Here, a rater might believe that differentiating ratings could lead to dissension and competition within the team, and so the rater chooses to distort the ratings in order to keep the work group intact.

The proposed model: Part II

The outcome of the PA model shown in Figure 6.1 is the public rating which is then shared with the employee or employees being evaluated. These evaluations often include a rating of overall performance, as well as ratings of tasks, or traits, or behaviors, that are presumably related to overall performance. This evaluation could be considered the end of the PA process, but the beginning of the PM process. The desired outcome of the PM process is an improvement in the performance of the employee being evaluated and, ultimately, in the performance of the organization, and that is the focus of the second part of our proposed model.

The Performance Management Process is modeled in Figure 6.2. Here we begin with the performance feedback given to the employee. This feedback generally indicates that there is some discrepancy between the observed level of performance in an area and the desired level of performance. This desired level of performance can be the result of established performance standards or earlier goal setting but, in any case, the critical issue is how to move the employee closer to that desired goal. Figure 6.2 suggests that various performance management interventions are designed to influence either the employee's ability to improve, the employee's motivation to improve, or both.

The process begins with the employee's acceptance of the feedback, and results in some change in performance that is (hopefully) closer to the desired performance level. Even if the employee is presently meeting her or his goals, the feedback might indicate that there is a need to increase those goals and so work harder. In any case, employee goals should determine (to a large part) the desired level of performance for the employee. Those goals, however, should also reflect larger corporate goals, or at least the goals of the next highest level in the organization. If this is done, then over time, the employee (hopefully) comes closer and closer to the desired level of performance, and so reduces the discrepancy between desired and observed performance. This progress is indicated by subsequent appraisals which produce additional feedback and closer approximations to the desired level of performance in a feedback loop similar to the type used in Control Theory (Carver and Scheier, 1981). As individual goals are met, then, corporate (or higher level) goals should also be met. Note that the system is not designed properly if individual goals can be met without there being any progress toward the achievement of organizational goals and, presumably, the improvement in organizational performance. In theory, the correct alignment of employee goals with organizational goals can then lead to improvements in organizational performance as well. This process continues until all goals are met. Then, the cycle begins again with new, more difficult individual goals that reflect new and more

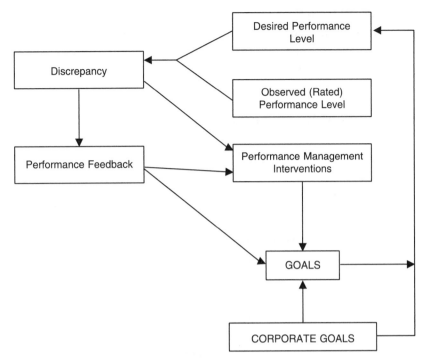

Figure 6.2 A model of the performance management process

difficult corporate goals, and which will result in even higher levels of corporate performance.

Note that, in our proposed model, discrepancies between observed performance levels and desired performance levels lead to both performance feedback and potential PM interventions. Many PM interventions involve some sort of goal setting, and ratees who receive unfavorable evaluations might set goals on their own that will influence their future performance. But, while goals are important, they are not the only mechanism by which PM interventions might work. Changes in the reward structure could also help, especially when the reward system is set up so that it rewards the "wrong" behaviors.

However, most PM interventions are focused on ways to motivate an employee to perform better. In some cases, the problem may not be one of motivation at all. Instead, the employee may not have been properly trained, or he or she may lack the basic ability or the skills needed to do better on the job. In other cases, the employee may need to overcome other constraints set by the organization. Thus, PM interventions, especially those based on goals, may not always be the best way to improve performance.

There are many other factors that could limit the effectiveness of performance management interventions. For example, there is some evidence that performance feedback does not always have the desired effect on employee motivation and that, in some cases, the presence of feedback (regardless of the sign of the feedback) can actually hurt subsequent performance (e.g. Kluger and DeNisi, 1996). In addition, poor communication of goals and expectations or failure to monitor performance can result in the employee not achieving his or her goals and, ultimately, the employee must have some incentive to improve if the process is to be successful.

Recommendations for research

As we noted at the outset it was not our goal to propose a new model of the PA process. We discussed several such models earlier, and there are others not explicitly addressed here that have discussed appraisals within the framework of more global systems (e.g. Budhwar and Sparrow, 2002). Nor did we undertake a complete review of the relevant literature – such a goal would require far more than this chapter. Rather, we present a framework, based on appraisal research, that can be used for discussing various appraisal systems. Nevertheless, the proposed model points to some directions for future research, and we turn to those to close this chapter.

Beginning with more distal factors, research aimed at describing "best practices" under different sets of circumstances would be useful. But in order to truly be instructive, it would first be important to develop a generalizable taxonomy of situational factors. Without such taxonomy, it might be difficult to determine exactly why a certain type of system is more successful in one country than in another, and whether there are lessons to be learned from cross-country comparisons of appraisal systems. The factors proposed here could be the beginning of such taxonomy, but there are surely other models that could be used as well.

Factors such as those described as "proximal" in our model should also be related to different measures of appraisal effectiveness. Specifically, if an organization uses appraisals primarily for purposes seen as legitimate by most employees, and organizational norms are such that everyone seeks to be as fair and accurate in rating as they can be (which should lead to the widespread acceptance of appraisals), those appraisals should be more effective in reaching organizational goals than in organizations where these conditions are not met. Thus, we would expect appraisals to be associated with improved individual performance as well as improved organizational performance. It may also be the case that perceived fairness and acceptability are the prerequisites for introducing changes in the way appraisals are conducted and used, or for introducing less traditional appraisals systems.

There has already been substantial research on the role of our "intervening" factors (see, for example, Murphy and Cleveland, 1995). There has also been a number of studies dealing with "judgment" factors (see, for example, DeNisi, 1996), and there may be decreasing returns from carrying out more studies of the roles of these specific factors. However, we do believe that the interactions among the various factors identified in our model have been under-studied, and that considering the way these factors combine may still yield considerable benefits.

The area in our proposed model where there has been very little research, and yet there is the potential for many interesting ideas, lies in the translation of judgments into ratings and feedback. There has been almost no research on intentional distortion that might occur as part of this process. More importantly, although many authors have suggested that such distortion exists, there are almost no data suggesting the exact variables that lead to distortion or to the specific nature of any distortion. This is fertile ground for future research in a national setting, as well as in a global setting, since different factors may lead to different types of distortion as we move around the world.

The benefit of developing an overall framework for discussing appraisal research and practice is that it provides a common language and frame of reference for making sense of the similarities and differences in appraisal systems across national and cultural boundaries. We hope the framework described here will prove useful for drawing insights from the chapters that follow.

References

Budhwar, P. and Sparrow, P. (2002) An integrative framework for determining cross-national human resource management practices, *Human Resource Management Review* 12: 377–403.

Carver, C. S. and Scheier, M. F. (1981) *Attention and Self-regulation: A Control Theory Approach to Human Behavior*, New York: Springer.

Cleveland, J. N., Murphy, K. R. and Williams, R. E. (1989) Multiple uses of performance appraisal: prevalence and correlates, *Journal of Applied Psychology* 74: 130–35.

DeCotiis, T. and Petit, A. (1978) The performance appraisal process: a model and some testable propositions, *Academy of Management Review* 3: 635–46.

DeNisi, A. S. (1996) *Cognitive Processes in Performance Appraisal: A Research Agenda with Implications for Practice*, London: Routledge.

DeNisi, A. S., Cafferty, T. and Meglino, B. (1984) A cognitive view of the performance appraisal process: a model and research propositions, *Organizational Behavior and Human Performance* 33: 360–96.

Feldman, J. M. (1981) Beyond attribution theory: cognitive processes in performance appraisal, *Journal of Applied Psychology* 66: 127–48.

Folger, R., Konovsky, M. A. and Cropanzano, R. (1992) A due process metaphor for performance appraisal. In B. M. Staw and L. L. Gummings (eds.) *Research in Organizational Behaviour*, Greenwich, CT: JAI Press, Vol. 14, pp. 129–77.

Huselid, M. A. (1995) The impact of human resource management practices on turnover, productivity, and corporate financial performance, *Academy of Management Journal* 38(4): 635–72.

Kluger, A. N. and DeNisi, A. S. (1996) The effects of feedback interventions on performance: historical review, meta-analysis, a preliminary feedback intervention theory, *Psychological Bulletin*, 119: 254–84.

Landy, F. J. and Farr, J. L. (1980) Performance rating, *Psychological Bulletin* 87: 72–107.

Longenecker, C. O., Sims, H. P. and Gioia, D. A. (1987) Behind the mask: the politics of employee appraisal, *Academy of Management Executive* 1: 183–93.

Murphy, K. R. and Cleveland, J. N. (1995) *Understanding Performance Appraisal: Social, Organizational, and Goal-based Perspectives*, Thousand Oaks, CA: Sage.

Wexley, K. N. and Klimoski, R. (1984) Performance appraisal: an update, in K. Rowland and G. Ferris (eds.) *Research in Personnel and Human Resources* (Vol. 2.), Greenwich, CT: JAI Press, pp. 134–65.

Whetten, D. A. (1987) Organizational growth and decline processes, *Annual Review of Sociology* 13: 335–8.

Whetten, D. A. and Cameron, K. S. (1983) *Organizational Effectiveness: A Comparison of Multiple Methods*, New York: Academic Press.

Part II

7 Performance management in the United States

ELAINE D. PULAKOS, ROSE A. MUELLER-HANSON AND RYAN S. O'LEARY

Nearly every type of industry and organization exists in the United States, from multibillion dollar, multinational corporations, to government agencies employing hundreds of thousands of people, to the smallest of nonprofit and family-owned businesses, and everything in between. As such, there is no "American style" of performance management (PM). Rather, there is enormous variety in the performance management systems (PMSs) used in the U.S. The goal of this chapter, therefore, is to describe the general trends and factors that impact the vast majority of PMSs in the U.S. To provide the context for this discussion, we begin with a brief summary of the socioeconomic and political factors that have shaped how PM is conducted in the U.S.

U.S. history is a story of independence and self-determination. The country was born out of a desire for freedom from foreign rule and a belief that all individuals "are created equal" and endowed with certain inalienable rights, namely, "life, liberty, and the pursuit of happiness." As the U.S. has matured, these principles have endured. Despite the wide diversity of its citizenry, the U.S. has retained a surprisingly robust national culture built upon the ideals of individualism, capitalism, and democracy. These ideals translate into several commonly held beliefs, including the importance of "personal responsibility" for one's actions, the expectation that wealth and status can be achieved through intelligence and hard work, and the right of individuals to determine their own futures and to elect their own leaders.

The strong individualistic nature of U.S. culture is manifested in PMSs as a conviction that employees ought to be evaluated on their individual performance and contributions. As such, performance evaluation in the U.S. is largely focused on the performance of individual employees rather than the performance of teams or work units. As a capitalist country, workers in the U.S. largely expect that their rewards will be a direct result of their individual contributions. As a result, there are competitive aspects to many PMSs in which only the top performing employees receive the greatest rewards. Capitalism has also created fierce competition for organizations and the people in them to be industry leaders. Pressure from stockholders, leaders, and boards of directors generate organizational climates that are results-oriented and driven to be highly successful and profitable. At the same time, as a democratic country in which everyone has a voice in government, citizens expect fair and transparent systems and processes. For employees, this translates into the expectation that PMSs will be administered in a fair and transparent manner and that employees will also have input into how their performance is evaluated. This expectation is reinforced by the U.S. legal system, which allows employees to easily seek redress if they feel they have been treated unfairly.

A primary goal of this chapter is to discuss key factors and challenges that impact the vast majority of PMSs in the U.S. Three key factors have had a particularly strong impact: a focus on results, automation, and the legal environment. These factors are a direct outgrowth of the national culture in the U.S. and the business environment and dynamics that characterize U.S. organizations. For example, a focus on results is an outgrowth of the desire and beliefs of U.S. citizens and organizations that they can compete successfully, attain wealth, and succeed. A key factor in achieving these goals is ensuring that businesses operate as efficiently, effectively, and profitably as possible, a key reason why U.S. businesses have been at the forefront of automation. Finally, the legal environment is an outgrowth of the democratic principles of fairness and justice that form the foundation of the U.S. While the three key factors that strongly impact PMSs in the U.S. are neither positive nor negative, they represent major trends with significant implications for PM design and implementation.

In contrast, the key challenges are decidedly not neutral. The challenges represent intractable problems that have plagued PMSs almost from their inception. While there is no "quick fix" for these issues, a thorough understanding of these and their implications is the first step toward mitigating them. Three top challenges faced by U.S. organizations include: viewing PM as an administrative burden rather than a strategic business tool, the reluctance of managers and employees to engage in candid performance discussions, and judgment and time factors that impede effective appraisal.

We begin with a brief history of how PM has evolved in U.S. organizations. Next we explore potential uses of PA information – decision-making versus development – and how the purpose affects important outcomes. The key factors and challenges are discussed next, followed by a best practice model of PM. While no single model can capture the full array of diverse PM practices in the U.S., the model presented in this chapter does reflect current writings and state-of-the-art practices used today in many U.S. organizations.

History of PM in the U.S.

The practice of using formal PMSs in the U.S. is fairly recent and its history is quite brief. Below is a brief outline of key events and trends that have helped to shape the way PM is conducted in the U.S. This outline provides a context for the discussion of current PM practices in this country.

● In the early 1900s, Frederick Taylor and other industrial engineers developed the principles of "scientific management" which emphasized the importance of defining standards for performance (Muchinsky, 1997). This movement has been widely recognized as the genesis of PM.

- During World War I (1914–18), Walter Scott and others conducted performance ratings of Army officers with a focus on officer ability (Muchinsky, 1997). These early efforts began to solidify the use of PMSs in government and industry and marked the first large-scale use of judgmental assessment.
- Following World War I, much of the work to define and measure performance was for the purpose of validating personnel selection methods (e.g. Bingham, 1926). As a result, considerable attention was paid to the development of standardized measures of performance for use as criteria (e.g. objective, personnel data, judgmental). In 1922, Patterson introduced the Graphic Rating Scale. This scale provided a metric on which to rate a trait or factor rather than making purely qualitative judgments. However, defining performance criteria proved difficult and the problem has plagued PM ever since (Austin and Villanova, 1992).
- The 1950s and 1960s saw continued development and expansion of the criterion domain with the use of multiple and composite criteria (e.g. Dunnette, 1963; Guion, 1961), which allowed for the expansion of the performance domain and the combination of objective and judgmental assessment of performance.
- The critical incident technique was introduced by Flanagan in 1954. This technique moved the focus of performance assessment away from global traits and factors toward job behavior.
- The Behaviorally Anchored Rating Scale (BARS; Smith and Kendall, 1963) was developed in the 1960s followed by several variants in the late 1970s and early 1980s [e.g. Behavioral Summary Scales (Borman, 1979); Behavioral Observation Scales (Latham and Wexley, 1981)]. These scales allowed for the quantification of behavioral performance.
- The civil rights movement of the late 1950s and early 1960s brought attention to the fact that minorities had systematically been denied equal opportunity in areas such as housing, education, and employment. The Civil Rights Act of 1964 and subsequent legislation, passed to help rectify these inequities, prohibited discrimination in employment practices. PAs, which often serve as the basis for employment decisions such as promotions and terminations, were required to be job-relevant, a requirement reiterated in 1978 with the publication of the *EEOC Uniform Guidelines on Employee Selection Procedures*.
- In the 1960s and 1970s, a considerable amount of research focused on alternative rating sources such as peers and customers (e.g. Lawler, 1967). Developing out of earlier work in the 1940s (e.g. Williams and Leavitt, 1947), this marked a movement away from reliance primarily on supervisory ratings.
- In the early 1990s, multisource or 360-degree feedback emerged out of rating source research and organizational movements such as employee involvement, self-managed work teams, and an increased focus on customer satisfaction. It quickly gained widespread popularity in the workplace (Hedge, Borman and Birkeland, 2001).
- Through the 1990s and into the 2000s, organizations increasingly adopted integrated

competency-based human capital systems. As a result, many PMSs incorporated competencies and behavioral-based standards to evaluate those competencies.

Uses of PM in the U.S.

Currently, most U.S. organizations use their PMSs for decision-making (e.g. for pay, bonuses, promotions, assignments, reductions in force). Fewer use PM to guide employee development, including training, mentoring, and other experiences to help employees develop their capabilities. The choice of whether to use a system for decision-making or development is a critically important one that has implications for the system's design and implementation.

Murphy and DeNisi (in Chapter 6) note the importance of the actual and perceived purposes of appraisal in their model: as a proximal factor (purpose of appraisal), an intervening factor (perceived use and purpose of appraisal), and as a distortion factor (consequences of appraisal). Because there are both advantages and disadvantages to using PMSs for decision-making versus development, neither option is uniformly better than the other. The decision about the purpose of PMSs needs to be based on the organization's PM goals. However, the real and perceived consequences of appraisal have significant implications, such as the following:

- **Rating distributions:** Research has shown that the purpose of appraisal affects the resulting rating distributions (Greguras, Robie, Schleicher and Goff, 2003). Ratings used for decision-making tend to be lenient, with most employees receiving ratings on the high end of the scale. Ratings for development tend to be more variable, reflecting both employee strengths and development needs.
- **Type of rating:** If a system is used for decision-making, numerical ratings are important. If a system is strictly developmental, there is less need for numerical ratings and, in fact, these may detract from development. This is because employees tend to be more concerned about their "score" than understanding their development needs. Rather than use numerical ratings, some developmental systems simply identify whether each competency "is a development area" or "is not a development area" for purposes of focusing developmental effort and goal setting.
- **Use of rating narratives:** From a developmental perspective, narratives tend to provide more useful information than numerical ratings. Even when performance is rated against defined standards, the ratings scores do not convey what the employee did or did not do in sufficient detail to be meaningful. Alternatively, rating narratives can be rich, customized, and useful sources of feedback because they tend to provide more specific examples that aid employees in understanding their evaluations. While rating narratives can also be useful for decision-making, they should not be used alone as a basis for decision-making. Without accompanying standards and ratings, narrative descriptions are often unstructured, unstandardized, and can reflect the motivation and writing skills of the manager more than the performance of the individual being rated.

- **Rating source:** Evaluations obtained from managers, peers, direct reports, or customers is often referred to as 360-degree feedback. Multisource assessments tend to be viewed as particularly credible for communicating development needs. Also, with multiple raters, the manager is not the "sole judge and evaluator" and can assume a greater role as a coach and helper. Using average ratings from at least three raters of a given type (e.g. peer) protects the anonymity of individual raters, which is important for obtaining accurate evaluations (Ghorpade, 2000; Waldman and Atwater, 1998). If performance information is to be used for decision-making, managers are typically the best source of information. While managers should collect performance information from other sources, it is important that they serve as gate-keepers, judging its credibility and quality and balancing it against other available information. This is important because raters from different sources often do not have the qualifications, experience, complete perspective, or motivation to make accurate evaluative ratings. In fact, research has shown decrements in the quality in multisource ratings when they are used for decision-making versus development purposes (Greguras *et al.*, 2003).
- **Equivalency across managers:** In systems used for decision-making, it is important for managers to calibrate their ratings to ensure that the same standards are being applied across employees. In developmental systems, rating calibration can be helpful but is not essential.

Although many organizations desire to implement a PMS that serves both decision-making and development purposes well, this is difficult to achieve in practice (Rotchford, 2002). For example, envision an organization where employees' pay and stock options are tied to performance. Although development is supposed to be included in the process, the range of pay increases and stock options is large, thereby allowing managers to make meaningful links between performance and rewards. With so much at stake, the majority of the PM process focuses on rewards justification by both parties, rather than on how the employee can develop. The decision-making consequences of PM are, by default, given more emphasis than development. Thus, for a PMS to achieve its maximum potential, it is best to choose one purpose – decision-making or development – and customize the system to best achieve that purpose.

Key factors impacting PM in the U.S.

Whether used for decision-making, development, or both, three key factors that are so pervasive that they impact essentially all performance management systems in the U.S. are:

- a focus on results,
- implementation of automated human resource systems, and
- a legal environment that allows challenges of employment practices.

Results focus

The U.S. has long been driven by bottom-line results, and this focus has increased in recent years, likely due to intense international competition that U.S. corporations have recently faced. As one example, to better compete in their market, IBM underwent performance-based restructuring in the 1990s. This "results focus" has not only affected private sector organizations but a similar trend has been observed in public sector and not-for-profit organizations as well – organizations that have not traditionally been driven by bottom-line results. For, example, in the 1990s the Internal Revenue Service (IRS), Federal Aviation Administration, and Government Accountability Office all initiated pay-for-performance systems, each of which focus on achieving results. More recently, the U.S. Departments of Defense (DoD) and Homeland Security (DHS) have begun to develop similar programs.

The value of results and their use to drive performance has been a cornerstone of many performance management trends, such as Management by Objectives (MBO) systems that were popular in the 1970s (Rodgers and Hunter, 1991). A current U.S. trend in this area is the use of cascading goals and objectives, where the organization's strategic goals are cascaded down to every level in the organization. Thus, each employee is accountable for accomplishing specific objectives that are aligned with the organization's mission (Hillgren and Cheatham, 2000), a concept that is also reflected in Murphy and DeNisi's PM process model. Employee performance is evaluated on the extent to which these objectives are met. The rationale behind this approach is that all organizational members are focused on work that is directly contributing to the organization's mission.

Although this approach seems imminently logical in theory, there are a number of potential problems in using objectives as the basis of PA (Borman, 1991). One issue is that inconsistency among managers can result in objectives that are too easy, unattainable, or unsystematic across individuals who occupy the same jobs (Jamieson, 1973; Strauss, 1972). For example, assume one employee's objective is to perform a simple information cataloguing project, while another in the same job is given the objective of managing the design and implementation of a complex information management system. If the value of different objectives has not been established and managers have not been trained on how to set appropriate objectives, both of these employees could be considered to be performing equally well, if they both met their defined objectives.

Another problem is that setting objectives in advance may be extremely difficult for some jobs (Cascio, 1998; Levinson, 2005). This is especially true today, as globalization has pushed the economy's focus from manufacturing toward knowledge and service work. The more varied and subtle the work, the more difficult it is to pin down objectives that represent more than a fraction of an individual's effort. Consider, for example, the difficulties one might encounter in setting objectives in R&D jobs where one cannot predict when discoveries will occur, in jobs that require extensive teamwork and interdependence with others, or in jobs that have unpredictable, fluid, and ever-changing performance requirements. To address the inherent difficulties in setting goals, some organizations are establishing an agreed upon set of cascading goals, where it is possible to do so, that are assigned to all employees in a particular work entity (e.g. unit, group, etc.). Additionally, managers and employees need to be prepared to make adjustments to the objectives during the year as the situation or priorities may change.

A third issue is assessing whether the objectives have been met or exceeded. Jobs that lend themselves best to setting objectives have static performance requirements and hard productivity measures (e.g. dollar volume of sales, profitability, or amount produced) rather than subjective indicators (e.g. manager ratings). Differences in results may be indicative of differences in opportunities that are available to different employees. For example, one employee may have more modern equipment than another and thus be able to produce a higher volume of product, irrespective of how hard either individual works. A similar example is that one employee may have sales territory in Wyoming and another in New York City. Certainly, based on the volume and proximity of potential customers, the individual in New York will have more opportunity to make sales than the one in Wyoming.

Finally, an exclusive focus on results can yield a deficient performance assessment because no consideration is given to *how* employees achieve their results. While one can achieve impressive results, overall performance is not effective if individuals are extremely difficult to work with, unhelpful, or cause problems. To address this issue, many organizations use systems that assess behaviors via the use of rating scales. One important advantage of using ratings to collect performance information is that all of a job's performance requirements can be described on the scales, thereby mitigating the deficiency problems often inherent in objective measures (Borman, 1979). Also, by focusing on behaviors that lead to effective performance, the problems associated with unequal opportunities to perform are also alleviated.

Although ratings circumvent several of the problems inherent in objective measures, concern has been expressed that this approach can miss an important aspect of work – namely, whether important results are actually being achieved. Therefore, a best practice today in the U.S. is to include a mix of results (what was achieved) and behavioral (how it was achieved) assessments in PMSs.

Implementation of automated human resource information systems

To achieve maximum results, the U.S. has a long history centered on efficiency of operations in organizations. From the advent of repetitive flow production in the early 1900s, to the use of Total Quality Management in the 1980s, to the recent trend to outsource non-mission critical functions (i.e. alternative service delivery), organizations are continually striving to increase efficiency. This has recently resulted in widespread implementation of automated Human Resource Information Systems (HRIS) in the U.S. to more efficiently deliver the vast majority of human resource-related business functions. Vendors such as SAP, PeopleSoft, and Oracle offer HRIS that allow employers to track and manage employees as they move through the employment lifecycle from pre- to post-hire. Typically, these systems automate human resources functions, such as time and attendance, leave, benefits, pay, recruiting, and staffing (Dorsey, 2002). Increasingly, PM has also become integrated into these large systems as more and more tools and platforms have been made available that automate all aspects of the appraisal process.

The movement to automated PMSs, a distal factor in Murphy and DeNisi's model, has both positive and negative potential consequences. On the positive side, automation greatly facilitates the PM workflow and substantially reduces the paperwork associated with the process, which should provide extra time for managers and employees to focus on activities that drive results (e.g. performance conversations, developmental activities). A cautionary note, however, is that in making evaluations easier to complete, automation may also result in a propensity for managers to get their PM responsibilities done as quickly as possible and perhaps not spend the extra time on performance-related interactions with employees.

Automated PMSs have also proved invaluable for the administration of multisource or 360-degree feedback systems, which are inherently more complex from an administration standpoint than traditional supervisory evaluations. They have allowed for efficient selection of raters (e.g. peers, customers, subordinates), the collection and integration of information from these multiple sources, and the automated development and delivery of feedback reports (Summers, 2001).

Finally, automated systems are useful because they efficiently capture data, creating a repository of easily accessible information that heretofore was difficult and time consuming to collect. While this facilitates HRM and reporting, such readily accessible data may also ultimately lead to increases in litigation, reinforcing the importance of conducting PM activities in accordance with legal and professional standards.

Legal environment

The U.S. is a particularly litigious society, where equal employment opportunity and fair employment practice laws (e.g. Title VII of the Civil Rights Act, Equal Pay Act) make it possible to challenge employment decisions. Many of these laws allow for jury trials and the collection of compensatory and punitive damages and may lead to high-profile class action lawsuits. While litigation related to employment practices has been occurring for over 30 years, activity has recently proliferated (Malos, 2005).

As discussed, PAs are frequently relied upon as a basis for making employment decisions and, as such, they are often the subject of employment litigation. In fact, it is very likely that some aspect of an organization's PMS will be the focus of an employment litigation lawsuit at some point. This occurs in cases where procedural aspects of the PMS are challenged (e.g. specificity and subjectivity of performance criteria, procedural standardization) and when the results of PM are used to challenge or defend employment practices (e.g. establish an employment relationship in "at will" employment cases, substantiate claims for overtime in Fair Labor Standards Act cases, substantiate hostile work environments and harassment claims).

The propensity for PMSs to be the focus of employment litigation makes it important for practitioners to be familiar with the laws and professional guidelines pertinent to the design and implementation of these systems. An in-depth discussion of legal issues and associated case law is beyond the scope of this chapter (see Malos, 1998 and Malos, 2005 for an in-depth review of legislation and case law related to PM; see Kahn, Brown and Lanzarone, 1996; Martin, Bartol and Kehoe, 2000; SIOP, 2003; UGESP, 1978 for further information on legal issues). However, Table 7.1 below provides a summary of guidelines derived from case law and standards for professional practice that have important implications for PMSs in the U.S.

Key challenges facing effective PM in the U.S.

PM is often referred to as the "Achilles Heel" of HRM. A survey by Watson Wyatt showed that only 30 percent of workers felt that their company's PMS helps to improve performance. Less than 40 percent said their systems established clear performance goals, generated honest feedback, or used technology to streamline the process. While these attitudes might be attributed to poorly designed systems, it is usually not poorly developed tools and processes that cause difficulties with PM. Rather, difficulties arise because, at its core, PM relies on human interactions and is an extremely difficult process to implement effectively. While there are many challenges associated with implementing effective PMSs in the U.S., three are particularly problematic:

- Organizational members view PM as an administrative burden to be minimized rather than an effective strategy to obtain business results,
- Managers and employees are reluctant to engage in candid performance discussions, and
- Judgment and time factors impede accurate performance assessment.

Table 7.1 Guidelines for addressing legal requirements in the United States

- Employees must be evaluated on job-relevant factors
- Employees must be told what is expected and the standards for evaluation
- There must be a standard, documented procedure, with defined roles and responsibilities for employees and managers
- Managers and employees should be trained to implement the process effectively
- Managers should document effective and ineffective performance to substantiate their evaluations
- Managers should be held accountable for providing feedback in a timely manner
- Performance evaluations should be reviewed by a higher-level manager or panel
- Employees should be allowed to comment on and appeal their performance evaluations
- Employees should be notified of deficiencies and afforded opportunities to correct them
- If performance evaluations are used for decision-making, the evaluation should be consistent with decisions (i.e. higher pay raises for higher rated staff)

The view of PM as an administrative burden

Many U.S. managers and employees don't believe the benefits of PM outweigh its costs, complaining that their PMSs are cumbersome, bureaucratic, and too time consuming. This leads them to treat PM as a necessary evil of work life that should be minimized rather than an important process that helps achieve key individual and organizational outcomes.

In order for a PMS to be effective, organizational members, especially managers, must view the system as one that helps them get work done. To put it plainly, if management does not view PM as an important strategic tool for driving results and managing work, the system will not be used properly, and, consequently, it will not yield its potential value. The key challenge, then, is to determine how to demonstrate and convince leaders about the strategic and business value that effective PM can have if sound practices are implemented and reinforced within an organization.

One approach to this issue has been to develop a competency-based PMS where competencies are linked to strategic goals and objectives. Such a system not only communicates a consistent set of expectations, but it also strives to measure performance on factors that are critically important to the organization's mission. However, the challenge is convincing managers to use the system as an active tool to actually manage the day-to-day performance of their employees (e.g. through regular expectation setting, monitoring, and feedback). More typically, managers use the systems only once a year when completing formal appraisals. Organizations need to consider this reality in the design of their systems to encourage and hold managers accountable for effectively managing the performance of their employees.

The reluctance of managers and employees to exchange candid information

The U.S. national culture tends toward egalitarianism and low power distance between supervisors and their direct reports. Consequently, managers are generally reluctant to have honest performance discussions with employees for fear of reprisal or damaging relationships with the individuals they count on to get work done. In addition, the individualistic and achievement oriented aspects of U.S. culture may be a factor in employee reluctance to discuss their development needs for fear that this will impact their rewards and advancement. These tendencies are exaggerated when the primary purpose of PM is to support pay, promotions, or other important HR decisions. The challenge is how to promote meaningful, candid performance conversations and exchange of performance information that is of value to both the organization and employees.

Judgment and time factors that interfere with accurate assessment

As Murphy and DeNisi discussed in their chapter, there are several judgment factors that present key challenges to effective PM, including managers' opportunity to observe performance, accurate recall of performance information, time pressure, and use of common evaluative standards. Although there is wide recognition in the U.S. that leadership is a critical function, the reality in many organizations is that managers are frequently overworked and have numerous responsibilities aside from managing people. It is not uncommon for managers to have full-time job responsibilities in addition to "people management" tasks such as evaluating performance, providing feedback, and developing the skills of their employees. Additionally, most managers have multiple direct reports and most PMSs cover at least six months to a year, yielding significant amounts of performance information that is difficult, if not impossible, to recall accurately.

These factors contribute to managers who base their appraisals on general impressions of employees developed over time, which may be reasonably accurate or may be fraught with bias. Irrespective of how accurate these developed impressions are, providing feedback to employees based on impressions rather than actual performance examples causes difficulties when managers are challenged to explain exactly what the employee did that deserved a particular rating.

Another factor that can interfere with accurate judgments is the opportunity to observe performance. With the rise in telecommuting and alternative work schedules in the U.S., managers are increasingly in positions where they see only a fraction of employees' work behavior because there are limited opportunities to observe performance. The challenge here is how to gain sufficient performance information on which to form a judgment and provide useful performance feedback when opportunities to observe performance are limited.

A final challenge is that different managers have different standards about what constitutes effective and ineffective performance. When managers are applying different standards to evaluating employees, it is difficult to calibrate evaluations from these managers and ensure consistency in evaluations across employees. If a performance measure is used, for example, that assesses whether an employee "meets expectations" without articulating exactly what those expectations are, some managers will inevitably expect more than others. The result is that employees holding the same job at the same level may be held to different standards, which is unfair. Similarly, a scale that asks managers to rate employees from "ineffective" to "highly effective" suffers the same problem. Thus, the challenge is how to help managers develop a common frame-of-reference and use similar standards in evaluating employees.

A model performance management process

While we have discussed trends, issues, and challenges that impact PM in the U.S., there is enormous variability in both the types of organizations and in the systems used by different organizations. Accordingly, it is not possible to present a PM model that is applicable to the myriad of U.S. organizations. Thus, we have opted to discuss an approach to PM that is based on best practice companies in the U.S. and current writings on PM practice.

Effective PMSs have a well-articulated process for accomplishing evaluation activities, with clearly defined responsibilities for managers and employees. Especially in organizations that use PM for decision-making, it is important that all employees are treated in a fair and equitable manner. This is not only important for procedural justice reasons but also to comply with legal guidelines that govern HR processes in the U.S. Based on examining PMSs in several organizations and the literature, most systems contain some variation of the following process (see Figure 7.1):

Performance planning

The PM cycle typically begins with a discussion of what is expected of employees in terms of results and behaviors. This step is important because it helps employees understand what is expected of them, requires articulating evaluation standards, thereby increasing transparency and fairness. Research has shown that it is important for employees to perceive that the PMS is fair, which mitigates negative feelings associated with less favorable outcomes (Gilliland and Langdon, 1998).

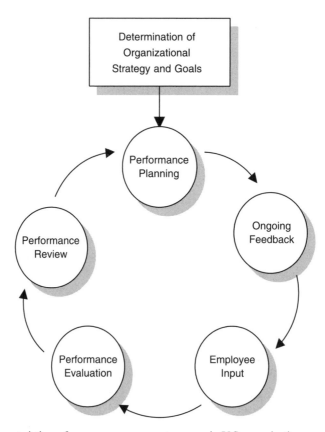

Figure 7.1 Characteristic performance management process in U.S. organizations

Ongoing feedback

During the rating cycle, performance needs to be discussed and feedback provided on an ongoing basis. For feedback to be effective, it must be a two-way communication process and the joint responsibility of managers and employees (Wexley, 1986; Cederblom, 1982). The managers' role is to provide feedback in a constructive, candid, and timely manner. The employees' role is to understand how they are performing and react to feedback in a positive manner. Having effective, ongoing communication between managers and employees is a key determinant of whether a PMS will achieve its potential benefits.

In some organizations, there is a culture that supports providing candid, regular feedback to achieve continuous improvement. More often, however, there is hesitancy among both managers and employees to engage in candid performance discussions, especially if these might damage relationships or reduce rewards. One recent trend in the U.S. has been to take steps to increase performance communications (i.e. feedback) between managers and subordinates. This has been accomplished primarily through training programs that focus on communicating the value of ongoing, informal feedback throughout the rating cycle. These training programs are geared to both managers and employees, teaching them about the value of ongoing performance discussions and their joint responsibilities in conducting them. The goal of the training is to remove some of the formality and discomfort around the concept of feedback and to make ongoing performance discussions more accepted and regular in the workplace.

Of course, irrespective of the training received or the climate for feedback, an important intervening factor noted by Murphy and DeNisi is the interpersonal relationship between the manager and employee. If the manager–employee relationship is not characterized by a basic level of trust and motivation to engage in effective performance conversations, it is unlikely that their communication and feedback processes will be productive or lead to positive results.

Employee input

Employee input can be invaluable for enhancing ownership and acceptance of the PM process. Gathering employee input also helps to increase understanding, resulting in fewer disconnects between managers' and employees' views of the employees' contributions. Employees are sometimes asked to provide input via self-ratings, which are then compared to the manager's ratings and discussed. However, experienced practitioners have found that this approach can lead to unnecessary defensiveness and disagreements between employees and managers, if managers ultimately rate employees less effectively than they have rated themselves.

An alternative to self-ratings is to ask employees to prepare statements of their most meritorious accomplishments at the end of the rating period. This process not only reminds managers about the results employees have achieved, but employee accomplishments can be used as input for pay or promotion decisions. Research has shown that employee accomplishments are effective predictors of how successfully employees will perform at higher job levels, and they thus provide useful input for promotion decisions (Hough, Keyes and Dunnette, 1983).

Performance evaluation

Evaluating behaviors

Today, many organizations in the U.S. are using competency models as a basis for their PMSs (Spencer and Spencer, 1994). Competency models articulate the knowledge, skills, abilities, and other personal characteristics that are most instrumental for achieving positive organizational outcomes. An advantage of competency models is that they typically include the full array of factors associated with success – technical, leadership, and interpersonal. Job analysis techniques, such as job observations, interviews, focus groups, and surveys, are often used to identify key competencies and associated critical work behaviors (Schippmann, 1999). For PM purposes, best practices define the competencies in terms of behavioral performance standards.

Evaluating results

As discussed above, the specific results to be achieved will vary for different employees, depending on the nature of the individual's job and assignments. An issue associated with evaluating results is determining the relative contributions of different results, for example, a cost-savings result compared to a leadership result. An effective strategy is to develop scaled

Table 7.2 Example performance standards for communication competency

Below expectations	*Meets expectations*	*Role model*
Fails to prepare timely, clear, organized, and concise communications on complex topics; communications require moderate to extensive revisions.	Effectively prepares timely, clear, organized, and concise communications on complex topics; communications require some revisions.	Effectively prepares timely, clear, organized, and concise communications on highly complex, sensitive, or controversial topics; communications require minimal revisions.
Fails to effectively adapt communication style and materials to communicate complex information.	Effectively adapts communication style and materials to communicate complex information.	Effectively tailors communication style and customizes materials to communicate highly complex, sensitive, or controversial information.

criteria that describe different levels of complexity, difficulty, contribution, and impact. Such standards help managers compare different accomplishments by putting them on a common scale that facilitates evaluation. Furthermore, the use of individualized performance objectives without scaled evaluation criteria can result in a system that fails to effectively differentiate between employees who are contributing more or less on the job and for differentially rewarding them (Muczyk, 1979).

Performance review

Assuming that ongoing feedback has been provided during the rating period, the formal performance review session is nothing more than a recap of performance during the rating period and developmental planning (Wexley, 1986). While identifying developmental needs can be easy with the right performance management tools, knowing how to address these needs effectively is not always obvious. To facilitate this process, "developmental handbooks" have been included in several U.S. performance management systems. These booklets contain on-the-job learning experiences, formal training, and other developmental resources (e.g. books, websites) that are targeted to different competencies and address development needs.

PM system implementation

Experienced practitioners uniformly agree that having an effective process is a necessary but not sufficient condition for having an effective PMS. It is equally, if not more, important that a system be implemented effectively and that managers and employees take it seriously, because this is what determines whether the PMS will yield positive results. Murphy and DeNisi similarly discuss acceptance of the appraisal system (proximal factor) and rater motivation (intervening factor), which are related factors. Technology (a distal factor) is also an important implementation variable.

Table 7.3 Example performance standards for evaluating results

Low impact	Moderate impact	High impact
The efficiency or effectiveness of operations remained the same or were only minimally improved.	The efficiency or effectiveness of operations were significantly improved.	The efficiency or effectiveness of operations were improved tremendously.
The quality of products remained the same or was only minimally improved.	The quality of products improved significantly.	The quality of products was improved tremendously.

User acceptance and buy-in

The literature shows that effective program implementation depends on management commitment – the stronger the commitment, the greater the program's success (Rodgers *et al.*, 1993). For PM, an organization with a committed top management team that models effective PM and establishes clear PM expectations has a much higher probability of success than one that does not do these things. Effective communications and a solid change management strategy are also essential for gaining buy-in and properly motivating system users (Mohrman, Resnick-West and Lawler, 1989).

Automation

Evaluations of automated PMSs have shown that they are viewed positively by users, decrease workload, ensure widespread access, and provide a standardized format for collecting and storing performance data. Basic automated functions typically include the ability to capture performance ratings, including interfaces for displaying performance standards and rating-process information. More advanced features include prompting managers and employees about PM events, routing documents between employees, providing access to forms, and providing automated reports. To make informed decisions about the extent of automation, organizations need to balance time, resource, development, and maintenance costs.

Training

Training helps to ensure that employees and managers are able and motivated to use the PMS effectively. There are a number of training formats that can be used for PM, including classroom training, job aides, or web-based training, each with its advantages and disadvantages. Most U.S. companies invest in at least a minimum amount of training to ensure that users understand the system; however, many invest considerably more resources into PM training. While no studies have specifically investigated the effects of the amount and type of training on PM outcomes, more extensive training is believed to send a positive message about the importance of PM.

Conclusion

Throughout this chapter, we have highlighted several important concepts for designing and implementing effective PMSs in the U.S. First, the system needs to be aligned with and support the organization's direction and critical success factors. Second, well-developed, efficiently administered tools and processes are needed to make the system user-friendly and well-received by organizational members. Third, and most important, is that both managers and employees must use the system in a manner that brings visible, value-added benefits in the areas of performance planning, performance development, feedback, and achieving results.

References

Austin, J. T. and Villanova, P. (1992) The criterion problem: 1917–1992, *Journal of Applied Psychology* 77: 836–74.

Bingham, W. V. (1926) Measures of occupational success, *Harvard Business Review* 5: 1–10.

Borman, W. C. (1979) Format and training effects on rating accuracy and rating errors, *Journal of Applied Psychology* 64: 410–21.

Borman, W. C. (1991) Job behavior, performance, and effectiveness, in M. D. Dunnette and L. M. Hough (eds.) *Handbook of Industrial and Organizational Psychology* (vol. 2), Palo Alto, CA: Consulting Psychologists Press, pp. 271–326.

Cascio, W. F. (1998) *Applied Psychology in Human Resource Management*, Upper Saddle River: Prentice-Hall.

Cederblom, D. (1982) The performance appraisal interview: a review, implications, and suggestions, *Academy of Management Review* 7: 219–27.

Dorsey, D. W. (2002) Information technology, in J. W. Hedge and E. D. Pulakos (eds.), *Implementing Organizational Interventions*, San Francisco: Jossey-Bass, pp. 110–32.

Dunnette, M. D. (1963) A note on the criterion, *Journal of Applied Psychology* 47: 251–4.

Flanagan, J. C. (1954) The critical incident technique, *Psychological Bulletin* 51: 327–58.

Ghorpade, J. (2000) Managing the five paradoxes of 360-degree feedback, *Academy of Management Executive* 14(1): 140–50.

Gilliland, S. W. and Langdon, J. C. (1998) Creating performance management systems that promote perceptions of fairness, in James W. Smither (ed.) *Performance Appraisal: State of the Art in Practice*, San Francisco: Jossey-Bass, pp. 209–43.

Greguras, G. J., Robie, C., Schleicher, D. J. and Goff, M. (2003) A field study of the effects of rating purpose on the quality of multisource ratings, *Personnel Psychology* 56: 1–21.

Guion, R. M. (1961) Criterion measurement and personnel judgments, *Personnel Psychology* 4: 141–9.

Hedge, J. W., Borman, W. C. and Birkeland, S. A. (2001) History and development of multisource feedback as a methodology, in D. W. Bracken, C. W. Timmreck and A. H. Church (eds.) *The Handbook of Multisource Feedback*, San Francisco: Jossey-Bass, pp. 15–32.

Hillgren, J. S. and Cheatham, D. W. (2000) *Understanding Performance Measures: An Approach to Linking Rewards to the Achievement of Organizational Objectives*, Scottsdale, AZ: WorldatWork.

Hough, L. M., Keyes, M. A. and Dunnette, M. D. (1983) An evaluation of three "alternative" selection procedures, *Personnel Psychology* 36: 261–76.

Jamieson, B. D. (1973) Behavioral problems with management by objective, *Academy of Management Review* 16: 496–505.

Kahn, S. C., Brown, B. B. and Lanzarone, M. (1996) *Legal Guide to Human Resources*, Boston: Warren, Gorham and Lamont, 6–2 to 6–58.

Latham, G. P. and Wexley, K. N. (1981) *Increasing Productivity Through Performance Appraisal*, Reading: Addison-Wesley.

Lawler, E. E. (1967) The multitrait-multirater approach to measuring managerial job performance, *Journal of Applied Psychology* 51: 369–81.

Levinson, H. (2005) Management by whose objectives? In *Harvard Business Review on Appraising Employee Performance*, Boston, MA: Harvard Business School Publishing Corporation, pp. 1–28.

Malos, S. (1998) Current legal issues in performance appraisal, in J. W. Smither (ed.) *Performance Appraisal: State of the Art in Practice*, San Francisco: Jossey-Bass, pp. 49–94.

Malos, S. (2005) The importance of valid selection and performance appraisal: do management practices figure in case law? In F. J. Landy (ed.) *Employment Discrimination Litigation*, San Francisco: Jossey-Bass, pp. 373–409.

Martin, D. C., Bartol, K. M. and Kehoe, P. E. (2000) The legal ramifications of performance appraisal: the growing significance, *Public Personnel Management* 29(3): 379–406.

Mohrman, A. M., Jr., Resnick-West, S. M. and Lawler, E. E. III (1989) *Designing Performance Appraisal Systems: Aligning Appraisals and Organizational Realities*, San Francisco: Jossey-Bass.

Muchinsky, P. M. (1997) *Psychology Applied to Work: An Introduction to Industrial and Organizational Psychology*, Pacific Grove, CA: Brooks/Cole Publishing Company.

Muczyk, J. P. (1979) Dynamics and hazards of MBO application, *Personnel Administrator* 24: 51–61.

Patterson, D. G. (1922) The Scott Company graphic rating scale, *Journal of Personnel Research* 1: 361–76.

Rodgers, R. and Hunter, J. E. (1991) Impact of management by objectives on organizational productivity, *Journal of Applied Psychology* 78: 51–155.

Rodgers, R., Hunter, J. E. and Rogers, D. L. (1993) Influence of top management commitment on management program success, *Journal of Applied Psychology* 78: 51–155.

Rotchford, N. L. (2002) Performance management, in J. W. Hedge and E. D. Pulakos (eds.) *Implementing Organizational Interventions*, San Francisco: Jossey-Bass, pp. 167–97.

Schippmann, J. S. (1999) *Strategic Job Modeling: Working at the Core of Integrated Human Resource Systems*, Mahwah, NJ: Lawrence Erlbaum Associates.

Smith, P. C. and Kendall, L. M. (1963) An approach to the construction of unambiguous anchors for rating scales, *Journal of Applied Psychology* 47: 149–55.

Society for Industrial and Organizational Psychology (SIOP) (2003) *Principles for the Validation and Use of Personnel Selection Procedures: Fourth edition*, Bowling Green, OH: author.

Spencer, L. and Spencer, S. (1994) *Competence at Work*, New York, NY: John Wiley.

Strauss, G. (1972) Management by objectives: a critical review, *Training and Development Journal* 26: 10–15.

Summers, L. (2001) Web technologies for administering multisource feedback programs, in D. W. Bracken, C. W. Timmreck and A. H. Church (eds.) *The Handbook of Multisource Feedback*, San Francisco: Jossey-Bass, pp. 165–80.

Uniform Guidelines on Employee Selection Procedures (UGESP) (1978) *Federal Register* 43: 38295–38315.

Waldman, D. and Atwater, L. E. (1998) *The Power of 360-degree Feedback: How to Leverage Performance Evaluations for Top Productivity*, Houston, TX: Gulf Publishing.

Wexley, K. N. (1986) Appraisal interview, in R. A. Berk (ed.) *Performance Assessment*, Baltimore: Johns Hopkins University Press, pp. 167–85.

Williams, S. B. and Leavitt, H. J. (1947) Group opinion as a predictor of military leadership, *Journal of Consulting Psychology* 11: 283–91.

Websites

www.clc.executiveboard.com
www.opm.gov
www.shrm.org

8 Performance management in Mexico

ANABELLA DAVILA AND MARTA M. ELVIRA

"Performance appraisal is not the final outcome."
Jesus Alarcon-Zertuche, HRM Consultant

"Performance evaluation is the initial kickoff for almost all HR processes."
Marcelo Romani, HR Director, Tenaris North America

Mexican management practices have received considerable attention from international researchers and practitioners, although few studies have explored performance appraisal (PA) systems. Specifically, we know little about how PA is influenced by contextual, organizational or individual factors in Mexico. These factors, as Murphy and DeNisi state in Chapter 6, affect appraisals and can illuminate both the research and practice of PA within international organizations.

Prior to our call for a contextual approach to human resource management (HRM) in Mexico as part of the Latin American region (Elvira and Davila, 2005b), knowledge about PA in this country focused on two areas. First, PA is rarely used as an incentive for individual performance (Milliman, Nason, Zhu and De Cieri, 2002) and, second, managers typically overrate the performance of employees who meet their assumptions about proper employee behavior, highlighting the role of subjectivity in PA (DeVoe and Iyengar, 2004).

Lacking other research on PA practices in Mexico, we started by reviewing the specialized business press[1] and then conducted six in-depth interviews with senior human resources (HR) executives from different organizations operating in Mexico. Interviews were conducted individually in each executive's office and lasted 85 minutes on average. (Table 8.1 shows the profiles of the executives interviewed. Appendix A shows the interview protocol.)

In this chapter, we start by exploring how contextual and organizational factors influence overall HRM in Mexican organizations and by extension their PA systems. Then we explore current PA processes and management in Mexico. Finally, we examine the assumptions underlying how companies and individuals approach PA and we identify the challenges to improving the design and implementation of PA systems.

Table 8.1 Profile of the executives interviewed

Business background experience	Industry experience	Origin	Performance management experience
HR Consultant, former CEO, former HR director	Steel, beverage, processed food	Mexican MNC	Undergraduate research thesis on sales merit systems
HR VP, former CEO, former logistics engineering	Beverage	Mexican MNC	MBO, EVA, 360-degree
HR Manager subsidiary	Health equipment, energy	U.S. MNC	PA manager, 360-degree, Basic homemade tools – excel
HR Regional North America Director	Steel	Argentinean MNC (former Mexican)	Relative comparative
HR Manager subsidiary	Beverage	Mexican MNC	Human values system, critical success factors, point scales systems
HR Consultant, former HR VP	Glass, energy	Mexican and U.S. MNC	PA manager

Contextual and organizational factors

Regarding contextual issues that affect an organization's practices, Murphy and DeNisi's Model of the Appraisal Process (Chapter 6) categorizes them into distal, proximal, intervening, judgment, and distortion factors. *Distal factors* refer partly to the national level, such as the economy, work culture, labor systems or technological infrastructure, but also include organizational variables such as firm strategy and performance. Distal factors are fixed and act as constraints or parameters for organizational actions that, in turn, affect PA. *Proximal factors* develop from the organizations' assumptions for managing performance, including organizational norms, purpose and acceptance of the PA systems. *Intervening factors* derive from distal and proximal factors' impact on PA management, such as issues arising from rater–ratee relationships. *Judgment factors* include the cognitive aspects of raters judging employee performance. Finally, *distortion factors* refer to the characteristics of the situations that alter a rater's evaluation due, for example, to organizational reward systems or the consequences of the appraisal for the employee. We start by examining distal factors.

Economic factors

Mexico's economy is ranked fourteenth in the world and third among emerging economies in terms of foreign direct investment (INEGI, 2006b; KPMG-AMECE, 2006). The active economic population represents 59 percent of the 104 million total, with 96.4 percent of them employed or an unemployment rate of 3.6 percent. The average formal education is nine years of schooling. The minimum wage in Mexico is 48.80 pesos per day ($4.46 dollars per day); and GDP per capita is U.S.$7,983.51 dollars (INEGI, 2006b).

The Mexican economic environment has changed dramatically since the recurrent economic crises – in 1976, 1979, 1982, 1986, and 1994 – that devastated industrial activity and citizens' quality of life. Mexico started to open its economy in 1986 and today macroeconomic conditions are seen as positive because of the prevailing stability since 1995. Foreign direct investment has increased, infrastructure has reached international standards, and business competitiveness is acknowledged by the international business community (KPMG-AMECE, 2006).

This market-oriented strategy has nevertheless not produced the expected results. Mexico has grown at 3 percent on average since 1990. The country has not benefited from proximity to the United States, international trade agreements or leadership within Latin American economies. Though manufacturing companies with an export orientation have reaped benefits, exports abound in low value-added products (Phillips, Mehrez and Moissinac, 2006).

International Monetary Fund research suggests that Mexico's implementation of economic and political policies limits its success (Phillips *et al.*, 2006). Specifically, the country needs legal reforms to provide incentives to private investment and improve business and labor competitiveness. However, social reforms – i.e. labor, health or education – are not in place yet. Furthermore, low economic growth in the country prevents the government from investing enough resources in social development. Economic history shows that businesses have acquired this responsibility, beyond providing workers' compensation and benefits (Castañeda, 1998).

The opening of the economy was an abrupt change for the country and business organizations. Businesses had to learn how to compete under economic and political uncertainty, having to adapt their management and manufacturing systems continuously. Some traumatic consequences followed with the downsizing of firms' operations and personnel during the 1980s and 1990s. Labor markets contracted severely, resulting in low job security and a growing informal economy (Bensusan, 2006).

HRM practices, particularly PA, reflected these changes. For example, firms that linked financial rewards predominately to the performance evaluation system suppressed rewards during economic turnarounds; thus employees developed negative perceptions, doubting the purpose of evaluation during these periods (Davila and Elvira, 2007). Some organizations even used PA to downsize and increase efficiency. For instance, GIS[2], a diversified business group in house appliances and ceramics, used performance evaluations to downsize (lowest performers were dismissed), when introducing a lean manufacturing system (Carlos, 2004).

Cultural factors

Existing cultural studies of management have limited application in Mexico because they typically assume that culture is stable, has precise boundaries and can be explained using universal dimensions (Hofstede, 1982). In studying Mexican work culture we propose using the concept of a hybrid system (Davila and Elvira, 2005). Our rationale follows the country's historical development, which passed through conquest and colonization sociopolitical processes, experiencing a flow of values and norms that made one culture nurtured by the other (Garcia-Canclini, 1990) and that is currently exposed to another type of cultural migration: socioeconomic globalization.

The hybrid view of Mexican work culture identifies leadership style with certain traits, such as *benevolent paternalism* in which a supervisor has the personal obligation to protect his/her subordinates and, often, safeguards the personal needs of workers and their families (Davila and Elvira, 2005). Research suggests that this style generates dependency behaviors in subordinates and, therefore, reduces their decision-making ability at work (Martinez, 2005). In turn, this trait prevents subordinates from entering into conflict or confrontation with a superior in public, because critiques could be considered offensive to the superior as well as to other colleagues (Diaz-Saenz and Witherspoon, 2000). This cultural norm preserves social differentiation between superiors and subordinates, yet jeopardizes hierarchical communication (Lindsley, 1999) which is key to effective PA. Simultaneously, superiors show an egalitarian sense and use leadership behaviors and symbols to reduce excessive power distance (D'Iribarne, 2001). Thus, the optimal leadership style in Mexican work culture provides intense mutual support and knows when to use managerial authority to give orders, criticize and control (Davila and Elvira, 2005).

Supporting this benevolent paternalism style of leadership is the structure of *social relationships*. The emotional content of such relationships requires face-to-face interaction and communication for in-group loyalty development (Davila and Elvira, 2005).

The cultural sensitiveness of the PA process is key for all the actors involved. How superiors and subordinates respond to authority and mutually rely on social relationships is critical for accepting the evaluation and contributes to protecting loyalty. Research shows that organizations use PA systems in Mexico as a forum for employee expression rather than for compensation adjustment. That is, employees perceive the purpose of PA as a means to express their views and their aspirations for career development (Milliman *et al.*, 2002). This is another manifestation of hybridism in Latin American management: the PA feedback interview enables subordinates' communication within a high-power distance society, because it is the social space where superiors and subordinates can engage in social exchanges related to performance (Martinez, 2005).

Labor relations

Mexico is a federal republic where labor and employment relations are regulated by Federal Labor Law. The law establishes equal working conditions, obligations and rights for workers regardless of company size, employee union type, and nationality, gender, religion or race (KPMG, 2006).

Labor regulations in Mexico have been characterized as rigid and costly, imposing expensive restrictions in the hiring and dismissal of workers. Non-wage costs are estimated at 47.2 percent of payroll. (These costs include benefits that cover the basic needs of the worker and his/her family.) Nonetheless, high dismissal costs generally prevent firms from downsizing in cyclical downturns and from optimal hiring during upswings. Workers might also avoid looking for more productive jobs due to the risk of losing severance pay. Therefore, low turnover rates reduce workers' incentives to train and acquire new skills (Phillips *et al.*, 2006). Although job security costs are high in Mexico, research suggests that firms do not bear these costs because labor laws are only weakly enforced and thus noncompliance is commonplace (Bensusan, 2006).

Regarding the use of PA to reward performance, we note that Mexican laws require employers to distribute a percentage of yearly profits among all employees. This compensation is variable and based upon annual profitability, providing an institutionalized link between individual and organizational performance. The issue for most executives (e.g. those we interviewed) becomes how to associate individual appraisal instruments with this yearly profit-sharing system.

Penalties for unsatisfactory performance could include denial of salary increases or even dismissal. Because of the high cost, firms resist dismissing workers for low performance. Thus, employees assess the extent of potential penalty and develop their own interpretations of employment terms and conditions. Consequently, managers usually avoid accurate PA and rewards could be considered as the only actual outcome of appraisal systems.

Organizational factors

Business historians describe large Mexican organizations as successfully managed despite the country's weak economy and unstable political conditions (Castañeda, 1998). To perform well in this environment, organizations have evolved and adapted. Because of low government resources, businesses have developed a set of economic and social strategies not only to protect but also to develop employees and the community. Take the case of FEMSA[3] (*Fomento Empresarial Mexicano*), a 115-year-old Mexican family firm and the largest beverage conglomerate in Latin America. FEMSA employs 30,000 people across its businesses of beer (*Sol, Indio, Dos Equis*), soft-drinks (*Coca-Cola*) and convenience stores (*Oxxo*). The company has been listed among the top "10 most admired Mexican companies" since 1996 for its contribution to economic and social development. In 1918 the company created a nonprofit association responsible for offering and managing different benefits for employees, their families, and relatives. Today, this association, named *Sociedad Cuauhtémoc y Famosa*, offers medical services, home loans, saving accounts, and food coupons, while also promoting sports, cultural activities, and specialized training programs. The association has state-of-the-art facilities that include a health center, sports club, and nursing home for retired employees. FEMSA has not had any strikes in more than 100 years (Elvira and Davila, 2005b). How can FEMSA devote organizational resources to the development of its employees and community while obtaining outstanding performance?

The governance of Mexican organizations is not only based on nuclear but also on the extended family that links one organization to another, conforming to diversified business groups (Castañeda, 1998) and making relational capital their main competitive advantage (Sargent, 2005). Organizational structures at these companies tend to be rigidly tied because they prevent organizations from favoring individualism over the collectivist Mexican mentality (Hofstede, 1982). In this context, bureaucratic mechanisms are complemented by social norms and rituals that make organizations function (Davila and Garcia, 2004). We find, for example, numerous social networks – vertical and horizontal – within and outside organizations. Failing to build HRM practices on the collectivist logic of this social structure would end in rejection or distortion of such practices. For example, Alejandra Gomez, GE Capital Mexico quality leader, stressed that a common mistake of Mexican executives is to abandon projects once they see that these worked – that was the case with Six Sigma methodology (*Personal Computing*, 2000). Modern management practices that are not culturally embedded tend to be adapted via local interpretations during implementation.

In sum, organizations accept modern management models and practices imported from developed countries while simultaneously using traditional approaches of community logic to demonstrate their competency in the collectivistic Mexican environment. In contrast, organizations reject imported bureaucratic practices that are based on the logic of individualism. These are the features of a hybrid management model characteristic of Mexican firms (Davila and Elvira, 2005), and could explain which PA methods and tools best fit this organizational context.

Technology factors

Technology plays a limited role in Mexican HR practices (Elvira and Davila, 2005a). However, some international firms in Mexico – i.e. PeopleSoft (today Oracle[4]) and SAP[5] – provide complex information technology (IT) services including HR inventories, personnel selection tools, benefits and compensation, PA, organizational charts, job evaluations, psychometric evaluations, and training (*Notimex*, 2003; *Personal Computing*, 2000).

Despite the universal approach to HR practices embedded in technology, the cultural context matters. In particular, we note the impact of e-HR practices on social relationships in Mexico. As outlined earlier, social ties govern Mexican employment relationships within organizations and need to be considered when changing HR practices (Davila and Elvira, 2005). For example, PeopleSoft Mexico's Strategy Product Manager thinks that hiring with HRMS tools will allow the company to identify the proper job for each person's profile and skills, and to provide needed training even before an individual joins the firm: "Employees must be seen as an asset of the company, as a good, as an investment of the company; it is the firm's responsibility to help and make him/her understand that he/she is the only one responsible of his/her own development"[6] (cited in *Personal Computing*, 2000). Manpower Mexico introduced co-sourcing in 2003 based on 360-degree evaluations. A key benefit of co-sourcing lies in allowing rapid responses to changes in the PA strategy and methodology within the company (*El Norte*, 2003). The challenge, however, is effectively implementing these systems with a culturally sensitive approach. In other words, the goals of an e-strategy need to be achieved through HR methods that differ from what has typically been socially acceptable (Olivas-Lujan, Ramirez, Zapata-Cantu, 2007).

The availability of complex IT tools for small and medium-size firms is also doubtful. Thus international consulting firms target these smaller companies. For example, *Excelencia en Factor Humano* provides advice on PA systems and organizational climate through software, including feedback for firms' personnel on 360-degree surveys (*El Financiero*, 2006). Yet it is unclear how many small and medium-size firms can afford this investment. In the short term inequality in IT human capital management among firms is likely to prevail in Mexico.

For larger, highly centralized organizations a cultural perspective could help understand the impact of IT tools. Implementing an e-HR strategy could help decentralization by allowing employees to own their information. Employees can access their salaries and benefits, and even plan their career development. Regarding PA, information derived from the evaluation could be computed in real time and from any place without schedule restrictions. Similarly, IT tools allow the simultaneous use of multiple-source, 360 evaluations. The resulting information of appraisal tools could be easily matched to the employee's salary (Plata, 2004). From a cultural perspective, this way of obtaining feedback might overcome the challenge of typically conflictive PA meetings (Davila and Elvira, 2005). Managers and employees could avoid the confrontation of a feedback interview by using IT. The question arises: to what extent would HR managers accept decentralization of their authority through e-HR? And how willing are employees to forgo personal interaction with HR administrators? This dynamic again manifests the hybrid management model characteristic of Mexican organizations.

In closing this section, we note that for a Mexican company to exploit IT advantages in e-HR systems, there remains the challenge of providing employees with extensive technological training. Computer literacy levels are very low, mainly because of the lack of resources to acquire equipment. Official statistics report that only 10 percent of Mexican homes have access to the World Wide Web (WWW) and 20 percent have a computer at home (INEGI, 2006a).

PA in Mexico

PA processes are also affected by *proximal factors* (Murphy and DeNisi, Chapter 6), including organizational norms, purpose and acceptance of the PA system. In Mexico, management practices developed during the first stage of the country's industrialization mainly related to increasing foreign investment, and during the economic transition from agriculture to manufacturing (Davila and Elvira, 2005). HR practices have thus been widely influenced by dominant global theories or foreign multinationals' imported practices. For example, multinationals such as GE Mexico use the Six Sigma methodology for continuous improvement. Also, numerous local and federal government initiatives promote international management systems such as ISO certification, offered to small and medium-size firms by the Ministry of Economy (*Personal Computing*, 2000).

Today, different agents import international HR practices for business use. For example, HR consultants introduce management systems in their activity. KPMG Mexico uses the Balanced Score Card as the management model that organizations need to monitor their strategy and produce reliable metrics, creating in Mexican executives a sense of business urgency. However, Pedro Payan, KPMG Mexico Risk Consulting Services Manager, states that many Mexican organizations only use metrics to monitor performance in terms of efficiency and forget to measure effectiveness, that is, the extent to which they meet goals and objectives in their progress toward their vision and mission (*El Economista*, 2005).

International authors also introduce their theories through business books. For instance, Gary Cokins and his book *Performance Management* were promoted by SAS Mexico in 2005 (*Notimex*, 2005). Similarly, Robert Kaplan presented Balanced Score Card principles at the ExpoManagement 2006 in Mexico City (*INFOchannel Mexico*, 2006). Press coverage of these conferences ignored how the national context could alter the main assumptions in which those practices are based. Thus, HR consultants not only import HR practices but also contribute to the homogeneity of organizations regardless of a country's contextual and organizational factors.

While it might be generally assumed that a systemized PA is critical to measuring employee productivity, this practice is not common in Latin America. Bumeran.com, an Argentinean virtual employment services agency, estimates that 44 percent of Mexican companies do not evaluate their employees' performance (Vizcaino, 2002). And research shows that when companies evaluate performance, they do so based on team work skills, attitudes and results (Suarez, 2004). Perhaps companies lack appropriate parameters for employee performance evaluation, or perhaps they lack interest in this HR function. These studies contrast with findings from a KPMG-AMECE 2006 survey reporting that organizational performance management (PM) is a strategic priority for top managers in Mexico. A gap seems to exist between organizational PM and employee PA systems in Mexican organizations.

HR consultants do urge businesses to redefine their HR policies, aligning them to appropriate rewards and recognition (Estrada, 2006). A survey of 3,500 workers in Mexico by bumeran.com suggests that employees abandon their jobs because they receive low compensation (46.5%), experience inadequate organizational climate (28.3%), or conflict with their supervisors (25.1%). HayGroup Mexico[7] also reports that two in three employees do not feel their contributions are recognized; four in ten do not know what is expected from them and, therefore, lack development opportunities; and six in ten workers perceive inconsistency between their work and income (Rivero, 2005b). It appears that a proper combination of psychosocial recognition and financial rewards could help create an organizational climate that fosters workers' loyalty and commitment in Mexican organizations. However, a paradox arises as organizations try managing rewards and recognitions in the absence of formal evaluation systems.

Developing a culture of PA in this context is challenging. However, it can be accomplished by joining the forces of HR consultants, governmental agencies, and businesses. Some initiatives illustrate this effort. For example, *Conocimiento y Direccion*,[8] an Argentinean business magazine operating in Mexico, started giving awards for innovative HR projects in 2006. According to the magazine's president Marcelo Andrea Natalini, organizations receiving awards demonstrated that people are their main asset. The Federal Labor Ministry (STPS) was recognized for a PA system based on Business Process Management, a method designed to evaluate organizational process and human competencies simultaneously. According to the STPS, this system allows public servants to identify their objectives, capabilities and indicators and produce their job description electronically (*El Economista*, 2006).

One executive interviewed by the authors indicated that this PA evolution typically starts with management systems "in fashion," which unwittingly lead HR to lose credibility in Mexican organizations. This same executive views PA as unrelated to organizational performance, or to the organization's business plan. From his viewpoint, PA instruments are no longer descriptive but rather evaluative, leaving many gaps for subjective judgments by both superiors and subordinates.

In summary, Mexican firms have implemented modern PA practices through imported methods and tools, yet the effectiveness of these practices is determined by the country's economy, work culture and organizational structures, all of which affect the purpose and acceptance of PA systems.

Methods and tools of PA

To identify *intervening factors* in the PA process we looked at methods and tools used in Mexico. Intervening factors derive from the impact of distal and proximal factors on different aspects of PA management, such as issues involving the superior–subordinate relationship or the motivation and acceptance of the appraisal (Murphy and DeNisi). By examining the methods and tools used in Mexico we aim to understand superiors' and subordinates' perceptions and the dynamics of their relationship.

Consider the performance evaluation method at American Express Mexico,[9] which received the 2001 Mexican National Quality Award and is a pillar of its quality model. Marcela Genis, quality director, describes the PM system as based on individual and group activities with a dialog between superiors and subordinates at the heart of the system (Cortes, 2002). This system consists of several sub-processes including:

1 The establishment of objectives: objectives are targeted to stakeholders, clients and employees.
2 Individual development: it includes comparative performance evaluation with past

performance, current job requirements and expectations, career development and employee's future aspirations.

3 Coaching and feedback: the superior needs to offer continuous coaching and feedback during the performance process.

4 Performance evaluation: it assesses individual and group contribution toward objective accomplishment, leadership competencies, development planning, and precise feedback between superiors and subordinates (Cortes, 2002).

The process starts at the beginning of the year, with a mid-evaluation period six months later and a final performance evaluation scheduled in December (Cortes, 2002). This PM system process includes the employee's self-evaluation, the superior evaluation, and the dialog between them, encouraging the actors to negotiate shared decisions about performance improvements.

Business press writers and HR executives interviewed for this study described PA tools and instruments in a hierarchical context. Top managers, for example, are evaluated in terms of their contribution to organizational performance, while clerical or manufacturing employees are evaluated in terms of merit and mastery of job duties.

Management by objectives is generally linked to compensation strategies that align the organization's financial objectives across all business units. This method assigns weighted percentages to organizational objectives. In some cases, objectives in executives' areas of responsibility have low importance, because the firm aims to reach forecasted business results. That is, rewards for individual results depend on the organization's global performance. For example, hotel NH Kristal Mexico[10] rewards its executives with variable pay tied not only to annual individual objectives but also to the performance of its international operations, making global business results a responsibility shared by all executives (Cortes, 2005). Siemens Mexico evaluates executives on behavioral factors such as leadership skills or willingness to help the career development of his/her collaborators. Through PA feedback, this company had learned that their relatively high employee turnover was due to a lack of adequate career plans. So they have added this facet to managers' responsibility (Cortes, 2002).

Acle-Tomasini, HayGroup Mexico director, argues that PA is a managerial tool developed to enhance businesses' productivity and that this tool is being erroneously applied in Mexico because organizations mistakenly judge the goals of employee PA. Most people view PA as a simple process by which superiors and subordinates establish and agree on an objectives matrix and meet yearly to evaluate the matrix. According to Acle-Tomasini, PA is a direct responsibility of each executive and his/her team. Yet before evaluating employees' performance superiors need to develop an appropriate organizational "microclimate" that fosters employee competencies through: allowing employees to balance his/her work and personal life; promoting employees' identification with the company; having a positive relationship with the supervisor; and allowing the supervisor to play a mentor role (cited in Estrada, 2006).

Along similar lines, HayGroup surveyed managers in 200 companies and found that an awareness that communication between superior and subordinates led to improving the achievement of individual objectives. While managers are good at developing plans and defining objectives, goals are often unmet because they are unclear to subordinates. Inefficient communication results from superiors insufficiently explaining how to link organizational and individual objectives. HayGroup's study found that only 54 percent of the employees know what to expect during the PA interview (Jaramillo, 2006).

Merit-based instruments are used at the lower employee levels, and present some conceptual problems. When the appraisal is qualitative employees are rated on scales ranging from very good, good, neutral, bad and very bad; or using achievement or non-achievement ratings. In the simplest method, percentiles are used (e.g. achieving 80% or 100% of goals). All our interviewees critiqued these rating methods because scales force front-line managers to classify their employees rigidly. HR executives recognized that front-line managers tended to avoid rating employees in the average range, requiring them to use normal distribution curves. They questioned the validity of this method, which automatically devalues employees who are equally effective yet have to be classified as underperforming.

This form of appraisal, also known as comparative/relative evaluation, forced curve, or Top Talent ranking, is the most common appraisal method according to the executives interviewed. Ultimately, these instruments offer a range for individual performance classification. The ranking system is based on individual merits. This system was introduced in Mexico by GE and clashes with the Mexican working culture of collectivism and group loyalty.

The appraisal meeting

Murphy and DeNisi's model speaks of *distortion factors*; those which help identify situations that might make the rater change his or her rating because of the organization's rewards systems or due to the potential consequences for ratees.

Given that PA systems are increasingly promoted as fundamental to managerial decisions (e.g. rewards and recognition), chances are that PA becomes established as an end in itself in Mexico. AOM Consulting, an HR consulting firm, reported in a recent study that 95 percent of Mexican companies surveyed base salary increases only on PA (Cortes, 2005). This frustrates the HR executives interviewed because it limits the use of flexible incentives such as salary adjustments or extraordinary bonuses to retain high-potential employees. Thus, HR executives know that supervisors find themselves tempted to manipulate the outcome of appraisal instruments in order to justify additional compensation for retaining key personnel, thus distorting appraisal's value for PM. As an interviewee stated: "With globalization we have to enhance the flexibility of HR systems, to facilitate retaining competitive talent and the valuable human capital that we have in our organizations, without trying to manipulate the instruments, and recognizing that there can be special cases."

The executives interviewed showed greatest concern about supervisors' reluctance to document and explain their appraisals personally to employees. This reluctance could be due to the difficulty superiors face in justifying the appraisal given. The appraisal may be favorable, but the superior feels that he or she lacks the ability to give adequate explanations for the subordinate. When the conversation is unpleasant or difficult, superiors may prefer to avoid sensitive topics. One of the interviewees said: "When managers see those months approaching [the evaluation period] they feel very uncomfortable because not all news is good news." Much of this problem is due to a lack of management training on how to conduct an adequate feedback session.

Consistent with our interviews, HP Mexico detected through PA that beyond training, subordinates need a leader to mentor and support their careers. The company established a "shadow" program by which a consultant follows the employee for a week in all his/her activities in order to help him/her develop skills and attitudes (Cortes, 2002).

Building on this theme, interviewees consistently discussed the impact of Mexican work culture on PA. Specifically, this work culture tends to associate assessment with a threat to personal or private interests, due possibly to low self-esteem, rather than as a potential source for individual or collective development. This trait, which we label *cultural* following prior research, leads to avoiding PA by managers as well as employees, and frustrates HR efforts to make compensation dependent on compliance. Some superiors treat the process as a superficial artifact or an informal task to complete at the last minute, quickly and carelessly. The need for compliance elicits a controlling response by HR managers that makes them take ownership of the PA process to the detriment of supervisors' commitment to organizational performance evaluation.

Recommendations for managing PA in Mexico

We have followed Murphy and DeNisi's model of the PA process and described contextual and organizational factors reported to influence the PA process in Mexico. Our research uncovers several challenges to enhance PA management and opens avenues for research in other Latin American economies.

Our initial recommendation is to acknowledge the challenge of managing PA practices and their relationship with organizational performance in an unstable economic and political environment such as Mexico. HR executives recognize that for PA to have strategic value it must derive from the organization's business. Yet business plans are threatened when organizations face high instability, and financial rewards may be suppressed in any period without notice. Therefore, organizations should carefully plan the consequences of PA. Evidence shows that one alternative is to link PA not only to financial rewards (i.e. salary increases or variable pay) but also to career plans (i.e. training or promotion) or other types of incentives. A career-performance system could positively impact labor competency and during turndowns could be limited only to the absence of promotions. Training for career advancement could increase the functioning of low educational level Mexican workers. Moreover, managerial conditions that promote an appropriate psychosocial culture could help to create an organizational climate that fosters workers' loyalty and commitment that ultimately could lead to improved individual performance.

Regarding work culture in Mexico, several challenges emerge. Much of the evidence on PA systems suggests that methods and tools encourage individual appraisal and, consequently, performance. Moreover, these methods and tools rest on the assumption of individual accountability. Methods and tools that classify employees tend to conflict with the collectivist culture of the country and the dependency behavior of subordinates toward authority figures. This might undermine PA systems' usefulness for enhancing employee performance. In order to minimize PA rejection, ensure individual performance and promote organization-wide coherence with Mexican collectivistic values, we suggest introducing collective purposes in PA. For instance, objectives could include desired cross-hierarchical – vertically and horizontally – or sub-group performance.

Some features of the superior–subordinate appraisal meeting could also undermine the effectiveness of PM systems. For example, the centralization of the appraisal in the supervisor or HR area could create distortions such as the subordinates' perception of inequalities within the organization. We do not know the extent to which PA methods and tools discriminate between employees' contribution and their willingness to satisfy the superior. With low compliance regarding labor laws that protect and warrantee the employment relationship and facing economic turnarounds that jeopardize jobs, superiors and subordinates could engage in psychological contract dynamics to mutually protect their jobs. These distal factors could shape proximal factors and influence raters' willingness to give high appraisals. Perhaps the institutionalization of the PA practice in Mexican organizations, and especially through information technology tools, could facilitate the spread of the PA logic.

In this chapter we have approached PM systems from the angle of contextual and organizational factors. This perspective provides insights for performance management in Mexico beyond a narrow preoccupation with measuring individual performance. It could also help understand challenges in the future of HRM in Mexico and guide future research on the culturally sensitive practice of performance evaluation.

Appendix A

Interview questionnaire

1   Could you briefly describe your career development path?
2   Let us go back to the beginning of your career. At that time, what instruments were used for PA?
3   Could you describe what the early PA was like?
4   In other companies where you have worked, how were PA processes and instruments managed? How are those managed today?
5   What appraisal methods were used at non-managerial levels of the organization, such as clerical or manufacturing jobs? Which ones are used today?
6   Over the length of your career, what are the three main organizational issues that you can identify regarding PA?

7 What are three main issues that you see with respect to PA concerning the superior–
   subordinate relationship?
8 How is PA related to other HR practices in this organization?
9 How do the instruments you have described differ from those used at other companies?

Notes

1 The main data base consulted was *Infolatina*, a subsidiary of ISI Emerging Markets, a division
   of Euromoney Institutional Investor.
2 http://www.gis.com.mx/
3 http://www.femsa.com/
4 http://www.oracle.com/global/lad/
5 http://www.sap.com/mexico/
6 Original statement in Spanish and translated to English by the authors.
7 http://www.haygroup.com.mx/
8 http://www.revistacyd.com.ar/
9 http://www.americanexpress.com/mexico/
10 http://www.nh-mexico.com.mx/

References

Bensusan, G. (2006) Las reformas laborales en America Latina (pp. 367–84). [Labor reforms in Latin
   America], in E. De la Garza Toledo (ed.) *Teorias Sociales y Estudios del Trabajo: Nuevos
   Enfoques* [Social Theories and Labor Studies: New Approaches], Cuadernos A. Temas de
   Innovacion Social Anthropos. Mexico: UAM-I.
Carlos, L. (July 13, 2004) Afila GIS tactica contra asiaticos [GIS sharpens its tactic against Asia].
   Palabra, Capitales. Retrieved on 04/04/2007 from ISI Emerging Markets: http://
   www.securities.com/doc.html?pc=MX&sv=CORP&doc_id=59171416.
Castañeda, G. (1998) *La Empresa Mexicana y su Gobierno Corporativo: Antecedentes y desafios para
   el Siglo XXI.* [The Mexican Enterprise and its Corporate Governance: Background and
   Challenges for the 21st Century.], Mexico: Universidad de las Americas-Puebla y Alter Ego
   Editores.
Cortes, A. (2002) Evaluacion del desempeno [Performance evaluation]. *Brenix*, Contacto de Union
   Empresarial. Retrieved on 04/04/2007 from ISI Emerging Markets: http://www.securities.com/
   doc.html?pc=MX&sv=CORP&doc_id=27628491.
Cortes, A. (2005) Atraer y retener talentos [Attracting and retaining talent]. *Brenix*, Contacto de
   Union Empresarial. Retrieved on 04/04/2007 from ISI Emerging Markets: http://
   www.securities.com/doc.html?pc=MX&sv=CORP&doc_id=92457757.
Davila, A. and Elvira, M. M. (2005) Culture and human resource management in Latin America
   (pp. 3–24), in M. M. Elvira and A. Davila (eds.) *Managing Human Resources in Latin America:
   An Agenda for International Leaders*, London: Routledge.
Davila, A. and Elvira, M. M. (2007) Psychological contracts and performance management in Mexico,
   International Journal of Manpower, Special Issue, Best HRM practices in Latin America, 28(5):
   384–402.
Davila, A. and Garcia, E. (2004) Cultural symbols as change agents: International joint ventures in the
   Mexican context (pp. 373–86), in V. Gupta (ed.) *Transformative Organizations: A Global
   Perspective*, New Delhi/California: Sage.

D'Iribarne, P. (2001) Administración y culturas políticas [Management and political cultures], *Gestion y Politica Publica* [Management and Public Policy], *X*(1): 5–29.

DeVoe, S. E. and Iyengar, S. S. (2004) Managers' theories of subordinates: a cross-cultural examination of manager perceptions of motivation and appraisal of performance, *Organizational Behavior and Human Decision Processes* 93: 47–61.

Diaz-Saenz, H. R. and Witherspoon, P. D. (2000) Psychological contracts in Mexico, in D. M. Rousseau and R. Schalk (eds.) *Psychological Contracts in Employment: Cross-national Perspectives*, Thousand Oaks, CA: Sage, pp. 158–75.

El Economista (June 27, 2005) Rompiendo paradigmas en gestion del desempeño [Breaking up paradigms of performance management]. Valores y Dinero. Retrieved on 04/04/07 from *ISI Emerging Markets*: http://www.securities.com/doc.html?pc=MX&sv=CORP&doc_id=79629505

El Economista (November 27, 2006) Premian a empresas innovadoras en recursos humanos [Awards for organizations innovating in human resources]. Empresas y Negocios. Retrieved on 04/04/2007 from ISI Emerging Markets: http://www.securities.com/doc.html?pc=MX&sv=CORP&doc_id=120892623.

El Financiero (October 11, 2006) Seleccion deficiente de personal causa perdidas a 50% de empresas [Inefficient personnel selection causes losses for 50% of firms]. Economia. Retrieved on 04/04/07 from *ISI Emerging Markets*: http://www.securities.com/doc.html?pc=MX&sv=CORP&doc_id=115529428.

El Norte (2003) Propone la Division Contactpower trabajar con el modelo co-sourcing [Contacpower Division proposes use of the co-sourcing model]. *Terra Networks, S. A. de C. V.* Retrieved on 04/04/2007 through ISI Emerging Markets: http://www.securities.com/doc.html?pc=MX&sv=CORP&doc_id=49430709

Elvira, M. M. and Davila, A. (eds.) (2005a) *Managing Human Resources in Latin America: An Agenda for International Leaders*, London: Routledge.

Elvira, M. M. and Davila, A. (2005b) Emergent directions for human resource management research in Latin America, *International Journal of Human Resources Management* 16(12): 2265–82.

Estrada, J. (October 30, 2006) Satisface mas al empleado el clima laboral que salario [Organizational climate satisfies workers more than salary]. *Milenio Guadalajara*. Retrieved on 04/04/2007 through: ISI Emerging Markets: http://www.securities.com/doc.html?pc=MX&sv=CORP&doc_id=117697271.

Garcia-Canclini, N. (1990) *Culturas Hibridas. Estrategias para Entrar y Salir de la Modernidad* (Nueva Edicion) [Hybrid cultures. Strategies to enter and exit modernity (New Edition)], Mexico: Grijalbo.

Hofstede, G. H. (1982) *Culture's Consequences. International Differences in Work-related Values. Abridged Edition*, Newbury Park, CA: Sage.

INEGI (2006a) *Estadisticas sobre Disponibilidad y Uso de Tecnologias de Informacion y Comunicacion en los Hogares* [Statistics on the Availability and Uses of Information and Communication Technologies at Homes]. Mexico: Instituto Nacional de Estadistica, Geografia e Informatica (INEGI) [National Institute for Statistics, Geography and Informatics]. Retrieved on 30/04/2007 through http://www.inegi.gob.mx/prod_serv/contenidos/espanol/bvinegi/productos/encuestas/especiales/endutih

INEGI (2006b) *Numeralia* [Statistics]. Mexico: Instituto Nacional de Estadistica, Geografia e Informatica (INEGI) [National Institute for Statistics, Geography and Informatics]. Retrieved on 01/04/2007 through: http://www.inegi.gob.mx/inegi/contenidos/espanol/acerca/inegi324.asp?c=324.

INFOchannel Mexico (July 7, 2006) Robert Kaplan y la mejora en procesos [Robert Kaplan and process improvement]. Retrieved on 04/04/2007 through ISI Emerging Markets: http://www.securities.com/doc.html?pc=MX&sv=CORP&doc_id=108218467.

Jaramillo, C. (March 15, 2006) Trabajan juntos, pero no se hablan [They work together, but do not speak to each other]. *Mural*, Negocios. Retrieved on 04/04/2007 through ISI Emerging Markets: http://www.securities.com/doc.html?pc=MX&sv=CORP&doc_id=99311864

KPMG. (2006) *Investment in Mexico 2006*. Mexico: KPMG. Retrieved on 26/04/2007 through: http://www.kpmg.com.mx/publicaciones/libreria/mexico/ft-investment(2006).pdf

KPMG-AMECE. (2006) *Perspectivas de la Alta Direccion en Mexico* [Top management perspectives in Mexico]. Retrieved on 23/04/2007 through http://www.kpmg.com.mx/publicaciones/libreria/mexico/fs-amecekpmg(0406).pdf

Lindsley, S. L. (1999) Communication and "the Mexican way": stability and trust as core symbols in maquiladoras, *Western Journal of Communication* 63(1): 1–31.

Martinez, P. G. (2005) Paternalism as a positive form of leadership in the Latin American context: leader benevolence, decision-making control and human resource management practices, in M. M. Elvira, and A. Davila (eds.) *Managing Human Resources in Latin America: An Agenda for International Leaders*, London: Routledge, pp. 75–93.

Milliman, J., Nason, S., Zhu, C. and De Cieri, H. (2002) An exploratory assessment of the purposes of performance appraisals in North and Central America and the Pacific Rim, *Human Resource Management* 41(1): 87–102.

Notimex (2003) Encabeza SAP sector de aplicaciones de software de recursos humanos [SAP leading in human resources software applications]. Financiero. Retrieved on 04/04/2007 through ISI Emerging Markets: http://www.securities.com/doc.html?pc=MX&sv=CORP&doc_id=46429473.

Notimex (August 1, 2005) Necesario integrar metodologias para eficiencia de empresas [The need to integrate methodologies for business efficiency]. Retrieved on 04/04/2007 through ISI Emerging Markets: http://www.securities.com/doc.html?pc=MX&sv=CORP&doc_id=83634184.

Olivas-Lujan, M. R., Ramirez, J. and Zapata-Cantu, L. (2007) e-HRM in Mexico: Adapting innovations for global competitiveness, *International Journal of Manpower*, Special Issue, Best HRM practices in Latin America, 28(5): 418–34.

Personal Computing (November 6, 2000) Mida su empresa [Measure your company]. *Servicios Editoriales Sayrols, S. A.* Retrieved on 04/04/2007 through ISI Emerging Markets: http://www.securities.com/doc.html?pc=MX&sv=CORP&doc_id=12547112.

Phillips, S., Mehrez, G. and Moissinac, V. (2006) *Mexico: Selected Issues*. Country Report. Washington, DC: International Monetary Fund. Retrieved on 01/05/2007 through https://www.imf.org/external/pubs/ft/scr/2006/cr06351.pdf

Plata, S. (2004) Hacia la era de los e-empleados [Towards the e-employees era]. *Revista Expansion en Linea*. Retrieved on 04/04/2007 through ISI Emerging Markets: http://www.securities.com/doc.html?pc=MX&sv=CORP&doc_id=59178581.

Rivero, A. (April 8, 2005a) Evaluan mal el desempeño [Poor Performance evaluation]. *Reforma*, Negocios. Retrieved on 04/04/2007 through ISI Emerging Markets: http://www.securities.com/doc.html?pc=MX&sv=CORP&doc_id=72446895.

Rivero, A. (April 12, 2005b) Crea descontento desercion laboral [Job desertion causes dissatisfaction]. *El Norte*, Negocios. Retrieved on 04/04/07 from ISI Emerging Markets: http://www.securities.com/doc.html?pc=MX&sv=CORP&doc_id=72586052.

Sargent, J. (2005) Large firms and business groups in Latin America: Towards a theory based contextually relevant research agenda, *Latin American Business Review* 6(2): 39–66.

Suarez, G. (August 5, 2004) Minimizan calificar desempeño [Performance evaluation is minimized]. *Mural*, Negocios. Retrieved on 04/04/2007 through ISI Emerging Markets: http://www.securities.com/doc.html?pc=MX&sv=CORP&doc_id=60020794.

Vizcaino, A. (2002) Piden evaluar personal [Requests for personnel evaluation]. *Reforma*. Retrieved on 04/04/2007 through ISI Emerging Markets: http://www.securities.com/doc.html?pc=MX&sv=CORP&doc_id=28443661

9 Performance management in the U.K.

PAUL SPARROW

This chapter covers four main issues. First, it provides a summary of the socioeconomic and legal context surrounding the employment relationship, followed by a historical review of the development of performance management systems (PMSs) in the U.K. Second, it identifies the key comparative factors that impact PMS practices in the country. Third, where appropriate, it makes links to the Murphy and DeNisi model, presented in Chapter 6, throughout these opening sections. Fourth, the chapter summarizes the current challenges facing effective PMSs in the U.K. as identified by both the research and practitioner communities, using the evidence base of a library search through ABI Inform from the years 2000 to 2006.

Socioeconomic, legal and political background of the U.K.

U.K. employment levels have risen over the past three decades from 24.6 million in 1971 to 28.8 million in 2005. As of February 2007, 74 percent of people of working age were in employment, and official unemployment as a percentage of the economically active is 5.5 percent. The Labour Cost Survey for 2000 notes that wages and salaries account for 83 percent of costs; employers' social contributions for 15 percent; and other labor costs for 2 percent (non-wage labor costs therefore amount to 17 percent). Managers and senior officials are the largest occupational group in the U.K., with 15 percent of people employed in this group. Twenty percent of males are employed in skilled trades compared with only 2 percent of females. Employment in the public sector stands at just under 6 million. The percentage of teleworkers doubled between 1997 and 2005 from 4 percent to 8 percent of the total workforce.

The employment relationship is governed by three imperatives: a complex mix of individual and collective agreements; implicit and explicit understandings; and rights and obligations enshrined in legal statutes. A legal framework surrounds the contract of employment with implied and express terms within it. Contract and common law (established by judges' decisions not statute) is used to establish whether a person is regarded as an employee in the first place, whether the employer is entitled to exercise control over what the employee does and how he or she does it, whether the employee is integrated into the structure of the organization, whether there is a mutual obligation to supply and accept work and, if yes, whether they can be considered an employee and so claim entitlements. In the U.K. there has long been a principle of "voluntarism" and state abstention from the employment relationship. Relatively few interactions have the force of law, although recent harmonization with EU legislation has changed this situation.

British statute law impinges on the nature of PMSs in three ways: through a "floor of rights" that have been established, structural support for collective bargaining, and through restrictions on boundaries of lawful action. The floor of rights covers rights for the individual on matters such as: unfair dismissal, redundancy, equal opportunities, maternity leave, employment rights for the disabled; confidentiality of computerized data; health and safety at work. EU law takes effect in two ways: regulations which affect member states (i.e. override domestic law), and directives concerning social rights and interests of employees, which have to be implemented in the public sector, but impact private sector firms when national courts take account of the purpose of a directive when interpreting national legislation. Therefore, some statutory principles have been enacted in response to European directives and some employee protection exists in parallel with rights accumulated through the precedents of common law, where rights have been established through judicial reviews over time.

The centre of gravity with regard to employment law has shifted therefore in recent years. There has been a return of a regulatory and collectivist orientation, signaled by the requirement to recognize unions for the purpose of collective bargaining if a majority of the workforce vote for it. The provision for a statutory minimum wage has signaled the return to a legal principle of providing a safety net for the low paid. The implementation of employee share ownership plans has promoted higher levels of employee involvement.

European directives have introduced a range of regulatory effects on U.K. employment, including measures relating to works councils, maximum working hours, full employment rights for part-time work and parental leave. Health and Safety has been elevated as a policy area demanding systematic and planned approaches on the part of employers, and the broadened definition of health concerns now encompasses factors such as stress, smoking and harassment. Finally, discrimination legislation has been extended from sex, race and disability into the arena of age discrimination. The legal context that surrounds the employment relationship in general, and therefore also the conduct of PMSs, is both complex and clearly also a significant factor.

Historical development of PM in the U.K.

If we recall the original Harvard model of HR (Beer *et al.*, 1984), it stressed four outcomes through which an HR system should be judged: cost effectiveness, competence, commitment, and coherence. There are still many U.K. organizations today that struggle to implement even the most basic PMSs although there were some organizations back in the 1980s that could claim fairly sophisticated systems. Nonetheless, if we look back over the main developments in practice amongst U.K. organizations, then it has evolved through successive stages given in order of attention to:

- cost effectiveness (exerted in the form of top-down systems based on narrow specifications of performance as measured through outputs such as objectives) in the 1980s;
- a more developmental agenda focused around the enablement of competence and broader performance specifications by the early 1990s;
- by the late 1990s, greater concern about the need for mutual employer–employee understanding about – and commitment to – performance, often in the context of change programmes (what has been called "engagement");
- finally, by the early 2000s, concern about broad strategic imperatives that might be hindered by a poorly designed PMS, and attention to the need for coherence between PMS and other HR agendas such as talent management and total rewards management.

Clearly, then, in relation to Murphy and DeNisi's model (see Figures 6.1 and 6.2), the norms relating to the distal factor of purpose (the frequency, source and use of PMSs) have developed over time. Attention to the importance of PMSs in the U.K. first developed in the 1980s. At the time, U.K. organizations were being subjected to considerable competitive threat and HR systems were developing under this impetus (Hendry, Pettigrew and Sparrow, 1989). Performance management was one of the many U.S. concepts that began to exert an influence on U.K. practice. Existing thinking about the nature of PMSs was already relatively advanced and so was quickly incorporated into professional training. Of course, there was a significant gap between the intent behind systems and the quality of their execution (problems were experienced with Murphy and DeNisi's proximal factors of both the purpose and acceptance of systems).

The response was more attention being given to the different purposes that might be served by PMSs. Randall *et al.* (1984) distinguished three roles typically seen in U.K. firms at the time: performance (concentrating on, improving and maintaining performance); potential (assessing what individuals were capable of in the future and giving attention to development needs); and reward (allocation of monetary and non-monetary rewards). It was pointed out that most organizations (inappropriately) attempted to handle all three decisions in a single process such as the appraisal interview, and that the efficiency of the process was very dependent on the individual skills of managers. In practice, the tendency was that appraisers used different appraisal styles such as "tell and sell," "tell and listen," "listen and support" and "joint problem solving" (these relate both to Murphy and DeNisi's proximal factor of purpose and to the way in which judgments were made). Joint problem solving is the recommended approach and textbook solution. However, in practice, surveys of the time showed that 61 percent of U.K. organizations were using PA for management training and development needs, and 57 percent for the assessment of potential. Around 40 percent of organizations used appraisal for clerical staff (Torrington and MacKay, 1986; Neale, 1991).

Given early concerns about the capability of narrowly-defined appraisal processes to handle the complex decisions needed of a PMS, the conceptualization of PMSs was soon broadened out. Using Murphy and DeNisi's language, the distal factor of Strategy and Firm Performance was made more visible within systems. Philpot and Sheppard (1992) identified eight successive layers of activity, each making its own contribution to HRM:

1 mission statements (defining the business territory and necessary direction);
2 business strategies and objectives (providing explicit guidance on future behaviours);
3 values statements (saying what was important to the organization in terms of how it conducted its affairs);
4 critical success factors (spelling out factors that contributed to effective performance);
5 performance indicators (where job-level critical success factors were translated into individual-level factors);
6 appraisal processes (the forum in which individual performance, qualities and competencies were evaluated);
7 pay reviews (where performance might be explicitly linked to rewards);
8 performance improvement processes (where training, career development, coaching and counselling could be used to handle under-performance).

PMS were then seen as part of a top-down cascading process that carried advantages of clarifying the nature of individual support for strategic objectives, educating the workforce about the nature of business performance, the monitoring of such performance, and the identification of factors that accounted for over-achieving and under-achieving performance.

However, there were soon debates about the most appropriate performance criterion that might be used for PMSs. Organizations began to identify the most appropriate contingencies that supported the use of systems (Sparrow and Hiltrop, 1994) which could be output-based (measuring what was achieved through objectives, standards and targets); input-based (measuring how employees performed through behaviors, values and competencies); stakeholder-based (measuring the expectations of key stakeholders such as the internal teams that received the output of an individual or customers); or more simple task/process-based (measuring the conduct of prioritized sequences of activities). There was much experimentation with systems that combined these elements with different weightings. Clearly, in terms of Murphy and DeNisi's judgment factors, the opportunity to observe performance ("who says" you are doing a good job) requires the involvement of different sets of people. Attention was also given to the source of evidence upon which performance assessment was based (Redman and Snape, 1992), which in practice could be: grandparent (skip-one-level manager); aunt/uncle (internal customer); client (external customer); subordinate (upward); other manager (peer); parent (immediate supervisor); or manager (self-appraisal). Again, multiple variations existed in terms of how these sources of evidence were being combined. In short, complexity was the order of the day and surveys that simply assessed the presence or not of a PMS were of limited value. This still carries implications today for much survey-based comparative studies of HRM, which inevitably can only make high-level comparisons of practice.

Although by this time it was (reluctantly in some sectors such as public services) accepted that appraisal systems were a feature of HRM, Murphy and DeNisi's intervening factors of rater–ratee relationship, motivation and quality of leader–member exchange, and judgment factors in terms of standards, still presented problems. Two adages characterized U.K. thinking about PMSs within professional training circles at the time: "there is nothing better than a well-designed PMS, but there is definitely nothing worse than a poorly-designed one" and "even the best-designed PMS will be destroyed by incompetent managers." With regard to the latter quip, line managers were considered to need a series of competencies in order to be able to "handle" even a simple PMS: objective setting; assessment; coaching; delegating; supporting; communication, and motivation. The effective introduction of PMS was therefore seen as part of a politically-determined HR strategy, crucially dependent upon the prior demonstration of basic HR capabilities. The ICL PMS of the time typified the nature of the more complex systems. An organizational capability review was influenced by four outputs from the appraisal process: (i) a personal job improvement plan (where the appraisal process highlighted deficiencies in business process, not the person); (ii) a career development plan; (iii) a training plan; and (iv) a performance rating. The performance rating was fed into a separate (in time) pay review. The organization capability review formed one of the major inputs into the business strategy setting process, so that strategy was always analyzed in the context of the limitations of capability. The next year's individual objective setting process then flowed top-down from the business strategies. Such horizontal and vertical linkages between strategy and across HR processes were common of the time. Nonetheless, there was widespread dissatisfaction with PMSs in the U.K., especially the appraisal element, with surveys showing that between 68 percent to 80 percent of organizations using appraisal were dissatisfied with it (Bowles and Coates, 1993; Fletcher, 1993).

By the early to mid-1990s some new life was put into PMS via the growth of management competencies and the pursuit of values-based HR strategies. These developments created a new context for PMSs. Organizations were giving more attention to the nature of effective (managerial) performance and had initially introduced competencies into their resourcing processes (notably in terms of external recruitment and internal career assessment processes). The competency approach proved very popular, but naturally led to the argument amongst line managers that "if you are going to decide whether or not to recruit me on competencies, and whether I get promoted on this basis, then I assume that you believe that they are good enough to pay me for them?" In short, pressure was exerted on PMSs to make sure that they did not just measure outputs (for example, the achievement of objectives, targets or standards) but also inputs (such as the values that an employee brought to a job, or the behaviors or competencies they were capable of demonstrating). Attention was given to the role that PMSs played in competency-based HR strategies (Torrington and Blandamer, 1992). Amidst various claims of using PMSs for this purpose – by 2003, 89 percent of U.K. organizations that had competency-based HR systems claimed to use these competencies for performance appraisal and management (Industrial Relations Services, 2004) – it became clear that there were some important distinctions to be made. There was a difference between PMSs that were competency-linked (somewhere within the

PA an assessment of behaviors or competencies might be made and this number, in conjunction with other factors such as the achievement of outcomes, might influence the final assessment of performance in some unprescribed way) and PMSs that were competency-based (where the effective display of competency led to a score that was directly linked to a final performance and rewards outcome (Sparrow, 2002)). Very few organizations pursued the latter option, although the professional press tempted people to believe otherwise. Whether competency-based or more indirectly competency-linked, PMSs were clearly seen to serve a strong developmental agenda.

By the late 1990s the context for PMSs shifted again (there was another shift in Murphy and DeNisi's strategy and firm performance factor). Organizations gave more attention to the link between values and the execution of strategy and the need for person–organization fit in values terms. The introduction of values (a "how you do it" or input-type performance outcome) into PMSs was motivated by one of three situations:

1   On the basis of prior work which established that the strategy could only be executed through the display of these values (a typical example would be customer service values), that is, there was no choice but to inculcate the values and the task of the PMSs was to "educate" managers and employees into this reality.
2   As a counter-weight to a strongly "what you achieve" PMS (i.e. to ensure that the inescapable targeting, standards and objectives were hopefully constrained to a degree by some specification of "how you should perform" (values)) there was risk management motivation introduced into PMSs to counter over-excessive concentration on outputs rather than inputs.
3   Where it was wholly evident that the existing culture did not display the prescribed values, so a mechanism was needed to legitimate discussion of them, that is, the PMS served as a re-education, not just education, mechanism.

There have, then, been three "faces" to values-based PMS in the U.K.

Moreover, in the context of discussions about a changing psychological contract at work and ever-increasing demands for greater flexibility, it was appreciated that whilst line managers may be able to direct the performance of their employees, they often had very limited insights into the personal needs and desires of their employees and the factors that might, or might not, persuade them to commit strongly to the organization. More attention was given to Murphy and DeNisi's rater–ratee relationship factor. Organizations began to understand the power of their PMSs as a vehicle for re-engaging their workforce behind a "new deal" at work. For example, NatWest, a major U.K. retail bank, pioneered a process of renegotiating the "deal" at work with their employees – what the organization expected of employees and what the employees expected of the organization in return for this. This new deal was established through a one-off process of focus groups and one-to-one interviews with staff, but it was understood that in order to sustain the relevance of a more individualized performance negotiation, line managers would need to adopt and adapt existing HR processes so that they could understand and manage employee sentiment. Improving the quality of the PMS in terms of the honesty of the dialogue that it contained seemed an obvious mechanism for achieving this (Herriot, 1998). In general terms, the focus had shifted from the need for PMSs to provide sophisticated evaluation and appraisal skills, toward a broader agenda of improving performance, and then into a mechanism for enabling more open and honest communications about behaviors and outcomes, issues and problems surrounding the execution of strategy, and the need to engage and motivate employees behind this. Three other HR developments reinforced this shift in focus:

- talent management
- employee segmentation
- total rewards management models

The first was the growth of talent management. The developmental agenda that PMS had served so well in the early 1990s was being replaced by attention to a much narrower cadre of "talented" employees. McKinsey's work on The War for Talent had proved influential in this regard. In the U.S., this was associated with a greater emphasis on PMS that differentiated performance through lavishing significant rewards at the high end of performance and exerting more punitive control over poor performance (the "rank and yank" systems that were to cause much controversy in terms of their potential for discrimination). In the U.K. the political debates were quite similar, and the absence (at the time) of age discrimination might have made the introduction of such systems easier, but what appeared to happen was that the more contentious issues were removed from PMSs. Decisions about the identification of talent (and by default, likely access to development resources) were increasingly made through separate talent management forums or processes. The PMS was instead mobilized as a way of helping think about a more individualized performance contract.

The second was increasing attention given to employee segmentation (Matthewman, 2003). Under this philosophy, organizations identify those segments of their employees whose performance really drives return on investment. It involves the application of customer relationship management principles to the organization's own workforce, and is used to identify the optimal workforce required to match customer expectations. It is important to note that Murphy and DeNisi's factor of rater–ratee relationship is too narrow to capture this development – this is an employee-as-consumer to organization relationship. Large U.K. employers such as Tesco, Marks and Spencer, Vodafone and Royal Bank of Scotland are known to have pursued this strategy. For example, in 2003 Tesco, the leading U.K. supermarket and food retailer, acknowledged that it knew more about its customers than it did its employees. On the basis of consumer research, staff were placed into one of five categories or employee segments (want it all, live to work, work to live, pleasure-seekers, and work–life balancers) in a bid to be more receptive to employees' needs (Watkins, 2003). They ascertained what staffs wanted from a career in Tesco and provided a series of what were termed "for me" solutions to enable staff to tailor their hours and employment relationship to their needs. Staff was surveyed twice a year to link their engagement scores to improvements in other areas. In short, PMSs were seen as part of a two-way communication process that played an important role in building levels of employee engagement.

The third development was the growth of "total rewards management" models. Closely linked to the need to develop more idiosyncratic or individualized "deals" within the employment relationship, it was considered necessary to reward performance through a total assessment of desired rewards, which in practice might include tangible factors (competitive pay and benefits, ownership potential, recognition and fairness); quality of work (perceived value, challenge, autonomy, quality of work relationships); growth opportunities (quality of feedback, learning and development opportunities beyond the job); work–life balance demands; and inspirational/emotional needs (the quality of leadership; the values and behaviors "lived" by the organization; communication, risk sharing; and the potential for reputation enhancement).

Compare the factors argued here as being essential ingredients of a PMS with the 1984 model of Randall *et al.* that differentiated discussion about performance, potential and reward. In theory at least, PM discussions, particularly in the more sophisticated U.K. organizations, are now highly integrated with higher-level organizational concerns of employee engagement and individualized reward.

Key factors that impact on PM in the U.K.

From a comparative HRM perspective, the latest Cranet 2004 data show that 90 percent of U.K. organizations formally assess managers through the use of a PA scheme, compared to 88 percent in Greece or Sweden, 81 percent in Germany but only 65 percent in Slovakia (Brewster, Sparrow and Vernon, 2007). What sorts of factors account for such differences? There are obvious issues such as levels of organizational autonomy and the consequent ability to introduce more flexible HR systems with less concern about industrial relations issues. Demographics associated with the industrial sector play an important role; see, for example, the fairly significant size of the public sector (which began to implement PMSs at about the same time that such systems had come into criticism in the private sector) and a relatively high number of very large organizations on the one hand and small and medium-sized enterprises on the other (which impacts the level of formality of HR). In addition to such factors, Sparrow and Hiltrop (1994) also identified three comparative HR features that could be linked to the nature of PMSs:

1 The role of specific cultural values
2 The efficiency of the manager–subordinate relationship
3 The level of strategic integration and devolvement of HRM

At a macro level, two of Hofstede's cultural dimensions (uncertainty avoidance and power distance) can be associated with the nature and conduct of PMSs in the U.K. Not only are there cross-national differences in the efficiency of the dialogue (Murphy and DeNisi's rater–ratee relationship factor), but national culture has an impact on the nature of the dialogue (their perceived use and purpose factor). The dialogue that takes place in the appraisal process becomes what Sparrow (1998) called the "stake of a different game." As noted above, in the U.K. early PASs were characterized as a "joint problem solving" activity with decentralized responsibility over how individual objectives may be met (Randall *et al.*, 1984). From a cultural point of view this was not surprising. In the U.K. and U.S. (but also in Denmark, Sweden, Norway and the Netherlands) the national culture combines low-power distance with low-uncertainty avoidance. Power distance touches upon the extent to which superiors can influence the behavior of subordinates and vice versa. Low-power distance is associated with a greater acceptance of equality, participation and co-operation between those in higher and lower organizational positions (Fletcher, 2001). It also means that the boss can be by-passed and rules bent so that the employee can get things done. Therefore the independence and self-realization of the employee is an issue. The "boss" therefore may need to find out the details of the subordinate's tasks (again, the role of managers in a U.K. context is to manage and to be an effective manager; you do not have to know the technical detail of your subordinate's tasks, whereas in, for example, France, managers are expected to be able to answer detailed questions about their subordinates' jobs). In the U.K., the low-power distance is blended with low uncertainty avoidance, which is associated with a higher tolerance of risk and acceptance of dependencies in performance, a reliance on resourcefulness and adaptability in achieving goals and a tendency to be reactive rather than proactive feedback.

It is not surprising that in this "game" it is legitimate to make the PA discussion a joint problem-solving activity and, moreover, that British firms could also consider a process such as psychological contracting as feasible within their existing PMSs (Sparrow, 1998). Fletcher and Perry (2001) also draw attention to the role of Hofstede's individualism–collectivism construct, with individualism being associated with people acting more in their own self-interest and initiative.

At an institutional level, the efficiency of the manager–subordinate relationship (Murphy and DeNisi's rater–ratee relationship) has a powerful impact on the nature of PMSs, as too does the level of devolvement of HR. Bournois and Chauchat (1990) gave attention to the presumed efficiency of the manager–subordinate relationship. They mapped European countries on two dimensions: the estimated level of management talent and levels of worker motivation. At the time, the U.K. scored badly on both dimensions, underperformed only by Spain, Greece and Portugal. In relation to PMSs, at the time, four out of five PMSs were considered to be failing (Fletcher and Williams, 1992) on the grounds that: the system was not used, modeled or supported at the top of the organization; line managers viewed the system as an administrative burden; performance objectives were subjective and subject to change; or managers were incapable of giving effective and constructive feedback or dealing with conflict. A decade later, Renwick and MacNeil (2002) argued that the devolvement of HR to line managers in the U.K. was still associated with a sense that HR managers had not just given PM away, but had given it up, with evidence of poor levels of partnership between the HR function and line managers. Much activity inside U.K. organizations since this period may be seen in the context of attempting to improve the efficiency of the employment relationship and historically high levels of PMS failure. To be fair, it could also be argued that U.K. managers were somewhat more honest about the failings of PMSs!

The third comparative factor concerns the strategic role of HR functions. Using data from the Cranet survey, the U.K. was originally characterized as having a "professional mechanic" approach to HR strategy (Brewster and Larsen, 1993). The level of strategic integration of HR into the business strategy was low, and the level of devolvement of HR to the line was also low. Since this time, there has been considerable devolvement of HR to line managers, fuelled by shared service HR models and the growth of business partner roles. In modern HR functions, the capability of line managers to conduct effective PAs is a major determinant of the ultimate credibility of the system.

However, such macro factors aside, the best way to understand which factors impact on the nature of PMSs in the U.K. is to consider the main "design choices" that organizations make when thinking about the shape of their systems, and then look at the factors that most likely influence these choices.

Key challenges in PM in the U.K.

As should be clear throughout this chapter, PMS now represents a fairly mature HR technology in the U.K. (IRS, 1994, 1999; Freemantle, 1994; Industrial Society, 1997). By the 1990s they were widespread in the U.K. A 1994 Industrial Relations Service survey (IRS is an employment intelligence provider) reported that 90 percent of respondents used an appraisal system and by 1999 this figure had reached almost 100 percent. The design of PMSs is still debated in terms of micro issues of fairness, assessment validity and strategic sensemaking. The issue of fairness has been discussed in terms of three topical issues (in order of appearance):

1 Concerns about the link between PA scores and the length of hours worked (i.e. work–life balance issues and rater bias)
2 An increasingly diverse domestic workforce (in terms of immigration and ethnic groups) has returned as a focus of professional attention (Income Data Service, 2006) and
3 The recent introduction of age discrimination legislation in the U.K. and concerns for the absence of bias.

Despite remaining issues relating to fairness, the design of PMSs today is however judged more in terms of coherence – how it supports macro corporate imperatives, such as the delivery of an appropriate customer experience. In order to identify both the evidence base and the key challenges in PM in a U.K. context, a library search through ABI Inform has been carried out using key word searches of PM and PA from the years 2000 to 2006. Those papers involving U.K. authors are reported on here. In addition, publications by the U.K. professional body the Chartered Institute of Personnel Development have been searched from 2003 to 2006 under the same headings to assess the developing professional debate.

The professional rhetoric around the topic has become increasingly sceptical. For example, Brown (2003: 25), reporting on CIPD data and research, noted that the understanding of the topic amongst U.K. managers is based on an ". . . outdated model of strategy . . . many HR strategies were 'illusions in the boardroom' . . . the realities of people management and performance HR strategies are dry, over-engineered plans that have been developed by a small coterie of 'experts' in the rarefied atmosphere of the boardroom. They assume simplistic relationships and fail to involve line managers and staff, taking no account of the realities of their daily lives." The need to realign PMSs after the damage created by ill-thought-out processes of downsizing, outsourcing, insourcing, acquisition or cost cutting has also been discussed by Drumm (2005). This brought with it heightened importance to elements of PMSs that signaled the (new) job purpose and the (often poorly understood) consequences connected to performance in the surviving roles. Perhaps not surprisingly, the quality of management is considered to be key to transforming performance in organizations (Mahony, 2003) and this has led to ". . . an evolutionary change in this area, with organizations seeing it as an opportunity for coaching rather than judging individuals . . . Performance management systems went hand in hand with a leadership and communications programme" (Glover, 2003: 9). Much of the professional focus has moved away from the issue of PM towards that of talent management. Moreover, PMS is one of those HR processes that can be e-enabled, and so attention to it has been subsumed within a broader move to automated transactions, capability development and strategic support.

In many senses, the academic research needs and priorities that surround PM have remained the same as they ever were. Fletcher (2001: 473) noted that as "performance appraisal . . . widened as a concept and as a set of practices and . . . the form of performance management [became] part of a more strategic approach to integrating HR activities and business policies" research has shifted away from its traditional focus on measurement issues and accuracy toward more social and motivational aspects. In conducting the review of published papers through ABI Inform it was clear that in the English language management journals there is a predominance still of U.S. writers on the topic, followed by U.K., Dutch, Australian and some Spanish. This reflects strong industrial and organizational psychology communities in these countries. The U.S. concerns are still mainly focused on issues of rater accuracy and perceived fairness. The U.K. writers focus much more on user (dis)satisfaction and the political context of PMS usage, perhaps reflecting concerns associated with the relatively more recent introduction of PMS into public sector settings.

Some work on measurement accuracy in a U.K. context still persists, however. Reflecting the adoption of more varied and complex systems, as argued above, attention has been given to the validity and utility of multiple-source multiple-rater feedback, the conduct of 360-degree feedback and individual perceptions about the validity of such systems (see, for example, Mabey, 2001; Bailey and Fletcher, 2002; Morgan, Cannan and Cullinane, 2005). Bailey and Fletcher (2002) studied some of the dynamics that result from such schemes. They point out that the benefits of this have largely been untested, but lie on assumptions that individuals learn what is the best specification of effective task performance, gain insight into how it is demonstrated, and build the accuracy of self-perception and subsequent corrective behaviors. The study of 104 managers receiving feedback on 50 behaviors over two years in an automobile breakdown service organization showed mixed benefits. The positive findings were that on average self-raters, first and second-level subordinates and bosses all saw improvements in competencies, development needs were perceived to decrease and there were dramatic changes in the perceptions of first and second-level subordinates in terms of the congruency of self- and other-ratings. Self-perceptions also became a more important predictor of actual appraisal scores over time. On the negative side, greater congruence in scores between peers, self and individual level largely resulted from subordinates changing their assessment of target managers – the managers' self-perceptions did not change much over time.

The context for the introduction of 360-degree feedback can be very important, and there has been a range of research in the U.K. looking at issues such as employee perceptions and existing organizational culture (in terms of levels of trust and openness). Mabey (2001) studied the introduction of 360-degree appraisal systems in the Open University, finding that many managers did not believe they had developed any greater (or had changed) self-perceptions, and raising questions about whether feedback should be public or not in terms of motivation to be self-accountable for feedback. Commentary by the Industrial Relations Service (2000) drew attention to the role of levels of trust and openness in organizational culture, arguing 360-degree systems fail where this is not present. Based on case study analysis in the Civil Service, Morgan, Cannan and Cullinane (2005) argued that the self-awareness is not a motivation for employees, however. In the U.K. public sector, strategic pursuit of goals such as "modernization," "reformulation" and "new public management" mean that the introduction of new pay and appraisal systems are intended to create more transparency in performance and a greater emphasis on consumer (the public) needs. However, in practice, there are tensions between a system (360-degree) based on an assumption of autonomous management (and therefore opportunity to self-correct) and an organizational system (Civil Service) characterized by complex and competing stakeholder demands on strategy and diffuse management authority.

Cook and Crossman (2004) have picked up on the U.S. focus on the link between perceived fairness of the PMS (the system, the process and the outcome) and user (or subject) satisfaction (this focus assumes subsequent impacts on motivation, individual performance and organizational performance). They measured satisfaction with all three forms of justice in 382 employees in a U.K. government agency, finding that overall satisfaction with the PMS was explained in order of importance by system, process and only then outcome justice. Respondents were not normally distributed. It is often assumed in the U.K. that appraisees either love or hate PMS, but often on ideological grounds. This study showed that a wide range of demographic factors predicted satisfaction, but not surprisingly those whose performance rating fell from year 1 to year 2 were more dissatisfied with the fairness of the process!

Academic focus on the role of PMS and disciplinary processes designed to address under-performance in public sector settings is also seen in the study of U.K. teacher assessment by Earnshaw, Marchington, Ritchie and Torrington (2004). Based upon telephone interviews with 520 head teachers and 100 interviews across 45 school case studies, under-performance was only an issue for around 1.2 percent of teachers, with 50 percent of those affected off sick and 80 percent of the absences due to stress-related illnesses. Corrective PMS capability-building processes for under-performers were found to be a necessary evil, but complicated, combative and emotionally draining for the head teacher (all for the removal of around 1 percent of performers).

Simmons and Lovegrove (2005) have also conducted case study research, looking at the introduction of PA in two U.K. academic institutions. They use stakeholder theory to consider the implications of the fact that there are often multiple constituencies that have legitimate performance expectations on an organization in terms of strategy, governance and accountability. The case study reveals some of the complexities involved in executing PM in a system where there are reciprocal rights and obligations between multiple stakeholders, and the view that within a knowledge-based organization there are dynamic and interactive systems between interest groups (Simmons and Iles, 2001), which mean that PMSs have to be seen as delivering effective governance logics, rather than a perception of control over groups that need to be "managed."

On the theme of stakeholders, attention has also been given to the alignment between PMS and strategic imperatives such as Total Quality Management (TQM) (Soltani, van der Meer, Gennard and Williams, 2004; Soltani, van der Meer, Williams and Lai, 2006). Soltani *et al.* (2006) asked whether quality-driven organizations in practice adjusted their PASs (original protagonists of the TQM approach argued that PASs were counter-productive). Based on a sample of 64 organizations, they concluded that only 42 percent of organizations believed their PMS had an impact on the longer-term performance of their organization. The majority of respondents did not believe that their PMSs were sufficiently integrated with quality-related aims (despite the growing use of balanced scorecards).

Conclusion

The field of PMS in the U.K. is a mature one. Organizational practice has clearly evolved through successive concerns for cost effectiveness, competence, commitment and coherence. The more recent focus of attention on values-based HRM and person–organization fit brings with it three potentially different "faces" for PMS. From a comparative HRM perspective, a range of factors can be linked to the nature of PMS in the U.K., including individual values orientations, the (in)efficiency of the employment relationship, and levels of devolvement of HR to line management. The professional dialogue has become increasingly skeptical, but new avenues of practice that serve PM aims are opening up. The interests of U.K. academics are unique and have moved away from the U.S. dialogue around accuracy and fairness toward political context and user acceptability. The focus of study (but equally validity and generalizability of the dialogue) has also moved away from private toward public sector settings. It is also clear even from existing work that a number of issues surrounding PMS remain broadly untested. Notably, these include:

1   the varied motivations to introduce PMS (which may be cloaked under headings such as self-development, culture change, or performance, and linked more or less explicitly to other strategic outcomes);
2   the level of internal consistency (such as the range of competencies that exist in other

parts of the HR system and total-system alignment with the logics contained in the PMS initiatives);

3 the ability of new PMSs to produce higher levels of employee engagement (as opposed to just more self-awareness or measurement accuracy);

4 the level of alignment between rewards (in their broadest sense) produced by the PMSs and the varied needs of diverse employee segments, who may be working to very different psychological contracts;

5 the extent to which standalone PMSs contribute directly to value-creation in the organization, or rather serve more to protect value by managing only marginal risks (extremely high or low performance, the identification or management of which may well be handled through other processes such as business process modifications, team socialization processes, or talent management/calibration exercises).

The field of management in the U.K. will contain many lively debates for several years to come.

References

Bailey, C. and Fletcher, C. (2002) The impact of multiple source feedback on management development: findings from a longitudinal study, *Journal of Organizational Behavior* 23: 853–67.

Beer, M., Spector, B., Lawrence, P., Mills, D. and Walton, R. E. (1984) *Managing Human Assets*, New York: Free Press.

Bournois, F. and Chauchat, J. H. (1990) Managing managers in Europe, *European Management Journal* 8(1): 3–18.

Bowles, M. L. and Coates, G. (1993) Image and substance: the management of performance as rhetoric or reality? *Personnel Review* 22(2): 3–21.

Brewster, C. and Larsen, H. H. (1993) Human resource management in Europe: evidence from ten countries, *International Journal of HRM* 3(3): 409–34.

Brewster, C., Sparrow, P. and Vernon, G. (2007) *International Human Resource Management*, 2nd edn, Wimbledon: CIPD Publishing.

Brown, D. (2003) Orchestral manoeuvres in the dark, *People Management* (15th May): 25.

Cook, J. and Crossman, A. (2004) Satisfaction with performance appraisal systems: a study of role perceptions, *Journal of Managerial Psychology* 19(5): 526–41.

Drumm, G. (2005) Putting the pieces back together to realign performance in the organisation, *Performance Improvement* 44(6): 26–30.

Earnshaw, J., Marchington, L., Ritchie, E. and Torrington, D. (2004) Neither fish nor fowl? An assessment of teacher capability procedures, *Industrial Relations Journal* 35(2): 139–52.

Fletcher, C. (1993) Appraisal: an idea whose time has gone? *Personnel Management* (September): 34–7.

Fletcher, C. (2001) Performance appraisal and management: the developing research agenda, *Journal of Occupational and Organizational Psychology* 74: 473–87.

Fletcher, C. and Perry, F. (2001) Performance appraisal and feedback: a consideration of national culture and a review of contemporary and future trends, in N. Anderson, D. Ones, H. Sinangil and C. Viswesvaran (eds.) *International Handbook of Industrial, Work and Organizational Psychology*, Beverly Hills, CA: Sage, pp. 127–44.

Fletcher, C. and Williams, R. (1992) The route to performance management, *Personnel Management* 24(10): 42–7.

Freemantle, D. (1994) The performance of "performance appraisal" – an appraisal, Windsor: Superboss.

Glover, C. (2003) Performance is key to success, *People Management* (17th April): 9.

Hendry, C., Pettigrew, A. and Sparrow, P. R. (1989) Linking strategic change, competitive performance and human resource management: results of a U.K. empirical study, in R. Mansfield (ed.) *Frontiers of Management Research*, London: Routledge, pp. 195–220.

Herriot, P. (1998) The role of the HR function in building a new proposition for staff, in P. R. Sparrow and M. Marchington (eds.) *Human Resource Management: The New Agenda*, London: Financial Times Pitman Publications, pp. 106–16.

Income Data Services (2006) Equality and performance appraisals, *IDS Diversity at Work*, Issue 26: 13–19.

Industrial Relations Service (1994) Improving performance: a survey of appraisal arrangements, *Employment Trends* 556: 5–14.

Industrial Relations Service (1999) New ways to perform appraisal, *Employment Trends* 676: 7–16.

Industrial Relations Service (2000) A rounded view, *IRS Employment Review* 705: 5–9.

Industrial Relations Service (2004) Benchmarking survey of the 11th Competency Survey, *Competency and Emotional Intelligence 2003/2004 Benchmarking Report*, London: IRS Eclipse Group.

Industrial Society (1997) *Appraisal. Report No.37*, London: Industrial Society.

Mabey, C. (2001) Closing the circle: participant views of a 360-degree feedback programme, *Human Resource Management Journal* 11(1): 41–53.

Mahony, C. (2003) On good authority, *People Management* (6th March): 28.

Matthewman, J. (2003) Strong division, *People Management* (20th February): 34.

Morgan, A., Cannan, K. and Cullinane, J. (2005) 360 degree feedback: a critical enquiry, *Personnel Review* 34(6): 663–80.

Neale, F. (ed.) (1991) *Handbook of Performance Management*, Wimbledon: Institute of Personnel Management.

Philpot, I. and Sheppard, L. (1992) Managing for improved performance, in M. Armstrong (ed.) *Strategies for Human Resource Management*, London: Kogan Page, pp. 98–115.

Randall, G. A., Packard, P. M., Shaw, R. L. and Slater, A. J. (1984) *Staff Appraisal*, London: Institute of Personnel Management.

Redman, T. and Snape, E. (1992) Upward and onward: can staff appraise their managers? *Personnel Review* 21(7): 32–46.

Renwick, D. and MacNeil, C. M. (2002) Line manager involvement in careers, *Career Development International* 7(7): 407–14.

Simmons, J. and Iles, P. (2001) Performance appraisal in knowledge based organizations: implications for management education, *International Journal of Management Education* 2(1): 3–18.

Simmons, J. and Lovegrove, I. (2005) Bridging the conceptual divide: lessons from stakeholder analysis, *Journal of Organizational Change Management* 18(5): 495–513.

Soltani, E., van der Meer, R. B., Gennard, J. and Williams, M. T. (2004) Have TQM organizations adjusted their performance management (appraisal) systems? A study of U.K.-based TQM-driven organizations, *TQM Magazine* 16(6): 403–17.

Soltani, E., van der Meer, R., Williams, T. M. and Lai, P. (2006) The compatibility of performance appraisal systems with TQM principles – evidence from current practice, *International Journal of Operations and Production Management* 26(1): 92–112.

Sparrow, P. R. (1998) Re-appraising psychological contracting: lessons for employee development from cross-cultural and occupational psychology research, *International Studies of Management and Organization* 28(1): 30–63.

Sparrow, P. R. (2002) To use competencies or not to use competencies? That is the question, in M. Pearn (ed.) *Handbook of Individual Development in Organizations*, London: Wiley, pp. 107–30.

Sparrow, P. R. and Hiltrop, J. M. (1994) *European Human Resource Management in Transition*, London: Prentice-Hall.

Torrington, D. and Blandamer, W. (1992) Competency, pay and performance management, in R. Boam and P. R. Sparrow (eds.) *Designing and Achieving Competency: A Competency Based Approach to Developing People and Organizations*, London: McGraw-Hill, pp. 137–45.

Torrington, D. and MacKay, L. (1986) Will consultants take over the personnel function? *Personnel Management* 18(2): 34–7.

Watkins, J. (2003) Tesco tailors working conditions, *People Management* (29th May): 10.

10 Performance management in France and Germany

CORDULA BARZANTNY AND MARION FESTING

Introduction

Performance management (PM) has been described in many ways. There is no single definition scholars working in this field have agreed on. The performance domain thus seems to be rather multifaceted (Cascio, 2006; see also DeNisi, 2000; den Hartog *et al.*, 2004). Armstrong and Baron (1998: 7) have defined PM as ". . . a strategic and integrated approach to delivering sustained success to organizations by improving the performance of the people who work in them and by developing the capabilities of teams and individual contributors."

As with many other human resource (HR) measures, PM very much follows the example of U.S. companies (see for example Pudelko, 2005, 2006; Claus and Briscoe, 2006). This can be observed in large companies in Europe, among them those in France and Germany, the two countries under investigation in this chapter. It seems that a kind of best practices system has emerged (Brewster, 1995). It has become popular, especially in multinational organizations, to define a common set of values or competencies, which are supposed to apply within the worldwide organization. Based on these criteria selection, appraisal, development and compensation practices are designed (Festing, Eidems, Royer and Kullak, 2006).

Another very common approach is the use of the balanced scorecard (Kaplan and Norton, 1992, 2006) in PM. This measure, which also originated in the United States, is adapted to the needs of human resource management (HRM) and furthermore to the respective corporate and local contexts (Becker, Huselid and Ulrich, 2001; Phillips, Stone and Phillips, 2001; Huselid, Becker and Beatty, 2005). For the French context Bourguignon *et al.* (2004) discuss the balanced scorecard, which has not received a particularly warm welcome and where the *tableau de bord* has been used for at least 50 years. This may be explained in terms of ideological assumptions, since these management tools tend to be somewhat consistent with the local ideologies in the countries of origin. Therefore, mainly larger, multinational corporations have introduced the balanced scorecard in France.

In order to address the criticisms and hindrances of the balanced scorecard implementation into the French corporate context, Oriot and Misiaszek (2004) furnish an interesting case study of a European space company. They found that despite the estimated influences of national culture, the most important factor posing barriers to balanced scorecard implementation was the professional context. This is linked to a strong engineering background with a lack of short-term cost-consciousness in the observed company.

Regarding the measures applied for PM in large French and German organizations, at first it is difficult to identify significant differences from the measures in the Anglo-American PM literature. However, this does not mean that the systems are identical. On the contrary, country-specific dimensions can be identified (Dowling, Festing and Engle, 2008), especially in the way PM processes are carried out. While we find the same vocabulary and similar agendas, the different environments firms are operating in have a strong influence on the implementation process (Radin, 2003). The aim of this chapter is to describe and explain different country-specific approaches for dealing with PM and to outline their possible implications. In this chapter, we will particularly address the various factors highlighted in the model proposed by Murphy and DeNisi (see Chapter 6), since their model is designed to analyze in detail PA, performance process, and PMSs across organizations, nations, and cultures.[1]

First of all, the European context is described, with France and Germany as rather important countries that are closely tied together in European history and in the present. Then we will analyze some particularities in the examples of France and Germany. The approach is to first take a broader look at the underlying HRM model and then concentrate on the PM field, which we will outline in the context of the respective institutional and cultural environments. The Murphy and DeNisi model provides an excellent basis for summarizing our findings while structuring the possible communalities and differences in the systems with respect to distal, proximal, intervening, judgment and distortion factors. At the end of the chapter a discussion about possible convergent or divergent developments will conclude the analysis.

The European context for PM in France and Germany

Based on the model outlined by Murphy and DeNisi, it can be argued that the European context includes *distal* factors, which may have an impact on European PMSs. However, Europe is far from being a homogenous group of countries. Although the European Union (EU) is striving for common, supranational regulations, its countries include differences in the ideological, political, legal, social and cultural environment (Nikandrou, Apospori and Papalexandris, 2005; Brewster, 1994). Nikandrou *et al.* state that Europe is ". . . characterized by internal variation among various clusters of countries and, at the same time, by external uniformity compared to the rest of the world" (2005: 542).

Within the course of discussions centering on the concept of HRM in the 1990s it became clear that this concept is difficult to apply in the same way that it is used in the U.S., where the concept was developed (Brewster, 1995; Guest, 1994). Guest (1994) states that the unitarist perspective contradicts the prevailing European tradition of pluralism. Furthermore, the strong individualist orientation inherent in this concept is difficult to realize in societies characterized by a higher degree of collectivism and more emphasis on social welfare and social responsibility for the more disadvantaged in society. Other barriers include differences in the ownership and control systems of organizations in Europe and the strong legal environment in many countries (Guest, 1994). Brewster (1994) suggests that limited organizational autonomy is of major importance, too (see also Lawrence, 1993).

Brewster (1994, 1995, 1999) emphasizes the need to pursue a contextual paradigm (i.e. addressing explicitly the external context of firms). Other researchers have confirmed the impact of the country-specific institutional or socioeconomic background (see, for example, Gooderham, Nordhaug and Ringdal, 1999) or of cultural values (see, for example, Lindholm, 2000; Papalexandris and Panayotopoulou, 2004; Cascio, 2006) on HRM. To sum up it can be said that "a single universal model of HRM does not exist" (Pieper, 1990: 11).

> Clearly, the European evidence suggests that management can see the unions, for example, as social partners with a positive role to play in HRM: and the manifest success of many European firms which adopt that approach shows the, explicit or implicit, anti-unionism of many American views to be culture-bound.
>
> (Brewster, 1994: 81; see also Pudelko, 2005)

With respect to PM this research perspective has led to the development of the Murphy and DeNisi model outlined in Chapter 6 of this book. It provides a broad framework that takes into account a variety of factors in which European diversity can be expressed.

Although France and Germany are neighboring European economies, sharing a common border and strong economic ties (half of all intra-EU Community trade is with the other partner), there is no common understanding of HRM. The historical, cultural and environmental factors in each country still play decisive roles that account for differences. Historically, Germany and France grew as competitors and enemies until the industrial revolution. Nationalist ideologies threw Europe and notably France into conflict and war against Germany several times until the end of World War II, and then the daring project of European integration saw its inception in the treaties of Paris (1951) and Rome (1957). Ever since, the French and German economies have played a major role in European integration and economic cooperation. However, both countries have had a different background since World War II because France was among the victorious countries whereas Germany was defeated. This had an important impact on the social, corporate and industrial relations systems. France continued the historically more hierarchical and conflict-intensive governance and behavioral mechanisms while (Western) Germany had to completely recreate all political, social and economic systems, assisted by the governance examples in the allied countries, notably the Anglo-Saxon ones such as the U.S. and U.K.

As an example, in Europe social factors play an important role in career systems (Alexandre-Bailly, Festing and Jonczyk, 2007). There is a high emphasis on a broad general education (Pudelko, 2000b), which becomes especially visible in the French system of the *classes préparatoires* providing general knowledge for another two years after the *baccalauréat* which is equivalent to a high school degree in the USA. Only students who have successfully completed a corresponding exam get the chance to study in the prestigious *Grande Ecole* system. Furthermore, empirical studies have shown that social class still matters to a high extent with respect to careers (Hartmann, 2003). In contrast, in Germany paths to higher education follow a more egalitarian principle, offering the same chances to every person. The reputation of the universities is not as important as in France but individual performance counts. The emphasis is much more on technical knowledge than on social networks. However, this does not mean that social networks do not play a role in career systems but the role is less important than in France (Alexandre-Bailly *et al.*, 2007). Additionally, Germany appears to be linked to the Northern European tradition which, when compared to Southern European countries, also tends to be driven more by equality.

Specificities characterizing PM in France

HRM in France started from a personnel administration and legal background position. The primary mission was to ensure that the firm complies with all legal provisions and avoids lawsuits and government inspections. Therefore, the personnel departments of corporations have been obliged to maintain a high level of legal expertise (Gooderham *et al.*, 1999). In a rather conflict-driven tradition of labor relations where union power is limited to collective bargaining, cooperation with unions is limited. Training is another important aspect of HRM in France, since firms are legally obliged to invest 1.6 percent of annual payroll into the training of employees, if they wish to avoid penalty taxes. Overall French HRM and its evolution is described by Jenkins and van der Wijk (1996) as *"hesitant innovation."* The management of performance in this context entered rather late into the area of people management and HRM. Historically, PM in France was either linked to physical and mechanical performance of processes in industrial manufacturing or, since the 1960s, to stock market portfolios of shares. PM – particularly its measurement at the level of the firm – is mainly developed in accounting and executive remuneration. It was in the 1980s that PM entered into HRM on a larger scale, notably with a more structured PA and the evaluation of employees. Since then, PM in French organizations has seen an evolution from a tool based on measurement toward an instrument used for motivating people in the firm as well as evaluating intellectual capital. More recent evolutions of PM integrate aspects of coaching, competence-based management and the knowledge worker in the wider area of HRM (Devillard, 2001; Klarsfeld and Oiry, 2003; Defélix, Klarsfeld and Oiry, 2006). Particularly emphasizing the measurement aspects, PM using the balanced scorecard is also related to quality in the French management literature (Iribarne, 2003). Today, PM is strongly linked to employee involvement as well as governance aspects. In this context PM is further related to the individual's responsibility, accountability and trust (Saglietto and Thomas, 1998) and re-emerges as an important motivational instrument of HRM.

Meysonnier (1994), for example, proposes a model tested with a sample of 271 French SMEs where economic performance of the firm is influenced by the social performance of the human resources. He shows that quality in HRM seems to matter for the firm's general outcome in the largely independent family-owned sample. Therefore, strategic HRM with its drive of social performance, which means fostering the non-financial "people" relationships for higher organizational achievements, is a determinant of firm performance increasing the motivation and involvement of employees on the individual, as well as on the team level (Côté and Tega, 1980; Besseyre des Horts, 1988; Kieser and Kubicek, 1992).

In their empirical study of PM in French companies, Bescos and Cauvin (2004: 195) state that the four perspectives of the balanced scorecard (financial, customer, internal, learning and growth) tend to be an example of the relations between financial and non-financial measures but differ from a model of a PMS. The authors underline that "this implies an adaptation of the Balanced Scorecard to the context of a firm or a country." Interestingly, the study shows that indicators related to employee satisfaction or shareholder value do not play an important role in France as they do elsewhere.

The French context appears rather specific, notably with regard to cultural norms as a critical factor of differentiation. France is one of the most inventive countries with respect to high technology research & development (ranked fourth in the world according to OECD & Eurostat in 2006), more particularly in life sciences and biotechnology as well as in computer sciences with new Information and Communication Technologies (OSEO, 2006). This also leads to a high acceptance of technology in the workplace in general. The use of Information and Communication Technology (ICT) is fostering innovative collaborative work and management, and tends to enhance productivity, which emphasizes a direct link with performance. Interestingly, the Latin world appeals more to direct and face-to-face contacts rather than dialogue through keyboard and screen. Nevertheless the use of ICT enables managers to deal with the traditionally significant amount of administrative and procedural issues particular to the French system. ICT also helps by offering some sort of "playground" for using and supporting French creativity; the very conceptual and continuous modeling emphasis in the educational system of France also drives the use of electronic simulation tools. Here it may be of interest that the majority of French corporations are led by CEOs with an engineering background, and engineering graduate training is perceived as the most prestigious and desired qualification for a professional career in French business (see also, Maurice, Sellier and Silvestre, 1982; Alexandre-Bailly *et al.*, 2007).

Another important factor to be observed is the country-specific legal as well as institutional system. Its impact will be discussed in the next section, also as part of the *distal* factors outlined in the Murphy and DeNisi model, which have implications for other model-related factors.

Impact of the legal environment on PM in France

In France, the impact of the legal environment on PM can be seen as minimal if there is any impact at all. French labor law gives large flexibility to assess and evaluate performance of employees so long as basic principles of merit and non-discrimination are respected. In a comparative study, the French system has been included in the group of moderately-regulated countries in Europe. In contrast, the German legal system, which is described on p. 156, is in the group of highly-regulated countries (Nikandrou, Apospori and Papalexandris, 2005).

From the institutional side the French Ministry of Industry is calling attention to quality and performance since 2006 by offering a prize to the best performers in industry and services (*Prix Français de la Qualité et de la Performance*). The idea behind this prize is to involve not only large corporations but also small and medium-sized enterprises in industry and services and to support a comprehensive overall drive toward excellence in quality and performance in organizations. Performance is still strongly related to quality, notably if it is considered on the level of the whole organization. While large corporations seem to follow more global approaches of PMSs, dominated mostly by U.S., medium and small enterprises in France appear to be more reserved with respect to the implementation of those systems. Specifically, PA systems and their strategic HRM elements tend to be generated, if at all, by visionary individuals at these firms, notably the founders or the head of the organization. Meysonnier's study (1994) has demonstrated the positive effect of a qualitative HRM strategy on firm performance by testing a model of interdependencies between social, organizational and economic performance in SMEs. With regard to careers and training, France represents, on the one hand, employees with poor basic and manual skills training at the bottom of the corporate ladder and, on the other hand, very high-brow generalists, notably engineers, as leaders of the firm.

In conclusion we can see that the particularities of various factors, not only for the French case of PMSs, but more generally, play a crucial role, as we will emphasize with the framework of Murphy and DeNisi's model along the different groups of distal, proximal, intervening, judgment and distortion factors in the next section.

Impact of the cultural environment on PM in France [2]

According to Hofstede's dimensions (1980, 2001), France is characterized high on power distance, high on uncertainty avoidance, high on individualism and moderate on the masculinity index with a rather feminine attitude. The first and the last dimension differentiate France very clearly from Germany. Such dimensions as part of the *distal* factors seem to be identified with the least difficulties per country and society.

As discussed in the section on historical developments, the French culture is – compared to other European countries – relatively high on power distance (Hofstede, 2001), valuing hierarchy (House *et al.*, 2004), manifested by a rather unequal power distribution in society. High power distance leads to an elite system that still prevails in education, administration, the management of organizations and overall society. Appreciation and appraisal of performance, for example, are strongly influenced by this context.

With regard to *proximal* factors many French firms dispose of appraisal schemes with formal annual interviews and assessment. The respective outcomes have an impact on remuneration and other benefits of the appraised individual (Rojot, 1990). But how the process of appraisal is finally carried out seems to show the variance between formally acclaimed PMSs and processes and the reality in French organizations, which leads to the intervening factors of Murphy and DeNisi's model.

An example of the *intervening* factors, according to Murphy and DeNisi's model, understood as results of the effects of distal and proximal factors, is the fact that PAs in France tend to be influenced by the prevailing elite system [see Brunstein (1995) for an overview of an elitist and Tayloristic approach in French firms]. This is manifest in the following way: if the individual to be evaluated comes from a more prestigious background, the PA will be more positive because of a priori more favorable expectations. This effect is even stronger when both the evaluator and the person to be evaluated share a similar higher educational background. Therefore, the often used management by objectives as a base for measuring possible performance indicators seems to be subjective according to this context following the national ranking of higher education establishments (*Grandes Ecoles* and universities). The basis of a fair PMS (Besseyre des Horts, 1991) is the measurement and the possible measurability of objective indicators. Therefore, the appraisal mechanisms and systems enter into the focus of attention (Longenecker *et al.*, 1987). Unfortunately, in France they are also often used with the aim of confirming and justifying the impact on someone's remuneration of rather subjective criteria, and their evaluation [see also Bourguignon (1998)]. This sometimes leads to limited motivation of individuals who have high performance potential despite the fact that their graduate studies were achieved in a second-tier school in France. The outcome may be that organizations are pulling themselves away from people performance inside their own firms. On higher levels of the organization this is, for example, often vested in countervailing power games. Here we observe an interesting impact of *judgment* factors with private evaluation of a person's performance in some areas (Murphy and Cleveland, 1995; see also Bourguignon, 2004).

High power distance in France leads to a very low degree of openness and lack of transparency between both parties in evaluation processes. "French companies are described as being based on the principle of control with power concentrated at the top" (Gooderham *et al.*, 1999: 513). Overall the employee–manager relationship is characterized by a lack of trust and circumvention of direct feedback. According to van der Klink and Mulder (1995) and Lane (1994) the lack of trust manifests itself through the managers' reluctance to share information "[. . .] since asymmetric information is a precondition for maintaining power" (Gooderham *et al.*, 1999: 513–14). This affects the objective-setting process as well as performance feedback, often leaving employees with a feeling of ambiguity and unfairness in the process and its outcomes and a perception of special, more favorable treatment for certain individuals according to the superior's will, mood and network. In PAs a manager tends to have the final word with a strong tendency to assign job objectives (Schuler, Jackson and Luo, 2004) without clear negotiation, leading to a more ambiguous formulation and, furthermore, a fuzzier relationship.

The difference in power distance may also explain the stratification of average income from bottom to top across industrial organizations varying by a ratio of 1 : 15 in France whereas Germany displayed a factor of 6 (Maurice, Sellier and Silvestre, 1982).

As in most continental European countries, French employees value stability and longer lasting, stable employment relationships. France is actually the EU country with the highest percentage of civil servants among the working population (Eurostat). People are rather averse to change, which impacts their preference and choice of employers as well as types of employment desired (public vs. private sector). These facts might reflect a high level of uncertainty avoidance.

The more feminine score of France compared to Germany is reflected in the definition of careers and the importance of professional progression. In a quasi-Latin environment like France's work climate, quality of life and work–life balance tend to be valued higher than basic economic considerations. This also has an influence on cooperation at work; French employees, on average, prefer a job placement with challenging interpersonal interaction and a positive climate since they focus on people relationships. Since interpersonal ties and networks tend to be very important, open criticism of others, notably along the hierarchical line, is avoided in order to have at least superficial harmony prevailing in work groups. This also impacts feedback, which is often only given when improvements and corrections are requested by the superior. The more qualified the professional category of employee, the fuzzier the goals and objective-setting become. Since in France the generalist profile prevails, the appraisal process takes this into account and also expects a rather diverse human development potential.

Since organizational norms do not necessarily contribute significantly to the accuracy of the PA process and overall PM, we observe a stronger impact from the rater–ratee relationship as well as rater motivation which represent *intervening* factors in Murphy and DeNisi's model. The perceived uses of a performance rating system lead to a rather average rating of all employees in a department, firm or corporation with little discrimination among ratees.

With regard to *distortion* factors, we see a rather low impact of PA on promotion, pay rises, etc., in the traditional French company and corporate hierarchy because of the social differentiation between employees already existing independent from actual professional performance. Interestingly, the variance of performance ratings tends to be small and around the average in each professional group. Nevertheless, higher qualified and more prestigious graduate degrees influence performance raters more positively and work experience with demonstrated performance often counts less than social and educational background.

The fact that most private organizations in France have introduced PA schemes is corroborated by the Cranet data (Hegewisch and Larsen, 1996; Brewster, Mayrhofer and Morley, 2004). Interestingly, this is not necessarily valid for the public sector following a much slower evolution. Overall, "effectiveness and further uptake in France have been hampered by both management and trade union opposition, who see appraisal as a threat to their traditional autonomy" (Hegewish and Larsen, 1996: 13; see also Bournois, 1996).

Performance-based pay is introduced in France mainly for senior managerial staff and follows U.S. examples (see, for example, Bournois and Tyson, 2005; Peretti and Roussel, 2000) in order to give performance incentives to corporate leaders. Interestingly, the acceptance of variable pay schemes appears rather high in private companies and French managers display willingness to take risks in this regard, because the basic social security and safety net ensure a rather high level of assistance for the individual (Sire and Tremblay, 1996, 1998).

In sum, we perceive the French historical cultural underpinning as a major influence for PMSs as well as for PA processes. Influences of globalization, corporate culture, and organizational norms appear to be rather weak in the French case, even if corporations in France, particularly larger ones, formally adopt the U.S. and Anglo-Saxon example of PMSs.

To contrast two European countries, in the next section the German specificities will be covered highlighting again the factors of Murphy and DeNisi's model.

Specificities characterizing HRM and PM in Germany

The main elements of the institutional framework in Germany are the German labor market institutions of collective bargaining, co-determination, and vocational training (Müller, 1999). Considering these factors it has to be stated that Germany not only reveals important differences compared to the U.S. or Japan but also when looking at other European countries (Pudelko, 2000a, b, c). As Dickmann (2003) states, the historical evolution, the cultural and institutional environment as well as the industry structure (i.e. the *distal* factors as identified by Murphy and DeNisi) are features which clearly distinguish Germany also from other European countries. He identifies the rather collectivist culture combined with the tight institutional framework as a major feature of the German system. Gooderham *et al.* (1999: 513) conclude that "German work life is characterized by powerful labor representative bodies and strong work legislation, and the personnel function has to deal with detailed and comprehensive regulations and is therefore highly operative oriented."

However, it cannot be said that the German HRM model is characterized by outstanding specificities that have had a direct influence on HRM role models in other countries such as the U.S. The German model seems to be less subject to stereotypical consideration than, for example, the American model, which can be described as "short-term performance efficiency based on flexible market structures and profit orientation" or the Japanese model interpreted as "long-term behavioral effectiveness based on cooperative clan structures and growth orientation" (Pudelko, 2005: 2067). According to Pudelko (2005, 2006) this is mainly due to a lack of information, which makes it even more important to take a special look in this chapter at the HRM practices of this country, focusing on PM.

Insofar as HRM in Germany is concerned, there is always a special interest in the legal system as part of the institutional environment of German firms. Very often the system of co-determination is the center of interest (see, for example, Warner and Campbell, 1993; Pudelko, 2005). These aspects will be described in the next section.

Impact of the legal environment on PM in Germany

As has been outlined in the introduction about the specificities of the HRM system in Germany, the German situation is characterized by a rigid legal environment. As in France, it also emphasizes non-discrimination. However, complex labor laws, contractual agreements with the unions, a system of co-determination including participation, consultation and information rights on the level of the works councils (*Betriebsrat*) limit managerial discretion to a high extent (Müller, 1999; Conrad and Pieper, 1990; Pudelko, 2005; Tempel, 2001; Wächter and Müller-Camen, 2002).

In Germany, five levels of regulation concerning the industrial relations system can be identified: the state level, the collective bargaining level, the company level, the plant level and individual workplace and work contracts. "The German state guarantees unions' and employers' associations freedom in concluding collective labor contracts and does not interfere actively in day-to-day activities" (Conrad and Pieper, 1990: 124). This is the most important precondition for the functioning of the German industrial relations system.

With respect to PM the most important industrial relations level is the plant level. Here, the system of legally guaranteed co-determination is relevant.

> Employees may exercise their influence through elected works councils . . . Works councils have almost no rights in the economic management of the company but have various options in influencing a company's HRM policy. Whereas in some matters they only have to be consulted, they may participate in the decision-making process in others (participation rights) or even have to approve management decisions (genuine co-determination rights).
>
> (Conrad and Pieper, 1990: 126)

The latter is the case when regulations for assessment and thus for PM are concerned. This means that any introduction or change of a PMS including all details is subject to co-determination (i.e. needs the approval of the works councils). According to Dickmann (2003), this should lead to co-operative behavior and thus to the consensus orientation further discussed below.

Besides the industrial relations system, the social market economy is an important feature of the German economy. It is seen as the basis for a "consensus philosophy, self-reinforcing socio-cultural institutions and a distinct approach to business management" (Dickmann, 2003: 266). It aims at a high level of job security for staff members and ". . . acts as an incentive for companies to use long-term career and succession planning and puts an onus on vocational training and staff development to increase functional flexibility" (Dickmann, 2003: 267). PM is a central element of the abovementioned features such as career and succession planning. Thus, there is a strong link between the social market economy system and the importance of PM in the German economy, associated with long-term developmental strategies in international HRM. These may even be fostered by the quality-orientation typically associated with German firms (Vitols *et al.*, 1997) leading to highly valued specialist knowledge, often acquired within so-called "chimney careers" (Dickmann, 2003), that is, the career of a specialist (see also Alexandre-Bailly *et al.*, 2007).

To sum up, the insights gained from the short discussions about the industrial relations system as well as the social market economy indicate that a cooperative orientation and long-term developmental HR strategies are a central feature of the German HR system, indicating the strategic importance of performance management systems (see also Child, Faulkner and Pitkethly, 2001). This is underlined by an extensive vocational training system, which provides employees with broad basic qualifications and should indicate a long-term perspective in the employment relation (Conrad and Pieper, 1990; Brewster, 1995; Warner and Campbell, 1993; Lawrence, 1993).

Impact of the cultural environment on PM in Germany

There is evidence that cultural differences have an impact on HRM and also on the specific field of PM (Conrad and Pieper, 1990; Lindholm, 2000). In terms of the four dimensions identified by Hofstede (1980, 2001), the German culture can be described as relatively low on power distance, high on uncertainty avoidance, high on the masculinity index and high on individualism. In this section we will outline the impact of cultural values on selected *proximal* as well as *intervening* factors.

Power distance seems to have an impact on the process of how an agreement on job objectives is reached. In German companies, setting objectives in the PA process is the result of a negotiation between superior and employee (for this relationship, see also Schuler, Jackson and Luo, 2004). The same is the case, for example, in Sweden (Tahvanainen, 1998). Both countries are characterized by a relatively low power distance (Hofstede, 1980). The low degree of power distance is also associated with a rather high degree of openness between both parties in the rater–ratee relationship, not only during the objective setting process but also where performance feedback is concerned (Schneider, 1988). In Germany, performance feedback seems to be an ongoing process of a dialogue between superior and subordinate including also many informal elements (Pudelko, 2000b). In contrast, in many Asian countries a high level of power distance leads to a clear assignment of job objectives by the manager and often to a more formal relationship between superior and employee (Lindholm, 2000). This more formal relationship is also valid for France.

The highly regulated work environment is often attributed to a high level of uncertainty avoidance in Germany (Conrad and Pieper, 1990; Warner and Campbell, 1993). With respect to PM, Germans expect such a system to be highly integrated in a set of precise rules: performance evaluations should be formalized in terms of defining goals or criteria, time frames, measurement methods and consequences (e.g. for training or pay decisions).

According to an interview with a German HR expert, the system is close to being over-regulated.[3] The standards set for this process are important *judgment factors* in the sense of Murphy and DeNisi's model.

Feedback is provided in a way that includes open confrontations – an approach that would not be acceptable, for example, in Asian countries. In Germany it is mainly based on individual achievements that often can be clearly measured, for example, in MBO-systems. *Distal* factors such as strategic goals of the firms are transferred into goals relevant for the individual depending on his or her position. This reflects a high level of individualism in the German culture. In summary, the role of PM is significant for German managers. It indicates a high importance of career progression for the individual as well as within the society, which reflects the high score on Hofstede's masculinity index (Lindholm, 2000). From an organizational perspective the major goal is coordinating all activities according to the major strategic goals of the firm.

Another feature that may explain the high importance of PM in German companies is the aforementioned long-term orientation in Germany (Dickmann, 2003; Ferner, Quintanilla and Varul, 2001). Many Germans still value long-term employment relationships (Child, Faulkner and Pitkethly, 2001; Festing, Müller and Yussefi, 2007). In this context, seniority plays an important role as in many German companies there is a comparatively high number of managers who still pursue life-long careers within one firm (Pudelko, 2000b, c). PM has a central function here in providing feedback and especially in outlining avenues for future development within the firm. This indicates the importance of the strong link between PA and HR development. PM would have a different meaning in a culture characterized by a short-term orientation.

In contrast, the link to performance-based pay has to be seen critically: while in the last few decades performance-based pay has also been of increasing importance to German firms (Child, Faulkner and Pitkethly, 2001; Müller, 1999; Brewster and Hegewisch, 1994), it does not have the same meaning as in other countries. This may be due to the fact that German companies – like most of their European counterparts (Ferner and Varul, 2000) – have introduced performance-related pay practices much later than British and U.S. firms, probably also due to the respective institutional and cultural environments.[4] One of the major reasons for this is that in German companies the introduction of performance-based pay systems needs to be approved by the works council (Müller, 1999). However, performance-based pay is also an expression of a rather short-term orientation (Pudelko, 2005), which contradicts the assumption that Germans are rather long-term oriented. Thus, in many companies we see the adoption of a typical feature of the Anglo-Saxon HRM system. However, as it is not fully compatible with German traditions and values, its adoption seems to have been realized only to a modest extent. In summary, although there is a high acceptance of PMSs and their impact on career development, the direct link to performance-based pay at this stage cannot be described as typical for all companies. This might be different in multinational corporations where there is a need to have worldwide standards in executive compensation (Festing, Eidems and Royer, 2007; Dowling *et al.*, 2008).

Concerning pay distribution, we usually find a normal distribution centering around the 100 percent mark with a low standard deviation. This is in line with information from a German HR expert who states that the willingness to discriminate between ratees is still low compared to other countries such as the U.S. This also leads to evaluations which are closer to the average than to the extreme poles of the evaluation scale. The underlying reason for this result may also lie in the highly egalitarian German system described above.

To sum up, it can be said that in German firms PA is of high importance in the context of long-term employment relationships. It has a long tradition in Germany (Oechsler, 2006) and very often includes behavioral dimensions (input factors) as well as output factors (Pudelko, 2000b). However, the emergence of integrated PMSs is rather recent. In integrated PMSs (Verweire and van den Berghe, 2004) appraisal is usually linked to the fields of management development and managerial pay. The investment in training based on PA results especially seems to differentiate Germany from other countries such as the U.S., where often up-or-out systems are favored (Pudelko, 2000b). The consequences of PA are discussed as *distortion* factors in the Murphy and DeNisi model. It becomes clear that the financial consequences especially may not be as important as in other countries (Child, Faulkner and Pitkethly, 2001).

While the German system seems to be very close to the Anglo-Saxon system, the preceding analysis has revealed a number of German particularities. In the French case representing a different approach compared to the German system, management is still able to pursue a tradition of autonomous, non-consultative decision-making (Gooderham *et al.*, 1999: 514).

Concluding remarks on future developments of the German PMS

Some researchers have found evidence that the German HRM model is in a process of change. While for a long time after World War II the economic conditions were more or less stable (Streeck, 1997, 2001) and characterized by growth, enabling the development of a social market economy, recently external factors inducing change have emerged. Among these are German reunification and the opening of new markets for labor as well as for products in Central and Eastern Europe and, of course, the worldwide-encompassing phenomenon of globalization (Ferner and Varul, 2000). These factors seem to be forcing German companies to intensify their internationalization processes, which compared to their U.S. and U.K. counterparts have started comparatively late (Ferner, Quintanilla and Varul, 2001). There are indicators that this process is associated with a further adoption of Anglo-Saxon HRM practices, partly starting in subsidiaries outside Germany and then being transferred back to the headquarters in the sense of reverse diffusion (Ebster-Grosz and Pugh, 1996; Müller, 1999). A long list of examples is given based on case study research in German MNEs by Ferner and Varul (2000). They state that

> as German companies move beyond their classic export platform strategy to become
> international players, they are much more likely to absorb the prevailing business-cultural

practices of companies well versed in the deregulated rules of the international economy than they are to transmit their own peculiarities to others.

(Ferner and Varul, 2000: 136)

Due to globalization, firms feel a need to standardize their HRM practices on a worldwide level and this is also true for PM (Festing, Eidems and Royer, 2007). Thus, as has been discussed before, in large MNEs there may be more evidence for integrated global PMSs following the same pattern worldwide.

However, it has to be considered that in the European Economic Area (EEA) less than 1 percent of enterprises are large ones, the rest are small and medium-sized enterprises (SMEs). Two-thirds of all jobs in this region are in SMEs, while one-third is provided by large enterprises (UNECE, 2007). In Germany, the percentage of jobs in SMEs even rises to more than 70 percent (Institut für Mittelstandsforschung, 2004). Consequently, in these companies PM rather follows a local pattern, being mainly based on PA. Although it is recommended that SMEs offer systematic career management related to a PMS, this area very often is neglected due to a lack of resources (Festing, 2007). Consequently, there are still German particularities deeply rooted in cultural values and in the specific institutional context, which lead to a different PM reality than in other countries although the measures and agendas might have similar names. Pudelko speaks about a "compromise formula" (2005: 2067), which is difficult to describe and to distinguish. We will come back to this point at the end of the chapter discussing the tendencies for convergence and divergence in Europe.

Conclusion

The presentations and discussions of the PMSs in France and in Germany have clearly shown that it is most important to include environmental factors in order to understand the particularities of each system as indicated by the contextual paradigm by Brewster (1999) or as in the model developed by Murphy and DeNisi. Below, key arguments concerning the impact of the French and German institutional and cultural environment on PM are summarized and structured according to the dimensions outlined by Murphy and DeNisi. At the end of the conclusion we will briefly discuss possible tendencies of convergence or divergence of HRM systems and especially PMSs in Europe.

From the analysis it has become clear that the *distal factors* differ to a high extent between France and Germany. The legal environment with the system of co-determination in Germany has a strong influence on the emergence of PMSs while in France legal aspects play only a minor role. Thus, discretionary choices seem to be higher in France. With respect to national educational institutions we can observe a far stronger tradition in Germany than in France to invest in training and professional development of employees. This may stem from the German "dual vocational training system" of alternating on-the-job training and formal education in professional schools (apprenticeships), which offers well-qualified intermediate professionals. This may explain the strong link between PA, training and career development as well. Such training and development systems are lacking in France. Besides the analysis of the institutional environment, the specificities of the German and French culture have also led to important insights in the PM process in both countries. It has been outlined that major differences were related to the power distance and femininity/masculinity dimensions identified by Hofstede (1980). For example, while the high power distance in France leads to objectives set by the superiors, the rather low power distance in Germany is associated with negotiations in the objective setting process in the context of PM. The strong masculine dimension attributes high importance to the notion of vertical careers in Germany. For the individual, and his/her status within the society this is most important. While career success is important in France as well, there is another dimension resulting from the high degree of femininity. Well-being in the working environment seems to play a relatively more critical role in France than in Germany. This may explain why one very important goal in the PM discussion is not to damage the personal relationship. Lebas (1995) has argued that performance measurement is intertwined with PM and cannot be separated. The context of the management relationships has a decisive impact that seems to be more personalized in France compared to more factual and task-orientated relationships in Germany. As outlined in the model by Murphy and DeNisi the distal factors have an impact on the proximal factors as well as on the intervening factors related to PMSs. This will be highlighted below.

With respect to the *proximal factors*, the purpose of appraisal seems to be more control-oriented in France while the emphasis in Germany is on coordination and cooperation for reaching common organizational and, in the best case, also individual goals. This, of course, is reflected in the rater–ratee relationship which, due to cultural differences, has a high potential to differ between Germany and France. Furthermore, it indicates differences in rater motivation. However, in both countries the willingness to discriminate among ratees is low. In France it is very common from school age on to give average grades, even if the performance is outstanding. Similar tendencies can be observed in Germany. It seems that appraisal systems are accepted to a higher degree in Germany than in France because they have a direct individual value if they are well managed. Differentiated open, direct and fair *feedback* is very much appreciated by the individuals in the German context.

More similarities were found when analyzing the *intervening factors* in both countries. The frequency of appraisal is, of course, very much dependent on the organizational system and inherent norms. As has been mentioned above, the organizational size and the degree of internationalization play important roles here as well. However, in many cases there seems to be a PA at least once a year in German and in French organizations, which is carried out by the superior. Depending on the purpose, this information can be used for making decisions about promotion, performance-based pay and personnel planning. This is, for example, the case in the "Leadership Evaluation and Development" concept of DaimlerChrysler Corporation. Here, individual assessments by the superior are in a next step discussed in Performance Validation Meetings on higher hierarchical levels. Furthermore, this information is used in Executive Development Conferences and supports succession planning procedures (Ring, Groenewald and Varga von Kibed, 2003). However, as we have outlined above, there are many cases where PA is not directly linked with other HR decisions and this is sometimes perceived as being free from *distortions*, which may occur due to the consequences of appraisals such as forced distribution because of certain budget constraints. In the first case the *judgment* is based on the individual and less on the organizational requirements.

Using the model developed by Murphy and DeNisi we were able to draw a differentiated picture about the commonalities and differences in PMSs in France and in Germany. The question that emerges from the identification of the differences in the PM practices in Germany and France is whether signs for convergence or divergence of the different systems can be identified. Gooderham *et al.* (1999: 526) state that ". . . the German regime [. . .] appears to be relatively unreceptive to international developments within the personnel management in general and collaborative practices in particular." Katz and Darbishire (2001), Streeck (2001) and Pudelko (2006) discuss converging divergences in employment systems. With respect to the employment system within each country they see an increasing divergence. However, in terms of workplace patterns at least Katz and Darbishire (2001) have identified a growing convergence. This is confirmed by research from the Cranet-network, mainly focusing on Europe (Brewster, 2006). Brewster, Mayrhofer and Morley (2004) give a more differentiated perspective. They distinguish between directional convergence and final convergence. The first is concerned with the question whether the same trends can be observed in different countries; the latter addresses the results. Their conclusion, based on the Cranet data, is as follows:

> From a directional point of view, there seems to be a positive indication of convergence. However, when one looks at the question from a final convergence point of view, the answer is no longer a clear positive one. None of the HR practices converged at the end of the decade. Rather, the maximum point of convergence is reached in the middle of the decade with signs of divergence after that.
>
> (Brewster, Mayrhofer and Morley, 2004)

Thus the results concerning the convergence or divergence of HRM systems including performance management systems are mixed. There is no clear tendency, although in an empirical study concerning the convergence–divergence debate in HRM, Pudelko (2005) concludes that the majority of the HR managers investigated (in Germany, the U.S. and Japan) expect a convergence of HRM systems.

These results of the convergence/divergence discussion are very much in line with the findings of this chapter indicating an isomorphism, maybe even a mimetic isomorphism (DiMaggio and Powell, 1983), with respect to the adoption of PMSs especially in large multinational organizations in Europe taking the example of the Anglo-Saxon world. However, there seems to be room for local adaptations in this process. As Fletcher (2001) has stated in his seminal article, the context is important and requires adaptation to make sense of professional PMSs in respective environments (see also Delery, 1998). This poses ongoing challenges for strategic human resource management with global thinking and local action.

Notes

1 For a detailed description see Chapter 6.
2 Our analysis and observations were corroborated with three interviews of HRM professionals of MNCs based in France and who are in charge of implementing and managing PMSs at corporate and business unit levels. The interviews consisted of open-ended questions concerning the PM practices in the firms.
3 The interview was conducted by one of the authors with an HR manager of a German MNE who is involved in the development and application of the company performance management system at the corporate and business unit level. The interview mainly consisted of open-ended questions concerning the PM practices and the impact of differing institutional and cultural environments within the respective MNE. It took place in October 2006 and lasted for approximately one hour.
4 For an analysis of the institutional environment with respect to the development and spread of stock options in Germany see Sanders and Tuschke (2007).

References

Alexandre-Bailly, F., Festing, M. and Jonczyk, C. (2007) *Choix et formation des dirigeants en France et en Allemagne*, in F. Bournois, J. Duval-Hamel, S. Roussillon and J. L. Scaringella, *Comités Exécutifs*, Paris: Groupe Eyrolles: 245–50.

Armstrong, M. and Baron, A. (1998) *Performance Management: The New Realities*, London: Institute of Personnel and Development.

Becker, B. E. and Gerhart, B. (1996) The impact of human resource management on organizational performance: progress and prospects, *Academy of Management Journal* 36(4): 770–802.

Becker, B. E., Huselid, M. A. and Ulrich, D. (2001) *The HR Scorecard: Linking People, Strategy, and Performance*, Boston, MA: Harvard Business Press.

Bescos, P.-L. and Cauvin, E. (2004) *Performance Measurement in French Companies: An Empirical Study*, in M. J. Epstein and J.-F. Manzoni (eds.) *Performance Measurement and Management Control: Superior Organizational Performance*, Studies in Managerial and Financial Accounting, Vol. 14, Oxford: Elsevier Jai: 185–202.

Besseyre des Horts, C.-H. (1988) *Vers une gestion stratégique des ressources humaines*, Paris : Les Editions d'Organisation.

Besseyre des Horts, C.-H. (1991) *L'appréciation comme pratique fondamentale de développement de l'équité en GRH*, Paris : cahier de recherche CCI.

Bourguignon, A. (1998) *L'évaluation de la performance: un instrument de gestion éclaté*, Rapport de recherche ESSEC-CR-DR – 98–042.

Bourguignon, A. (2004) Performance management and management control: evaluated managers' point of view, *European Accounting Review* 13(4): 659–87.

Bourguignon, A., Malleret, V. and Nørreklit, H. (2004) The American balanced scorecard versus the French tableau de bord: the ideological dimension, *Management Accounting Research* 15(2):107–34.

Bournois, F. (1996) Industrial relations, source of economic and social performances of a company, in A.-M. Fericelli and B. Sire (eds.) *Performance et Ressources Humaines*, Paris: Economica.

Bournois, F. and Tyson, S. (2005) *Top Pay and Performance – Strategy and Evaluation*, Oxford: Butterworth-Heinemann.

Brewster, C. (1994) European HRM. Reflection of, or challenge to, the American concept, in P. S. Kirkbride (ed.) *Human Resource Management in Europe. Perspectives for the 1990s*, London and New York: Routledge, pp. 56–92.

Brewster, C. (1995) Towards a "European" model of human resource management, *Journal of International Business Studies* 26(1): 1–21.

Brewster, C. (1999) Strategic human resource management: the value of different paradigms, *Management International Review* 39: 45–64.

Brewster, C. (2006) *International Human Resource Management: If there is no "best way", how do we manage?*, Inaugural Lecture, Henley Management College U.K.

Brewster, C. and Bournois, F. (1991) A European perspective on human resource management, *Personnel Review* 20(6): 4–13.

Brewster, C. and Hegewisch, A. (eds.) (1994) *Policy and Practice in European Human Resource Management. The Price Waterhouse Cranfield Survey*, London and New York: Routledge.

Brewster, Ch., Mayrhofer, W. and Morley, M. (eds.) (2004) *Human Resource: Evidence of Convergence?* London: Elsevier.

Brunstein, I. (1995) "France", in I. Brunstein (ed.) *Human Resource Management in Western Europe*, Berlin, New York: Walter de Gruyter, pp. 59–88.

Cascio, W. (2006) Global performance management systems, *Handbook of Research in International Human Resource Management*, Cheltenham, U.K., and Northampton, USA: Edward Elgar Publishing, pp. 176–96.

Child, J., Faulkner, D. and Pitkethly, R. (2001) *The Management of International Acquisitions*, Oxford, U.K.: Oxford University Press.

Claus, L. and Briscoe, D. (2006) Employee performance management across borders: a review of relevant academic literature, *Paper presented at the Annual Conference of the Academy of Management, Atlanta, GA*.

Conrad, P. and Pieper, R. (1990) Human resource management in the Federal Republic of Germany, in R. Pieper (ed.) *Human Resources Management. An International Comparison*, Berlin: de Gruyter, pp. 109–39.

Côté, M. and Tega, V. (1980) *La démocratie industrielle*, Montréal: Les Presses HEC et les Editions agence d'Arc.

Defélix, C., Klarsfeld, A. and Oiry, E. (eds.) (2006) *Nouveaux regards sur la gestion des compétences*, Paris : Vuibert.

Delery, J. (1998) Issues of fit in strategic human resource management: implications for research, *Human Resource Management Review* 8(3): 289–309.

den Hartog, Deanne, Boselie, Paul and Paauwe, Jaap (2004) Performance management: a model and research agenda, *Applied Psychology: An International Review* 53(4): 556–69.

DeNisi, A. S. (2000) Performance appraisal and performance management : a multilevel analysis, in K. J. Klein and S. Kozlowski (eds.) *Multilevel Theory, Research and Methods in Organizations*, San Francisco: Jossey-Bass, pp. 121–56.

Devillard, O. (2001) *Coacher, efficacité personnelle et performance collective*, Paris: Dunod.

Dickmann, M. (2003) Implementing German HRM abroad: desired, feasible, successful? *International Journal of Human Resource Management* 14(2): 265–83.

DiMaggio, P. and Powell, W. (1983) The iron cage revisited: institutional isomorphism and collective rationality in organisational fields, *American Sociological Review* 48(4): 147–60.

Dowling, P., Festing, M. and Engle, A. (2008) *International Human Resource Management. Managing People in a Multinational Context*, 5th edn., London: Thomson.

Ebster-Grosz, D. and Pugh, D. (1996) *Anglo-German Business Collaboration. Pitfalls and Potentials*, Basingstoke: Macmillan.

EUROSTAT: *http://epp.eurostat.cec.eu.int/*

Ferner, A. and Varul, M. (2000) "Vanguard" subsidiaries and the diffusion of new practices: a case study of German multinationals, *British Journal of Industrial Relations* 38(1): 115–40.

Ferner, A., Quintanilla, J. and Varul, M. (2001) Country-of-origin effects, host-country effects, and the management of HR in multinationals, *Journal of World Business* 36(2): 107–27.

Festing, M. (2007) Globalization of SMEs and implications for international human resource management, *International Journal of Globalisation and Small Business* 2(1): 5–18.

Festing, M., Eidems, J. and Royer, S. (2007) Strategic issues and local constraints in transnational compensation strategies: an analysis of cultural, institutional and political influences, *European Management Journal* 25(2): 118–31.

Festing, M., Müller, B. and Yussefi, S. (2007) Careers in the auditing business – still ballroom dance?! Static and dynamic perspectives on the psychological contract in the up-or-out system. Paper to be Presented at the 23rd EGOS Colloquium, Vienna, July 2007.

Festing, M., Eidems, J., Royer, S. and Kullak, F. (2006) *When in Rome Pay as the Romans Pay. Considerations about Transnational Compensation Strategies and the Case of a German MNE*, Working Paper No. 22: ESCP-EAP European School of Management, Berlin.

Fletcher, C. (2001) Performance appraisal and management: the developing research agenda, *Journal of Occupational and Organizational Psychology* 74: 473–87.

Gooderham, P., Nordhaug, O. and Ringdal, K. (1999) Institutional and rational determinants of organizational practices: human resource management in European firms, *Administrative Science Quarterly* 44: 507–31.

Guest, D. (1994) Organizational psychology and human resource management: towards a European approach, *European Work and Organizational Psychologist* 4(3): 251–70.

Hartmann, M. (2003) Nationale oder transnational Eliten: Europäische Eliten im Vergleich, in S. Hradil, and P. Imbusch (eds) *Oberschichten? Eliten? Herrschende Klassen*, Opladen: Leske und Budrich: 273–98.

Hegewisch, A. and Larsen, H. H. (1996) Performance management, decentralization and management development: local government in Europe, *Journal of Management Development* 15(2): 6–23.

Hofstede, G (1980) *Culture's Consequences: International Differences in Work-related Values*, Beverly Hills, CA: Sage.

Hofstede, G. (2001) *Culture's Consequences. Comparing Values, Behaviours, Institutions, and Organizations Across Nations*, 2nd edition, London: Sage. [1980]

House, Robert, Hanges, Paul J., Javidan, Mansour, Dorfman, Peter W. and Gupta, Vipin (eds.) (2004) *Culture, Leadership and Organizations. The GLOBE Study of 62 Societies*, Thousand Oaks: Sage.

Huselid, M. A., Becker, B. E. and Beatty, R. W. (2005) *The Workforce Scorecard, Managing Human Capital to Execute Strategy*, Boston, MA: Harvard Business Press.

Institut für Mittelstandsforschung (2004) *SMEs in Germany. Facts and Figures 2004*, Bonn: Institut für Mittelstandsforschung.

Iribarne, P. (2003) *Balanced Scorecard et qualité, le couple gagnant*, Paris: AFNOR.

Jenkins, A. and van der Wijk, G. (1996) Hesitant innovation: the recent evolution of human resources management in France, in Timothy Clark (ed.) *European Human Resource Management*, Oxford: Blackwell, pp. 65–92.

Kaplan, R. and Norton, D. (1992) The Balanced Scorecard. Measures that drive performance, *Harvard Business Review* 70(1): 71–9.

Kaplan, R. and Norton, D. (2006) *Alignment: Using the Balanced Scorecard to Create Corporate Synergies*, Boston, MA: Harvard Business Press.

Katz, H. and Darbishire, O. (2001) Review symposium. Converging divergences: worldwide changes in employment systems, *Industrial and Labor Relations Review* 54(3): 681–716.

Kieser, A. and Kubicek, H. (1992) *Organisation*, 3rd edition, Berlin, New York: Walter de Gruyter.

Klarsfeld, A. and Oiry, E. (eds.) (2003) *Gérer les compétences: des instruments aux processus: cas d'entreprises et perspectives théoriques*, Paris: Vuibert.

Lane, C. (1994) Industrial order: Britain, Germany and France, in Richard Hyman and Anthony Ferner (eds.) *New Frontiers in European Industrial Relations*, Oxford: Blackwell, pp. 167–95.

Lawrence, P. (1993) Human resource management in Germany, in S. Tyson, P. Lawrence, P. Poirson, L. Manzolini and C. F. Vicente (eds.) *Human Resource Management in Europe*, London: Kogan Page, pp. 25–41.

Lebas, M. (1995) Performance measurement and performance management, *International Journal of Production Economics* 41(1/3): 23–35.

Lindholm, N. (2000) National culture and performance management in MNC subsidiaries, *International Studies of Management and Organization* 29(4): 45–66.

L'industrie en France 2005–2006, Rapport du ministère de l'Industrie [report of the French Ministry of Industry] notably chapter 8 on R&D available on: *http://www.industrie.gouv.fr/portail/chiffres/index_etudes.html*, consulted 14/10/2006.

Longenecker, C. O., Sims, Jr., H. P. and Gioia, D. A. (1987) Behind the mask: the politics of employee appraisal, *Academy of Management Executive* 1(3): 183–93.

Maurice, M., Sellier, F. and Silvestre, J.-J. (1982) *Politique d'éducation et organisation industrielle en France et en Allemagne*, Paris: Presses Universitaires de France.

Meysonnier, F. (1994) *Stratégies de gestion des ressources humaines et performance dans les PME – Résultats d'une recherche exploratoire*. Rapport de recherche FR CESREM – CR-94–12.

Müller, M. (1999) Unitarism, pluralism and human resource management in Germany, *Management International Review*, special issue 39(3): 125–44.

Murphy, K. and Cleveland, J. (1995) *Understanding Performance Appraisal: Social, Organizational, and Goal-oriented Perspectives*, Newbury Park, CA: Sage.

Nikandrou, I., Apospori, E. and Papalexandris, N. (2005) Changes in HRM in Europe. A longitudinal comparative study among 18 European countries, *Journal of European Industrial Training* 29(7): 541–60.

OECD: *http://www.oecd.org/*

Oechsler, W. (2006) *Personal und Arbeit – Grundlagen des Human Resource Management und der Arbeitgeber-Arbeitnehmer-Beziehungen*, 8th edn., München: Oldenbourg.

Oriot, F. and Misiaszek, E. (2004) Technical and organizational barriers hindering the implementation of a balanced scorecard: the case of a European space company, in M. J. Epstein and J.-F. Manzoni (eds.) *Performance Measurement and Management Control: Superior Organizational Performance*, Studies in Managerial and Financial Accounting, Vol. 14, Oxford: Elsevier Jai, pp. 265–301.

OSEO (2006) *http://www.oseo.fr/informations_entreprises/actualites_d_oseo/bilans_sectoriels*, consulted 15/10/2006.

Papalexandris, N. and Panayotopoulou, L. (2004) Exploring the mutual interaction of societal culture and human resource management practices; evidence from 19 countries, *Employee Relations* 26(5): 495–509.

Peretti, J.-M. and Roussel, P. (eds.) (2000) *Les Rémunérations. Politiques et pratiques pour les années 2000*, collection Entreprendre, Paris: Vuibert.

Phillips, J. J., Stone, R. and Phillips, P. (2001) *The Human Resources Scorecard (Improving Human Performance)*, Woburn, MA: Butterworth-Heinemann.

Pieper, R. (1990) Human resource management as a strategic factor, *Human Resources Management, an International Comparison*, Berlin and New York: Walter de Gruyter.

Prix Français de la Qualité et de la Performance, *http://www.industrie.gouv.fr/dge/listeDiff/lettre17/lettre.htm issued* and consulted 16/10/06.

Pudelko, M. (2000a) *Das Personalmanagement in Deutschland, den USA und Japan*. Band 1: Die Bedeutung gesamtgesellschaftlicher Rahmenbedingungen im Wettbewerb der Systeme, Köln: Jörg Saborowski Verlag.

Pudelko, M. (2000b) *Das Personalmanagement in Deutschland, den USA und Japan*. Band 2: Eine systematische und vergleichende Bestandsaufnahme, Köln: Jörg Saborowski Verlag.

Pudelko, M. (2000c) *Das Personalmanagement in Deutschland, den USA und Japan*. Band 3: Wie wir voneinander lernen können. Mit einer empirischen Studie über die 500 größten Unternehmen der drei Länder, Köln: Jörg Saborowski Verlag.

Pudelko, M. (2005) Cross-national learning from best practice and the convergence–divergence debate in HRM, *International Journal of Human Resource Management* 16(11): 2045–74.

Pudelko, M. (2006) A comparison of HRM systems in the USA, Japan and Germany in their socio-economic context, *Human Resource Management Journal* 16(2): 123–53.

Radin, B. (2003) A comparative approach to performance management: contrasting the experience of

Australia, New Zealand, and The United States, *International Journal of Public Administration* 26(12): 1355–76.

Ring, M., Groenewald, H. and Varga von Kibed, G. (2003) Leadership evaluation and development – die Einführung des LEAD-Konzeptes bei DaimlerChrysler Japan, W. Dorow, and H. Groenewald (eds.) *Personalwirtschaftlicher Wandel in Japan*, Wiesbaden, Gabler: 457–75.

Rojot, J. (1990) Human resource management in France, in R. Pieper (ed.) *Human Resources Management, an International Comparison*, Berlin and New York: Walter de Gruyter: 87–107.

Saglietto, L. and Thomas, C. (1998) Gestion des ressources humaines et enjeux de l'économie post-industrielle: L'histoire d'une reconquête de la performance fondée sur la responsabilisation et la confiance, *Revue de gestion des ressources humaines* 28: 15–25.

Sanders, W. M. G. and Tuschke, A. (2007) The adoption of institutionally contested organizational practices: the emergence of stock option pay in Germany, *Academy of Management Journal* 50: 33–56.

Schneider, S. (1988) *National vs. Corporate Culture: Implications for Human Resource Management*, Fontainebleau: Insead.

Schuler, R. S., Jackson, S. E. and Luo, Y. (2004) *Managing Human Resources in Cross-Border Alliances*, London/New York: Routledge.

Sire, B. and Tremblay, M. (1996) Perspective sur les politiques de rémunération des dirigeants en France, *Revue Française de Gestion*, No. 111, Nov./Dec: 230–8.

Sire, B. and Tremblay, M. (1998) Éclatement des politiques de GRH selon l'espace culturel: Une comparaison Internationale des politiques de rémunération, in J. Allouche and B. Sire (eds.) *Ressources Humaines: Une gestion éclatée*, Paris: Economica, pp. 335–52.

Streeck, W. (1997) German capitalism: does it exist? Can it survive? *New Political Economy* 2(2): 237–57.

Streeck, W. (2001) High equality, low activity: the contribution of the social welfare system to the stability of the German collective bargaining regime. Review Symposium. Converging Divergences, *Industrial and Labor Relations Review* 54(3): 698–706.

Tahvanainen, M. (1998) *Expatriate Performance Management*, Helsinki: Helsinki School of Economics Press.

Tempel, A. (2001) *The Cross-National Transfer of Human Resource Management Practices in German and British Multinational Companies*, München/Mering: Hampp Verlag.

UNECE (2007) *UN-ECE Operational Activities: SME – their role in foreign trade*. Available http://www.unece.org/indust/sme/foreignt.html (17 February 2007).

van der Klink, M. and Mulder, M. (1995) Human resource development and staff flow policy in Europe, in Anne-Wil Harzing and Joris van Ruysseveldt (eds.) *International Human Resource Management*, London: Sage, pp. 156–78.

Verweire, K. and van den Berghe, L. (2004) *Integrated Performance Management – a Guide to Strategy Implementation*, London: Sage.

Vitols, S., Casper, C., Soskice, D. and Woolcock, S. (1997) *Corporate Governance in Large British and German Companies: Comparative Institutional Advantage or Competing for Best Practice*, London: Anglo-German Foundation for the Study of Industrial Society.

Wächter, H. and Müller-Camen, M. (2002) Co-determination and strategic integration in German firms, *Human Resource Management Journal* 12(3): 76–87.

Warner, M. and Campbell, A. (1993) German management, in D. J. Hickson (ed.) *Management in Western Europe: Society, Culture and Organization in Twelve Nations*, Berlin and New York: Walter de Gruyter, pp. 89–108.

11 Performance management in Turkey

ZEYNEP AYCAN AND SERAP YAVUZ

In brief: socioeconomic and political background

Turkey, as an emerging economy, attracts significant attention for its geopolitical and strategic importance. Turkey is an independent republic, founded in 1923, occupying a region partly in Europe and partly in Asia. It plays a major role in world history as the crossroad of civilizations and the bridge connecting East and West. This characteristic allows the co-existence of both the modern and the traditional in its culture. Turkey adopted the Civil Code from Switzerland in 1926, which made her the only country with a Muslim population that is not governed by the Islamic Sharia rules (World Bank, 2003). Turkey has a parliamentary democracy and is currently led by a single-party government. The single-party government has brought political and economic stability to the country which has been led by coalition governments since 1987.

Since World War II the Turkish economy has been transformed by the steady growth of industry and services, and the consequent decline in the share of agriculture in national income. Beginning in the 1950s and peaking in the 1980s several developments advanced Turkey's modernization and transformed Turkish politics (Narli, 1999:1): "The result was a confrontation between provincial/traditional and urban/modern cultures, new social classes, and the fragmentation of the conservative electorate from the 1970s onward."

The decade of the 1980s marked a turning point in Turkey's socioeconomic structure and politics (Eralp, Tunay and Yesilada, 1993). Not only has the Turkish economy and societal structure changed, but also the political system and its external relations were altered by an economic austerity package and the 1980 military coup (Eralp, Tunay and Yesilada, 1993). In the early 1980s, after the initial meetings with the IMF, Turkey launched a program of structural change, stabilization and economic liberalization. However, since 1986, the achievements of the stabilization program in question have been overshadowed by high inflation rates and events like a major earthquake in 1999, the deep economic crisis in February 2001, and the events of September 11. The revision of the economic program with strong structural and social elements resulted in the recovery of the economy in 2002. The outlook for Turkish economy remains positive in 2007. Inflation dropped to almost single-digits from 110.2 percent in the early 1980s. Due to the strong activity in the private sector that continues to boost the economy, GDP growth in Turkey is expected to remain above 6 percent in 2006 and 2007 (OECD Economic Outlook, 2006). This argument has been supported by the latest growth rate results of 7.5 percent in 2006.

Turkey, one of the more developed Middle Eastern countries, was designated by the U.S. Commerce Department as one of the world's ten "Big Emerging Markets" and industrialization is still in progress. For more than two centuries Turkey has been experiencing political, cultural and economic engagement with Europe and has pursued an integration policy with western institutions. Turkey, as a full member of the European Union Customs Union, has been a candidate state for EU membership since the 1999 Helsinki European Council. Currently, the government of Turkey is engaged in harmonizing its legislation and institutional framework to match EU standards and requirements in accordance with western democratic forms, with the support of international financial institutions (e.g. the IMF).

Historical development of HRM and PMS in Turkey

Since performance management system (PMS) is a relatively new concept in Turkey, the development of HRM in general will be the focus of this section. Moreover, since there is a paucity of research in Turkey about the implementation of PMS, the specific findings of a few studies on HRM will be communicated. Longitudinal survey data (e.g. Arthur Andersen study, Cranfield research) on performance management (PM) will be helpful in understanding the developments of PMSs in recent years in Turkey. It should be mentioned that while these studies include findings on some aspects of PMSs, including performance appraisal (PA), training and development, career management and performance-reward contingency, they do not address other aspects of PMSs such as goal setting and coaching.

The importance of HRM as a key factor in maintaining competitive advantage has been recognized in Turkey, thanks to factors such as Turkey's adoption of a liberal economy, the changing nature of market structure, decrease in government intervention and increase in privatization, legal and economic changes that are geared toward EU membership, globalization, and change in workforce characteristics, as well as societal values. Such a dynamic environment requires Turkish business organizations to be more profit-oriented and maintain competitiveness locally as well as globally. Turkish organizations facing these challenges eventually realize the critical role HRM plays for their survival in fierce global competition. Moreover, due to the dramatic shift from a predominantly agricultural-based economy to an increasingly industrialized and service-based economy after the 1980s, the emphasis has also shifted from "production" to "human resource management" as the key success factor.

Until the 1950s, finance departments of organizations were in charge of personnel-related activities which were limited to fulfilling legally-required practices (Özden, 2004). Personnel departments emerged as subdivisions within finance departments around the 1960s

(Arthur Andersen, 2000). Although personnel departments were officially formed to carry out personnel-related tasks after the 1970s, the scope was still limited to compensation, tax and social security, and premiums (Dereli, 2001). In the 1980s, global competition brought by the liberalization movement made organizations recognize the importance of human resources as a competitive advantage. The term "human resources management," which was equated with "modern management," was adopted at the beginning of the 1990s (Kuzeyli, 2000). The changing role of HRM in Turkey is promising. While in 1998 "Human Resource Management Departments" existed in 56 percent of the organizations, by 2000 it was 65 percent (Arthur Andersen, 2000). This increase in the adoption of HRM departments in organizations is in a way a sign of institutionalization of this concept. However, the recent large-scale downsizings following the February 2001 economic crises harmed the positive sentiments toward HRM departments, which were blamed for large-scale layoffs at that time.

HRM is a developing field in a developing country like Turkey (Aycan, 2006a) and so is PMS, which, however, is not widely used in Turkey. Indeed, most of the Turkish organizations implement traditional PA as a stand-alone system, rather than implementing PMS as an integrative process comprising goal-setting, clarification of expectations, coaching, performance appraising and providing resources and assistance, regular performance reviews and rewards for performance (Spangenberg and Theron, 1997).

Arthur Andersen surveys of 1998 and 2000

The comprehensive survey of HRM carried out by Arthur Andersen demonstrates the changes in HRM practices of private sector organizations in Turkey over time. These surveys have been carried out in different waves to examine the differences in HRM policies and practices. In a 1998 survey 109 organizations from the private sector participated in the study, whereas in 2000 there were 307 organizations (Arthur Andersen, 2000). These organizations operate in a wide array of industries including finance, automotive, textile, health, IT, fast-moving consumer goods, metal, mass-media, durable goods, and construction. Because large-scale organizations comprised the largest group of participating organizations in both waves of the survey, Arthur Andersen's sample should not be considered as representing all Turkish organizations.

While almost all participating organizations (95%) reported that the main function of the HRM department included "recruitment and selection," "performance evaluation" was considered as one of the key functions by 79 percent of these organizations. With respect to PM practices, the survey included questions about the performance evaluation system, performance-based reward and career management. Performance-based rewards and promotions have brought dynamism to organizations in Turkey, where wage determination and promotion was decided solely on the basis of organizational seniority until the 1980s (Arthur Andersen, 2000). In the year 2000, 81 percent of participating organizations reported that they had a formal performance evaluation system. However, the existence of a PM system with a standardized evaluation form does not guarantee an objective and bias-free appraisal. Even though one-third of the organizations reported that they evaluated performance on the basis of both goals, competencies and behaviors, this would not ensure objectivity due to the lack of criteria that are properly operationalized and communicated. This might be the reason why only 30 percent of organizations agreed that their performance system fulfilled their needs.

In the majority of organizations, performance evaluations are conducted as a top-down process whereby only the superiors evaluate their subordinates. While this top-down process was established in 80 percent of the participating organizations in the 1998 survey, it increased to 92 percent in 2000. This could be expected and accepted in a high-power distance cultural context, which is prevalent in Turkey (Pasa, Kabasakal and Bodur, 2001). The interesting point with regard to performance evaluations is the use of individual performance evaluation (almost 63%) rather than group evaluation. Although this could be perceived to be against the collectivistic norms prevailing in the Turkish culture, it might be a reflection of a move toward a performance-oriented culture where performance excellence, achievement, and interpersonal competition are values that organizations want to develop in employees. Last but not least, although almost half of the organizations reported that they conduct an interactive PAS, where the superior and subordinate discuss the subordinate's performance, this would not necessarily imply that the system was participative. In the hierarchical societal and organizational culture of Turkey, even though superiors may ask the opinions of subordinates, the decisions are taken unilaterally. Moreover, 11 percent of organizations in Turkey (it was 13% in 1998 survey) did not show the evaluation results to employees. This non-participative performance evaluation approach might result from the fact that giving and receiving performance feedback is a challenge in cultures like Turkey where people take criticisms as personal attacks, get offended and emotional about it (see Aycan, 2005).

Another point worth mentioning here is that in Turkey allocation of rewards is based on criteria other than performance (e.g. age, seniority, loyalty). This conveys the message to the employees that working hard or performing the best would not necessarily lead to desired rewards. In such a context, the implementation of a performance-reward contingency is necessary to change the "entitlement" culture.

The surveys revealed that performance evaluation results are used as an input to multiple HRM areas. Almost half of the organizations reported that performance evaluation results provided input for decisions in three HRM areas – rewards, promotion and training need analysis. More than two-thirds of the organizations reported that they had a system to ensure performance-reward contingency. The most frequently administered rewards included bonuses and salary increases (almost 50%). Performance-based reward allocation is administered mainly for white-collar employees in 60 percent of organizations, including middle- and upper-level managers, compared to blue-collar employees (27%). In a collectivistic Turkish cultural context, rewards that single out high performers, such as selecting the "employee of the month," are not preferred, because this kind of rewarding is perceived as hurting other employees' feelings and disturbing group harmony (see Aycan, 2005).

Performance evaluations constitute input for decisions concerning career management and promotions. More than half of the organizations (58%) reported that they had a career management system in place in the 2000 survey and 85 percent of them reported that it was linked to the performance evaluation system, which means that half of all the participating organizations had a career management system linked to performance evaluations. This was 40 percent in the 1998 survey.

Need assessment on the basis of performance evaluation was one of the most widely used methods. However, only one-fifth of the organizations reported that they conducted need assessment on the basis of performance evaluations (21%). Interestingly, findings of the 1998 survey revealed that 63 percent of the organizations used performance evaluations in training need assessment. The above findings suggest that although PMS is a developing area in private sector organizations in Turkey, there are still problems with its implementation, which is not free from subjectivity and bias.

Cranfield Human Resource Management Surveys of 2000 and 2005

Cranfield Network on Comparative Human Resource Management (Cranet) Survey provides data on HRM practices across the world, which are collected by an international team of collaborators from top business schools and academic institutions (*www.cranet.org*). Cranet aims to provide a coherent and accurate picture of international and comparative HRM. Turkey has been included in the waves of Cranet survey collected in 1992, 1995, 2000 and 2005. PM data was collected from mainly private sector organizations in Turkey operating in various sectors. It should be noted that the profile of organizations agreeing to participate in this survey does not represent Turkish business organizations in general. The findings of 2000 and 2005 will be discussed here (Uyargil, Ozcelik and Dundar, 2001).

Consistent with Arthur Andersen's findings, the top-down evaluation process is found to be in use in most of the participating organizations. While in the 2000 survey 79 percent of the organizations reported that performance evaluations are conducted by first-line supervisors, this percentage increased to 96 percent in 2005. This encouraging finding relates to the involvement of employees themselves in the evaluation process. While 42 percent of organizations reported that employees played a role in the evaluation process, it almost doubled and increased to 77 percent in 2005. The findings on subordinate and peer evaluation were also promising. The percentage of organizations reporting the use of subordinate and peer evaluation tripled in five years, increasing to 38 percent, although it is still far from being at the desired level.

The performance evaluation was reported to provide input mainly to HR planning (53%), career-development (60%), promotion potential (60%) and individual performance-based reward allocation (51%) in the 2000 survey. The interesting finding was that none of the organizations reported that performance evaluation provided input to organizational training need analysis. The percentages demonstrated an increase in all these areas. In 2005, organizations reported that performance results were used in HR planning (82%), training and development need analysis (90%), career planning (87%) and performance-based pay (87%). These results are encouraging in the use of an integrated PMS.

Key factors that determine PMS in Turkey

Cultural context

Turkey was situated in the cluster of high-power distant and collectivist countries in Hofstede's well-known research (1980). However, the socio-cultural environment of Turkey is changing toward being less collectivistic (e.g. Goregenli, 1997; Aycan, Kanungo, Mendonca, Yu, Deller, Stahl and Khursid, 2000), somewhat less hierarchical (Aycan *et al.*, 2000), and less uncertainty avoiding (e.g. Kabasakal and Bodur, 1998). A recent GLOBE project also demonstrated that Turkey is below the world average on performance and future orientation (Kabasakal and Bodur, 1998). Another salient cultural characteristic of Turkey is paternalism (Aycan *et al.*, 2000).

The impact of the socio-cultural environment on work culture and HRM practices, specifically PM in Turkey, has been examined in few studies. Aycan *et al.* (2000) conducted cross-cultural research to test the Model of Culture Fit, the theoretical model linking culture to HRM practices, at the cultural level. Yavuz (2005) tested the relationship between values and PM practices at the individual level. The basic rationale of the Model of Culture Fit is that HRM practices are based on managerial beliefs and assumptions about two fundamental organizational elements (the task and the employees), which form the internal work culture (Aycan *et al.*, 2000). Managers implement HRM practices based on their assumptions about the employees and the nature of the task. These managerial assumptions (i.e. internal work culture) are influenced by the socio-cultural context as well as the enterprise environment (e.g. size of the organization, ownership status, industry) within which the organizations operate. The antecedent variables in the Model of Culture Fit resemble the distal factors, especially the norms operating at the level of nation and organization, proposed by Murphy and DeNisi.

Aycan *et al.* (2000) found that HRM practices emphasizing performance-reward contingency were based on managerial assumptions concerning the possibility of change and improvement in employee skills and behaviors (i.e. malleability assumption). Managers holding this assumption were found to be working in non-fatalistic cultures where people believed that it was possible to control the outcomes of individuals' actions (Aycan *et al.*, 2000). The findings also showed that paternalism as a socio-cultural value had a positive impact on the participation assumption of managers (i.e. the assumption that employees want to participate in decisions), but a negative impact on the proactivity assumption (i.e. the assumption that employees are proactive, rather than reactive, in their work); participation and proactivity assumptions were positively related to performance-reward contingency. Because managers build family-like relationships with subordinates, they are involved in the decision-making of personal and professional matters in their employees' lives. Paternalist leaders are trusted as elderly family members and relied upon as "authority figures" who can give the right decisions that would benefit employees. Hence, employees prefer to be "reactive" rather than "proactive" in their stance toward their jobs. The dark side of paternalism, however, is the differential treatment in organizations, which is reflected in the lack of performance-reward contingency. Those who are closer to the paternalistic leader get the rewards regardless of their performance (Aycan, 2006b). At this point, it is also worth mentioning that the links between distal, proximal as well as intervening factors (Murphy and DeNisi, see Chapter 6) can be identified in the findings of these studies. For example, the above finding reveals that paternalistic value orientation, a cultural norm corresponding to the distal factor, has an effect on the rater–ratee relationship intervening factor, which is proposed as having a strong and close relationship with the ratings made in the PM process (Murphy and DeNisi, this volume). The closer the employee's relationship with the manager, the higher the performance ratings and rewards that he/she would receive. The paternalistic value orientation (i.e. the distal factor) has an influence on managers' participation assumption (i.e. an organizational norm as a proximal factor), which results in the top-down appraisal process.

Another study, which is the only study that assessed all aspects of PMS, tested the link among values, assumptions and HR practices at the individual level and examined not only the impact of managerial values and assumptions on managerial implementation of PMS, but also the effect of enterprise environment on this relationship (Aycan and Yavuz, 2006; Yavuz, 2005). The study empirically tested the contingencies likely to influence managers' PM practices. More specifically the focus was on how individual psychological factors (i.e. managerial values and assumptions) as well as work unit characteristics (e.g. size, technology) interacted to predict managers' PM practices. The rationale was that managers' socio-cultural values would shape their employee-related assumptions which, in turn, would lead them to implement certain practices. However, the characteristics of the enterprise environment they worked in (e.g. size, technology adopted) were expected not to allow them to implement certain practices, despite their values and assumptions. Hence, including work unit characteristics as a moderator was expected to enhance our understanding of the mechanisms underlying variations in PM practices.

This study had a sample of 214 middle- and upper-level highly educated Turkish managers from 214 different organizations. Organizations included in the current study represented a wide range of industry, sector, and size. Participating managers completed a self-administered questionnaire which assessed five managerial values (i.e. performance orientation, collectivism, paternalism, power distance and fatalism), five dimensions of employee-related managerial assumptions (i.e. malleability, obligation toward others, participation, goal orientation and proactivity), four work unit characteristics (i.e. unit size, technology, formalization and job complexity), and PM practices. PM practices included goal setting, determination of performance criteria, determination of performance evaluation method, and consequences of performance evaluation (e.g. types of rewards for performance and use of performance outcomes in training and development decisions). These practices were grouped under three categories: structured and systematic PM (e.g. specifically setting goals, periodically objective and systematic evaluation of performance with written reports), performance-oriented criteria (e.g. emphasizing criteria like performance outcomes, job-related competencies, merit rather than criteria like age, seniority, loyalty, etc.), and participative PM (e.g. participative goal-setting, a multisource evaluation, participative need assessment for training). Fifty-one percent of managers reported that there was an established PMS in their organizations. The presence or absence of an established PM system in the organization was controlled for in the analyses.

Results revealed that even if there was an established PM system in organizations, the ways in which it was implemented and practiced by managers varied due to managerial values and assumptions (Yavuz, 2005). Managers' values and assumptions about employee nature were significantly related to their PM practices, above and beyond the established organizational systems and rules. For instance, managers who were high on fatalistic value orientation were more likely to assume that employees were reactive and did not want to participate in decisions concerning them. These managers, in turn, were less likely to implement participative PM (i.e. they did not invite employees to state their opinions about their own performance).

Results also illustrated that values and assumptions seem to be more influential than work unit characteristics on managers' implementation of PM practices. Only one work unit characteristic, technology, which has also been conceptualized as one of the distal factors in the PA process (see Chapter 6), had a moderator effect. Managers who assumed that employees were goal oriented and worked in units with non-routine technology were more likely to implement a structured and systematic PM. When managers assumed that employees wanted to have goals to achieve and they worked in units where there were non-routine tasks (i.e. unique tasks, unanalyzable work), they were more likely to implement structured and systematic PM (i.e. they set employees' goals specifically where employees knew what to do, when to do it and how to do it; they evaluate employee performance in an objective, bias-free and systematic way, periodically with written reports). However, no other work unit characteristic had an impact on managerial implementation of PM practices.

Institutional context

One of the most important institutional contextual factors affecting the implementation of PMS in Turkey is the legal system, namely the New Labour Law, another distal factor proposed by Murphy and DeNisi. The new labour law was accepted in May 2003 and replaced the one that had been in use since 1971. According to the new labour law, employers carry the burden of proof of inadequate performance in cases of dismissals. This requires that organizations assess performance of employees in a systematic and objective way and document it properly. By 2004, organizations started to focus on the formation of new PMS or on the already existing PMSs in accordance with the new law.

There are also some organizational level variables that are related to the use of effective PMSs. The private sector accounts for some 80 percent of Turkey's economy, in which the majority is comprised of family-owned small and medium-size enterprises. Due to the dominance of informal family norms (rather than institutional norms) in these family-owned organizations, basic HRM functions such as PMS cannot be implemented properly (Selcuklu, 2005). There is an ongoing tension between the top management who are focused on work output and the HR department, which is focused on employee development and satisfaction. For example, in these family-owned organizations, family-like environment and relationship-oriented organizational norms, as a proximal factor in Murphy and DeNisi's model, may result in subjective and less formal PMS rather than more objective and formal ones that aim at identifying and differentiating good versus poor performers. It is very difficult to replace the traditional management approach in these family-owned businesses with the modern one involving PMSs. Hence in comparison to private sector organizations and MNCs, SMEs and family-owned organizations are more likely to implement traditional stand-alone performance appraisal rather than an integrative PMS.

As can be seen from the previous sections, few studies conducted in Turkey portrayed the situation in private sector organizations. However, almost no study investigated the PMS in public sector organizations. Most large-scale private sector organizations and MNCs adopt the western style in PMS. For example, Turkish subsidiaries of organizations like Philip Morris, Honda, Ford, Unilever use an extensive performance evaluation system in which both quantifiable objectives and competencies of employees are evaluated and the results of these evaluations provide input to rewards and especially to training and development (Suzer, 2004).

Despite limited data, there is evidence that public sector organizations in Turkey are also becoming aware of the importance of effective PMS. A municipality in Istanbul, the metropolis of Turkey, broke ground and implemented, for the first time, a "performance evaluation and management system" based on customer satisfaction and rewarded its successful personnel. This system was developed to prevent waste of time and resources in the public sector, help employees to better focus on their work and assess the productivity of personnel. The mayor indicated that the public sector is entering into a new era in line with the enactment of new laws, and the implementation of this management system would set an example for other public sector organizations in managing and evaluating the performance of employees.[1]

Key challenges for PMS in practice

Suppose that you are a human resource manager in charge of the PM function in a large-scale Turkish organization. Top management asked you to develop an objective PM system to prepare for a 360-degree performance evaluation. You assigned a project group for this task, assessing quantifiable goals and competencies in an objective and systematic way and using performance evaluation results as an input to employee-related decisions such as compensation, promotion and training. You hired consultants from a well-known western consulting group to work with your local HR staff. After a year's work, the project group developed a less-than-perfect computerized PM system in which the objective performance of employees would be measured, twice a year, with formal written reports.

You had faith in this system; however, after the first implementation of the system, you started to have feelings that something was going wrong. It would not take long before you realized that not the systems but the people who used the systems were the key to its successful implementation. Turkish managers who evaluate their subordinates' performance could find a way to manipulate the system, because their values, beliefs and assumptions about what constitutes "good performance" are different from that which the system suggests. You find out that they take into account not just the objective, quantifiable outcomes, but also criteria like good interpersonal relationships, loyalty to the organization and good interpersonal relationships with supervisors and colleagues, etc.

Values held by managers are real challenges for the successful implementation of PMSs. Creation of a perfect PM system does not guarantee its successful implementation; this is reminiscent of law and enforcement. A country may have laws in place but they are useless if not enforced. Values shaped by the socio-cultural context might result in resistance to change and continuation of the traditional stand-alone performance appraisal, rather than an integrative PMS. Indeed, the term PM itself may not be an appropriate term in a country like Turkey. Since PM is an ongoing communication process that includes partnership of employees and supervisors and the establishment of clear goals and expectations about the job (Bacal, 1999), an open and continuous communication may be a challenge in a high power distant and high context culture.

Due to the reasons indicated above, the reliability of the evaluation criteria and the evaluation process can be at risk (Aycan, 2005). For example, organizations who attempt to adopt the 360-degree performance evaluation system get frustrating results, because employees find it very difficult to evaluate their superiors and colleagues, since it is perceived to be against the power distance as well as collectivistic norms of maintaining group harmony (Aycan, 2005). This raises the question of the *reliability* of the whole information used in PMS. The challenge here lies in the use of performance evaluation results that are biased and subjective as inputs in other HRM decisions. Not only is there a concern about the objectivity of the system, but also about the fact that the system mainly involves a top-down evaluation process, as indicated by the Arthur Andersen and Cranfield surveys.

Turkey's unstable economic and political environment (Nichols, Sugur and Demir, 2002) poses another challenge for HR practitioners in the implementation of the PMS. Performance evaluation and PM tend to be difficult and complicated in politically and economically unstable countries, because in many steps of PM (e.g. goal setting, evaluating and rewarding performance), the instability constitutes a barrier between setting goals and evaluating employees vis-à-vis the goals. Often, top management finds it difficult to foresee the future and set specific business goals for the organization and cascade them down to the work units and employees. They tend to revise the goals several times during the year and evaluate employees in light of their conjectures.

Last but not least, another challenge in HRM in general and PMS in particular is the tension created by the necessity to follow global trends, while at the same time trying to establish the basics of HRM in organizations. Organizations in Turkey closely follow the North American HRM systems. However, in terms of level of development of the field,

Turkey is at least 10 years behind the North American system. What is popular in Turkey (e.g. using multiple assessors in performance evaluation) was popular in North America 10 years ago. In order to implement the cutting edge developments in PM, one has to establish the basics of the process. For instance, in some cases where there is no performance evaluation system HR departments are asked to implement 360-degree appraisals. In particular, MNCs in Turkey have to consider the global–local balance in developing appropriate PMSs.

Websites

The readers can refer to the following websites to get more information about Turkey and Turkish HRM practices in general:

Turkey–EU relationships: *http://www.dtm.gov.tr/ab/ingilizce/turkeyeu.htm*
State Institute of Statistics: *http://www.die.gov.tr/english/SONIST/*
Government Institute of Statistics: *http://www.die.gov.tr/listTablolar.htm#eko*
Unemployment statistics: *http://www.die.gov.tr/ieyd/troecd/page9.html*
   http://www.tisk.org.tr/yayinlar.asp?sbj=ic&id=852
   http://www.turksae.com/face/index.php?text_id=18
   http://www.tisk.org.tr/isveren_sayfa.asp?yazi_id=793&id=47
Inflation statistics: *http://www.die.gov.tr/ieyd/troecd/page8.html*
Laborforce statistics: *http://www.die.gov.tr/english/SONIST/ISGUCU/160704/S1.htm*
Population & development indicators: *http://nkg.die.gov.tr/*
Organizational statistics: *http://www.die.gov.tr/TURKISH/SONIST/SIRKET/090804h.html*
Economic crisis: *http://www.belgenet.com/eko/21subat01.html*
   http://www.isguc.org/arc_view.php?ex=15
Education statistics: *http://www.meb.gov.tr/indexeng.htm*
Current government: *http://www.belgenet.com/secim/3kasim.html*
The new labour law: *http://www.isguc.org/arc_view.php?ex=130&hit=ny*
HRM sites: *http://web7.kariyer.net/KariyerRehberi/index.kariyer?arn=&sid=&xx02=2*
   http://www.yenibiris.com/CareerSupport/ArticleTemplate.aspx?sectionID=4
   http://www.personelonline.com/linkler.htm
   http://www.insankaynaklari.com/cn/index001.asp?SectionId=3&ShowAbs=ON
   http://www.geocities.com/jumptobetterjob/diger_hr.html
   http://www.ntvmsnbc.com/news/250272.asp
   http://www.aksam.com.tr/arsiv/aksam/2002/08/14/yazidizi/yazidiziprn1.html

Note

1 *http://www.tuzla.bel.tr/performans/tanitim/sayfa2.asp*

References

Andersen, Arthur (2000) *2001'e Dogru Insan Kaynaklari Arastirmasi (Human Resource Management Research towards 2001)*, Istanbul: Sabah Yayincilik.

Aycan, Z. (2005) The interface between cultural and institutional / structural contingencies in human resource management, *International Journal of Human Resource Management* 16(7): 1083–119.

Aycan, Z. (2006a) Human resource management in Turkey, in P. Budhwar and K. Mellahi (eds.) *HRM in the Middle East*, New Jersey: Routledge, pp. 160–80.

Aycan, Z. (2006b) Paternalism: towards conceptual refinement and operationalization, in K. S. Yang, K. K. Hwang and U. Kim, (eds.) *Scientific Advances in Indigenous Psychologies: Empirical, Philosophical, and Cultural Contributions*, London: Cambridge University Press, pp. 445–66.

Aycan, Z. and Yavuz, S. (2006) How does the interface between managerial values and work unit characteristics influence PM practices? Paper presented at the 26th International Congress of Applied Psychology, Athens, Greece, July.

Aycan, Z., Kanungo, R. N., Mendonca, M., Yu, K., Deller, J., Stahl, G. and Khursid, A. (2000) Impact of culture on human resource management practices: a ten country comparison, *Applied Psychology: An International Review* 49(1): 192–220.

Bacal, R. (1999) *Performance Management*, New York: McGraw-Hill.

Dereli, T. (2001) Peryon in its 30th Year and Human Resources Management (30. Yasinda Peryon ve Insan Kaynaklari Yonetimi), *Peryon Dergisi, Fall*, 22.

Eralp, A., Tunay, M. and Yesilada, B. (1993) *The Political and Socioeconomic Transformation of Turkey*, Westport, CT: Praeger Publishers.

Goregenli, M. (1997) Individualist-collectivist tendencies in a Turkish sample, *Journal of Cross-Cultural Psychology* 28(6): 787–94.

Hofstede, G. (1980) *Culture's Consequences: International Differences in Work-related Values*, Beverly Hills, CA: Sage.

Kabasakal, H. and Bodur, M. (1998) Leadership, values and institutions: the case of Turkey, Paper presented at Western Academy of Management Conference, Istanbul, Turkey, June.

Kuzeyli, H. S. (2000) Human resources management in Turkey, in Z. Aycan (ed.) *Management, Leadership and HR in Turkey*, Istanbul: Turkish Psychological Association Press.

Narli, N. (1999) The rise of the Islamist movement in Turkey, *Middle East Review of International Affairs* 3(3).

Nichols, T., Sugur, N. and Demir, E. (2002) Beyond cheap labour: trade unions and development in the Turkish metal industry, *The Sociological Review* 50(1): 23–47.

OECD Economic Outlook (2006) *Country Summaries: Turkey, No. 79*. Retrieved from the World Wide Web on August 29, 2006: *http://www.oecd.org/dataoecd/5/51/20213268.pdf*

Özden, M. C. (2004) *Relations and Differences between Personnel and Human Resources Management (Personel ve Insan Kaynaklari Yonetimi Arasindaki Iliski ve Farklar)*. Retrieved from the World Wide Web on October 13, 2004: *http://www.mcozden.com/ikf10_pikyaivf.htm*

Pasa, S. F., Kabasakal, H. and Bodur, M. (2001) Society, organizations, and leadership in Turkey, *Applied Psychology: An International Review* 50(4): 559–89.

Selcuklu, H. (2005) *Turkiye'de Insan Kaynaklari (Human Resources in Turkey)*. Retrieved from the World Wide Web on August 29, 2006: *http://www.inisiyatif.net/document/22.asp*

Spangenberg, H. H. and Theron, C. C. (1997) Developing a performance management audit questionnaire, *South African Journal of Psychology* 27(3): 151–9.

Suzer, H. D. (2004) A'lari sirkete cek ve B ve C'yi gelistir. (Recruit As and develop Bs and Cs), *Capital Monthly Business and Economy Journal*. Retrieved from the World Wide Web on August 29, 2006: *http://www.capital.com.tr/haber.aspx?HBR_KOD=1113*

Uyargil, C., Ozcelik, A. O. and Dundar, G. (2001) *Cranfield Uluslararasi Insan Kaynaklari Yonetimi Arastirmasi: 1999–2000 Turkiye Raporu (Cranfield International Strategic Human Resource Management Survey: 1999–2000 Turkey Report)*, Istanbul: I.U. Isletme Fakultesi Yayinlari.

World Bank Report (2003) *Bridging the Gender Gap in Turkey: A Milestone Towards Faster Socio-economic Development and Poverty Reduction*, Poverty Reduction and Economic Management Unit, Europe and Central Asia Region.

Yavuz, S. (2005) *The Relationship of Managerial Values, Assumptions and Work Unit Characteristics with Performance Management*. Unpublished master's thesis, Koc University, Istanbul, Turkey.

12 Performance management in India

TANUJA SHARMA, PAWAN S. BUDHWAR AND ARUP VARMA

Introduction

At present, India is acknowledged as one of the fastest growing economies in the world (second only to China). Not surprisingly, the economic reforms initiated in the early 1990s have resulted in numerous changes in policies and practices employed by Indian organizations (Kapur and Ramamurti, 2001). Furthermore, numerous multinational corporations (MNCs) continue to set up operations in India (Bjorkman and Budhwar, 2007). The competition presented by the MNCs (both for market share and for qualified employees) has forced Indian organizations to re-visit their systems, with a view to staying competitive and competing at the global stage. In this chapter, we present a critical overview of the Indian context regarding one of the most crucial HR systems in organizations, namely, the performance management system (PMS).

A large variety of both forms and designs of PMSs are in use in Indian organizations. However, as one might expect, the nature and content of PMSs in the Indian context differ in different types of organizations, that is, private, public and foreign firms (Amba-Rao *et al.*, 2000; Budhwar and Boyne, 2004; Saini and Budhwar, 2007). With the growth of the Indian economy, more and more Indian organizations are emphasizing development of effective PMSs. Of course, while there are some commonalities in the emerging PMSs, it is rather difficult to generalize, given the scope of a diverse and varied country like India. Indeed, while India has emerged as a leading exporter of computer software, and a major global outsourcing hub for IT and IT-enabled services, its economy continues to be a mixture of traditional village farming and handicrafts on the one hand, and a wide range of modern industries including chemicals, food processing, steel, and a multitude of other services on the other (see Budhwar, 2001). Ironically, the existing literature on PM is rather scarce, and fails to provide a clear picture of the PMSs in use in Indian organizations. We believe our chapter helps fill this gap.

A review of the existing literature (e.g. Basu, 1988) reveals that PMS practices in India range from "no appraisal" to "sophisticated multipurpose, multi component web-based performance management systems." Some of the key factors influencing performance appraisal (PA) management in India are (i) changes in the economic environment resulting from the integration of Indian economy into the global economy, (ii) cultural diversity, and (iii) the on-going technology revolution. Furthermore, Indian organizations are facing several challenges, as they attempt to establish formal PMSs. These include, though are not limited to, (i) transparency in the appraisal process, (ii) establishing clear linkages between performance evaluation and rewards, and (iii) a multitude of labor laws, many of which have not been updated for decades.

In this chapter, we initially outline the history of the development and acceptance of PA/management systems in India. This is followed by a discussion of the current scenario of PMSs in Indian organizations. Next, we explore the key factors that impact PMSs in India, and finally, we highlight the challenges faced by organizations in establishing effective PMSs.

History of PMSs in India

The literature (e.g. Basu, 1988) reports that leading private sector organizations such as Union Carbide started using PAs for managerial personnel as far back as 1940, followed by other well-known organizations, such as the Tata Iron and Steel Company, Voltas, and Bata India, which introduced such systems in the 1950s. On the other hand, public sector enterprises adopted a confidential reporting system, which has been used by the government to evaluate its bureaucrats since India achieved independence in 1947. Furthermore, personality- and trait-based systems of evaluation were in use prior to 1947 in the Indian armed forces and the civil services, though these were primarily used for merit pay and promotion-related decisions.

In a 1968 survey (see Bolar, 1978), 49 of 82 companies reported having some form of formal performance evaluation system in place, though 20 of the 49 companies reported that while they had the systems in place, these were rarely used. Furthermore, graphic rating scales were the most popular form of evaluation in use at the time. In the mid-1970s, Rao and Pareek (1996) developed an open-ended PAS that included performance planning and analysis, identification of development needs, participatory planning, culture building, competence building, and upward appraisal and review for Larsen and Toubro. Although this system was simply called performance appraisal, its focus was on managing overall performance and development. Many other organizations subsequently developed and implemented open-ended appraisal systems similar to the one in use at Larsen and Toubro (for details see Rao, 2004).

In the late 1970s and early 1980s, most Indian organizations were using PAs to regulate employee behavior and help develop employee capabilities. These were known by various names, such as "work planning and review system" in the Life Insurance Corporation, and "performance planning and review system" in the National Dairy Development Board. In later years, performance appraisal systems were revamped to incorporate quality initiatives such as total quality management. Indeed, organizations such as Xerox (India) became well known for incorporating quality dimensions into their performance review systems, whereby individual performance reviews reflected the input of customers (both internal and external), and "quality of work" and "customer service" were some of the critical dimensions on which both employees and executives were appraised (Parker and Datta, 1996). By the late 1980s, some clear trends in PMSs began to emerge – such as a shift away from closed and confidential evaluations, to open dialogue and discussion-based systems. In addition, there was a discernible move from a purely numeric evaluation format to qualitative, interactive, and improvement-oriented systems (Rao and Pareek, 1996).

Overall, performance appraisal/management had been an under-emphasized function in Indian businesses until very recently (e.g. Amba-Rao et al., 2000). It was only in the early twenty-first century that most Indian organizations started emphasizing the development of effective PMSs (Rao et al., 2001). As these authors note, it was around this time that the PM processes started incorporating development-oriented tools, as well as feedback and counseling systems. By 2004, with continuing economic liberalization and enhanced competition, a majority of Indian organizations reported using various methods of performance appraisals/management. Indeed, numerous organizations such as Infosys, Titan, Tata Steel, Bharat Petroleum, Dr Reddy's Lab and the National Stock Exchange are known to use some of the most sophisticated forms of PMSs. For example, the appraisal system in Voltas recognizes communication and counseling as important aspects of development through self-improvement and encourages raters to be objective during the evaluation process. At Larsen and Toubro, the use of facilitators is a unique part of the evaluation and development system. Furthermore, peer rating and assessment of values and potential are also incorporated in the PMS (see Rao and Rao, 2006).

Ironically, in spite of the major changes sweeping the Indian economy, and the consequent professionalism introduced by these changes, informal and confidential appraisals by the immediate supervisor continue to be a part of the evaluation process, especially in public sector organizations. However, there are some notable exceptions, such as the Life Insurance Corporation, the National Dairy Development Board, and the National Thermal Power Corporation. These public sector organizations are well-known for their use of progressive, open-ended performance appraisal/management systems for almost three decades (Rao, 2004).

Current scenario

Over the past few years, there has been a rather impressive move by Indian companies to go global. From major international acquisitions by leading organizations such as Tata Steel and United Breweries, to operations in numerous countries, the truly global Indian corporation is now a reality. A logical outcome of this is the need to manage performance in numerous countries, as well as the need to manage a multicultural workforce. Many HR professionals now admit a new-found respect for PMSs in India, viewing them as a tool for transforming the organization through promoting high performance. As an example, the HR team at Ranbaxy Laboratories, an Indian pharmaceutical multinational, uses an electronic performance management system for development purposes by incorporating their "Values-in-Action" leadership competencies into the PMS. The company is also using PMSs for promoting the notion of employee ownership of tasks, by linking the PMS with its business processes, and providing employee mentoring through coaching. Not surprisingly, almost all IT and IT-enabled organizations in India now use e-PMS (for details see Budhwar *et al.*, 2006).

Recently, Hewitt Associates conducted a comprehensive salary survey for 2004–5, covering 652 organizations across all industries and business sectors in India. They reported that 99.5 percent of the sample firms in India are using some form of PMS (*Hewitt Report*, 2005). According to this report, the most commonly used system for performance management in Indian organizations is the Target Based Evaluation/MBO. Furthermore, balance scorecards and 360-degree tools are also being used increasingly, as these help to provide linkages with business processes.

Furthermore, 96.8 percent of the participating firms link their salary increases to performance ratings. Annual performance reviews are conducted by 60 percent of the sample organizations, while one-third of the respondent firms conduct biannual reviews. In 89 percent of the firms, a variable pay program is in practice and the emerging trend is toward higher component of variable pay for executive compensation. For senior/top management, variable pay as a percentage of total cost to company is highest among all employee groups, and was estimated at 23.7 percent for the year ending 2006.

Another interesting finding of the survey is the effort by organizations to establish a linkage between incentives and business results. Of the sample organizations, 60 percent indicated that individual performance awards have the most significant effect on improving business results. Other types of awards and their perceived impact are presented in Table 12.1.

A subtle but definite shift toward preference for individual gains, in terms of immediate cash, has been also reported in the Hewitt survey. Individual performance awards are offered by 60 percent of the respondents, though other awards such as "business incentives," "team awards," both long term as well as short term, were also deemed to have meaningful impact in achieving business results (see Table 12.2).

PMS of MNCs in India

The above discussion concentrated on PMSs in Indian organizations in general; however, it is important that we separately examine PMSs in MNCs operating in India. In this connection, Budhwar and Singh (2004) conducted an in-depth study of HRM systems in 102 MNCs operating in India. With reference to PMSs in MNCs, they report that (i) most MNCs in India follow a formal and structured approach to performance appraisal, (ii) the appraisal or assessment system is typically developed in their corporate office(s) and imported, and adapted, for use in India, and (iii) in most cases, the appraisals are conducted once a year. It should be noted that some firms (e.g. Hyundai) conduct bi-annual appraisals, while others (e.g. GlaxoSmithKline Beecham) conduct quarterly appraisals. All

Table 12.1 Performance management system (PMS) in India

Types of Performance Management System in Place	Percentage (n = 639)
Annual review by supervisor/manager	11
180 performance review	1
360 performance review	12
Balanced score card	14
Informal review	12
Peer review	6
Target-based evaluation/MBO	25
Others	19
99.5% of respondents have PMS in place	
96.8% of respondents link salary increases to performance ratings within the PMS	

Source: Compiled from *Hewitt Report* (2005)

participating firms have a structured format and a clear set of parameters for appraisals. In many cases, the ratee is required to fill out a self-appraisal, whereby s/he is able to list his/her achievements and future plans/goals for development. Next, the rater (i.e. the immediate supervisor) is required to meet with the ratee to discuss his/her performance, and compare the ratee's self-appraisal with the rater's evaluation, and arrive at mutually accepted ratings and evaluation(s). This discussion is designed to help resolve the discrepancy between the ratee's own evaluation and that of the rater as well as allow the ratee to explain contextual factors that may have affected his/her performance. In practice, of course, things often work out differently. The general trend seems to be that the immediate supervisor of the employee fills out the form, allows the employee to read it, and then asks him/her to countersign it, after which the form is sent to the head of the department/division. In addition to evaluation of performance for the period under review, most organizations also use the appraisal system to identify employee training needs.

Finally, most MNCs have an individual-based PMS, though some (e.g. Whirlpool) also use team-based evaluations. Almost all the firms use some kind of rating scale, grading or ranking system and set targets for appraisals. For senior managers, many firms employ more comprehensive evaluation systems, such as the 360-degree feedback mechanism. Such a comprehensive PMS has some drawbacks as summarized in the comments of the HR manager from Hughes Software Systems:

> What happens is that implementation of appraisal is something which nobody likes, it is almost like a necessary evil that everyone has to see. I have not seen in my career someone who is willing to do that. So we have to at times give the bad news or we have to be tough, which people do not like doing. So no matter how objective it becomes, how transparent it becomes, doing a tough part of evaluating a person is something that people do not like. That is the bad part of the whole thing.

The above quote clearly is the "bad news" – the fact that most people continue to feel that

Table 12.2 Effects of variable pay/rewards on business results in India (1–5 Scale and %)

Awards	Helped in Business Results (1)	(2)	Had no Effect (3)	(4)	Hindered Business Results (5)	n
Individual performance	60	26	5	5	3	336
Team based	48	33	11	4	3	183
Gain sharing/productivity	35	35	18	6	5	65
Cash profit sharing	49	18	19	5	9	79
Business incentives	54	27	12	6	2	142
Special recognition	47	33	14	5	1	235
Stock option	39	30	24	4	3	162

89% of the responding organizations (n = 639) have a variable pay in place

Source: Compiled from *Hewitt Report* (2005)

appraisals (and all that goes with appraisals) are really a waste of time, and should be "eliminated from the face of the earth," as per Deming. The good news is that a majority of HR managers are convinced of the utility of comprehensive PMSs, and report that most employees seem to accept the system rather quickly, and treat it as a "way of life" in their organizations. However, what is clear is that the system can be further improved. For example, the way PMSs are currently implemented in MNCs, the ratee's involvement is rather limited, especially in terms of goal setting (though, not surprisingly, many organizations claim that the process is expected to be fully participative). This is further true in the Indian BPO sector where systems are strongly data driven (see Budhwar *et al.*, 2006). Perhaps this is reflective of the hierarchical nature of Indian society (see Kakar, 1971; Sparrow and Budhwar, 1997). To help us better understand how factors such as power distance affect the Indian workplace, the following section presents a discussion of the key factors influencing PMSs in India.

Factors influencing PMSs in India

Economic factors

As mentioned above, over the last few years, India has emerged as one of the fastest growing economies in the world (with an average annual growth rate of 8 percent over the past three consecutive years). The fundamentals of the Indian economy are being reported as strong and stable as measured by indicators such as growth rates, foreign exchange reserves, foreign direct investment and inflation and interest rates. Indeed, several key forecasting agencies such as the Economist Intelligence, the Confederation of Indian Industry, and Citigroup have predicted a sustained GDP growth of 7.2–8.2 percent in the coming years (Consensus Economics and media reports). Furthermore, as is now globally acknowledged, the service industry in India is the fastest growing sector and the most consistent performer, particularly the IT/ ITeS sectors, having grown at a rate close to 10 percent over the past couple of years. Overall, the key environmental factors shaping the Indian economy are globalization, profitability through growth, technology, and intellectual capital.

The continued growth of the Indian economy, and the need to sustain this rate of growth, are putting tremendous pressure on industry leaders and HR professionals to better manage both their financial and human resources (e.g. Budhwar and Sparrow, 1998; Saini and Budhwar, 2007). As a result, many organizations are recognizing and emphasizing the critical role played by various HR processes, including PMSs. Relatedly, the contribution of initiatives such as goal setting, decision-making, conflict resolution and OCTAPACE (Openness, confrontation, trust, autonomy, proaction, authenticity, collaboration, and experimentation) in helping increase motivation and maintain the morale of employees is being appreciated by the Indian organizations. Indeed, the use of the PMS as a mechanism to improve a firm's performance has increased drastically over the past few years (e.g. Amba-Rao *et al.*, 2000; Bordia and Blau, 1998).

In this connection, the relationship and impact of distal factors like norms, strategy and firm performance (see Murphy and DeNisi's model; Chapter 6 of this volume) on performance appraisal is being re-visited and clearly defined and communicated to employees during the initial stages of their employment. Furthermore, both private and public sector organizations are clearly setting individual and department goals (Key Performance Areas), and use of appraisal information for decision-making is on the increase (Rao, 2004). Moreover, positive correlations have been indicated in a study conducted on tracing linkages between the employee's perceptions of PMS in the use and external customer's perceptions of service quality delivered to its customers in the banking sector (see Sharma, 2006).

Cultural factors

The impact of cultural factors on both macro (distal factors) and micro levels (proximal factors) of PMS is also increasingly evident in the Indian workplace (see Budhwar, 2000). India represents a "major socio-historic entity representing one idea of one civil society that is composed of a small set of closely inter-related attributes" (Kothari, 1997: 7 cited in Chhokar, 2007). As a result, the business environment in India is not only complex but also full of contrasts; for example, there are significant variations between industry sectors (see Budhwar, 2001; Budhwar and Boyne, 2004).

The extremely rich history and cultural heritage of the country coupled with its recent economic successes has added to the complexity and diversity of Indian society and culture. In this connection, a number of scholars (e.g. Sinha, 2004; Sparrow and Budhwar, 1997) have written extensively on leadership, motivation, PMS and compensation philosophy in the Indian business context. Furthermore, scholars (e.g. Gupta, 2000) have conducted in-depth studies of concepts such as "nurturing-task leadership" and "araam" (leisure, relaxation), to better understand the evolving Indian workplace culture and ethos. In order to better understand how the Indian culture affects individuals and their workplace experience, it is important that we explore India's standing relative to other nations on critical contextual factors that may influence business decisions.

In this connection, GLOBE, a major cross-cultural study covering 63 countries, has observed that in India "it is not easy to find manifestations of 'Indian' culture which are: (a) common to the entire country without exception, and (b) unique to the country insofar as these are not found in other countries" (Chhokar, 2007). Based on continuing traditional rituals and ceremonies, the concept of time, respect for age, and the prevalence of family-owned businesses, India is often categorized as a traditional and collectivist society. Indeed, the GLOBE results place India high on collectivism and humane orientation. Furthermore, it is placed in the top one-third among all nations in terms of performance orientation, future orientation, and power distance. In terms of gender egalitarianism, India seems to continue to be a male-dominated society. India ranks 26 out of 53 nations on the measure of uncertainty avoidance. Given the above, it is not surprising that Trompenaars (1993) classifies India as a "family culture," marked by a person-oriented and hierarchical culture which tends to be power oriented. Here, the leader, or manager, is seen as a caring parent, and power tends to be moral and social in nature and is rooted in broad status. In addition, the corporate culture tends to be high in context, and the thrust is on intuitive development. Finally, the focus is on effectiveness and not efficiency (Pattanayak *et al.*, 2002: 474–5).

Overall, the few published studies on India indicate a presence of collectivist and individualist values and the adoption by many Indian organizations of the formal systems of management in a *vertical collectivist* culture. This often creates unpredictability in managerial and decision-making styles, whereby the practices may seem similar to many western managerial practices, though their basic causes or driving forces are quite different, given the diversity of the Indian nation.

It should be noted, for example, that Indians are very proud of their "secular," multireligious, multicultural and multilingual country (e.g. Budhwar, 2001). The multiplicity of languages (e.g. 15 official languages recognized by the Indian constitution and hundreds of dialects) adds to the complexity of the nation and its workplace. Also, in the absence of a strong legal system and its clear implementation which can define the scope of various HR policies and practices, it is rather difficult to develop a common and comprehensive PMS for such a diverse nation. In summary, PM in India, particularly in local and national public and private sector firms, is deeply affected by the high context, power oriented, hierarchy-driven mindset of Indian managers. As the literature documents, their style of leadership and management is paternalistic in nature, and often causes employees to look for detailed and continuous guidance, in order to achieve the defined goals (Sparrow and Budhwar, 1997). Thus, adherence to norms and managerial directives is emphasized. Furthermore, supervisor–subordinate relationships play a huge role in determining the ratings of individual employees. In this connection, Varma, Pichler and Srinivas (2005) reported that subjectivity in ratings had a significant impact on the ratings awarded to employees, such that raters tended to inflate ratings of poor performers whom they liked.

Performance is linked to both compensation and promotions; however, all performance rewards must be validated by the senior management team and HR department. Finally, confidentiality of information is maintained at many levels in the entire process, thus depriving individual employees of a clear understanding of the process and the outcomes.

At a macro level, distal factors like norms, strategy and firm performance clearly have played a role in the evolution of industry in India, and on their HR practices and policies. For example, public sector units in the country are an outcome of India's first prime minister Jawaharlal Nehru's vision of a mixed economy, emphasizing both private and public enterprise. The Indian PSUs are governed by welfare objectives and tend to focus on generating employment, skilling Indian labor and making India self-reliant by producing and distributing goods and services. In addition, the policy of life-time employment and the active participation of unions have had the effect of taking away the focus from productivity and profits, instead emphasizing sustenance and governance (also see Budhwar and Boyne, 2004).

As a result, HR systems in the public sector units are often maintenance-oriented, rather than progressive. For example, PMSs in public sector units are typically used only for promotion purposes, and reward/outcomes are often not clearly linked to performance and productivity. As a result, the acceptance of the PMS is extremely low, further confounded by the fact that PMSs in PSUs are typically operated under a "closed system." Also, many researchers have reported distortions in rating and promotion decisions (e.g. Amba-Rao *et al.*, 2000; Sharma, 2006).

On the other hand, findings of an empirical study conducted on Indian banks to map the role of PMSs (Sharma, 2006) indicate that the private banks (both foreign banks and Indian private banks) show higher correlation between four important dimensions of the PMS – performance planning, feedback and coaching, performance review and rewards with internal service climate and external customer's perception of service quality. Focus on performance planning has been the strength of private banks. Performance orientation and training given for communication during induction also played an important role. On the other hand nationalized banks follow the policy of considering seniority as the main factor for promotions, and performance review only has a limited role in supporting such decisions.

Key challenges facing effective PMSs in India

As is clear from the above discussion, performance appraisal/management practices have been continually improving, with considerable innovations and changes, but can be further improved by new interventions (see Bolar, 1978). Based on the above discussion, we present a list of key action items that can help further improve PMSs in the Indian context. For one, mismanagement of the PMS is sometimes in evidence. Research also indicates that very few managers are proficient in performance planning. Typically, organizations attach higher priority on acquiring technical competencies (such as in the fields of operations management, accounting, marketing) rather than on HR competencies of determining performance objectives, providing feedback and administering performance-contingent rewards. These activities are often seen as unnecessary and time-consuming by both managers and employees. In addition, the haphazard administration and confidential nature of PMSs lead to conflict between raters and their ratees.

One key factor that is often overlooked is that Indian organizations are not homogenous. Thus, although all types of Indian firms implement PMSs, the process varies significantly depending on the nature and size of the firm. Perhaps the biggest challenge before Indian organizations today is to ensure that the whole process of performance management is not reduced to a simple form-filling exercise, a mistake repeatedly made by managers (Rao, 2004). Furthermore, the dyadic nature of performance seems to have been almost completely ignored, for the most part, with most evaluation and feedback mechanisms being top-down.

Not surprisingly, there are numerous issues related to problems with ratings. For example, ratings are subject to bias and often colored by the nature of the relationship between supervisors and subordinates. Also, supervisors are often willing to inflate ratings to avoid having to give negative feedback. Clearly, this is an area that needs attention from both managers and HR departments, so that feedback can be used as a mechanism to help improve performance (Sharma, 2006).

Another challenge facing organizations is performance management in a team environment. Effective systems need to be developed so that individuals in teams can receive fair and equitable evaluations. In this connection, Rao and Pareek (1996) have argued that in order to draw the best from employees, the following attributes need to be in place:

1 a high degree of entrepreneurship and global thinking;
2 cost-effectiveness and high performance standards;
3 quality-consciousness in products and services to match international standards; and
4 an emphasis on values that help kindle hidden talent.

They maintain that "performance appraisal systems have a catalytic role to play" (1996: 7) to meet the objective of putting these attributes in place. These authors also emphasize that to meet international standards, integration of quality into performance development has been a challenge for all Indian organizations.

Next, the confidential nature of appraisals and the lack of direct and obvious connection between one's performance and the rewards remain as strong de-motivating factors. Organizations need to establish transparent systems such that employees can see the link between performance and rewards, and trust the system to be fair to them.

With globalization and liberalization sweeping India, optimum use of money and machines has more or less been achieved. Technological developments have accelerated this achievement manifold by creating a global village. Competitive advantages are being actualized by outsourcing work and processes throughout the world. The major challenges before firms are to maximize employee performance and achieve the highest level of quality output. Perhaps this is clearly evident in the Indian BPO sector which is now maturing and where firms are having a difficult time retaining employees and consistently improve their performance (Budhwar et al., 2006). This requires an intrinsically motivated workforce in a more meaningful context, which helps them grow in self-esteem while simultaneously allowing for the growth of business enterprise. Thus redefined, the role of management clearly becomes that of a provider of correct and timely information about organizational goals, resources, technology, structure and policy. This would create a context that has multiplicative impact on employees, their individual attributes, competency and willingness to perform, goal clarity and sense of ownership, by the continuous participation of employees in work efforts and feedback, together with outcome and rewards, leading to higher self-esteem and greater involvement. Systemic support in terms of performance planning, coaching, feedback and a correlation between performance and the desired rewards or outcome thus would seem critical. Thus, a well-designed PMS which can act as a strategic tool for attaining quality employees' output, leading to their retention and continued association and involvement of both internal and external customers, which significantly contributes to the survival of organizations, should be the aim in the long run.

References

Amba-Rao, S. C., Petrick, J. A., Gupta, J. N. D. and Von der Embse, T. J. (2000) Comparative performance appraisal practices and management values among foreign and domestic firms in India, *International Journal of Human Resource Management* 11(1): 60–89.

Basu, M. K. (1988) *Managerial Performance Appraisal in India*, Delhi: Vision Books.

Björkman, I. and Budhwar, P. (2007) When in Rome . . .? Human resource management and the performance of foreign firms operating in India, *Employee Relations* 29(6): 595–610.

Bolar, M. (ed.) (1978) *Performance Appraisal: Readings, Case Studies and a Survey of Practices*, India: Vikas Publishing.

Bordia, P. and Blau, G. (1998) Pay referent comparison and pay level satisfaction in private versus public sector organizations in India, *International Journal of Human Resource Management* 9(1): 155–67.

Budhwar, P. (2000) Factors influencing HRM policies and practices in India: an empirical study, *Global Business Review* 1(2): 229–47.

Budhwar, P. (2001) Doing business in India, *Thunderbird International Business Review* 43(4): 549–68.

Budhwar, P. and Boyne, G. (2004) Human resource management in the Indian public and private sectors: an empirical comparison, *International Journal of Human Resource Management* 15(2): 346–70.

Budhwar, P. and Singh, V. (2004) Dynamics of HRM systems of foreign firms operating in India. Paper presented at the *Annual Academy of Management Conference*, 6–11 August, New Orleans.

Budhwar, P. and Sparrow, P. (1998) Factors determining cross-national human resource management practices: a study of India and Britain, *Management International Review* 38, Special Issue 2: 105–21.

Budhwar, P., Varma, A., Singh, V. and Dhar, R. (2006) HRM systems of Indian call centres: an exploratory study, *International Journal of Human Resource Management* 17(5): 881–97.

Chhokar, J. S. (2007) India: diversity and complexity in action, in J. S. Chhokar, F. C. Brodbeck and R. J. House (eds.) *Culture and Leadership Across the World: The GLOBE Book of In-depth Studies of 25 Societies*, Mahwah, NJ: Lawrence Erlbaum Associates, pp. 971–1020.

Gupta, R. K. (2000) *Requisite Organizational Design in Towards the Optimal Organization: Integrating Indian Culture and Management*, New Delhi: Excel Books.

Hewitt Report (2005) Salary increase survey, New Delhi: Hewitt.

Kakar, S. (1971) Authority pattern and subordinate behaviours in Indian organisation, *Administrative Science Quarterly* 16(3): 298–307.

Kapur, D. and Ramamurti, R. (2001) India's emerging competitive advantage in services, *Academy of Management Executive* 15(2): 20–33.

Parker, M. and Datta, R. (1996) Performance management system in Modi Xerox, in T. V. Rao and Udai Pareek (eds.) *Redesigning Performance Appraisal Systems*, New Delhi: Tata McGraw-Hill.

Pattanayak, B., Gupta, V. and Niranjana, P. (2002) *Creating Performing Organizations: International Perspective for Indian Management*. New Delhi: Response Book-Sage.

Rao, T. V. (2004) *Performance Management and Appraisal Systems – HR Tools for Global Competitiveness*. Response Books: Sage.

Rao, T. V. and Pareek, U. (1996) Performance appraisals in the new economic environment, in T. V. Rao and Udai Pareek (eds.) *Redesigning Performance Appraisal Systems*, New Delhi: Tata McGraw-Hill.

Rao, T. V. and Rao, R. (eds.) (2006) *360 Degree Feedback and Performance Management System*. Volume one, New Delhi: Excel Books.

Rao, T. V., Rao, R. and Yadav, T. (2001) A study of HRD concepts, structure of HRD departments, and HRD practices in India, *Vikalpa* 26(1): 49–63.

Saini, D. and Budhwar, P. (2007) Human resource management in India, in R. Schuler and S. Jackson (eds.) *Strategic Human Resource Management*, Oxford: Blackwell Publishing, 287–312.

Sharma, T. (2006) A comparative Audit of Performance Management System of selected banks in India and its contribution in delivering quality service to its Internal and External customers. Paper presented at 21st *Workshop at Strategic Human Resource Management*, March 30–31, Aston Business School, Birmingham, U.K.

Sinha, Jai, B. P. (2004) *Multinationals in India – Managing the Interface of Cultures*, New Delhi: Sage.

Sparrow, P. and Budhwar, P. (1997) Competition and change: mapping the Indian HRM recipe against world-wide patterns, *Journal of World Business* 32(3): 224–42.

Trompenaars, F. (1993) *Riding the Waves of Culture. Understanding Cultural Diversity in Business*, London: Economist Books.

Varma, A., Pichler, S. and Srinivas, E. S. (2005) The role of interpersonal affect in performance appraisal: evidence from two samples – U.S. and India, *International Journal of Human Resource Management* 16(11): 2029–44.

13 Performance management in China

FANG LEE COOKE

Introduction

Performance management (PM) is currently being promoted as a modern western HRM concept in China. This is in spite of the fact that performance appraisal (PA) practices have long existed in China with strong Chinese characteristics. This chapter first provides an overview of the human resource environment in China through a brief summary of the main characteristics of HRM and employment profile in China. It then traces the historical development of the PMS during the state-planned economy period and the ensuing economic reform period. A number of key characteristics and pitfalls in PA practices are identified. Some of them are generic in many parts of the world, others are unique to the Chinese cultural values. A most notable difference between the Chinese-style PA and that promoted in western HRM literature is the narrow focus of the former. The adoption of the western approach in China is further hampered by the lack of strategic orientation of many Chinese firms and the deficiency of HR skills to design and implement an effective PMS.

While a level of simplicity is inevitable in a chapter that is to summarize the PM practices of a vast country, this chapter avoids a broad brush approach as far as possible by drawing specific examples from primary and secondary empirical data. The primary empirical data came from the semi-structured interviews which I conducted during 2005 and 2006 with 64 government officials and civil servants at junior and mid-senior ranks from four large and medium-size cities in China. The secondary empirical data came from studies published in academic and practitioners' journals as well as scholarly books in both the English and Chinese languages. Together, these primary and secondary empirical data sets provide balanced information that covers organizations of different sizes and ownership forms, and different categories of employees and sectors. This spread of coverage is essential because these contingent factors may have significant influence in the way the PA system is designed, implemented, utilized and perceived by both appraisers and appraisees. For example, PA may be more widely used in government and civil service organizations partly because it is an established part of their HRM, but also because performance measurement can be more subjective due to the perceived need to emphasize the ideological dimensions and to the difficulties of quantifying performance level compared with other enterprises. It is these nuances that make the comparisons of PASs across different organizations and sectors in China more interesting and revealing.

Overview of China's human resource environment

Founded in 1949, Socialist China has less than 60 years of history. For the first three decades until the end of the Cultural Revolution in 1976, the PMS in China was highly centralized under the state-planned economy regime. PM during this period exhibited two major features in terms of its governance structure and substance of the personnel policy. First, the personnel policy and practice of organizations were strictly under the control of the state through the regional and local personnel and labour departments. Centralization, formalization and standardization of personnel policies and practices were the primary tasks of the Ministry of Labour (for ordinary workers) and the Ministry of Personnel (for professional and managerial staff). It was these ministries' responsibility to determine the number of people to be employed and sources of recruitment as well as the pay scales for different categories of workers. State intervention was also extended to the structure and responsibility of the personnel functions, including PM, at the organizational level. Managers at all levels were only involved in the administrative function and policy implementation under rigid policy guidelines (Child, 1994; Cooke, 2004). Second, jobs for life were the norm for the majority of employees in urban areas (Warner, 1996), regardless of the work attitude and performance outcome of the individual. Wages were typically low with only a small gap between each grade as a result of the egalitarian approach to redistribution. Monetary incentives and personal advancement were regarded as incompatible with the socialist ideology.

These characteristics were dominant in the PMS of the country because, until the 1980s, over three-quarters of urban employees worked in state-owned units (see Table 13.1). The situation of state dominance started to change in the late 1970s, following the country's adoption of an "open door" policy to attract foreign investment and domestic private funds in order to revitalize the nation's economy. Parallel with this economic policy, the state sector has witnessed radical changes in its personnel policy and practice as part of the Economic Reforms and the Enterprise Reforms begun in the early 1980s (Child, 1994). One of the major changes has been the rolling back of direct state control and the consequent increase of autonomy and responsibility at enterprise level in major aspects of their PM practice, including the wide adoption of performance-related bonus schemes to subsidize the low wages. These changes were followed by several rounds of radical downsizing in the state-owned enterprises and, to a lesser extent, in the public sector and government organizations, throughout the 1990s. This has led to a significant reduction of the state-sector and the radical growth of businesses in a variety of forms of business ownership (see Table 13.1).

Meanwhile, China's economic structure has undergone significant changes. Some industrial sectors have experienced slow growth or even contraction, whereas other sectors have seen

Table 13.1 Employment statistics by ownership in urban and rural areas in China*
(Figures in million persons)

Ownership	1978	1980	1985	1990	1995	1998	2000	2002	2005
Total	**401.52**	**423.61**	**498.73**	**647.49**	**680.65**	**706.37**	**720.85**	**737.40**	**758.25**
Number of urban employed persons	95.14	105.25	128.08	166.16	190.93	206.78	231.51	247.80	273.31
State-owned units	74.51	80.19	89.90	103.46	112.61	90.58	81.02	71.63	64.88
Collectively-owned units	20.48	24.25	33.24	35.49	31.47	19.63	14.99	11.22	8.10
Co-operative units	–	–	–	–	–	1.36	1.55	1.61	1.88
Joint ownership units	–	–	0.38	0.96	0.53	0.48	0.42	0.45	0.45
Limited liability corporations	–	–	–	–	–	4.84	6.87	10.83	17.50
Share-holding corporations ltd.	–	–	–	–	3.17	4.10	4.57	5.38	6.99
Private enterprises	–	–	–	0.57	4.85	9.73	12.68	19.99	34.58
Units with funds from Hong Kong, Macao and Taiwan	–	–	–	0.04	2.72	2.94	3.10	3.67	5.57
Foreign-funded units	–	–	0.06	0.62	2.41	2.93	3.32	3.91	6.88
Self-employed individuals	0.15	0.81	4.50	6.14	15.60	22.59	21.36	22.69	27.78
Number of rural employed persons	306.38	318.36	370.65	472.93	488.54	492.79	489.34	489.60	484.94
Township and village enterprises	28.27	30.00	69.79	92.65	128.62	125.37	128.20	132.88	142.72
Private enterprises	–	–	–	1.13	4.71	7.37	11.39	14.11	23.66
Self-employed individuals	–	–	–	14.91	30.54	38.55	29.34	24.74	21.23

Source: adapted from *China Statistical Yearbook*, 2003, pp.126–7; *China Statistical Yearbook*, 2006, p.125.

* Since 1990, data on economically active population, the total employed persons and the sub-total of employed persons in urban and rural areas have been adjusted in accordance with the data obtained from the 5th National Population Census. As a result, the sum of the data by region, by ownership or by sector is not equal to the total (original note from *China Statistical Yearbook*, 2003, p.123).

rapid expansion at different periods during the past two decades (see Table 13.2). In general, the weight of China's economic structure has been moving from agriculture and heavy industry toward the service sector. The growing diversity of ownership forms and business nature has different implications for PM as part of the HRM in different firms in China.

Historical development of the PMS

In line with the development of its personnel management system, the development of the PMS in China can be divided into two broad periods.[1] The first period was that of the state-planned economy during which PA for ordinary workers focused mainly on attendance monitoring and skill grading tests. The former was used as the basis for wage deduction and the latter for pay rise. Since wage increase was frozen during the Cultural Revolution period (1966–76), skill grading tests were in effect not carried out. In addition, personal character traits were used as part of the criteria in evaluating an employee's performance. For the professional and managerial staff (broadly classified as state cadres), PA was used primarily as a means for selecting and developing cadres and as evidence for promotion (Zhu and Dowling, 1998). In the early years of Socialist China, ideological and technical elites were promoted. However, during the Cultural Revolution period, political performance (e.g. loyalty to the Communist Party) and moral integrity were the key criteria of performance measurement rather than technical competence and output. Organizational leaders were not enthusiastic in conducting PA, partly because they lacked informative job specifications and performance indicators and partly because they found the exercise time-consuming (Chou, 2005).

The second period started from the early 1980s till the present (i.e. the period of market economic development). During this period, and particularly since the 1990s, PASs have been more widely and systematically adopted by organizations. For example, Björkman and Lu's (1999) study of 72 foreign-invested enterprises in China found that nearly half of them had adapted their western PASs to suit the Chinese culture. Ding et al.'s (1997: 611) study of 158 foreign-invested enterprises in southern China showed that "regular evaluation of individual employee performance and setting employee pay levels based on individual performance have become organizational norms." They also found that workers were receptive to individual-oriented PM and reward in order to maximize their income. However, it must be noted that performance review here is mainly used to determine pay. In fact, performance-related pay is the main method for setting pay rate in the majority of foreign-invested manufacturing plants where workers, many of them rural migrant workers, work excessively long hours in order to increase their wage income.

Lindholm's (1999) survey of 604 Chinese managerial and professional employees from MNCs in China found that they were satisfied with the western-styled PMS adopted in their company. They particularly liked the developmental approach in the system and were keen to participate in setting their performance objectives and to receive formal performance feedback. It must be noted that prestigious MNCs in China are attractive to those who have strong career aspirations and desire development opportunities.

Table 13.2 Number of employed persons at the year-end by sector in China*
(Figures in 1,000 persons)

Industry	1985	1990	1995	1998	2000	2002
Farming, Forestry, Animal husbandry & Fishery	311,300	341,170	330,180	332,320	333,550	324,870
Mining & Quarrying	7,950	8,820	9,320	7,210	5,970	5,580
Manufacturing	74,120	86,240	98,030	83,190	80,430	83,070
Electricity, Gas & Water Production & Supply	1,420	1,920	2,580	2,830	2,840	2,900
Construction	20,350	24,240	33,220	33,270	35,520	38,930
Geological Prospecting & Water Conservancy	1,970	1,970	1,350	1,160	1,100	980
Transport, Storage, Post & Telecommunication services	12,790	15,660	19,420	20,000	20,290	20,840
Wholesale, Retail Trade & Catering Services	23,060	28,390	42,920	46,450	46,860	49,690
Finance & Insurance	1,380	2,180	2,760	3,140	3,270	3,400
Real Estate	360	440	800	940	1,000	1,180
Social Services	4,010	5,940	7,030	8,680	9,210	10,940
Health Care, Sports & Social Welfare	4,670	5,360	4,440	4,780	4,880	4,930
Education, Culture & Art, Radio, Film & Television	12,730	14,570	14,760	15,730	15,650	15,650
Scientific Research & Polytechnic Service	1,440	1,730	1,820	1,780	1,740	1,630
Governmental Organizations, Party Agencies and Social Organizations	7,990	10,790	10,420	10,970	11,040	10,750
Others	13,190	17,980	44,840	51,180	56,430	62,450
Total	*498,730*	*647,490*	*680,650*	*706,370*	*760,850*	*737,400*

Source: adapted from *China Statistical Yearbook*, 2005, p.125.

* **Employed persons** refer to the persons aged 16 and over who are engaged in social working and receive remuneration payment or earn business income. This indicator reflects the actual utilization of total labour force during a certain period of time and is often used for the research on China's economic situation and national power (original note from *China Statistical Yearbook*, 2005, p.181).

Bai and Bennington's (2005) more recent study of the Chinese state-owned enterprises in the coal mining industry revealed that as a result of increasing pressure from intensified market competition, Chinese SOEs were utilizing modern PA measures as effective tools to enhance their management efficiency and productivity. Their study showed that whilst differences from western PA practices persist, significant changes were taking place in PA practices in China that depart from its traditional form.

PM also became a top priority in the management of government and civil service organizations since the mid-1990s, as part of the state's broader initiative of reforming its civil service function (Cooke, 2003). In particular, the "Provisional Regulations for State Civil Servants" was implemented in 1993 (hereafter "Regulations"). The Regulations placed great emphasis on the recruitment, performance appraisal and assessment, promotion, reward and disciplinary procedures in order to improve the transparency and efficiency of the personnel administration. The Regulations were replaced by the first Civil Servant Law of China which took effect on January 1, 2006.[2] The government officials and civil servants whom I have interviewed commonly reported that their municipal governments have adopted a type of "management by objective" scheme where performance targets are cascaded down from each level and reviewed on an annual basis.

Key factors influencing the PMS

A number of key factors influence the PMSs in China, mainly in the design of the performance indicators and the process of conducting PAs. While some factors are generic to PM in many parts of the world, others are specific to the Chinese cultural and institutional context.

The influence of organizational size, ownership and business nature

Variations in HRM practices tend to exist as a result of differences in organizational size, ownership forms and business nature of the firm. The same is true in the PMS in China (distal factors). For example, Chen et al.'s (2004) study of 100 enterprises of various sizes in the IT industry found that, compared with larger firms, smaller enterprises tended to focus on the individuals' quality and competence in their appraisal system, including attitude, work intensity, moral integrity and position, and neglect the evaluation of team performance or the quality of customer services. The study also revealed that employees in smaller firms paid more attention to the utilization of their competence, had lower demands for and expectation from the PAS, and were more easily satisfied and motivated than their counterparts in larger firms. In addition, appraisal outcomes in smaller firms were more heavily influenced by the subjective impression of the superior (rater), whereas the intervention of subjectivity was better avoided in larger firms.

Whilst sharing some similarities, the PMS applied to ordinary employees tends to differ from that for professional/managerial staff. These differences become even more significant between enterprises and government/civil service organizations. Generally speaking, PA for ordinary workers in China was mainly about linking their productivity and level of responsibility with their wage and bonuses in order to motivate them to work toward the organizational goals (see Table 13.3). This is in spite of the fact that an employee's moral behavior continues to be part of the appraisal in many state-owned enterprises. By contrast, results of PAs for professional and managerial staff, particularly those in government and civil service organizations, are often linked to annual bonuses and promotion. The state also has a much more hands-on role in designing the performance indicators for government officials and civil servants. In 1998, the Ministry of Personnel introduced a new PAS for evaluating civil servants (Chou, 2005). The scheme focused on four main performance indicators as criteria for assessing civil servants' performance: *De* (morality), *neng* (competence/ability), *qin* (diligence/work attitude), *ji* (achievement). Many organizations added another indicator *lian* (honesty/non-corrupted) to the four as corruption opportunities became relatively widespread amongst government officials and civil servants.

In principle, PA for all employees focuses on two aspects: behavior measurement and outcome measurement. These include the employee's moral and ideological behavior, competence, skill level and ability to apply skills and knowledge to work, work attitude, work performance and achievement, personal attributes, physical health and so forth. It has been noted (e.g. Chou, 2005; Cooke, 2008) that the importance of political integrity is now significantly downplayed by leaders in government organizations because of the need to have competent cadres to deliver government functions effectively.

Broadly speaking, PAs for ordinary employees in enterprises tend to be held on a more regular basis than that for government officials and civil servants. This is mainly because the outcome of the former is often directly linked to their financial reward and job security (proximal factors) (see Table 13.3). The methods of assessment/appraisal used for the ordinary employees in enterprises are also simpler, mainly between the supervisor and the individual being appraised. In some enterprises, the practice of "competing for the post" is implemented in which the employee who comes last in the test will be removed from the post, receive retraining before returning to the post and made redundant if he/she comes last again (Cooke, 2005). By comparison, annual PA (end-of-the-year) is the norm in government and civil service organizations. The PA procedure adopted is more sophisticated. It normally involves the initial self-appraisal, followed by a peer appraisal discussion meeting held collectively in the department as an act of democracy. Finally, the department leader will sign the form and submit it to the personnel department for record keeping.

Business nature, broadly defined, further influences the PMS. This is often the case across different departments within the same organization. For example, an observation shared by many government officials whom I have interviewed was that it is easier for heads of revenue-generating departments to get a good rating for their performance than those who are in charge of departments that are prone to public complaints no matter how hard they have worked and how much they have achieved. Police forces and municipal environment

Table 13.3 Key characteristics in performance assessment/appraisal practices in China

	Main characteristics for enterprise workers	*Main characteristics for government officials and civil servants*
Purposes of assessment (proximal factors)	Financial reward, job grading, job retention	Financial reward, routine appraisal, promotion and grading
Measurements of performance (proximal factors)	More quantifiable hard targets Effort (e.g. attendance, work attitude), output (e.g. productivity)	Hard as well as "soft" criteria Four or five norms *De* (morality), *neng* (competence/ability), *qin* (diligence/ work attitude), *ji* (achievement), *lian* (honesty/non-corruptness)
Methods of assessment	Top-down assessment, self-evaluation Tests to compete for posts – "last one in the assessment out" practices	Self-appraisal, collective/peer appraisal discussion meeting as acts of democracy, top-down assessment, bottom-up appraisal
Frequency of assessment (intervening factors)	Monthly, quarterly, six-monthly, and annual (end-of-the-year) appraisals	Six-monthly and annual (end-of-the-year) appraisals
Implementation process (intervening factors)	Relatively easier to conduct appraisal/assessment due to more specific purpose and outcome	More problematic to conduct appraisal due to less quantifiable criteria, more complex relationship with peers/superior, and organizational politics Greater level of subjectivity and intervention
Utilization of outcome (distortion factors)	Linked to financial reward Little link to training and development Little feedback from superior	Linked to bonus and promotion Little link to training and development Little feedback from superior
Persistent cultural influence v. adaptation of western HR practices (distal factors)	Harmonization, egalitarian norm More widespread adaptation of performance appraisal of western style as part of modernized HR practices to enhance organizational performance	Harmonization, egalitarian norm Less influenced by individualistic performance-related reward pressure More cautious adaptation of western HR practices due to sectoral and ideological differences
Acceptance of performance appraisal practices (proximal factors)	More receptive to performance-related reward due to job insecurity and the financial pressure of individuals	More resistant to performance appraisal due to greater level of subjectivity in appraisal criteria and intervention in process

cleaning and protection units are cases in point. However, interviewees also reported that municipal leaders are acutely aware of the need to "balance the situation" so that staff in the complaint-prone departments are not demotivated because their performance forms a vital part of the overall performance of the municipal government. Municipal leaders may intervene in the PA outcomes by rotating the top prize between departments (the leaders of which will be rewarded accordingly) or by offering some concessions or other benefits discreetly to those departments that are given lower ratings.

The influence of Chinese culture

PA is perhaps one of the HRM practices that display the most enduring influence of Chinese culture (distal factor). It has been widely noted that the Chinese culture respects seniority and hierarchy, values social harmony, and adopts an egalitarian approach to distribution (Hofstede, 1991; Takahara, 1992; Yu, 1998). It is a well-known fact that the Chinese respect age and seniority. In an organizational environment, this is often translated into the following assumption: older age → seniority → higher grade and higher organizational position → higher level of contribution and more value-added to the organization → higher income. Similarly, egalitarianism has long been recognized as a unique Chinese societal culture and continues to be used by some as a yardstick of fairness and equity in rewards, especially in the distribution of bonuses. It has been reported that those who were rated for the top prize had to share their bonuses with their colleagues in order to avoid jealousy and resentment. Employees have also been known to rotate the top award amongst themselves (Cooke, 2004). Since PA in China is often narrowly related to financial reward and promotion instead of training and development needs, these Chinese norms play a particularly influential role throughout the appraisal stages. The Chinese cultural norm of modesty and self-discipline (Bailey et al., 1997) is also reflected in the appraisal system because self-evaluation and criticism often forms part of the appraisal process and content, particularly in government and civil service organizations. In addition, Chinese employers tend to attach considerable weight to their employees' work attitude and the effort they have made in their work, often disregarding the outcome of their work. This norm is typically applied in the selection for promotion and bonus allocation.

The strong influence of the Chinese culture in PA has been confirmed by the findings of a number of empirical studies. For example, comparative studies on the PAS in Hong Kong, U.S. and U.K. have highlighted the fact that Chinese culture plays an important part in the design, implementation as well as the utilization of the PAS in Hong Kong (e.g. Snape et al., 1998; Entrekin and Chung, 2001). Hempel's (2001) comparative study of Hong Kong Chinese and western managers also points to the cultural differences between these two groups in their perceptions of PA and the differing emphasis they held on PA criteria. Similarly, Easterby-Smith et al.'s (1995) comparative study of eight matched Chinese and U.K. companies revealed that appraisal criteria in Chinese organizations focus not only on hard tasks but also on "moral" and ideological behavior. Self-evaluation and democratic sounding of opinions by peers and subordinates are the commonly used appraisal methods. Studies on PA practices in MNCs and joint ventures in mainland China further highlighted the tension between what is required to be effective in implementing the western approach to PA and the Chinese cultural tradition (e.g. Warner, 1993; Child, 1994; Lindholm *et al.*, 1999). Whilst the former requires individualistic goals setting, face-to-face feedback/criticism, and employee involvement, the latter respects age and hierarchy, values collectivism, and emphasizes the importance of maintaining "face" and harmonious relationships at the workplace (e.g. Lockett, 1988; Hofstede, 1991).

However, it must be pointed out that changes in cultural outlook are taking place in China, as mentioned earlier. For example, Bailey *et al.*'s (1997) comparative study of managers in U.S., Japan and mainland China found that whilst the collectivist culture remained pertinent among the Chinese managers surveyed, there was a discernible new trend for endorsing individual accountability and initiative in the Chinese enterprises as a result of transformational changes in China's economic policy since the late 1970s. Bai and Bennington's (2005) study also revealed that the Chinese cultural values did not impede the implementation of individual performance-related reward schemes, suggesting that the new materialism has overtaken traditional cultural forces.

Major challenges to effective PM

PM in China encounters a number of pitfalls and challenges, as it does in other countries. Some of these are universal, others accentuated by Chinese cultural values. This section discusses some of these issues.

Lack of strategic HRM, understanding of and managerial competence for PMS

An important element of a PMS is the alignment of the system with the strategic goals of the organization, because a fundamental task for the former is to ensure the fulfilment of the latter (Williams, 2002). However, the vast majority of Chinese organizations do not have any strategic goals, let alone cascading these goals to departmental and individual levels and designing comprehensive performance indicators based on these strategic goals (Chen, 2003; Yu, 2006). Moreover, the information system of many organizations is rudimentary and unable to provide adequate support to an effective PMS.

In the last few years, there has been much hype about the notion of HRM in China. Many HR concepts and practices were introduced as advanced western management philosophy and techniques, including PM, PA, management by objective, balanced scorecard, key performance indicators and so on. Not only have many personnel departments changed their title to HRM department, but also HR (personnel) managers started to apply these new HR concepts and tools to their organizations without a real understanding of what they mean and how they can be adapted to suit their organizational environment. An increasing number of organizations are reported to have adopted performance management schemes and implemented PA practices. However, the majority of appraisers and appraisees are not aware of what is being assessed and for what purposes. An important part of the PMS is to utilize the appraisal outcome to inform various aspects of the HRM, including career planning, employee training and development, job allocation and reward. Unfortunately, the majority of Chinese firms still lack a strategic approach to HRM, particularly in employee training and development. As a result, PA is often narrowly focused on reward (proximal factors) instead of utilizing the result to inform career planning and training and development (e.g. Chen *et al.*, 2004).

There is insufficient managerial thinking and skill in designing a PMS and conducting PAs. Discrepancies in performance measure criteria and standards often exist across departments within the same organization, causing grievances from employees when a similar level of performance is given different scores and financial rewards (Liu, 2005). A PM survey conducted by Deloitte Human Capital Consulting (China) in 2003 on 51 Chinese enterprises in a wide range of industrial sectors (cited in Chen, 2003: 28) found that performance indicators were designed by the senior management in 85 percent of the enterprises. Some 55 percent of the enterprises did not carry out due diligence in collecting performance data and made little use of performance information systems. Only 4 percent of the enterprises adopted a 360-degree appraisal system. About 55 percent of the enterprises gave feedback to appraisees on the areas requiring improvement and only 18 percent of the enterprises offered training relevant to appraisees in the areas that needed improving. PA outcomes were used for bonus distribution (by 88% of the enterprises), promotion, job reallocation or redundancy (77%), wage adjustment (49%), training and development planning (49%). Nearly 8 percent of the enterprises did not make use of PA outcomes at all.

PM has not been fully accepted by managers as an effective tool in managing human resources. According to a study conducted by Zhang (2005), who surveyed the managers and workers across the five subsidiaries of a large stock market-listed state-owned enterprise, junior managers appeared to be more conservative and resistant than workers in terms of implementing a new PMS, aimed at relating performance more closely to financial rewards. More specifically, whilst 90 percent of the mid-ranking managers believed that differential rewards would be more effective than an egalitarian distribution system, over half of the junior managers believed that differential rewards should only be implemented when egalitarian elements were also incorporated in the differential scheme. While over 80 percent of the mid-ranking managers believed that recognition and incentive would have motivational effects, only 12 percent of junior managers felt this was the case. By contrast, over half of the workers surveyed had a positive attitude toward performance-related pay, and only a small minority of 10–15 percent felt that competition pressure and distributional variations should be minimized. In addition, whilst 64 percent of the workers believed that their reward was closely related to their group performance, the rest felt that their reward had nothing to do with group performance. This indicates that alignment of goals and performance level has yet to be made at all levels within the organization.

PA seen as a formality

A related problem is that PA is often seen as a waste of time and not taken seriously by either the appraisers or the appraisees (e.g. Chou, 2005). A manager from a tax bureau whom I interviewed disclosed that he distributed the annual appraisal forms to his staff for them to fill in rather than conducting the appraisal and writing the comments himself. All he did was to sign his name on the forms without checking them and forward the forms to the personnel department for record keeping. "I am too busy to do all that rubbish, especially at the end of the year. I don't want to upset my staff by giving them negative feedback. It is just a formality we have to go through once a year. It is not real work." A common feature in the performance appraisal process is that appraisal outcome is rarely fed back to the appraisee in qualitative comments and is seldom used for training and development purposes (Easterby-Smith *et al.*, 1995; Chen *et al.*, 2004). This is in part because line managers are reluctant to provide negative feedback to subordinates in order to avoid causing resentment and resistance from the staff concerned, which may impede motivation and performance further.

Avoiding criticism of bad behavior reflects the Chinese culture of neutrality, which leads to the tolerance of poor performers, thus demotivating good performers. The egalitarian and neutral approach to managing workplace relationships further results in the adoption of a broad band approach to performance rating. In most organizations, a quotas system is imposed by the senior authority in classifying employees' performance in their annual performance review. For example, according to the state guideline for government and civil service organizations, no more than 10 percent of civil servant employees should be rated "excellent" for symbolic purposes, the same is true for the last category "unacceptable." This broad band system and the small differentials in prize awards do not provide sufficient motivational or punitive effect to enhance performance level.

For some appraisees whose wage is not related to performance, the incentive impact of receiving a good rating is so small that it falls short of being inspirational, to say the least. A mid-ranking civil servant (a department chief of a traffic bureau) whom I interviewed held this view, which was shared by some other civil servants interviewed,

> Our annual performance appraisal is a pointless exercise. It has no value at all. I was rated as the best employee of the year by my colleagues in the bureau last year, but I did not want to take the title, because the reward was so trivial and meaningless. I did what I need to do and what I think I should do, not because I want to get the prize. I feel more comfortable without it.

The lack of utility of PA as perceived by appraisers and appraisees remains a severe barrier (intervening factor) to the effective implementation of PA, particularly in the public sector.

Subjectivity

It is recognized that subjectivity exists in PA, especially for jobs the performance of which is difficult to quantify and measure. The impartiality and competence of the appraiser in conducting appraisal also plays an important part in controlling the level of subjectivity. Since the majority of Chinese managers have limited HR training and knowledge, the level of subjectivity may be relatively high when they use their own judgment, experience and preference in conducting the PA and distributing reward. On the one hand, certain types of employees may be rated and rewarded favorably; on the other hand, Chinese managers may continue to feel the pressure to adopt a broad band in assessing performance level and an egalitarian approach to the distribution of rewards in order to maintain workplace harmony.

A number of difficulties in PA were revealed in a survey conducted by Deloitte Human Capital Consulting (China) in 2003 (Chen, 2003). Many of the difficulties are related to the subjectivity in performance measurement (see Table 13.4).

An added dimension of subjectivity in PA in China is the way performance measurement criteria are set. As discussed earlier, performance measurement criteria in China tend to be generic, broad and focus on effort and behavior instead of/as much as outcome. There is a lack of individualized performance measurement indicators to reflect the specific characteristics of different posts. The five major criteria for PA for government officials and civil servants are a case in point (see Table 13.3). The high level of subjectivity is reflected in a sarcastic saying that is going around, "If the leader says you are good, then you are good even if you are no good. If the leader says you are no good, then you are no good even if you are good." This subjectivity encourages some people to pretend to be busy and cultivate their relationship with their superior to gain promotion.

Table 13.4 Difficulties encountered in performance management – survey findings

Difficulties in performance management	*% reported in the sample*
Some tasks impossible to be measured objectively	82.4
Performance indictors were not given by superior and/or goal design was not fully communicated with employees	49.0
Employees' perceived subjectivity and incomprehensiveness of superior in handling performance evaluation	43.1
Difficulties in breaking down further the goals of performance indicators	41.2
Lack of scientific methods in setting performance assessment indicators	37.3
Ineffective in helping senior management team to identify problems in enterprises	35.3
Lack of enthusiasm from employees in participating in performance management tasks	33.3
Others	11.8

Source: Adapted from Chen (2003, p.28).

Interventions in the appraisal process

Ironically, the biggest hurdle in making PA really effective is perhaps the adoption of the collective peer appraisal method. It requires colleagues from the same group/department to gather together to give a self-appraisal and to appraise each other's performance, including that of their superior, in a face-to-face meeting. The collective peer appraisal, known as "democratic life meeting" during Mao's era, is often no more than a show. It provides prima facie evidence of fairness and transparency in the process. In reality, peers are unwilling to say anything negative to others face-to-face as a result of the Chinese norm of saving face for both parties. They are even less willing to criticize their superiors for fear of revenge. For example, a mid-senior ranking government official whom I interviewed described one of their collective appraisal events as below:

> Everybody in the whole department, about 12 of us, was in the meeting room having this end-of-year self-appraisal and collective-appraisal meeting. It is an annual joke for us. When we appraised ourselves, we all said we had been performing adequately and had tried our best. But there was still room for improvement and we would like to receive more criticism and guidance from our leaders and colleagues in order to improve ourselves next year. We would then give one or two examples of very trivial areas which we have identified as targets for improvement. Of course, we were not going to disclose or admit to any major failures because, apart from being face losing, they would go on your personnel record. It would give others excuses for allocating you to a lower category for the annual bonus . . . When it came to the appraisal of our chief, nobody dared say anything negative about him no matter how much we hated him, as we don't want him to take revenge on us. But we had to find some negative points to say about him to help him improve next year just as a formality. After a long silence, I made the speech. I praised the leader highly first and then said, "The only shortcoming of our leader is that he worked too hard and did not pay sufficient attention to his own health. Whilst this self-sacrificing spirit is commendable, it may be harmful to our department, because if our leader becomes ill, we will have nobody to lead us. That will be a great loss. So I urge our leader to work less hard and maintain his good health, so that we can all benefit from it." Then everybody in the room nodded, "Yes, we fully agree," and then the meeting ended to everybody's relief. When we came out of the meeting room, everybody gave me a little pat on my back and whispered, "That's a good one. Well done!"

Similar stories resonate in my interviews with other government officials and civil servants. It is clear that fear of negative consequences of appraisal (e.g. revenge by the superior if criticizing his conduct, or reduced bonus as a result of self-criticism) is an important distortion factor in the PA process.

Finally, it has been observed that annual appraisal report writing can be a literary exercise for supervisors and it may be the supervisor's literary skills, rather than the civil servants' performance per se, that determines the appraisal results. "Moreover, supervisors were not held responsible for falsifying civil servants' performance records" (Chou, 2005: 47).

Conclusions

This chapter has provided an overview of the historical development of performance management and appraisal systems in China. It has revealed that some form of PA has long existed in a Chinese style, with a narrower purpose and a different focus in its content (e.g. moral behavior) than what is being promoted in western literature on PMSs. In recent years, PM as a modern western HRM concept and technique is being embraced unquestioningly by an increasing number of Chinese firms. It is now evident that Chinese employees in enterprises are becoming more receptive to performance-oriented rewards and welcome career development opportunities through the implementation of a PMS.

However, the implementation of a PAS in China is challenged by a number of factors that are generic or cultural-specific. In particular, Chinese cultural values seem to have profound and enduring influence throughout the various stages of the PAS. This is especially the case in government and civil service organizations where state intervention remains relatively strong and performance outcomes are more difficult to quantify. It is perhaps in this sector where PA is seen more as a formality and punctuated with a greater level of subjectivity, compared with the reward-driven PAS in enterprises.

In general, the traditional PAS in China is reward driven and tends to focus on the person and behavioral performance, whereas the PAS promoted in western HRM literature takes a developmental approach and focuses on the alignment between individual performance and organizational goals. Nevertheless, recent studies on PA practices in China have detected a discernible trend that an increasing number of Chinese organizations are adopting a western-style PMS. Whilst a total transfer to western practices is not found, or indeed possible, a unique blending of both modernizing and traditional forces are at play in shaping the new PM practices in China (Bailey *et al.*, 1997). The continuing trend of adaptation of western PM practices is likely to lead to further behavioral changes from Chinese managers and employees that depart from traditional Chinese cultural norms exhibited in the Chinese-style PAS.

Notes

1   Also see Zhu and Dowling (1998) for a summary of the history of PA in China.
2   The Civil Servant Law (2006) applies to the management of government officials and civil servants in other public-funded organizations. There were nearly 6.4 million civil servants and over 30 million personnel working in the public-funded organizations in China by the end of 2003 (*China Daily*, 27 April 2005).

References

Bai, X. and Bennington, L. (2005) Performance appraisal in the Chinese state-owned coal industry, *International Journal of Business Performance Management* 7(3): 275–87.

Bailey, J., Chen, C. and Dou, S. (1997) Conceptions of self and performance-related feedback in the U.S., Japan and China, *Journal of International Business Studies* 28(3): 605–25.

Björkman, I. and Lu, Y. (1999) A corporate perspective on the management of human resources in China, *Journal of World Business* 34(1): 16–25.

Chen, H. (2003) A survey on performance management in Chinese enterprises, *Development and Management of Human Resources* 12: 28–31.

Chen, M. Z., Wang, L. P. and Dai, H. R. (2004) Performance appraisal criteria and implementation in small IT enterprises in China, *Development and Management of Human Resources* 3: 36–9.

Child, J. (1994) *Management in China during the Age of Reform*, Cambridge: Cambridge University Press.

China Daily, 27 April 2005, New law approved to improve China's civil servant system, internet source: *http://www.chinadaily.com.cn/english/doc/2005–04/27/content_438023.htm*, accessed on 23 October 2006.

China Statistical Yearbook, 2003, Beijing: China Statistics Publishing House.

China Statistical Yearbook, 2005, Beijing: China Statistics Publishing House.

China Statistical Yearbook, 2006, Beijing: China Statistics Publishing House.

Chou, B. (2005) Implementing the reform of performance appraisal in China's civil service, *China Information* XIX(1): 39–65.

Cooke, F. L., (2003) Seven reforms in five decades: Civil service reform and its human resource implications in China, *Journal of Asia Pacific Economy* 18(3): 381–405.

Cooke, F. L. (2004) Public sector pay in China: 1949–2001, *International Journal of Human Resource Management* 15(4/5): 895–916.

Cooke, F. L. (2005) *HRM, Work and Employment in China*, London: Routledge.

Cooke, F. L. (forthcoming, 2008) Women in management in China – a study of government and civil service organizations, in C. Rowley and V. Yukondi (eds.) *The Changing Face of Women Management in Asia*, London: Routledge.

Ding, D., Field, D. and Akhtar, S. (1997) An empirical study of human resource management policies and practices in foreign-invested enterprises in China: the case of Shenzhen Special Economic Zone, *International Journal of Human Resource Management* 8(5): 595–613.

Easterby-Smith, M., Malina, D. and Lu, Y. (1995) How culture-sensitive is HRM? *International Journal of Human Resource Management* 6(1): 31–59.

Entrekin, L. and Chung, Y. (2001) Attitudes towards different sources of executive appraisal: a comparison of Hong Kong Chinese and American managers in Hong Kong, *International Journal of Human Resource Management* 12(6): 965–87.

Hempel, P. (2001) Differences between Chinese and western managerial views of performance, *Personnel Review* 30(2): 203–26.

Hofstede, G. (1991) *Cultures and Organizations, Software of the Mind*, New York: McGraw-Hill.

Lindholm, N. (1999) Performance management in MNC subsidiaries in China: a study of host-country managers and professionals, *Asia Pacific Journal of Human Resources* 37(3): 18–35.

Lindholm, N., Tahvanainen, M. and Björkman, I. (1999) Performance appraisal of host country employees: Western MNEs in China, in C. Brewster and H. Harris (eds.) *International HRM: Contemporary Issues in Europe*, London: Routledge, pp.143–59.

Liu, H. X. (2005) Who should appraise the appraisers and who should monitor the monitors, *Development and Management of Human Resources* 11: 40–41.

Lockett, M. (1988) Culture and the problems of Chinese management, *Organisation Studies* 9: 475–96.

Snape, E., Thompson, D., Yan, F. and Redman, T. (1998) Performance appraisal and culture: practice and attitudes in Hong Kong and Great Britain, *International Journal of Human Resource Management* 9(5): 841–61.

Takahara, A. (1992) *The Politics of Wage Policy in Post-Revolutionary China*, London: Macmillan.

Warner, M. (1993) Human resource management with Chinese characteristics, *International Journal of Human Resource Management* 4(4): 45–65.

Warner, M. (1996) Human resources in the People's Republic of China: the "Three Systems" reforms, *Human Resource Management Journal* 6(2): 32–42.

Williams, R. (2002) *Managing Employee Performance: Design and Implementation in Organisations*, London: Thomson Learning.

Yu, H. (2006) Performance management of the Chinese style, *Development and Management of Human Resources* 1: 34–5.

Yu, K. C. (1998) Chinese employees' perceptions of distributive fairness, in A. M. Francesco and B. A. Gold (eds.) *International Organisational Behavior*, New Jersey: Prentice-Hall, pp. 302–13.

Zhang, L. H. (2005) A case study analysis of the remuneration change strategy of a state-owned enterprise, *Development and Management of Human Resources* 11: 47–9.

Zhu, C. and Dowling, P. (1998) Performance appraisal in China, in J. Selmer (ed.) *International Management in China: Cross-Cultural Issues*, London: Routledge, pp.115–36.

Useful websites

http://www.aphr.org
http://www.chinaHR.com
http://www.ChinaHRD.net
http://www.china-hr.org
http://www.China-training.com
http://www.51e-training.com
http://www.800hr.com

Performance management in South Korea

HYUCKSEUNG YANG AND CHRIS ROWLEY

Introduction

Performance management systems (PMSs) in South Korea ("Korea" from now on) can be best understood in the context of the transformation companies have gone through in the nature of their relationship with their human resources (HR) and HR management (HRM) as a whole within Korea's institutional and cultural context. This has several aspects to it, including the underpinning and content of HRM, and PMS within it, and two critical junctions in time – 1987 and 1997. We deal with these in the following sections. As such, our chapter deals with the development, features and issues of PMS and factors that are evaluated to influence its changing nature. It should be noted, however, that all the dimensions of PMS are not included, but the typical features, issues and factors conspicuous in Korea are explored.

Brief socioeconomic and political background

Korean society is influenced by its Confucianist traditions and background. This impacts on national and corporate culture, management and business through values and norms such as hierarchical paternalism, kinship and collectivism (Rowley, 2002; Rowley and Bae, 2003; Yang, Chang and Song, 2005). Emerging from under-development, poverty and the ruin of Japanese occupation and the Korean War, the post-1960s Korean economy boomed and transformed from an agricultural to manufacturing success and at the same time experienced social development. Korea was seen as one of the Asian "miracles," although its underpinnings and sustainability have been challenged (see Rowley and Fitzgerald, 1996; Rowley and Bae, 1998; Rowley *et al.*, 2002). We step aside from such debates and note that Korea has emerged as a producer of a range of products from "ships to chips" in global markets, from particular forms of capitalism to the *chaebol* – large, diversified, family-owned conglomerates. The 1997 Asian Financial Crisis seemed to expose these achievements and structures as a "mirage," but the economy quickly recovered (Rowley and Bae, 2004). The post-1950s political background can be divided into two phases. Following a succession of post-war military and authoritarian governments, in 1987 political democracy was achieved. The state has remained stable since then.

Development of PMS

PMS developed within this context and Korean HRM, which was characterized as paternalistic and collectivistic with a seniority-basis of lifetime employment and tenure-based pay (Rowley and Bae, 2001, 2003). Within that tradition, appraisals designed to differentiate between individual employees based on performance and competencies were not a critical component of HRM. Employees were paid and promoted based on their seniority. In seniority-based schemes a pay template reflecting job tenure within the firm was used without individual differences being considered in determining pay. Starting pay slots allocated in the pay template were determined by educational background and job experience in the external labor market. Once starting pay had been determined, pay moved up a pay ladder as job tenure increased. Individuals in the same slot in the pay template were collectively paid the same regardless of differences in job performance and roles.

Indeed, it was feared that differentiation among employees would actually damage teamwork and the communal nature of organizations. Records on employee performance-relevant characteristics were only kept for the purpose of justifying managements' decisions and protection against litigation or internal grievances. Measurement of those characteristics may not have been accurate because they were rarely challenged. Those characteristics were typically judged and recorded by HR staff and the data were typically kept in HR departments. They were not fed back to employees. In short, PA did not carry much real meaning and was predominantly under the control of HR departments, not line managers.

The reasons that made the existing PMS less workable were two-fold. First, the internal constraints inherent in seniority-based systems – such systems could be maintained while companies rapidly grew and the average tenure of workforces was relatively short. However, if growth and expansion slowed and tenure and seniority increased, the burden of labor costs under seniority-based systems rose steeply and inexorably (Kim, 2005). Paradoxically, a common corporate reaction of halting recruitment makes little difference as these are actually lower-paid staff. In addition, it was argued that systems lacked motivational effects and flexibility required under a fast changing business environment with heightened uncertainties.

Second, external factors gave further momentum – the most conspicuous were the 1987 Proclamation of Democratization and the 1997 Asian Financial Crisis (Rowley and Bae, 2004). Authoritarian governments had suppressed workers in favor of management (Yoo and Rowley, 2007). Democratization removed major restrictions on individual freedoms and rights to organize unions, bargain collectively and take collective action were granted. There was noticeable growth in labor disputes and strikes, new trade unions and wage increases all increased (see Table 14.1). Workers' collective voices, combined with labor market tightness, were big challenges to management.

The other external factor was the 1997 Asian Crisis, which bankrupted the economy and many companies and led to much debate as to its causes and implications. The International Monetary Fund's bailout required some policy changes and companies were forced to cut costs, reform and become more adaptable to environmental turbulence. The Crisis made companies realize how vulnerable they were to environmental uncertainties as well as threats of heightened global market competition and to reshuffle their organizational structures as well as their overarching management views (Rowley and Bae, 2004).

As a result of these factors, Korean companies began to shift their management orientation toward being more individualistic, contract-based and more meritocratic, emphasizing performance and competencies. Some managers tried to orient employees' mindsets away from seniority by establishing new PA systems with performance central to their criteria and linking pay to performance. Pay-for-performance systems ("*Yunbongje*" or "Annual Gross Pay System") were adopted, especially by large companies. These are regarded as pivotal for changing organizational culture as well as managing HR in a new fashion. Accordingly, PA became an important underpinning element for a newly oriented HRM system. Data on the performance of employees obtained from PA began to replace data on personal characteristics (e.g. seniority, educational and social backgrounds) in making decisions about important HRM issues such as pay, promotion, training, and so forth.

Table 14.1 GDP, unions and strikes growth rates in Korea

Year	Growth rates of real GDP (%)[a]	Number of unions[b]	Number of strikes[b]
1985	6.8	2,534	265
1986	10.6	2,658	276
1987	11.1	4,086	3,749
1988	10.6	6,142	1,873
1989	6.7	7,861	1,616
1990	9.2	7,698	322
1991	9.4	7,656	234
1992	5.9	7,527	235
1993	6.1	7,147	144
1994	8.5	7,025	121
1995	9.2	6,605	88

Sources: Adapted from:

[a]Bank of Korea, *http:/ecos.bok.or.kr*
[b] Stat-Korea, *http://www.stat.go.kr/statcms*

Factors associated with the PA process

Distal factors

Legal constraints on employment practices are two-fold. One category concerns employee discharge, and the other concerns employment discrimination. First, the Labor Standard Act (1953 and its amendments) restricted management's discretion to discharge employees. This contrasts with "employment-at-will" in countries such as the United States. Under Clause 30 employers should not discharge employees, suspend them from office, transfer them to another job, cut their pay, or discipline them without just cause. Due to this legal constraint, management needed to keep employees' (particularly low performers) performance records for legal defense purposes.

Second, discrimination in employment is prohibited mainly by the Equal Employment Act (1987 and its amendments) and the National Human Rights Commission Act (2001). These laws do not have a substantial binding power yet, because the penalties are not large enough. Therefore, discrimination issues have not been of much interest among employers (or the public) until recently. However, those legal restrictions are expected to gradually influence the way management conduct and utilize PA, as they gain more binding power.

As for the cultural environment, traditional Korean culture can be characterized by several features: emphasis on relationships with others, collectivism, respect for seniority, attaching importance to just cause and face-saving, and so forth (see also Rowley and Bae, 2003; Yang, Chang and Song, 2005), although some aspects of western culture are becoming popular among younger generations. Nevertheless, Korean culture attaches importance to affective rather than calculative relationships. Koreans' emphasis on affective relationships is often extended to contract-based relationships, such as employment relationships. Although the nature of the employment relationship is transactional and contract-based, Koreans are reluctant to explicitly define the relationship as such. Combined with paternalism, this emphasis on an affective relationship in the context of employment relationships was expressed as employees showing loyalty to employers with little concern about how much they were paid, while employers took care of employees in return.

Korean culture has also been seen as more on the side of collectivism as opposed to individualism (Hofstede, 1980). To Koreans, collectivism tends to be expressed in the form of carrying out one's obligations and responsibilities toward the group they belong to, exerting one's efforts to keep harmony with group members, trying to minimize differences and maximize common interests among group members, and regressing themselves to the mean rather than distinguishing themselves in the group. Associated with a hierarchical order within collectivism, Korean society places much importance on seniority. Older people have authority over younger people. Although having weakened gradually, especially in private companies which have merit-based systems, seniority-based mindsets remain strong and widespread in Korea.

In addition, face-saving and just causes are very important to Koreans and much more important to older Koreans. Sometimes they sacrifice their real interests to a just cause which is thought to save "face." Those who attach importance to just causes and face-saving tend to be concerned about how they are seen by others. These cultural factors make PA implementation in the Korean context different from that in other countries.

The Korean economy and companies faced many challenges in the 1990s: markets globalized, increasing market competition; information and communication technology proliferated rapidly, changing ways of running businesses; newly developing countries with abundant cheap labor, such as China and the South Asian countries. All of these developments forced companies to change their competition strategies from those based on cheap labor to those based on technologies or skills. Korean companies needed to switch from low to high value-added sectors. Many companies reported that they changed their business strategies from growth-seeking to profitability-seeking post-1997. According to one survey of 686 members, the ratio of companies with profit-maximizing strategies to those with sales volume-maximizing strategies changed from 40% : 60% before the Crisis to 77.1% : 22.9% after the Crisis and 42.1 percent changed their strategies from the latter to the former over the Crisis (Korea Chamber of Commerce & Industry, 2001 in Kim, 2005). These environmental changes have driven Korean companies to think differently about their ways of managing HR.

Proximal factors

Changes in the business environment and business strategies forced companies to transform their HRM, especially pay systems, which, as mentioned earlier, was the most direct factor that encouraged PMS in Korea. *Yunbongje*, a significant shift from traditional systems, has been more rapidly adopted, with the 1997 Crisis a critical moment, as shown in Table 14.2 (Ministry of Labor, 2005).

Key features of *Yunbongje* include the notion that differences in individual contributions to organizational success are reflected in pay, that many complex components (i.e. base pay, various allowances and fixed bonuses) are merged, and that performance as outcomes rather than seniority or job tenure as inputs are more emphasized in determining pay. *Yunbongje* has been adopted in the form of a merit pay system in which a merit increase is added to the following year's base pay or a merit bonus system in which a merit bonus is not added to the following year's base pay. Some 15.7 percent and 13.8 percent of the companies which adopted *Yunbongje* utilized it in the form of a merit pay system and merit bonus system, respectively, while 46.4 percent utilized it in a combined fashion of merit pay and merit

Table 14.2 Adoption rates of *Yunbongje* around the 1997 Crisis

Year	'96.11	'97.10	'99. 1	'00. 1	'01. 1	'02. 1	'03. 1	'04. 6	'05. 6
Adoption rate	1.6%	3.6%	15.1%	23.0%	27.1%	32.3%	37.5%	41.9%	48.4%

Source: Adapted from Ministry of Labor

bonus, and 21.3 percent used just a simple gross pay system without any merit pay or bonus (Ministry of Labor, 2004).

Another critical aspect of *Yunbongje* is that it strengthens both the flexibility of pay by increasing the proportion of performance-linked variable pay and competition among employees by differentiating their pay; and reduces labor cost pressure from increasing seniority. This is consistent with a neo-liberal perspective advocating market mechanisms in which contract-based employment relations, merit-based competition among individuals, flexibility and economic incentives as motivators are emphasized. Furthermore, *Yunbongje* adoption has been supported and legitimized by the argument that such systems are a global standard in competitive markets. Of course, we can question this assertion both theoretically and empirically (Rowley, 1998; Rowley and Benson, 2002; Rowley, 2003; Rowley *et al.*, 2004).

Nevertheless, these changes in pay systems helped move PMS from the periphery of HRM decision-making to the centre in Korea by forming links between performance ratings and valued outcomes (i.e. pay). Critically, linking pay to performance heightens the consequences of giving and receiving high or low performance ratings, which in turn have several effects on PA (Murphy and Cleveland, 1995: 340–44; Rowley, 2003).

As far as the purposes of PA systems implemented in Korea are concerned, an administrative purpose is dominant, although these have been gradually extended to feedback and developmental purposes. Traditionally, PA had been implemented for the purpose of justification for management's decisions about personnel such as dismissal, since management were required to justify their disciplinary decisions with just cause based on the Labor Standard Act. PA began to be newly looked at as *Yunbongje* spread. Now individual performance needed evaluating and differentiating in a substantive way. This indicates that new merit-based PA systems have been adopted first to serve the pay-for-performance system. However, the fact that the administrative purpose (i.e. justification for decisions) is dominant implies that people tend to be very sensitive to PA outcomes, although complaints about them are not explicitly expressed due to Korean culture.

Intervening factors

PA is typically conducted on an annual or biannual basis. Most organizations that conduct PA for an administrative purpose tend to evaluate their employees' performance on an annual basis, while organizations implementing management by objectives (MBO) tend to do so on a biannual basis, one for intermediate review of progress and the other for final evaluation. Among companies implementing MBO, 60.9 percent set individual employees' annual objectives based on agreement between individual employees and their superiors (KRIVET, 2005). In another 22.9 percent individual employees' objectives were set by superiors after a discussion session with each individual, while in another 6.3 percent they were set solely by superiors. On the other hand, in another 8.8 percent individual employees were allowed to set their own objectives after having a discussion session with their superiors, while the remaining 1.1 percent were allowed to do so by themselves (KRIVET, 2005).

The main source of PA information is a superior's observation and judgment. PA done by superiors is the dominant form in Korea. Meanwhile, some organizations have utilized multisource performance evaluations. For example, about 29 percent of organizations with 100 or more employees adopted multisource PA systems (KRIVET, 2005). The outcomes of multisource PAs are taken into account mainly for promotion and individual development. With less frequency, however, they are also reflected in pay raises.

In most organizations, raters' motivations underlying their rating behaviors have not been paid attention to seriously, although the fact that a "leniency tendency" was prevalent has been recognized among HRM professionals. Typically, raters are not well motivated to evaluate their subordinates' performance accurately. PA is regarded as a "dirty" job that superiors are obliged to do, but with high costs in the form of time and energy involved in collecting performance information or harming relationships with subordinates.

Judgment factors

Most Korean companies adopting PMS have not paid attention to raters' abilities to evaluate accurately and fairly. It has been assumed the abilities to appraise performance accurately are somehow "inherent," which is a common myth (Rowley, 2003). Few companies have provided raters with training on how to evaluate. According to one survey of the top 300 companies in Korea, the lack of raters' abilities to evaluate appropriately was a problem to be most urgently handled for improving PA systems (SERI, 2002). Of course, equipping raters with such abilities does not guarantee accurate and fair ratings since PA is a goal-directed, not a neutral, behavior (Murphy and Cleveland, 1995). However, raters' abilities to appraise accurately are a necessary, if not sufficient, condition for accurate and fair PA.

Distortion factors

To understand raters' behaviors fully it should be acknowledged that rating behaviors are goal-oriented (Murphy and Cleveland, 1995). It should not be assumed that raters would appraise ratees' performance as accurately as possible. Raters are inclined to maximize their interests, minimizing their costs incurred. PA as it is supposed to be conducted in the Korean context is anticipated to incur high costs with low benefits to raters. As mentioned earlier, lots of time and energy would have to be invested on the part of raters to collect accurate information on ratees' performance, and affective relationships with their ratees (typically subordinates) and teamwork are at risk as a consequence of PA. Also, reward systems for raters are not designed to compensate for the costs they have to bear. Although supervisors' ratings are reviewed by, or added to, ratings of superiors in a higher position, those in the higher position tend to have limited opportunities to observe ratees' performance. In sum, devices to prevent raters from distorting their ratings in their interests are rarely found in real settings. The only device to try to do this found in organizations is a forced distribution system, which will be discussed later.

Main features of PA

Traditionally PA was not taken seriously and attitudes toward companies and managers, rather than performance, were the main focus. This was understandable because loyalty mattered in paternalistic, seniority-based management. However, performance and competencies have dramatically gained importance as criteria. According to one survey of a representative sample of companies with 100 or more employees, performance and competency were included as criterion in 48.6 percent and 31.3 percent of companies, respectively, while attitude was included in only 13.9 percent (Ministry of Labor, 2005). This emphasis reflects some shift in HRM orientation from paternalism toward meritocracy.

Meanwhile, in most organizations that intended to utilize PA in a substantial manner, objective performance measures are eagerly sought. With little credit for raters' abilities and willingness to evaluate performance accurately, and inherent favoritism, subjective performance measures were common. Complaints about PA due to its subjective nature occurred. HRM staff in those organizations tried to find objective performance measures as an alternative in the hope that they would contribute to clearing up the fairness issues associated with PA. Thus, some organizations have adopted MBO. For instance, among companies with 100 or more employees, about 52 percent had adopted MBO by 2004 (KRIVET, 2005). However, it is too early to say that fairness issues have been overcome in relation to PA in Korea.

As far as how to allocate ratings is concerned, forced distribution systems that represent relative evaluation systems were common among companies that began to utilize PA along with *Yunbongje*. Here fixed percentages of ratees for each grading mark are predetermined (e.g. S for the top 5%, A for the next 20%, B for the following 50%, C for the next 20%, D for the next 5%) and raters are forced to place ratees along them (Rowley, 2003). Along with a fixed budget for merit pay increases, this system was supposed to encourage differentiation of individuals' performance. A forced distribution system has been seen as a method of avoiding problems, such as inflated ratings, and has also been preferred by management since it was expected to stimulate and reinforce zero-sum competition among employees for the predetermined percentages of high marks. For example, among companies with 100 or more employees, those that used an absolute evaluation system solely were only 14.8 percent of those reporting that they implemented PA, while those which used a relative evaluation system solely or in a combination with an absolute evaluation system were 82.3 percent (Ministry of Labor, 2003). A relative evaluation system combined with an absolute evaluation is nothing but a relative evaluation system since in the system ratees are usually assigned to a slot of a forced distribution scale based on their performance scores on an absolute evaluation scale.

As for feedback, PA results were provided to individual workers in 37 percent of companies with 100 or more employees (KRIVET, 2005). As regards the way feedback is provided, a majority (50.9%) of companies which reported that they were implementing a PA system provided PA results to individual workers through feedback sessions with superiors, and 16.1 percent provided the results only to those who wanted to get them. Another 10.2 percent of them provided PA results through e-mail, and the remaining 22.8 percent utilized an e-HR system where individual workers could see the results. However, Korean superiors tend to feel uncomfortable articulating what their subordinates have done on their jobs against performance criteria face-to-face. Superiors may feel that teamwork and relationships with subordinates might be damaged if they articulate their performance and differentiate them based on their performance. Although they have to rate their subordinates for their business purpose, they would prefer not talking with them about their performance directly.

Another important feature of PA implementation in Korea is that the state-of-the-art forms of PA systems are struggling in the local culture. The original intent of PA tends to be outwitted by raters who still feel uncomfortable with meritocracy and its individualism. They live in a culture emphasizing seniority and collectivistic solidarity among group members. Therefore, PA has been an arena where these two different perspectives – seniority and meritocracy – clash. Meritocracy forced by new PA combined with pay-for-performance was strange to those accustomed to a collectivistic, seniority-based culture. Often compromises were made such that the high grades required for promotion were assigned to those who would have been promoted if seniority had been applied. In those settings there is an implicit mutual understanding with management that employees would be promoted in order of seniority. Thus, even though top management were eager for meritocracy to take root in their companies and expected raters to differentiate individuals solely based on merit, middle managers or raters tried to maintain positive climates in their workgroups by keeping a culture that members feel comfortable with.

In addition, combined with a traditional seniority-based ranking system, a face-saving culture encourages people to care about their titles on their business cards that show whether they have been promoted in a timely manner in accordance with seniority. Even though senior employees accept the changing reality that they could be outpaced by junior employees in terms of pay and promotion, they want their face to be saved among their family members and acquaintances. This is why some companies trying to replace seniority with merit-based systems still keep traditional titles, although they have become detached from employees' roles and pay, and try to prevent morale from declining by letting employees use their traditional titles corresponding to their tenure.

Key challenges facing PA

Companies face a big challenge with cultural fit. In most companies that adopted new PA systems the systems were used as a key to transform traditional culture to meritocracy. However, challenging and transforming existing culture deeply rooted in ways of thinking and ways of life is very difficult since there is very strong inertia. One risk for PA is in being defeated by cultural inertia. For example, it has been mentioned that raters and ratees collaborate to outwit management's desire to bed down meritocracy by giving high marks to those who are due for promotion, based on their seniority.

Korean companies that adopted PA without taking into account cultural influences need to examine what the relationship should be between PA and the existing culture rooted in their employees. Some features of PA might need to be adjusted to cultural features which could be functional in building up organizational competitiveness, with others designed to overcome existing cultural inertia. For example, management needs to think about whether collectivism should be overcome or utilized as an anchor for building competitiveness. Some features of PA in Korean companies, such as individual-based PA, forced distribution and merit-based pay, seem to have been designed to overcome collectivism. Yet, some commentators, such as Deming, a founder of the TQM field, advocate team-based work organisation as desirable, condemning individualistic merit-based pay systems (Deming, 1982, 1994).

Fairness issues tend to be mentioned along with the subjective nature of PA and rater favoritism in Korea. PA based on subjective judgments is considered biased and unfair. Combined with prevalent favoritism in Korean society, subjective PA has been assumed to be highly vulnerable to rater arbitrariness or intentional distortions in rating performance. One reason why companies have tried to find objective measures for performance lies here. For some people, objective performance measures are themselves just or fair, while subjective measures are unjust or unfair. However, fairness is not guaranteed with more objective performance measures. If construct validity of, and controllability toward, a measured performance is not secured, fairness issues would not be ameliorated.

Rating inflation is another major concern in Korea. Management worries that raters engaging in lenient rating can defeat the desire to root meritocracy in organizations. Raters have a strong tendency to give ratings leniently since low ratings can lead to resentment and perceptions of inequity while lenient ratings are helpful in maintaining or improving a positive climate in the workgroup (Murphy and Cleveland, 1995). This phenomenon is understandable if we take into account that raters' goals are not necessarily consistent with the organization's goals. For raters it makes sense to maximize their own goals and minimize the costs that follow when conducting PA, although top management expect them to evaluate accurately for the organization's interests. For raters the ability to maintain positive interpersonal relationships with subordinates might be viewed as much more important than turning in accurate PAs (Murphy and Cleveland, 1995: 248).

As mentioned earlier, companies in Korea have tried to tackle rater leniency problems by forced distribution schemes, which assume employee performances within a rater's span of control follow a certain kind of probability distribution. However, forced distribution can bring side effects (Rowley, 2003). First, it can damage teamwork while reinforcing zero-sum competition. Co-workers are seen not as team members but competitors from an appraisee's point of view. Second, it can deprive raters of motivation to upgrade subordinates' skills and performances across the board since they remain forced to differentiate afterwards and thus end up facing resentment from those placed in lower grading marks. Third, it can distract attention away from more important causes of inaccurate and lenient rating behaviors. As Murphy and Cleveland (1995: 215) pointed out, PA is "a goal-directed communication process in which the rater attempts to use performance appraisal to advance his or her interests." Thus, inaccurate and lenient ratings need to "be understood in terms of the rater's rational pursuit of sensible goals rather than being understood in terms of errors and mistakes" (Murphy and Cleveland, 1995: 242). From the rater's perspective there are many reasons to provide inaccurate (typically inflated) ratings and, more importantly, surprisingly few good reasons to give accurate ratings (Murphy and Cleveland, 1995). This perspective implies that inaccurate ratings need to be corrected mainly by aligning raters' goals with the goals intended by the PA system. In this sense, a forced distribution system can be an easy, not a proper, solution for the rating inflation problem.

Conclusion

We have presented an overview the main features and issues of PMSs in Korea and some factors which affected their changing nature and were driven by critical events, particularly democratization and the Asian Crisis (Rowley and Bae, 2004). According to one survey, 60.6 percent of the companies that adopted *Yunbongje* pinpointed the lack of trust in PA outcomes as the most conspicuous problem in relation to its implementation (Ministry of Labor, 2005). Another survey also showed that the most urgent task for merit-based HRM systems was to stabilize PA (SERI, 2002). PAs, which are supposed to be an important hinge around which other HRM functions, including pay, operate, have not received full credit in measuring reliable and valid performance outcomes in Korea.

The "fertility" of the ground for PA in terms of culture and raters' motivation and competencies needs to be considered. Merit-based PA needs to be reconciled with existing culture in an appropriate manner. PA can operate in an unintended fashion, being outwitted by line managers who are supposed to play a critical role as raters. In this respect, several questions regarding the relationship between PA and cultural contexts need to be answered. These include the following. What should the relationship between PA and existing culture in Korea look like? What facets of existing culture need to be changed by PA and to what facets should PA be tuned? Which orientation of PA might be desirable taking into account the cultural context in Korea? More specifically, is PA that stems from individualistic contract-based traditions desirable in Korea or are there other possibilities in the existing culture? These are not easy-to-answer questions. In addition to the cultural context, it is also important that middle managers who are supposed to play a key role as raters be trained and motivated to evaluate accurately and fairly. If some managers are not ready for PA, a meritocracy cannot be rooted in organizations. In that sense, PA in Korea would be said to still be in flux.

References

Bank of Korea (2006) *Economic Statistics System*. Accessible at *http://ecos.bok.or.kr*

Deming, W. E. (1982) *Out of the Crisis*, Boston, MA: The MIT Press.

Deming, W. E. (1994) *The New Economics for Industry, Government, Education*, 2nd edn., Boston, MA: The MIT Press.

Hofstede, G. (1980) Motivation, leadership and organization: do American theories apply abroad? *Organizational Dynamics* 9: 42–63.

Kim, D. (2005) Human resource management in Korean firms after the foreign currency crisis, in G. Park *et al.* (eds.) *HRM in Korean Firms* (in Korean), Seoul: Pakyoungsa.

Korea Research Institute for Vocational Education and Training (KRIVET) (2005) *Human Capital Corporate Panel Survey (HCCP)*.

Ministry of Labor (2003, 2004, 2005) *Results of Survey on Yunbongje and Profit Sharing* (in Korean). Executive summary report. Available at *http://www.molab.go.kr/*

Murphy, K. R. and Cleveland, J. N. (1995) *Understanding Performance Appraisal: Social, Organizational, and Goal-based Perspectives*, Thousand Oaks, CA: Sage.

Rowley, C. (ed.) (1998) *HRM in the Asia Pacific Region: Convergence Questioned*, London: Frank Cass.

Rowley, C. (2002) South Korea management in transition, in M. Warner (ed.) *Culture and Management in Asia*, London: Routledge.

Rowley, C. (2003) *The Management of People: HRM in Context*, London: Spiro Business Press.

Rowley, C. and Bae, J. (eds.) (1998) *Korean Business: Internal and External Industrialization*, London: Frank Cass.

Rowley, C. and Bae, J. (2001) The impact of globalization on HRM: the case of South Korea, *Journal of World Business* 36(4): 402–28.

Rowley, C. and Bae, J. (2003) Culture and management in South Korea, in M. Warner (ed.) *Culture and Management in Asia*, London: Routledge.

Rowley, C. and Bae, J. (2004) HRM in South Korea after the Asian Financial Crisis: emerging patterns from the labyrinth, *International Studies of Management & Organization* 34(1): 52–82.

Rowley, C. and Benson, J. (eds.) (2002) *The Management of HR in the Asia Pacific Region: Convergence Reconsidered*, London: Frank Cass.

Rowley, C. and Fitzgerald, R. (eds.) (1996) *Greater China: Political Economy, Inward Investment and Business Culture*, London: Frank Cass.

Rowley, C., Benson, J. and Warner, M. (2004) Towards an Asian model: a comparative analysis of China, Japan and Korea, *International Journal of HRM*, 15, 4/5: 917–33.

Rowley, C., Sohn, T. W. and Bae, J. (eds.) (2002) *Managing Korean Business: Organization, Culture, Human Resources in Change*, London: Frank Cass.

Samsung Economic Research Institute (SERI) (2002) *Analysis of HR Competencies and Trend in Korean Firms* (in Korean). Executive summary report.

Yang, H., Chang, E. and Song, B. (2005) *Exploring Korean HRM Systems that Fit in with Positive-Sum Paradigm* (in Korean), Seoul: New Paradigm Center.

Yoo, K. S. and Rowley, C. (2007) Trade unions in South Korea, in J. Benson and Y. Zhu (eds.) *Trade Unions in Asia*, London: Routledge.

Websites

Bank of Korea: *http://www.bok.or.kr/* (in Korean or English)

Korea Chamber of Commerce & Industry: *http://www.korcham.net/* (in Korean) or *http://english.korcham.net/* (in English)

Korea Labour Institute: *http://www.kli.re.kr/* (in Korean or English)

Korea National Statistical Office: *http://www.nso.go.kr/*
Ministry of Labor: *http://www.molab.go.kr/* (in Korean) or *http://english.molab.go.kr/* (in English)
Samsung Economic Research Institute: *http://www.seri.org/* (in Korean)

15 Performance management in Japan

MOTOHIRO MORISHIMA

The purpose of this chapter is to present a model of the Japanese performance management system (PMS), whose strength lies in its ability to support employee and organizational learning. Beyond simple descriptions of "lifetime" employment, seniority wage and promotion (*nenko* practices), and enterprise unionism, recent observers have begun to describe Japanese human resource management (HRM) as a system in which learning new skills and acquisition of knowledge are supported and encouraged. PM practices such as extensive in-house training and compensation practices that reward both employee performance and skill development, and other supporting HRM practices, broad job structures and employee participation, are often cited as components of the Japanese HRM system (for example, Nonaka and Takeuchi, 1995; Koike, 1992; Morishima, 1996). Embeddedness of these practices in labor market institutions such as long-term employment and enterprise unionism is also often stressed (for example, Aoki, 1988).

In particular, two aspects of the PMS are often described as the core of this learning-centered HRM: employee evaluation and compensation based on competence development, and extensive in-house training. Many have argued that the combination of the two has provided a PMS that strongly encourages employee learning and skill/knowledge acquisition, especially at the workplace level in offices and factories (Koike, 1991; Morishima, 1996, 2006). The first section of this chapter describes this traditional model and its historical development in detail.

Yet, as has been discussed by a number of researchers (Jacoby, 2005; Morishima, 1995, 1996), the past 15 years has been a period of changes in white-collar HRM practices in Japanese corporations. In this period, many of the treasured principles of Japanese white-collar HRM practices are said to have been either modified or replaced by other principles. Not surprisingly, two PM practices that provided the basis of the learning-centered system were not exceptions.

First, employee evaluation and reward practices have shifted toward an emphasis on individual employees' performance from an emphasis on employees' skill and seniority, leading to a larger disparity in pay among employees. This is a departure from past practice in which substantial pay and other kinds of disparity were regarded as undesirable for employee morale and teamwork. Individual performance, as opposed to team and corporate performance, is now used as one of the major determinants of employees' compensation and, consequently, leads to larger wage disparity and fluctuation (see Morishima, 2002). This emerging practice is often called *seikashugi or* "performance-ism."

Second, another change is Japanese corporations' slow yet steady departure from the "lifetime" employment system. It is now not uncommon for firms to hire a large number of mid-career workers as full-time employees and to outsource work that used to be conducted by regular, full-time workers, to external service providers. A large number of part-time, temporary and other contingent workers are part of everyday office scenes in most corporations. Most importantly, regular advancement through and happy retirement from the firm that workers had chosen to enter in their younger days are now an outcome reserved only for a privileged few. In the second section of this chapter, these changes are described with implications for the learning-centered model.

Finally, the chapter ends with a discussion of procedural justice in the new system, an emerging issue in PM in Japan. This issue has become critical because the modifications in the system of PM just described involve a shift in psychological contract for employees from that based on the long-term relational nature to that based on the transactional relationship between employees and employers. Previous researchers have often argued that the importance of justice and equity is likely to be heightened when similar kinds of changes in PM are introduced and the shift in emphasis in the psychological contracts from relational to transactional (Cropanzano and Prehar, 2001). The issue now draws a great deal of attention in Japan where the strength of PMS has resided, in large part, in employees' high commitment to learning.

The traditional "learning-centered" model

The traditional Japanese PMS is often called "learning-centered," since, throughout the system, employee learning and skill/knowledge acquisition processes are explicitly encouraged. Two components are most critical: evaluation and reward on employees' ability and competence development, and extensive human resource development embedded in long-term employment. Two aspects – employee evaluation and reward and extensive in-house training embedded in long-term employment – are most critical in this system.

Rewards: compensation and promotion

In many Japanese firms, employees are assessed and their pay and promotions determined by a scheme called the skill-grade system which, using a set of very detailed criteria, assesses each employee as to what he/she is capable of performing, not what he/she actually performs (Koike, 1991). Supervisory assessments of employee competence and potential (*satei*) play a crucial role in the evaluations process (Endo, 1994). In this scheme, employees' capabilities are considered to be formed on the basis of cumulative on-the-job experience and internal training, and, therefore, strongly related to their tenure.

The skill-grade pay system encourages learning over the long span of one's career in a corporation. Since there are on average seven to eight skill grades for an employee's occupational category and it takes a few years for an employee to complete a skill grade, advancing through the entire skill-grade hierarchy could take more than 25 years. A survey conducted by the Ministry of Labour in 1990 shows that out of approximately 6,000 firms with employment size of 30 or more, 79.6 percent used the skill-grade system to determine at least some portion of their employees' take-home pay. It is almost 100 percent for large firms with employment size of 1,000 or more. Most firms use this system to determine white-collar workers' pay as well as blue-collar workers' pay.[1]

Increases in compensation due to skill and knowledge acquisition tend to be small since in a structured learning environment where the main method of teaching is on-the-job training, employees do not have opportunities to try substantially different kinds of tasks in a short period of time. Moreover, the differentials are especially small for those employees who have not had many opportunities for annual increases (i.e. those with relatively short firm tenure). Some have argued that compressed pay differentials have positive productivity effects when work is organized to take advantage of cooperation among lower-level employees (Levine, 1991).[2] Mitani (1992) found, however, that in higher-level grades, there are a number of employees who spend more than 10 years in a grade, thus creating large differences in pay between those who advance through grades quickly and those who do not.

In addition to advancement in skill grades and increase in pay, promotion (here defined as movements up to a higher position in the authority hierarchy) provides another incentive for Japanese workers, especially for white-collar workers. Many firms require advancement to a certain skill grade as a precondition for promotion to higher positions (that is, to be promoted to the position of, say, section head, one must be at least in grade, say, A5).

Yet, an important characteristic with the Japanese promotion practice is the speed with which selection of candidates occurs. Among white-collar managerial candidates who started employment at a company at the same time in a given year (see the section on hiring for details), the first differentiation occurs after seven to ten years of employment (Wakabayashi and Graen, 1989) and even then the differences in authority between those who were promoted and those who were not are minor. For blue-collar workers, this period is shorter and is about 3 to 5 years. Until then, cohort members make career progress within firms without much differentiation in authority, a practice often identified as "slow progress" (Wakabayashi and Graen, 1989) or "late promotion" (Koike, 1993).[3] In one important study on this issue, Yashiro (1995) showed that this system is conducive to a variety of HR outcomes, including maintaining motivation of most employees as long as possible, upgrading employees' skills through fierce competition, and staffing flexibility through multiple skilling.

Finally, in order to maintain the learning incentive value of promotions, the practice that used to be dominant, and is still practiced by a large number of Japanese employers, is that firms rarely staff higher-level positions with external hires.

Naturally, there are downsides to the system just described. Most importantly, since the Japanese assessment and evaluation system has focused mainly on the input aspect of employee performance – skills and abilities – Japanese employers have not expended a great deal of effort to measure and evaluate employee output.

In manufacturing, which is often referred to as the economic engine of the Japanese economy, this may not be such a serious problem. In blue-collar production situations, where the match of the Japanese HRM and production system has excelled (MacDuffie, 1995), output measurement was easier and the criteria clearer. In contrast, white-collar employees' (managers, research and development workers, etc.) output is more intangible. In addition, for white-collar professional and managerial workers, the link between employees' inputs (skills and abilities) and their performance output is not clear, thus making it difficult to assume that better qualified employees are always more productive workers. Simply focusing on employees' inputs does not necessarily identify productive and effective workers. Output depends on a variety of other factors, including motivation levels, technology, and collaboration among team members.

Consequently, in white-collar situations, performance assessment is not easy due to the nature of the work, and, therefore, a substantial amount of investment is needed on the part of employers to increase the accuracy and fairness of the performance evaluation process. U.S. firms, for example, have expended considerable resources on the development of appropriate assessment tools for white-collar workers. Japanese firms have not expended similar levels of resources on this issue.

Thus, the link between employee performance and compensation has become weak for a large number of white-collar workers. The increase of white-collar and professional workers and the increase in their average age have started to present a major problem to the Japanese HRM system.

Long-term employment and HR development

If employees are evaluated on the basis of the development of their skills and competencies, it is important that lower-level employees be given ample resources (time, money, and opportunities) to acquire high skills and knowledge about work processes within the firm. As many observers have pointed out, in Japanese organizations, internal training and HRD are considered pivotal HRM functions (Dore, 1989; Koike, 1988). It must also be noted that this heavy emphasis on internal training is embedded, partly, in the context of long-term employment practices. With less of a threat of losing trained employees, employers are more willing to invest in skill development.

Among the researchers who have focused on this aspect of the Japanese HRD system, Koike and his associates most convincingly show the contents and the process of skills/knowledge acquisition on the job in large Japanese firms (Koike, 1988, 1992; Koike and Inoki, 1991). According to their findings, most Japanese firms place a large amount of emphasis on problem solving and decision-making skills for routine, and especially non-routine, problems in the operation, and systematically use OJT to train workers to handle progressively difficult non-routine operations.

In particular, acquiring skills and knowledge to solve non-routine problems prepares workers both for planned adjustments arising from changes in operation plans and for unexpected problems that occur due to issues with technology (e.g. machine malfunctioning) and environment (e.g. customer demands). Since jobs are structured broadly and flexibly with employee involvement in mind, there is much room for incremental learning on the job. Koike argues that, in the end, workers are expected to acquire the ability to detect, diagnose and find solutions for problems, an ability which Koike calls "intellectual skills" (1994).

While the previous discussion appears to apply mainly to production workers in the manufacturing sector, Koike (1991, 1993) has recently expanded his analyses to white-collar workers. According to his findings, the development of managerial workers in large Japanese firms is quite similar, in principle, to that for blue-collar workers. One major finding that is worth noting, however, is that, especially for white-collar positions, training is a long process, which might last up to 10 years, involving a number of assignments within a broadly defined specialization (Koike, 1993). Morishima (1998) found that relative to managers in the U.S., rotation to a few multiple-functional specializations (e.g. sales, HRM and accounting) is a common career experience of middle and senior Japanese managers.

Frequent job assignment changes are also used to develop organizational skills, which are required for coordination of work within a firm, across divisions, departments, teams, and individual workers. These skills are even more important in Japanese organizations, since, as noted earlier, broad job classification and decentralization assigns a vital role to "horizontal" coordination among individual employees (Aoki, 1988). Communication and coordination skills are considered just as important as skills related to task execution (Kagono, Nonaka, Sakakibara and Okumura, 1985).

As noted earlier, these employees for whom employers make substantial investment in skill development are protected in a long-term employment contract. This group covers both production (blue-collar) and office (white-collar) employees who enjoy relatively secure employment status and the duration of their employment contracts are "unspecified," meaning that their contracts are not short-term or limited.

There are at least three reasons why the core employees of large Japanese corporations – those employees who are normally labeled as "regular status" employees – enjoy strong employment security. First, Japanese employment security is firmly grounded in legal precedents set by the Japanese court, which has made it almost impossible for employers to terminate or lay off their regular-status employees without the employees' (or their unions') consent. Second, both long-term employment and employment security are explicit policies of the Japanese government. For example, the Ministry of Labour, using its unemployment insurance funds, subsidizes up to two-thirds of wages for the employees in companies that engage in temporary shutdowns of operations instead of layoffs or terminations. Third, among the bargaining goals of Japanese enterprise unions, wage increases have always been considered in tandem with the protection of employment security for the firm's permanent workforce. Japanese unions' accommodating attitudes in wage negotiations are complemented by their strong insistence on employment security for their membership. For our purposes, one implication of this union behavior is the creation of a core workforce that is more or less "permanently" employed by the firm.

Socioeconomic background of the traditional model

Pre-World War II legacies

The origins of the current Japanese HRM practices go back to the turn of the twentieth century when Japanese industrialization began to take off and economic and technological advances generated pressure for more effective employment arrangements (Gordon, 1985: chs. 2 and 3). Government-owned firms and leading private sector firms in the heavy manufacturing industries, which were then the target industries of the Japanese government's industrialization efforts, were suffering from excessive turnover approaching 60 percent a year and facing difficulties retaining skilled machine operators who could handle complex machinery imported from other nations (Shimada, 1992). In response, these firms began to offer such personnel practices as company-sponsored internal training programs and seniority-based pay increases and promotion, which were intended to train and retain highly qualified machine operators (Shimada, 1992).

Between 1910 and 1940, these "new" practices began to spread to other sectors of the economy due to a variety of organizational and institutional reasons. Most importantly, the surge of militancy in the labor movement in the *Taisho* era (1912–1926), the Great Depression in the 1930s, and the Japanese government's war mobilization efforts in the period leading up to and through World War II all accelerated the "rationalization" of employment in Japanese firms. Rationalization often meant the adoption of employment internalization practices.

Period immediately following World War II [4]

The ten years after the end of World War II in 1945 marked an important era in the development of basic elements of the current Japanese HRM/IR system. The most important of these elements was the formation and rapid diffusion of enterprise unions. With the legalization of the labor movement by the Supreme Commander of the Allied Forces, unions were rapidly organized throughout the country, with the percentage of paid employees in organized labor unions climbing sharply from near zero to more than 46 percent in about two years. Up until the mid-1950s, however, the strategies chosen by these newly-born unions were far from peaceful and cooperative. The labor movement, often led by radical and militant unionists whose agenda centered around social revolution, frequently staged prolonged strikes. Work stoppages averaged 4.6 person-days lost per 10 employees per year in this period (Shimada, 1992).

After a decade of labor turmoil, however, the tide began to change, thanks largely to the efforts of employers led by the prominent *Nikkeiren* (the Japan Federation of Employers' Associations). Initially, these efforts were focused on replacing the politically-motivated labor leaders with unionists who embraced more business-oriented unionism.

Then, as labor relations became gradually pacified, the focus changed more to the development of the HRM/IR system that would subsequently help the Japanese economy plunge into its export-oriented phase. Specifically, by the end of the 1950s, Japanese corporations, especially those oriented toward exports, began to show increasing concern with improving firm productivity and product quality. In the manufacturing sector, these efforts led to the development of now-famous quality control activities, worker participation programs, the lean production system, and the like.

An important consequence of this campaign for quality improvement was that it required of employees both a fundamental grasp of technological knowledge and a recognition of the organizational implications of their contributions. This requirement prepared the groundwork for the development of the PMS focused on continuous learning by employees, to be described in the following sections. In addition, substantial energy was also expended to strengthen cooperative labor–management relations, which, firms considered, were the basis for the newly emerging learning-oriented PMS.

Rapid economic growth up to the 1970s

The rapid economic growth period, spanning the late 1950s through to the early 1970s, provided the right environment for large Japanese firms to strengthen their HRM system based on long-term employment security and continuous learning. In particular, the rapid growth of the economy translated, in most cases, into rapid growth of the firms themselves. Thus, firms were able to reward their employees with promotions and substantial wage increases year after year. One of the major requirements of the system based on continuous employment and learning is that employees continue to be rewarded for their skill upgrading and that their motivation is kept high by hopes for better lives. Japanese firms, with their rapid expansion of sales both at home and abroad, were able to provide opportunities for promotion and annual wage increases that averaged 8 percent to 9 percent during this period. The growth convinced both employees and employers of the legitimacy of the system.

Yet, sustained rapid economic expansion and people's expectations for future growth were brought to a screeching halt by the first oil crisis in 1973. Yet, the economic recession triggered by this and the second oil crisis in 1979 worked to strengthen, not weaken, the PMS, since all the parties concerned utilized the system to its fullest extent in their effort to ameliorate the impacts of the recession. Expressly, the system was used to facilitate reallocation of workers within and across firms to avoid layoffs and to convince workers to accept moderate wage increases and employers' cost-cutting measures.

Period up to the early 1990s (or the burst of the "bubble")

As a result of these efforts since the end of World War II, the "learning-centered PMS system" that we will see in the following sections had come to occupy an important place in Japanese management. It has also become ingrained in Japanese people's values about employment relationships: "good" employers are those that commit to long-term employment security and offer systematized training programs and periodic opportunities for advancement in status and wages, and "good" employees are those who develop their careers within one firm and share interests and goals with their employers.

Equally important, over the course of this development, the Japanese PMS became closely tied to the vested interests of the participants as well as to the institutional rules of the society. Most important among these institutional rules is the legal framework that provides an enormous amount of employment security to employees and makes it almost impossible for firms to terminate their regular employees.

Changes in HRM in Japan

This type of learning-centered HRM system for the core, regular-status employees working for large Japanese corporations – the main beneficiary of the HRM system described above – remained relatively stable, with a few modifications (Nakamura and Nitta, 1995) until the early 1990s.

However, the circumstances that helped create these formal arrangements for managing core employees in large Japanese firms – often referred to as internal labor markets – have changed. Pressured by global competition, rapid technological change and, most importantly, by the high cost of labor due to the ageing workforce, many employers have begun to question the effectiveness of current HRM practices. While the current commotion may mean yet another revision in the series of adjustments to the Japanese employment system that have been occurring since the 1960s, two trends are visible in the current attempts: the introduction of competitive appraisal practices which emphasize individual performance and output, and the externalization of core, regular-status employees (see Morishima, 1996 for details).

Output-based evaluation and individual differentiation

This change reflects a shift away from basing employee evaluation and rewards on criteria related to seniority and ability development (Koike, 1994), resulting in an increasing emphasis on the more careful evaluation of employees' contributions to the organization, through such practices as performance-based evaluation and management-by-objectives. The change is most visible in the arrangements for the compensation of middle and senior managers, although a number of firms have also introduced similar measures for a range of non-managerial workers. According to a survey conducted by the Ministry of Labour in Japan in 1996, approximately 7.9 percent of large firms (with over 1,000 employees) have built some type of pay-for-performance criteria into their compensation practices. Another 11.6 percent are considering doing so over the next five years.

Moreover, if the sample is restricted to the firms that play major roles in the Japanese economy, the proportion of firms adopting some type of pay-for-performance scheme increases substantially. According to an unpublished report by Tsuru, Morishima and Okunishi (1998), in a sample of 450 large firms whose stocks are traded in the public stock exchange, 54.0 percent of the firms have some type of pay-for-performance scheme for at least some segment of their workforce. The proportions are even higher for larger firms (65.8% in the employment >5,000 category) and among manufacturing firms (61.0%). The survey was conducted in June and July 1997.

As a result of these changes, employees are evaluated on the basis of both performance and ability/competence. A survey conducted by the Fuji Research Institute in 1998 suggests that firms assign approximately 40 percent of the weight to performance and about 25 percent to 26 percent to ability/competence. Use of ability/competence and performance in employee evaluation is one major characteristic of the Japanese PMS.

Another practice that is becoming more and more accepted is to assign employees early in their career with the firm to managerial and supervisory positions. This finding goes against the accepted practice that formal status differentiation among employees in the same cohort (defined by year of entry and occupational grouping) occurs only after 7 to 10 years of en masse advancement with little individual differentiation. This approach to promotion and employee advancement was considered necessary for careful screening of employees with managerial talent.

Two surveys conducted six years apart suggest that the timing at which firms introduce status differentiation may now be occurring earlier in employees' careers than previously was the case. In a Ministry of Labour survey conducted in 1987, more than 20 percent of firms reported introducing status and large pay differentials more than 10 years after the cohort entered the firm. Another 40 percent introduced such differentials after the cohort had been employed for 5 to 10 years. In a Japan Institute of Labour (currently, the Japan Institute of Labour Policy and Training or JILPT) survey conducted in 1997, the proportion of firms introducing such differentials after 10 years dropped to 7.6 percent. Similarly, the proportion of firms introducing differentials after the cohort had been employed 5 to 10 years dropped to 33.1 percent. In this survey, the largest proportion of firms (46.3%) reported that they would introduce large status and pay differentials after the cohort had been employed for three to five years. The same survey also indicates that these "early career" differentials are introduced on the basis of employees' potential and current performance. As noted earlier, these changes are called a move toward *Seikashugi*.

As a result of these changes, employees' salary differentials have begun to become larger. Using a 2005 JILPT corporate survey,[5] it is clear by looking at the results (not shown) of the logistic regression analysis where the controls were industry and size that both systematic and operational differentials are higher in companies that had introduced *Seikashugi* than in those that had not. Statistical analysis also confirms the accuracy of the general opinion that "*Seikashugi* increases the wage differential."[6]

Externalization of regular-status, core employees

The externalization of employment has been proceeding in Japan in a manner similar to that found in other industrialized nations. In particular, Japanese firms have begun to externalize core employees' positions not only through the increased use of part-time and temporary employees (Osawa and Kingston, 1996), but also by hiring limited-contract employees and sorting current employees into categories that have different levels of employment security. The goal has been to introduce mobility and to obtain a better match between employees and jobs. This goal is accomplished by reducing the likelihood of long-term employment and by giving both employees and employers more autonomy in choosing the "right" partners.

Some Japanese firms have also begun to utilize a variety of devices to sort core workers into employment categories with different levels of employment protection. According to surveys conducted by the Ministry of Labour in 1990 and 1996, the number of firms offering multiple-career tracks increased from 6.3 percent in 1990 to 11.5 percent in 1996. Firms having employees "retire" from managerial positions at a pre-set age increased from 11.8 percent to 15.8 percent during the same period. Finally, "specialist" career tracks were used in 19.9 percent of the firms in 1996, compared to 16.2 percent in 1990. "Specialists" usually enjoy less employment protection and their career tracks often have lower ceilings.

Also, many firms have started to remove their senior employees from their workforce permanently. Japanese firms often use *shukko* and *tenseki* to remove redundant workers from the company payroll. Some transfer destinations are affiliated in terms of capital or business transactions; others have no such affiliation (Sato, 1996). With *shukko*, employees are temporarily lent to other companies. With *tenseki*, their official employment status is permanently changed and they become employees of the receiving firms. Strategies to remove senior employees range from early voluntary retirement to aggressive outplacement counseling (called *Katatataki*). As a result of these approaches, Japanese core workers now find themselves in various places along the continuum from being strongly protected to being weakly protected.

In addition, there is some indication that many Japanese employers are reducing their emphasis on internal development of their employees. For example, the JILPT survey in 2005 indicates that only about 58 percent of the responding firms "have viewed employee development as a very important HRM activity" during the past five years. In addition, there is a great deal of anecdotal and statistical evidence that on-the-job training in Japanese workplaces has become weaker. For example, Ministry of Health, Welfare and Labour surveys indicate that programmed OJT was conducted in 42 percent of the workplaces in 2002. In 1993, the same proportion was 74 percent (Morishima, 2006).

Rising concern with procedural justice

Overall, the diffusion of increasingly competitive reward practices and the use of externalized employment arrangements represent attempts by Japanese employers to gain flexibility in employment systems and to control costs with regard to the management of their core employees. Consequently, performance management of Japanese white-collar and professional workers has become a lot more focused on their performance (output) with an expectation of short(er)-term relationships with one's employers.

As a result of these changes, the psychological contract between Japanese employees and employers has shifted from relational to transactional (Rousseau and Schalk, 2000). The employee–employer linkage that existed in the learning-centered system is of a relational nature and the new emerging model is of a transactional nature.

It is often claimed that under this type of shift in psychological contract from relational to transactional system-wide change, employees become much more concerned with the procedural equity with which their employers' PMS is operated (Cropanzano and Perhar, 2001). This is because in relational contracts, the balance between employee contribution and reward is established over a much longer period of time. Thus, when relational contracts are in place, employees tend to be less concerned with the fairness and equity of each transaction. When transactional relationships are in place, in contrast, employees tend to be concerned with justice and equity in every employee–employer transaction and, therefore, tend to pay much more attention to procedural justice they perceive in the performance management system.

Japanese performance management also seems to be going through such a transformation. Results shown in Table 15.1 indicate that procedural justice is likely to be a main factor in maintaining the traditional strength of high employee motivation while meeting the new challenges that demand flexibility in human resource management.[7] Thus, the acceptance and continued effectiveness of the new PMS in Japanese corporations are likely to depend on how employers respond to this increasing concern with procedural justice.

Yet, available evidence suggests that Japanese employers have not responded to these increasing demands by employees very well. Another JILPT survey conducted in 2005 asked about the extent to which firms have introduced personnel practices for fair evaluation of employee performance and disclosure of information regarding employee evaluation. Results in Table 15.2 show that only about 56 percent of the employers in the overall sample have introduced at least two of these measures and about 67 percent even in the sample of firms with *Seikashugi* in place.

Also, another question in this survey that asked about so-called "360-degree evaluation"

Table 15.1 Employee demand for procedural fairness in evaluation practices in Japan: % of managers wanting fair procedures (N=2,699)

	Have Your Evaluations Become More Performance-Based?	
	Yes	No
% of managers who want criteria for employee evaluation to be disclosed	63.9%	56.8%
% of managers who want opportunities to discuss evaluation results with their bosses	63.1%	56.0%

Source: Adapted from JILPT Survey, 2005

Table 15.2 Proportion of firms with practices intended to increase performance evaluation fairness in Japan

	Proportion of "being implemented" (%)		
Did your company introduce the following measures concerning employee assessment?	Total (N=2,699)	Introduction of *Seikashugi* (N=1,526)	Others (N=1,173)
1) Management-by-objectives system	64.1	65.2	34.8
2) Disclosure of assessment results to the person in question	48.4	60.0	40.0
3) Assessor training	49.4	55.8	44.2
4) Implemented at least two of the above-mentioned measures	55.9	66.6	33.4

Source: Adapted from JILPT workers' survey, 2005

indicates that this practice is adopted by only about 6 percent of the responding firms (not shown in Table 15.2). The proportion is 8.0 percent for employees with *Seikashugi* in place. While 360-degree assessment is not conducted solely for the purpose of increasing assessment fairness, the result indicates that Japanese employers have not adopted this option, either.

Finally, another major component of a fair evaluation system is the mechanism for handling appeals and complaints. When employees have a way in which to voice their discontent with the outcome of their evaluation, it is more likely that employees will see the evaluation system as being fair. The JILPT survey shows that only 11.1 percent of the responding firms have established a formal system for employees to file complaints regarding his or her evaluation. The figure is slightly higher at 16.1 percent when the sample is restricted to firms with *Seikashugi* in place.

These findings indicate that only a small number of firms provide formal mechanisms to handle complaints, and that dissatisfaction with evaluation outcome is handled through informal interactions with one's supervisors. Another indication that complaints regarding evaluation outcomes are handled interpersonally through face-to-face interaction may be the extremely limited use of formal mechanisms by managers. In the employee survey of the JILPT study, only about 3.6 percent of those respondents who said that their firms had a formal mechanism for handling complaints regarding evaluation (N=282) report that they have ever used the system. Japanese employers are still a long way from establishing practices for procedural justice in the new PMS to their employees' satisfaction.

Conclusions

The above discussion leads to four conclusions. First, the traditional Japanese PMS may best be described as focusing on encouraging employee organizational learning, especially with regard to core, long-term employees. In sum, the Japanese PMS has been a unique combination of appraisal based on ability/competence development and extensive in-house human capital development embedded in employers' commitment to long-term employment. This has, in turn, enabled Japanese employers to gain competitiveness, particularly in manufacturing.

Second, faced with globalization of the economy, an ageing workforce and other changes in the competitive environment, Japanese firms have started to place more emphasis on the current contribution and output of employees to the firm when evaluating and rewarding them. Similarly, they have also sought for ways to increase flexibility in employment by relaxing the unwritten rule of "lifetime employment" and bringing in more flexibility in the employment arrangements.

Third, as a result, the importance of having mechanisms that appeared to increase procedural fairness has increased. As has been the case in many other countries, short(er)-term transactional relationships have emerged in the Japanese PMS, making procedural justice one of the major concerns when employers want to maintain the strength of the system.

Fourth, Japanese firms have responded to some extent by instituting ways of disclosing to their managers information on the evaluation processes and outcomes, but its extent is still limited. For example, complaints and dissatisfaction regarding evaluation results are more likely to be dealt with through informal interaction with superiors than through formal mechanisms. While the importance of interactional justice (Folger and Cropanzano, 1998) will not become smaller, there will be a larger demand for HRM practices as the main mechanisms by which employees and managers resolve dissatisfaction with the outcomes of their appraisals and maintain the high motivation levels of Japanese workplaces. Japanese employers must respond to such employee demand, or they are likely to lose the high employee motivation and commitment that they have utilized so far as the basis of their competitive strength.

Further information

Further and current information regarding Japanese PMSs may be found in the publications by the Japan Institute of Labour Policy and Training (JILPT), a research agency funded by the Ministry of Health, Labour and Welfare. It continually publishes numerous research reports and policy papers on Japanese labor and human resource management issues both in Japanese and English. Its flagship English-language journal entitled *The Japan Labor Review* is published four times a year with the purpose of providing information on Japanese labor issues to a broad range of overseas readers. The organization's website may be found at *http://www.jil.go.jp/*.

Notes

1 As Koike (1988) notes, Japan is rather unique in that even unionized production workers are subject to merit assessments conducted by supervisors.
2 The negative effects include the relative lack of reward for those who are capable of learning more quickly and of contributing more to the organization than others.
3 Wakabayashi and Graen (1989), however, reveal that during this period of no apparent differentiation, large amounts of data are accumulated on individual employees. These data are used to determine who will be chosen to advance in the firm in the later stages of careers.
4 This section draws heavily on Shimada (1992: 270–79).
5 This survey, which will be used throughout the remainder of this chapter, is described in detail in JILPT (2005).
6 Refer to JILPT (2005), pp. 153–4. These facts support all three requirements for *Seikashugi* as introduced by Okunishi (2001).
7 More evidence may be found in Tatsumichi and Morishima (2007).

References

Aoki, M. (1988) *Information, Incentives, and Bargaining in the Japanese Economy*, New York: Cambridge University Press.

Cropanzano, R. and Prehar, C. A. (2001) Emerging justice concerns in an era of changing psychological contracts, in R. Cropanzano (ed.) *Justice in the Workplace* 2: 245–69.

Dore, R. P. (1989) Where we are now: musings of an evolutionist, *Work, Employment and Society* 3: 425–46.

Endo, K. (1994) Satei (personal assessment) and interworker competition in Japanese firms, *Industrial Relations* 33: 70–82.

Folger, R. and Cropanzano, R. (1998) *Organizational Justice and Human Resource Management*, Thousand Oaks, CA: Sage.

Gordon, Andrew (1985) *The Evolution of Labor Relations in Japan: Heavy Industry, 1853–1955*, Cambridge, MA: Harvard East Asian Monographs.

Jacoby, Sanford M. (2005) *The Embedded Corporation: Corporate Governance and Employment Relations in Japan and the United States*, Oxford: Oxford University Press.

The Japan Institute of Labour Policy and Training (2005) *Transforming Human Resource Management and Governance/Corporate Strategies*, JILPT Research Report No. 33 (in Japanese).

Kagono, T., Nonaka, I., Sakakibara, K. and Okumura, A. (1985) *Strategic vs Evolutionary Management: A U.S.–Japan Comparison of Strategy and Organisation*, Amsterdam: North Holland.

Koike, K. (1988) *Understanding Industrial Relations in Modern Japan*, London: Macmillan.

Koike, K. (ed.) (1991) *Human Resource Development of White-Collar Employees*, Tokyo: Toyo Keizai (in Japanese).

Koike, K. (1992) Human resource development and labor-management relations, in K. Yamamura and Y. Yasuba (eds.) *The Political Economy of Japan, Volume 1: The Domestic Transformation*, pp. 289–330, Stanford: Stanford University Press.

Koike, K. (1993) Human resource development among college graduates in sales and marketing, in K. Koike (ed.), *An International Comparison of Professionals and Managers*, JIL Report No. 2, pp. 42–64, Tokyo: Japan Institute of Labour (in Japanese).

Koike, K. (1994) Learning and incentive systems in Japanese industry, in Aoki Masahiko and Ronald Dore (eds.) *The Japanese Firm: Sources of Competitive Strength*, New York and Oxford: Oxford University Press, pp. 41–65.

Koike, K. and Inoki, T. (1991) *Skill Formation in Japan and Southeast Asia*, Tokyo: University of Tokyo Press.

Levine, D. I. (1991) Cohesiveness, productivity, and wage dispersion, *Journal of Economic Behavior and Organization* 15: 237–55.

MacDuffie, J. P. (1995) Human resource bundles and manufacturing performance: organizational logic and flexible production systems in the world auto industry, *Industrial and Labor Relations Review* 48: 197–221.

Ministry of Labour (1987) *Prospects on Changes in Japanese Employment Practices: A Survey Report*, Tokyo: Ministry of Finance Printing Office (in Japanese).

Ministry of Labour (1990) *Comprehensive Survey on Pay and Working Hours*, Tokyo: Ministry of Finance Printing Office (in Japanese).

Ministry of Labour (1996) *Shuro Joken Sogo Chosa* [Comprehensive Surveys of Work Conditions], Tokyo: Ministry of Labour (in Japanese).

Mitani, N. (1992) Job- and ability-based pay structure, in T. Tachibanaki (ed.) *Assessment, Promotions and Pay Determination*, pp. 109–36, Tokyo: Yuhikaku Publishing (in Japanese).

Morishima, M. (1995) Embedding HRM in a social context, *British Journal of Industrial Relations* 33: 617–40.

Morishima, M. (1996) Evolution of white-collar HRM in Japan, in David Lewin, Bruce E. Kaufman and Donna Sockell (eds.) *Advances in Industrial and Labor Relations*, Vol. 7, Greenwich, CT: JAI Press, pp. 145–76.

Morishima, M. (1998) Career development of Japanese and U.S. managers: differences in "Career Breadth", Working Paper, Faculty of Policy Management, Keio University, Fujisawa.

Morishima, M. (2002) Pay practices in Japanese organizations: changes and non-changes, *Japan Labour Bulletin* 41(4): 8–13.

Morishima, M. (2006) Evolution of white-collar HRM in Japan: an update, in H. Itami, H. Fujimoto, T. Okazaki, H. Ito and T. Numagami (eds.) *Japanese Corporate System: Readings*, Vol. 4, Tokyo: Yuhikaku Press, pp. 269–303 (in Japanese).

Nakamura, K. and Nitta, M. (1995) Developments in industrial relations and human resource practices in Japan, in Richard Locke, Thomas Kochan and Michael Piore (eds.) *Employment Relations in the Changing World Economy*, Cambridge, MA: MIT Press, pp. 325–58.

Nonaka, I. and Takeuchi, H. (1995) *The Knowledge-Creating Company*, Oxford and New York: Oxford University Press.

Okunishi, Y. (2001) Conditions for the introduction of "performance-based" wages, *Organizational Science* 34 (3): 6–17.

Osawa, M. and Kingston, J. (1996) Flexibility and inspiration: restructuring and the Japanese Labor Market, *Japan Labor Bulletin*, January 1: 4–8.

Rousseau, D. M. and Schalk, R. (eds.) (2000) *Psychological Contracts in Employment: Cross-National Perspectives*, Thousand Oaks, CA: Sage.

Sato, H. (1996) Keeping employees employed: Shukko and Tenseki job transfers – formation of a labor market within corporate groups, *Japan Labor Bulletin*, December 1: 5–8.

Shimada, H. (1992) Japan's industrial culture and labor-management relations, in Shumpei Kumon and Henry Rosovsky (eds.) *The Political Economy of Japan, Volume 3: Cultural and Social Dynamics*, Stanford: Stanford University Press, pp. 267–91.

Tatsumichi, S. and Morishima, M. (forthcoming) *Seikashugi* from an employee perspective, *Japan Labor Review*.

Tsuru, T., Morishima, M. and Okunishi, Y. (1998) Press Release on the 1997 Survey on the Assessment and Evaluation Practices of Large Japanese Firms. Unpublished Manuscript, Tokyo: Hitotsubashi University (in Japanese).

Wakabayashi, M. and Graen, G. (1989) Human resource development of Japanese managers: leadership and career investment, in A. Nedd, G. R. Ferris and K. M. Rowland (eds.) *Research in Personnel and Human Resources Management*, Suppl. 1, Greenwich, CT: JAI Press, pp. 235–56.

Yashiro, A. (1995) *Careers of White-Collar Workers in Large Japanese Firms*, Tokyo: The Japan Institute of Labour (in Japanese).

16 Performance management in Australia

HELEN DE CIERI AND CATHY SHEEHAN

The model of performance appraisal (PA) and performance management (PM) proposed by Murphy and DeNisi (Chapter 6, this volume) provides the context for our analysis of the major features of the Australian PMS in this chapter. Although the available research literature does not address all of the factors identified in the model, it is evident that the model provides a useful tool for the country-level analysis and comparison of PM across countries. In each section of this chapter, we also identify the relevant challenges associated with each of the factors in the model.

Consistent with Murphy and DeNisi's model, we view PMSs broadly as the process through which managers ensure that employees' activities and outputs are congruent with the organization's goals. PA is a major part, but not the only component of the broader process of PM. A PMS should link employee activities with organizational goals both at the level of strategic business objectives and at the operational level. PM typically involves processes of identifying performance objectives, defining performance required, facilitating performance, encouraging performance, measuring performance, and providing feedback on performance. PM should be both developmental and evaluative. The system must be flexible because when goals and strategies change, the results, behaviors and employee characteristics usually need to change correspondingly.

Distal factors influencing performance management

Murphy and De Nisi identify distal factors as those that operate at national or regional levels and are influential for performance management. In this section, we discuss examples of distal factors that influence PMSs in Australia.

The development of norms related to the PMS in Australia

To understand current norms that are relevant to PM, it is first necessary to be familiar with the historical development of PM in Australia. In the U.S. and in Britain during World War I, performance measurement approaches were initiated with the introduction of psychological testing and systems for monitoring (Dulebohn, Ferris and Stodd, 1995; Ling, 1965; Sofer, 1972). In Australia, however, due to the relatively small size of organizations and the restricted scale of manufacturing, it was not until the production demands of World War II that many employers invested in a permanent personnel function, and set about the task of systematically measuring work activity and developing bureaucratic procedures (Dunphy, 1987; Smart and Pontifex, 1993).

In the 1950s, manufacturing activities increased to account for about one-third of gross domestic product, moving Australia to a degree of industrialization comparable to the United States and Canada (Butlin, 1970). According to Lansbury (1995), during the 1950s PA was dominated by a measurement approach that focused on valid rating scale development rather than interactive PA interviews. It was not until the 1970s and 1980s that PA focused more on employee counseling and feedback. At the time, the Australian economy was experiencing a downturn. The export of agricultural products had come under threat and the manufacturing sector was pressured to improve efficiency and quality levels in order to match the increasing presence of multinational firms (Dowling and Boxall, 1994). The changes in the Australian economy in the 1980s made it clear that the future success of organizations depended more than ever on the quality of the management of people (Collins, 1987). In response, many managers recognized the potential returns from investment in employee development and more attention was given to the quality of the feedback given to employees (Lansbury, 1995).

In general, economic pressures to become more competitive in the 1980s led to refinement and sophistication of the appraisal techniques used (Lansbury, 1995). Problems identified with early and rudimentary forms of PA, such as rating scales, included concerns about the subjectivity and inconsistency in the way that supervisors were using scales, and the incidence of central tendency, with appraisers avoiding the extreme ends of the scales. A study conducted in the mid-1980s reported greater involvement of the appraisee, with almost 57 percent of Australian organizations including some form of self-appraisal in the appraisal process (Wood, Collins, Arasu and Entrekin, 1995). Used in conjunction with the appraisal interview, this participation allowed employees to voice their grievances and discuss development and training needs.

As well as a greater focus on employee participation and personal development within the PA process, the pressure on Australian companies to become more competitive led to a growing awareness of the need to build connection between PA and strategy. Dunphy and Hackman (1988) outlined the need for PA systems to contribute to organizational adaptability and flexibility. An outcome of the push for a more strategic contribution was the development of PMSs that incorporated a clearer focus on goal alignment. An example of this was the introduction by management of objectives systems to support corporate planning and budgeting targets.

Performance-related pay (PRP) also emerged as an issue for discussion when changes to regulation of the employment relationship led to the decentralization of the employer–employee relationship. A series of industrial relations reforms began with the formation of an Industrial Relations Accord in 1983 between the government at the time, the Australian Labour Party, and the Australian Council of Trade Unions. The collaboration provided the basis for a series of micro-economic reforms that included productivity growth encouragement at the enterprise level (Deery, Plowman, Walsh and Brown, 2001; Shelton, 1995). In March 1987 the centralized policy of wage fixation was abandoned and the Australian Industrial Relations Commission introduced a new two-tiered wage-fixing system that incorporated a general wage increase plus a second possible increase of up to 4 percent that was contingent on workplace efficiency improvements (McKenzie and Van Gramberg, 2002).

The focus on productivity at the enterprise level led a number of companies to introduce pay systems that included a performance component. A major Australian employer, the Commonwealth Bank, introduced a performance-payment system in 1987 that incorporated a yearly bonus contingent on the results of the PA. Similar systems were subsequently introduced in a number of other Australian banks (Wright, 1994). Further initiatives to decentralize the wage determination occurred in October 1991, when a framework for enterprise bargaining[1] was approved and was later supported in 1992 with amendments to the Industrial Relations Act (Deery, 1995). By 1991, PRP was in evidence in a number of industries. Results from the Australian Workplace Industrial Relations Survey (AWIRS) showed that in 1990 approximately 34 percent of workplaces with 20 or more employees had some form of PRP in place for non-managerial employees. By 1995, however, there was no increase with only 33 percent reporting some form of PRP. O'Donnell and Shields (2002) point out that in those workplaces only a small minority of employees were covered. In the majority of workplaces that had reported the use of PRP, only 25 percent of the workforce was covered and only 16 percent offered these payments to all of their employees.

Current norms and challenges for PMS in Australia

Since 1995, the level of PRP has increased, such that it may be considered the norm across Australian industries today. As reported by Long and Shields (2005), using a survey conducted in 1999, PRP for individual performance, particularly merit raises, is used by the majority of companies in Australia. The development of this first norm has been driven by changes in the legal employment framework. The *Workplace Relations Act 1996 (Cwlth)* 1996, and *Amendments to the Workplace Relations Act (Workchoices)* 2005, discussed earlier, have included changes aimed to create a more direct relationship between employers and employees. This legislation has dismantled the existing centralized system, which gave the Australian Industrial Relations Commission a central role in dispute settlement and the determination of employment conditions. The new approach gives primacy to Australian Workplace Agreements[2] and enterprise bargaining, which allow employers and workers to negotiate directly. A second norm resulting from the decentralization of the wage-setting system is that more decisions are now made at the workplace level. These decisions include, but are not restricted to, PM concerns.

A third identifiable norm in Australian industry is that efficiency and productivity demands are progressively connecting performance with reward. As a result, PMSs have become a key source of information in the determination of rewards levels.

These norms raise important challenges for PMSs in Australia. The focus on enterprise-level negotiations creates a need for employers and employees to have the requisite skills and knowledge, and for appropriate mechanisms for communication to be in place. With respect to research on the development of communication opportunities, Dowling and Fisher (1997) identified that 46 percent of a group of HR professionals surveyed in 1995 identified new HR programs in the area of joint consultation and participation. In a follow-up survey, Sheehan, Holland and De Cieri (2006) reported that new initiatives in this area had dropped to 24 percent. A total of 47 percent of respondents did, however, report the initiation of new grievance processes (this area was not a listed area in the 1995 survey). It would appear, therefore, that there is some evidence of attempts in Australian businesses to address the need to provide communication pathways between employees and employers.

Strategy and firm performance

The norms identified above in Australian industry have developed in the context of Australian industry striving to become more competitive in global markets. Therefore, a fourth trend, or emerging norm, over the past three decades, has been the increasing internationalization of Australian organizations. As Australia is a small domestic economy heavily dependent on international trade, Australian companies are vulnerable to the pressures of globalization. The movement of labor that has been concomitant with expansion of international business has meant that issues related to the management of a global workforce have become more critical to Australian employers. While many large firms originating in Australia, such as BHP-Billiton, News Corporation and Qantas, are already multinational corporations that span the globe, it is increasingly the norm for many medium-sized and small organizations to be involved in international business.

Another major development in Australian industry has been the shift away from manufacturing toward the services industry. Since the early 1970s, employment growth has been dominated by service-sector employment, which has culminated in more than 70 percent of the Australian workforce being employed in various service industries (Australian Bureau of Statistics, 2000; Walsh, 1997). Currently, retail trade has the largest percentage of employed persons, followed by property and business services, and manufacturing. Employment in the health sector and in hospitality (accommodation, cafés and restaurants) is rising (Australian Bureau of Statistics, 2006a).

Current challenges for firm strategy and performance

To be successful in the global marketplace, a major challenge for all businesses is to manage human resources in ways that will lead to effective performance across cultural and national boundaries (De Cieri, 2007; Fish and Wood, 1997). With respect to the emerging focus on services, research suggests that, to maximize customer service, companies in the service sector require progressive HRM approaches, including an emphasis on PM, to create a positive experience for the employee and the customer (Batt, 2002; Korczynski, 2002). More will be said in the next section about how diversity in the Australian workforce presents particular challenges for the growing services sector.

Cultural factors: workforce diversity in Australia

Australia is often characterized as a multicultural society. With respect to the composition of the Australian population, Australia has one of the most culturally heterogeneous societies in the world, due to several waves of migration from a broad range of cultural and geographic backgrounds (Wilkinson and Cheung, 1999). The social, economic and political implications of this multiculturalism are significant for organizations and Australian society in general. The workforce diversity is particularly interesting when taking into account the relatively small size of the Australian resident population [in June 2004, the population was 20.1 million people. This is projected to increase to between 24.9 and 33.4 million by 2051, and to between 22.4 and 43.5 million by 2101 (Australian Bureau of Statistics, 2006b)].

Indigenous Australians have one of the oldest cultures in the world, with a presence dating back at least 60,000 years. European settlement from 1788 had a dramatic and largely negative impact on indigenous Australians, who were disadvantaged and marginalized by the social, economic and political policies of European colonists. These disadvantages remain in terms of literacy rates, unemployment, health and housing problems (Human Rights and Equal Opportunity Commission, 1997). Recent research examining current practices and emerging opportunities for indigenous Australians in the workforce has shown that significant obstacles remain (Australian Bureau of Statistics, 2004a; Schaper, 1999).

Prior to the 1960s, the majority of migrants to Australia came from Europe, particularly the United Kingdom. Historically, multiculturalism in Australia was regarded as a governmental social policy problem and attempts were made to reduce cultural heterogeneity by restricting immigration to white Europeans (Wilkinson and Cheung, 1999). There has, however, been increasing national awareness of the importance of Australia's Asian geographic positioning vis-à-vis European cultural heritage, with significant demographic change within Australia. In the current decade, there is intensification of debate around immigration. The dominant view among researchers and policy makers is that immigration yields overall long-term benefits to the economy, although there is recognition of the need for adjustments (Betts, 2003; Boreham, Stokes and Hall, 2004; Oslington, 1998).

Along with the broad representation of ethnic groups within the Australian population, other sources of diversity include an ageing workforce and greater representation of women. First, with respect to the ageing of the workforce, over the period from 2004 to 2051, the proportion of the population aged 65 years and over is projected to increase from 13 percent to between 26 and 28 percent (Australian Bureau of Statistics, 2006b, 2006c, 2006d; Munk, 2003).

Second, with respect to gender representation, during the past two decades the overall labor force participation rate has increased slowly, rising from 60 percent in 1984–5 to 64 percent in 2004–5 and the main force behind the long-term rise in the labor force participation rate has been an increase in the female participation rate, including an increase in the proportion of women with family responsibilities who are in the workforce (Australian Bureau of Statistics, 2006a). Women dominate the part-time and contingent workforce. Currently, women represent around 25 percent of managers and administrators in Australian workplaces (Australian Bureau of Statistics, 2004a; Preston and Burgess, 2003). However, the higher the level of management, the fewer women to be found: it has been reported that women represent only 8 percent of executive management. Recent surveys show that only in large organizations (those employing more than 100 staff) have we seen substantial increases in the number of female managers. For example, Westpac Corporation, one of the major Australian banks, reports a strong commitment to increasing the representation of women at all managerial levels, through processes of cultural change and a comprehensive approach to gender equality (Beck and Davis, 2005). The more general trend shows that, over the past ten years, the number of women in management has been relatively stable (Australian Bureau of Statistics, 2004b). Overall, PMSs need to be designed to deal with the diverse composition of the Australian workforce and the expectation that all workers will be dealt with fairly and equitably.

Challenges of a diverse workforce

The demographic changes in the workforce have led to several challenges for PMSs. First, PMS should provide adequate developmental opportunities for women, minorities and contingent workers. Brown and Heywood (2005) have provided some interesting insights into the way that PASs are applied to the female workforce in Australia. Using data from the AWIRS in 1990 and 1995, these writers make the point that PA is more likely in Australian establishments with more women workers and without large proportions of long-tenure workers. This result is used to support the hypothesis that, for these groups of workers, the purpose of appraisal is simply to monitor performance and provide appropriate rewards. Their analysis is interesting in light of the statistics showing increasing numbers of women in the workforce, although not at senior levels. It suggests that these female workers may not be benefiting from the developmental opportunities that are often part of broader PMSs.

Second, as mentioned above, the growth of jobs in the service sector has led to several challenges for the management of employees, particularly for PM. Specifically the supply of individuals with the necessary education and training is not meeting the emerging job demands of the Australian economy. Two problems are evident with regard to skills: new entrants to the workforce who come from diverse backgrounds and the current dominance of women in the labor force. New entrants to the labor force often arrive without the skills needed for success, and therefore require training. This is especially a problem for small businesses (with fewer than 200 employees), which comprise around 90 percent of Australian employers. The implications of the changing labor market for managing HR are farreaching. As labor-market growth will be primarily based on females and people with English as a second language, Australian employers need to ensure that PMSs are free of bias to capitalize on the perspectives and values that a diverse workforce can contribute to improving product quality, customer service, product development and market share. The reliance on high quality of performance in the service sector presents a particular challenge for employers as, concurrent with the demographic and other changes in distal factors noted above, working life in Australia is changing.

Technology and the rise of contingent work

Across Australian industry, there is increasing diversity in employment arrangements, increasing use of information technology, more flexible working time patterns, and more people working part-time hours (Australian Bureau of Statistics, 2006d). The contingent workforce, which includes temporary, part-time and self-employed workers, is growing. Australian studies suggest evidence of the common pattern seen in other industrialized countries: employment is moving from the "traditional" forms of full-time, permanent, work toward a wider variety of working arrangements (Kalleberg, 2000; Van den Heuvel and Wooden, 1997). In 2004–5, 71 percent of employed people were working in full-time employment. Full-time workers are those who usually work 35 hours or more per week in all jobs, or, although usually working less than 35 hours a week, actually worked 35 hours or more during the reference week of the survey. Part-time workers are those who usually work less than 35 hours a week. Part-time employed persons now account for 28 percent of all employed persons. Women dominate the part-time workforce (Australian Bureau of Statistics, 2006a).

The increase in the number of contingent workers is occurring for several reasons (Burgess and Connell, 2006). Erosion of the traditional employment contract, typically thought to be based on lifetime employment for dedicated service, is evident. Employers can no longer guarantee job security for their employees. Many companies have reduced the number of full-time employees to lower the associated labor costs and give the organization the flexibility to contract for skills when needed. Companies that use contingent employees from temporary agencies and contract firms are likely to experience a reduction in the administrative and financial burden associated with HRM because the agencies take care of selecting, training and compensating the workers. Contingent work can be attractive from the worker's perspective. Many employees have decided to work on a contingent basis as a result of interests, values and needs. Another emerging trend in Australian work patterns is that more work is being done outside the traditional office or worksite (i.e. distributed work or telecommuting) and it includes work done at home, while traveling, or anywhere a person can connect to the office or colleagues using information technology (Lindorff, 2000).

Challenges related to technology and contingent work

The increasing use of technology and contingent work creates several challenges for PM. For example, research by Lowry (2001) suggests that contingent work is more likely to be based on a transactional relationship between employer and employee, and has been associated with an under-investment in employee development, particularly for casual workers. Furthermore, distributed work brings particular challenges for managing employee performance. Employees need to be trained in using information technology to share data, information and ideas with peers, managers and customers. Companies need to adapt types of employee appraisal to fairly and accurately assess performance.

The Australian legal system

In Australia, there are six major legal issues associated with PM. These issues relate to: documentation of PA for legal protection; implications of condoning poor performance by inaction; anti-discrimination and equal employment opportunity legislation; an employer's duty of care to a poorly performing employee; provision of adequate warning before dismissal of an employee; and termination of employment (De Cieri, Kramar, Noe, Hollenbeck, Gerhart and Wright, 2005). These issues are outlined below.

First, it is possible for dismissed employees to use PA records to challenge the decision to terminate their employment. Therefore, employers are advised to retain all material relating to performance in a formal record, particularly documentation relating to poor performance and counseling provided to an employee.

Second, where an employer has tolerated poor performance for a long period of time without starting formal review procedures, the employer may face legal action against unfair dismissal. It could be argued that the employer has condoned the poor performance as adequate.

Third, anti-discrimination and equal employment opportunity legislation prohibits discrimination on several grounds. Therefore, any decisions based on a performance assessment that was judged to be discriminatory would be unlawful. This discrimination does not have to be conscious or intentional and it may result from a manager's attitudes or beliefs. Employers are advised to ensure that: appraisal criteria are job-related and appropriate; appraising managers and supervisors are trained in appraisal processes; and there are no direct or indirect forms of discrimination.

With regard to the latter three issues, legislation regarding unfair dismissal specifies that employers have a duty of care to employees with poor performance. Employers are prohibited from forcing an employee to resign or making work conditions unpleasant enough to resign; these actions would be interpreted as dismissal. The *Workplace Relations Act 1996 (Cwlth)* 1996, and subsequent *Amendments to the Workplace Relations Act* (*Workchoices*) 2005, require employers to conduct and document regular performance assessments. These requirements prohibit an employer from dismissing an employee without valid reason (Sheldon and Junor, 2006). Employers are required to give an employee an opportunity to defend any allegations as well as give adequate notice to the employee. Employees are entitled to procedural and substantive fairness whenever any action is taken in response to a negative assessment of performance. These actions could include a warning, direction, suspension, transfer, demotion or removal of benefits.

Challenges associated with the legal system

The requirements of the legal system raise challenges and obligations for both employers and employees. For example, employers' legal obligations regarding fairness can be met by ensuring the:

- development of a transparent PAS that can be consistently applied;
- review of performance made against clearly specified criteria (e.g. a position description and performance goals);
- results of previous performance assessments are taken into account;
- systems to deal with counseling and warnings are in place;
- nature and duration of the actions are clear and the reasons as to why the actions have been taken are clear;
- duration of the actions and the reasons as to why the actions have been taken are clearly explained to the employee;
- employee understands how his/her performance could be improved and how this improvement would be assessed; and
- employee is informed of the consequences of not improving performance and the procedures to be followed if this occurs (De Cieri *et al.*, 2005: 364).

Proximal factors influencing PM

Current research into PMSs in Australia indicates that many organizations have introduced systems aimed to gather performance information, for a variety of purposes. In this section, we review the major proximal factors for PM that are of current concern for researchers and practitioners in Australia. Proximal factors include acceptance of appraisal systems and purposes for which appraisal systems are used.

Prevalence and acceptance of PMSs

The use of PAs in Australia increased in the 1990s; these are now widespread (Patrickson and Hartmann, 2001). The findings of a 2006 study of PMSs conducted through the Australian Human Resources Institute found that from the sample of 992 respondents across a range of organizations, almost all of the respondents (96%) indicated use of a PM or PA system. This is perhaps not surprising, given the recent legislative developments.

Research by Sheehan *et al.* (2006) also indicates widespread uptake of PM in Australian organizations. When HR professionals were asked to identify areas in which there had been new policy programs or system development in the past 5 years, 75 percent reported HR development in PA initiatives for managers and 69 percent reported attention to PA for non-managers.

Purpose and types of PMSs

Kramar's (2000) national survey established that organizations typically use the information from the PA component of a PMS for administrative purposes, rather than strategic purposes. This is consistent with international research findings (Brewster, Tregaskis, Hegewisch and Mayne, 1996; Milliman, Nason, Zhu and De Cieri, 2002). In Australia, the primary purpose of information from PAs has been found to be for making decisions about improving employee performance in their current job, rather than for making decisions about organizational training needs or future career and organizational training needs (Kramar, 2000; Nankervis and Leece, 1997).

More recently, Nankervis and Compton's (2006) review of the status of performance systems established that the main purposes of PMs are almost equally distributed across training and development needs (89.2%) and the appraisal of past performance (88.9%) and to a lesser extent alignment of objectives (75.5%). In an attempt to explore in more detail the strategic element of the PMS, Nankervis and Compton (2006) reviewed the uptake of the balanced scorecard (BSC) amongst Australian organizations. These researchers argued that the BSC makes explicit links between performance measures and organizational objectives and strategies and as such is worthy of particular investigation. A total of 25.5 percent of total respondents reported using the BSC and 95 percent of this group felt that their performance measures are consistent with their organizations' missions, visions and long-term goals strategies. Most of the respondents using a BSC approach felt therefore that their performance measures were generally consistent with organizational goals and strategies. Following on, despite the overall quite low level of uptake of these strategically focused systems, respondents indicated a projected increase in the use of the BSC as well as 360-degree/multi-rater feedback, and a fall in support for forced rankings and the use of the bellcurve.

Employers in Australia are most likely to use PAs for managers, professionals and technical employees, with about 95 percent using them for these employees. Although not as widely used for clerical and manual employees, 89 percent of organizations used PAs for clerical staff and almost two-thirds used them for manual employees (Kramar, 2000).

Challenges associated with proximal factors

Despite the increasing use of formal PMSs, it remains a challenge to reach uniformity or common standards across industry. The extent of formalization of PMSs appears to vary;

64 percent of surveyed organizations reported having a formal PM policy manual (Nankervis and Compton, 2006). A second, and related, challenge for PMSs is that, despite the managerial interest in PM, there is some debate in the literature around whether these systems are achieving their strategic purpose. Without alignment with organizational strategic purposes, the effectiveness of PMSs will be somewhat restricted.

Intervening factors

Murphy and De Nisi recognize in their model that intervening factors, such as rater skills and motivation, and rater–ratee relationships, may influence PM processes. For example, Nankervis and Compton (2006) report that, although there is an increase in the use of 360-degree feedback or multi-rater systems, joint discussions between employees and their supervisors are still very widespread (65%). Work group or team performance is included in only 11 percent of the respondents' systems. The heavy reliance on the interview, therefore, places high expectations on the objectivity and reliability of the interaction between employees and their supervisors. Furthermore, the quality of this interaction is in large part driven by the interpersonal skills possessed by the manager. There has been concern in the literature, however, about the lack of interpersonal and communication skills of Australian managers. In 1995 the industry task force on leadership and management skills in Australia, chaired by David Karpin, reinforced the need for Australian managers to develop an emphasis on what they referred to as "soft skills." The task force made the point quite clearly that even though Australian managers rated highly on functional skills, there has been a lack of attention to skills that address the flow of communication between employees and management (*Enterprising Nation*, 1995).

Challenges associated with intervening factors

Despite awareness of the need to improve managerial skills, a recent study by Connell and Nolan (2004) proposed that Australian managers still lack proficiency in providing meaningful feedback to employees. The research used a qualitative case study approach of two multinational organizations. The companies were chosen as they had been voted in the top twenty Australian organizations in HR and it could be expected, therefore, that these companies would be characterized by well-developed approaches to PA. The researchers concluded, however, that PMSs were used primarily for political purposes and did not result in open and useful communication. It was considered that this was exacerbated by the lack of supervisory skills to enact more direct and meaningful interactions with employees.

Conclusion

PMSs are influenced by the national context – institutional, economic, political, legal and social factors all influence the development and design of organizational systems such as those for PM. Within an organization, a PMS serves strategic, administrative and developmental purposes – their importance cannot be overestimated. Further, as global integration and competition builds, issues related to PM have become critical to organizational sustainability and success. While there have been noteworthy developments in PM in Australia over recent decades, there remain many challenges for the development of this field of research and practice, and the opportunities for progressing this field are substantial.

Overall, as for many areas of management, on some issues related to PM, it is evident that a research-practice gap exists, with research needed to analyze areas such as the implications of new legislation and the current needs of HR practitioners and managers. This gap may not be easy to fill, as there are complex issues to define, measure and address. There is also a practice-research gap, with PM in some aspects lagging behind developments in research knowledge (Rynes, Bartunek and Daft, 2001). We encourage knowledge sharing between academics and practitioners, to bridge these identified gaps and develop the field.

Websites

1   To view information about the PMS used in the Australian Public Service, go to: http://www.apsc.gov.au/publications01/performancemanagement.htm
2   Numerous consultants provide PM services to organizations operating in Australia. Some examples are:
   ● http://www.peoplestreme.com/
   ● http://www.iedex.com.au/

Notes

1   Enterprise bargaining is the formation of employer and employee agreements conducted at the level of the enterprise. The product of the process, an enterprise agreement, may exist as a supplement or complement to existing awards or it may be a complete substitute. In the case of agreement about wages, these may be adjusted to suit changes in work value and productivity (Fox, Howard and Pittard, 1995: 583).
2   An employer and employee may make a written agreement called an Australian Workplace Agreement that deals with matters pertaining to the relationship between an employer and an employee. An AWA is similar to an individual contract of employment, except that its content is subject to scrutiny and approval by the Employment Advocate and is enforceable in public law (Deery et al., 2001: 278–9).

Further reading

Brown, M. and Heywood, J. S. (2005) Performance appraisal systems: determinants and change, *British Journal of Industrial Relations* 43(4): 659–79.

Kulik, C. T. and Bainbridge, H. T. J. (2006) HR and the line: the distribution of HR activities in Australian organisations, *Asia Pacific Journal of Human Resources* 44: 240–56.

Long, R. and Shields, J. (2005) Performance pay in Canadian and Australian firms, *International Journal of Human Resource Management* 16: 1783–811.

Nankervis, A. and Compton, R. (2006) Performance management: theory in practice? *Asia Pacific Journal of Human Resources* 44(1): 83–101.

Sheehan, C., Holland, P. and De Cieri, H. (2006) Current developments in HRM in Australian organizations, *Asia Pacific Journal of Human Resources* 44(2): 132–52.

Sheldon, P. and Junor, A. (2006) Australian HRM and the *Workplace Relations Amendment (Work Choices) Act 2005*, *Asia Pacific Journal of Human Resources* 44: 153–70.

References

Australian Bureau of Statistics (1999) *Yearbook Australia 1999 special article – Older Australians*, Catalog no. 1301.0, Canberra: Australian Bureau of Statistics.

Australian Bureau of Statistics (2000) *Australia now – a statistical profile. Industry overview*, Canberra: Australian Bureau of Statistics.

Australian Bureau of Statistics (2004a) *Labour force, Australia, detailed May 2004*. Catalog no.6291.0.55.001, Canberra: Australian Bureau of Statistics.

Australian Bureau of Statistics (2004b) *Yearbook Australia 2004*. Catalog no. 1301.0, Canberra: Australian Bureau of Statistics.

Australian Bureau of Statistics (2006a) *Yearbook Australia 2006*. Catalog no. 1301.0, Canberra: Australian Bureau of Statistics.

Australian Bureau of Statistics (2006b) *Population projections, Australia 2004–2101*. Catalog no. 3222.0, Canberra: Australian Bureau of Statistics.

Australian Bureau of Statistics (2006c) *Labour force, Australia*. Catalog no. 6203.0, Canberra: Australian Bureau of Statistics.

Australian Bureau of Statistics (2006d) *Australian social trends 2006*. Catalog no. 4102.0, Canberra: Australian Bureau of Statistics.

Batt, R. (2002) Managing customer services: human resource practices, quit rates, and sales growth, *Academy of Management Journal* 45: 587–98.

Beck, D. and Davis, E. (2005) EEO in senior management: women executives in Westpac, *Asia Pacific Journal of Human Resources* 43(2): 273–88.

Betts, K. (2003) Immigration policy under the Howard Government, *Australian Journal of Social Issues* 38(2): 169–92.

Boreham, I., Stokes, G. and Hall, R. (eds.) (2004) *The Politics of Australian Society: Political Issues for the New Century* (2nd edn.), Frenchs Forest, NSW: Pearson Longman.

Brewster, C., Tregaskis, O., Hegewisch, A. and Mayne, L. (1996) Comparative survey research in human resource management: a review and an example, *International Journal of Human Resource Management* 7: 585–604.

Brown, M. and Heywood, J. S. (2005) Performance appraisal systems: determinants and change, *British Journal of Industrial Relations* 43(4): 659–79.

Burgess, J. and Connell, J. (2006) Temporary work and human resource management: issues, challenges and responses, *Personnel Review* 35(2): 125–40.

Butlin, N. G. (1970) Some perspectives of Australian economic development, 1890–1965, in C. Forster (ed.) *Australian Economic Development in the Twentieth Century*, Sydney: Australasian Publishing, pp. 266–327.

Collins, R. (1987) The strategic contributions of the human resource function, *Human Resource Management Australia* (November): 5–19.

Connell, J. and Nolan, J. (2004) Managing performance: modern day myth or a game people play, *International Journal of Employment Studies* 12(1): 43–63.

De Cieri, H. (2007) Transnational firms and cultural diversity, in P. Boxall, J. Purcell and P. Wright (eds.) *Handbook of Human Resource Management*, Oxford: Oxford University Press, pp. 509–32.

De Cieri, H., Kramar, R., Noe, R., Hollenbeck, J., Gerhart, B. and Wright, P. (2005) *Human Resource Management in Australia. Strategy – People – Performance* (2nd edn.), Sydney: McGraw-Hill.

Deery, S. (1995) Industrial relations, in G. O'Neill and R. Kramar (eds.) *Australian Human Resources Management*, Melbourne: Pitman Publishing, pp. 53–76.

Deery, S., Plowman, D., Walsh, J. and Brown, M. (2001) *Industrial Relations: A Contemporary Analysis* (2nd edn.), Sydney: McGraw-Hill.

Dowling, P. J. and Boxall, P. F. (1994) Shifting the emphasis from natural resources to human resources: the challenge of the new competitive context in Australia and New Zealand, *Zeitschrift für Personalforschung* 8: 302–16.

Dowling, P. J. and Fisher, C. (1997) The Australian HR professional: a 1995 profile, *Asia Pacific Journal of Human Resources* 35(1): 1–20.

Dulebohn, J. H., Ferris, G. and Stodd, J. T. (1995) The history and evolution of human resource management, in G. R. Ferris, S. D. Rosen and D. T. Barnum (eds.) *Handbook of Human Resource Management*, Oxford: Blackwell Business, pp. 18–41.

Dunphy, D. (1987) The historical development of human resource management in Australia, *Human Resource Management Australia* 25: 40–47.

Dunphy, D. C. and Hackman, B. K. (1988) Performance appraisal as a strategic intervention, *Human Resource Management Australia* 26(2): 23–34.

Enterprising Nation [The Karpin Report] (1995) *Report of the Industry Task Force on Leadership and Management Skills*, Canberra: Australian Government Printing Service.

Fish, A. and Wood, J. (1997) Cross-cultural management competence in Australian business enterprises, *Asia Pacific Journal of Human Resources* 35(1): 37–52.

Fox, C., Howard, W. and Pittard, M. (1995) *Industrial Relations in Australia: Development, Law and Operation*, Melbourne, VIC: Longman.

Human Rights and Equal Opportunity Commission (1997) *Bringing Them Home: Report of the National Inquiry into the Separation of Aboriginal and Torres Strait Islander Children from their Families*, Sydney: Human Rights and Equal Opportunity Commission.

Kalleberg, A. (2000) Nonstandard employment relations: part-time, temporary and contract work, *Annual Review of Sociology* 26: 341–65.

Korczynski, M. (2002) *Human Resource Management in Service Work*, London: Palgrave.

Kramar, R. (2000) *Cranfield-PricewaterhouseCoopers Survey on International Strategic Human Resource Management*, North Ryde, NSW: Macquarie University.

Lansbury, R. (1995) Performance appraisal: the elusive quest, in G. O'Neill and R. Kramar (eds.) *Australian Human Resources Management*, Melbourne: Pitman Publishing, pp. 123–44.

Lindorff, M. (2000) Home-based telework and telecommuting in Australia: more myth than modern work form, *Asia Pacific Journal of Human Resources* 38(1): 1–11.

Ling, C. (1965) *The Management of Personnel Relations: History and Origins*, Chicago: Irwin.

Long, R. and Shields, J. (2005) Performance pay in Canadian and Australian firms, *International Journal of Human Resource Management* 16: 1783–811.

Lowry, D. (2001) The casual management of casual work: casual workers' perceptions of HRM practices in the highly casualised firm, *Asia Pacific Journal of Human Resources* 39(1): 42–62.

McKenzie, D. and Van Gramberg, B. (2002) Legal regulation of employment, in J. Teicher, P. Holland and R. Gough (eds.), *Employee Relations Management: Australia in a Global Context*, Frenchs Forest, NSW: Pearson Education, pp. 235–41.

Milliman, J., Nason, S., Zhu, C. and De Cieri, H. (2002) An exploratory assessment of the purposes of PAs in North and Central America and the Pacific Rim, *Human Resource Management* 41(1): 87–102.

Munk, K. (2003) The older worker: everyone's future, *Journal of Occupational Health and Safety – Australia and New Zealand* 19(5): 437–46.

Nankervis, A. and Compton, R. (2006) Performance management: theory in practice? *Asia Pacific Journal of Human Resources* 44(1): 83–101.

Nankervis, A. and Leece, P. (1997) Performance appraisal: two steps forward, one step back? *Asia Pacific Journal of Human Resources* 35(2): 80–92.

O'Donnell, M. and Shields, J. (2002) The new pay: performance-related pay in Australia, in J. Teicher, P. Holland and R. Gough (eds.) *Employee Relations Management: Australia in a Global Context*, Frenchs Forest, NSW: Pearson Education, pp. 406–34.

Oslington, P. (1998) Australian immigration policy and unemployment, *Australian Journal of Labour Economics* 2(2): 91–104.

Patrickson, M. and Hartmann, L. (2001) Human resource management in Australia: prospects for the twenty-first century, *International Journal of Manpower* 22(3): 198–206.

Preston, A. and Burgess, J. (2003) Women's work in Australia: trends, issues and prospects, *Australian Journal of Labour Economics* 6(4): 497–518.

Rynes, S., Bartunek, J. and Daft, R. (2001) Across the great divide: knowledge creation and transfer between practitioners and academics, *Academy of Management Journal* 44(2): 340–55.

Schaper, M. (1999) Australia's Aboriginal small business owners: challenges for the future, *Journal of Small Business Management* 37(3): 88–93.

Sheehan, C., Holland, P. and De Cieri, H. (2006) Current developments in HRM in Australian organizations, *Asia Pacific Journal of Human Resources* 44(2): 132–52.

Sheldon, P. and Junor, A. (2006) Australian HRM and the *Workplace Relations Amendment (Work Choices) Act 2005*, *Asia Pacific Journal of Human Resources* 44: 153–70.

Shelton, D. (1995) Human resource management in Australia, in L. F. Moore and P. D. Jennings (eds.) *Human Resource Management on the Pacific Rim*, Berlin: Walter de Gruyter, pp. 31–60.

Smart, J. P. and Pontifex, M. R. (1993) Human resource management and the Australian human resources institute: the profession and its professional body, *Asia Pacific Journal of Human Resources* 31(1): 1–19.

Sofer, C. (1972) *Organizations in Theory and Practice*, London: Heinemann Educational.

Van den Heuvel, A. and Wooden, M. (1997) Self-employed contractors and job satisfaction, *Journal of Small Business Management* 35(3): 11–20.

Walsh, J. (1997) Employment systems in transition? A comparative analysis of Britain and Australia, *Work, Employment and Society* 11(1): 1–25.

Wilkinson, I. and Cheung, C. (1999) Multicultural marketing in Australia: synergy in diversity, *Journal of International Marketing* 7(3): 106–25.

Wood, R., Collins, R., Arasu, S. and Entrekin, L. (1995) A national survey of performance-appraisal practices, *Australian Personnel Management*, North Ryde, NSW: CCH.

Wright, C. (ed.) (1994) *Incentive Payments in Australia*, Department of Industrial Research Series, No. 9, Canberra: Australian Government Printing Service.

17 Performance management around the globe: what have we learned?

ANGELO DeNISI, ARUP VARMA AND PAWAN S. BUDHWAR

All modern organizations face the challenge of how best to manage performance. That is, they must determine the best ways to set goals, evaluate work and distribute rewards in such a way that performance can be improved over time. While *all* firms face similar challenges, the way a firm responds to those challenges may well depend on where the firm is located and the context within which it is operating. Differences in culture, technology, or simply tradition make it difficult to directly apply techniques that have worked in one setting, to a different setting (see, for example, Björkman, 2004; Hofstede, 1993). This, of course, is what the present volume is all about. We began with some "universals" in terms of issues, challenges, and a proposed model to help guide discussion, and then moved to solutions and performance management systems (PMSs) that have been used in various countries around the world.

In this chapter, we present brief synopses of the various chapters in the two parts of the book, comparing and contrasting key findings, as appropriate. The issue for the reader, after having read all the specific descriptions, is to determine what can be learned from these descriptions. Are countries really so unique that nothing can be learned by examining what has been done somewhere else? Or, on the other hand, are differences between countries disappearing (in our "flat world") so that we can focus on the universals and apply them wherever we need? The answer is, of course, that neither is completely true and perhaps some kind of "*crossvergence*" (i.e. blending of work practices, due to the active interface of diverse groups, in turn due to globalization) is taking place (see also Gopalan and Stahl, 1998). Thus, in this chapter, we examine where the similarities exist, and where the differences/uniqueness endure, and try to understand how these findings can help guide MNEs in setting up effective PMSs across the globe.

The first part of the volume was meant to set up the critical issues and provide a framework for discussion. As such, it was pretty much self-contained and self-explanatory. The opening chapter laid out the need for understanding PM in different settings, and explained the logic of the rest of the volume – including the rationale behind choosing which countries or regions to focus upon. The second chapter (Briscoe and Claus) went one more step toward setting the stage. As these authors argue, much of the global commerce in this day and age is carried out by multinational enterprises (MNEs). These large, global firms dominate the world business setting because they have the capacity to do business across a wide variety of settings. This is not to suggest that there is no place for national enterprises, or even for small businesses, but the role of these smaller operations has been largely to funnel goods and services to the multinationals who then trade and do business globally.

These multinationals are also the most interesting focus for a discussion about PM on a global scale. A local grocer in London, Mumbai or the suburbs of Chicago may need to implement a PMS, but they are not concerned with how such a system will translate across countries or cultures. They can simply implement the best English, Indian, or U.S. ideas on managing performance. They may learn about other systems and approaches, but they have the luxury of dealing (primarily) with individuals from one country in designing their programs. This is, of course, not the case for multinationals who may need to implement English, Indian and U.S. systems, along with Chinese and Italian systems, and all the while ensure that everyone is treated the same by the firm, regardless of where they live and work. These cultural challenges, as well as problems of transparency and communications, are the special issues that MNEs must face, and these are discussed in some detail by Briscoe and Claus in Chapter 2 of this volume.

The next three chapters deal with issues in the field of PM that, arguably, affect everyone, regardless of where they are doing business. Pritchard and DiazGranados focus on the basic issue of employee motivation. Why does any firm implement a PMS? Although there are a number of reasons, a major reason underlying all such systems is the attempt to improve performance. This means that the system must somehow motivate employees to exert effort in the directions the company desires, to help the company meet its goals. These authors rely on an earlier model of motivation (Naylor, Pritchard and Ilgen, 1980), which has subsequently been modified and used to form the basis for a major PM intervention known as ProMES (e.g. Pritchard *et al.*, 1989). Since their model builds upon a rational decision-making framework, it addresses issues that are relevant to anyone interested in motivating employees to exert effort at work. Nonetheless, the authors conclude with observations about how cultural difference may well influence the ways in which the links in their model operate.

Pichler, Varma and Petty discuss the ways in which the relationship between a rater and a ratee can influence PAs and PMSs. Thus, their chapter focuses upon potential sources of bias, and proposes how two constructs – interpersonal affect and leader–member exchange – might be sources of that bias. This discussion is extremely interesting in the present context because these models and constructs have been based, primarily, upon U.S. oriented research. There is evidence that these constructs have meaning in other cultures, but the exact nature of the bias and the source of the bias may well differ from country to country. Nonetheless, there is little question that, in all cultures, interpersonal relationships will play a role in the PM process.

Gerhart and Trevor, in their chapter, deal with another issue that is part of most PM programs – merit pay. They explain some of the basic concepts underlying any merit pay plan, as well as some of the mechanics for such a program. They end their discussion with a note concerning how culture can impact on the effectiveness of such programs by leading to a greater or lesser degree of variance among performance ratings. They argue that any merit pay plan, in order to be effective, must have substantial variance across ratings, and this will be hard to accomplish in some cultures.

Finally, this section of the volume ends with a chapter by Murphy and DeNisi, where they lay out a model of the PM process that is used as the framework for the discussion of the specific programs later on. Many aspects of the proposed framework (for example, both distal and proximal factors) have been used by contributors of the country-specific chapters. Their model deals with both the factors that are likely to impact upon ratings in an appraisals system and also the ways in which organizations seek to narrow the gap between rated performance and desired performance. Their model is rather comprehensive and allows other authors to use their model in presenting PMSs from around the world.

These six chapters provide an excellent backdrop for the remainder of the book. They address issues that are relevant to PM programs, wherever they might exist, and they raise issues that help to frame the discussions of specific programs in the subsequent chapters. These chapters also introduce a level of scholarship that is not typical of this type of book. These early chapters touch on issues and questions from the scholarly side of the field, which need to be addressed when discussing practical programs. We believe that this is one of the unique aspects of the present volume.

The discussion of specific programs begins with a description of PMSs in the United States (in the chapter by Pulakos, Mueller-Hanson and O'Leary). These systems are characterized by individual-based rewards, poor communications between parties, and a strong driving force provided by equal employment legislation. It is interesting to note that there are also strong legalistic forces operating in the systems we find in the United Kingdom (Sparrow), France and Germany (Barzantny and Festing), and Australia (De Cieri and Sheehan). Although the exact nature of the laws that affect PM is somewhat different in each setting, they are each settings where legal concerns are important. Thus, in each case, in addition to trying to improve performance, a real incentive for developing better PMSs is to avoid legal problems. Thus, even if fashions change and PMSs become less fashionable, these countries are always likely to have some form of PMS in place.

Perhaps related to the presence of legal pressures, is the fact that, in each of the above countries, diversity issues are growing more important. That is, even if certain practices might not be illegal, it is important for PMSs to overcome the differences found in increasingly diverse workforces (also see Vance and Paik, 2006). Finally, both sets of pressures make it more important to be concerned with issues of rater bias. That is, once there are clearly identifiable sub-groups in the population, there is the potential for bias toward the "out-group," whoever that may be in a given country. This tendency, of course, reinforces the need for legal checkpoints, and also leads to a need to train raters where it is possible to help them avoid bias and develop employees. Thus, it would seem that legal concerns and potential bias are the major issues that companies must deal with when implementing PMSs in countries such as these, which have had considerable experience with the field of PM.

It would also seem that the transfer of knowledge about PMSs across these countries would be relatively easy, given the individualistic nature of the countries (Hofstede, 1993). That is not to suggest that there are no differences across settings, since there are clearly important differences. For example, legal pressures on U.S. firms are confined to equal employment issues, while legal pressures on firms in Europe and the U.K. are also concerned with wealth re-distribution and the funding of social welfare programs. Furthermore, employees in those countries have much better established rights than do U.S. employees. Nonetheless, as we note above, the relatively individualistic nature of these cultures means that it is easier to get the kind of variance in appraisals needed for merit pay, and that rewards based on individual performance are more likely to be acceptable. In addition, hierarchical relations in these countries tend to be similar and similarities in their cultures also suggest that motivational processes should be similar across the countries.

PMSs in China (Cooke), South Korea (Yang and Rowley), and Japan (Morishima) share certain characteristics because all are functioning in collectivist cultures. But the differences in the levels of economic development result in few similarities in terms of what actually happens in PM. The Chinese system is much less formal, and the norms regarding "face" set the systems here apart from that of their neighbors. Of course, as suggested in the chapter, China is experiencing a period of tremendous economic growth, and it seems reasonable to expect that, over the next few years, the Chinese systems of PM will begin to look more and more like western systems. Specifically, the Chinese system is likely to evolve closer to the present state of affairs in Korea. That is, merit is likely to become a more important factor, relative to seniority, and individual merit and performance are likely to become even more important. In fact, it would seem as though, as China moves toward Korea in terms of PMSs, Korea is moving more toward Japan. The Japanese economic development is the most mature in the region and, although there are elements of traditional culture that are still present, the Japanese systems of PM have largely become very much like those in western countries.

In fact, it would seem as though economic maturity is a more important determinant of PMSs than is culture. As the economic systems of countries grow and become more sophisticated, the evidence would suggest that the PMSs become more focused on output, merit and individual performance, regardless of the country's specific cultural norms that might run counter to these trends (see, e.g., Vance and Paik, 2006). Thus, over the next ten years or so, we might expect to see the Korean system look very much like the PMS in present-day Japan, while the Japanese system will likely look even more like the systems in Western Europe, the U.S., and Australia. The Chinese PMSs may develop a bit more slowly, but we would expect them to look like those in present-day Korea over the next few years as well.

The situation in Turkey (Aycan and Yavuz) is also one in transition, but the transition seems to be slower than in the Asian countries we have just discussed. Personal relationships and subjective evaluations may take longer to disappear from Turkey than in some other countries, primarily because there are still strong cultural norms to retain these practices. It is interesting to note that although modern Turkey is a secular society, it is the only country represented in this volume that has come out of the tradition of Islam. These traditions have produced some friction in Turkey concerning the extent to which the country should remain strongly secular, and the resolution of this friction will probably be a strong determinant of the rate of economic growth in the country.

Developments in Mexico (Davila and Elvira) would seem to parallel those in Turkey although, of course, the cultures are very different. In Mexico, issues surrounding the social distance (or power distance) between supervisors and subordinates appear to be important for what little there exists in the way of PMSs. Overall, the situation seems to be one where everyone recognizes the need for PM, but few real examples or suggestions are available. Given the geographic proximity of the United States, one would expect that U.S.-based systems will be introduced – once the economy is ready for more serious PMSs.

Finally, India (Sharma, Budhwar and Varma) may be in the most unique situation of all the countries covered in this volume. Although India may technically be a collectivist society, it has also been strongly influenced by the British and their more individualistic culture. This background has been coupled with a huge explosion in foreign investment in India, and a huge wave of foreign innovations. As a result, PMSs, many of them adapted from western models, have become much more widespread and accepted in India. But the large number of small, family-owned businesses will also have to adapt to these changes over the coming years. However, if the current rate of globalization in India continues, India should find itself moving closer and closer to western PMSs (also see Björkman and Budhwar, 2007).

Thus, one conclusion that would seem reasonable from these various chapters is that, as a country becomes more economically mature, PMSs tend to move more closely toward the type of systems we find in the U.S. and Western Europe. It would seem reasonable to suggest that more particularistic systems are developed based on the culture of the country, but as a country's economic system becomes more complex and the country begins to compete on a global basis, the more basic needs of increasing productivity and measuring outcomes take over, and the PMS becomes less about the country's specific culture.

Since most of the world's MNEs are headquartered in North America or Western Europe (or Australia), such a trend would seem to be quite welcome. It would suggest that these firms only need to wait until economic development increases and then they can implement PMSs that are similar to those they have in their home countries. But that view is too simplistic. Instead, we believe that this pattern of findings really suggests that MNEs will face more pressure to implement uniform PMSs around the world and to ensure that those systems respect local cultures and customs. Therefore, even if the world moves to similar models for PA in the long term, in the short and intermediate terms there will still be a need to deal with collectivism, deference to seniority and issues of "face" while, at the same time, gradually introducing more western PMSs.

Where do we go from here?

The practice of PM will proceed in the way described in the various chapters in this volume, and, as noted above, this apparently will involve some shift toward western ideas about PA.

But what of future research in this area – especially the research dealing with PM in a global setting? These chapters suggest a number of research ideas that can contribute to our understanding of decision-making processes and also contribute to future implementation of PMSs.

The model proposed by Murphy and DeNisi clearly distinguishes between judgments a rater might make about an employee's performance, and the ratings that rater might give (also see Murphy and Cleveland, 1995 for a further discussion of this issue). The difference between judgments and ratings are due to a number of factors, but one of them certainly is bias. It is interesting to note that several chapters describing systems in somewhat less economically developed countries also discussed issues of bias and favoritism in ratings. Are biases based on social class and family ties more acceptable in these countries? The concept of *guanxi* in China certainly has counterparts in Latin America and possibly in India as well. That is, it may be quite easily accepted that raters should show favoritism toward family members in those settings. These countries also lack legal systems that might make such biases illegal, and so perhaps the question of bias in appraisals in these countries is less critical for now. Nonetheless, it would be interesting to learn how biases operate in these settings and how people react to those biases. There is a good chance that these processes will look different than they do in the U.S. or in Western Europe, but we really don't know. This information will become extremely important when the economies in those countries develop to the point that they can no longer afford this type of bias, and organizations must seek ways to eliminate it. Understanding the nature of bias in those cultures will provide invaluable information about the best ways to eliminate it.

Another important issue for future research concerns the effectiveness of feedback. Recent work in this area suggests that feedback interventions don't always work the way we plan (e.g. Kluger and DeNisi, 1996; most of the work cited in this paper was done in U.S. or Western European settings). A critical part of any PMS must be the provision of feedback to employees, but how to provide that feedback to ensure it is effective in different countries around the world? For example, would negative feedback be absolutely devastating in China, where maintaining "face" is so important? Do status differences that might exist between managers and subordinates in a country such as Mexico mean that feedback will trigger the wrong responses by subordinates, leading them to become defensive rather than leading them to improve their performance?

One of the more important findings in the Kluger and DeNisi (1996) paper was that, overall, feedback interventions are less effective than had been previously believed. This finding was surprising because there had been relatively few studies that actually evaluated the effectiveness of feedback interventions – but that was considering U.S. and western literature only. Is feedback ever effective in China or Korea? Is it more effective? Does goal setting work in Turkey? The point is that we really don't know much about the effectiveness of most PM interventions in non-U.S. settings. If some of the countries profiled in this volume begin to adopt U.S. and Western European models, they will be likely to do so without an independent evaluation of the effectiveness in each country. The fact that interventions such as feedback seem to be less effective than we had believed makes it even more critical that these interventions be evaluated in the other countries around the world where PMSs will become more formal over the next few years.

One specific type of feedback system – 360-degree feedback – is especially suspect in this global context. As noted in several chapters, not all countries accept peer evaluations, and the more hierarchical a society is, the less likely it is for that society to accept upward feedback. As with feedback in general, there is really little formal research evaluating the effectiveness of multisource feedback in U.S. settings. Once we leave U.S. or Western European settings we have absolutely no idea as to whether such programs might be effective or destructive. Thus, for all the various motivational components that are often part of PMSs, it is critical that we conduct research to determine if there are any unanticipated effects of these programs when we use them in settings where the cultural norms and values are much different from those where the programs were first proposed.

This brings us to a reasonable note upon which to end this chapter. The various chapters presented in this volume make it clear that, although there are clearly differences in the nature and extent of PMSs around the world, things seem to be moving in a certain direction. It would appear that, as economic and business systems become more complex, countries are moving more toward the type of PMSs that have been developed in the U.S. and Western Europe (perhaps some kind of "best-practice" mode). This may reflect some belief that these systems are better developed and more attuned with accountability and individual performance, or it may simply reflect a cultural norm that western things are better – witness the number of McDonald's and Starbucks all over the world .

In either case, these systems should not be adopted uncritically. It is very important that HR experts in the various countries develop enough understanding of U.S.-based PMSs to appreciate why they work when they do, and why they might not work in every setting. Furthermore, it is even more important that research determines how well these U.S.-based systems can be assimilated into cultures that are very different from that of the U.S. or Western Europe. As noted above, PM interventions developed in the U.S. have not always been critically evaluated in the U.S. – their introduction in Turkey or India or China could potentially be disastrous. Interventions designed to improve performance are important in all settings, and the chapters in this volume seem to indicate that there is a growing awareness of this fact. As more countries begin to introduce more PM techniques, then what is important is that they not blindly copy something that has worked somewhere else. Such a strategy might result in less effective PMSs, or it might actually result in systems that hurt productivity and performance.

Finally, visitors to India will find that the menu at McDonalds does not include its classic hamburger – instead the chain sells vegetable burgers. This "Indianization" of the hamburger seems to be exactly the approach we need in the area of PM. As countries develop more sophisticated systems they should learn from other countries, but also make sure that, where needed, they modify existing programs to fit with local "tastes."

References

Björkman, I. (2004) Transfer of HRM to MNC affiliates in Asia-Pacific, in P. Budhwar (ed.) *Managing Human Resources in Asia-Pacific*, London: Routledge, pp. 253–67.

Björkman, I. and Budhwar, P. (2007) When in Rome . . .? Human resource management and the performance of foreign firms operating in India, *Employee Relations* 29(6): 595–610.

Gopalan, S. and Stahl, A. (1998) Application of American management theories and practices to the Indian business environment: understanding the impact of national culture, *American Business Review* 16(2): 30–41.

Hofstede, G. (1993) Cultural constraints in management theories, *Academy of Management Executive* 7(1): 81–94.

Kluger, A. N. and DeNisi, A. S. (1996) The effects of feedback interventions on performance: historical review, meta-analysis, a preliminary feedback intervention theory, *Psychological Bulletin* 119: 254–84.

Murphy, K. R. and Cleveland, J. N. (1995) *Understanding Performance Appraisal: Social, Organizational, and Goal-based Perspectives*, Thousand Oaks, CA: Sage.

Naylor, J. C., Pritchard, R. D. and Ilgen, D. R. (1980) *A Theory of Behavior in Organizations*, New York: Academic Press.

Pritchard, R. D., Jones, S. D., Roth, P. L., Stuebing, K. K. and Ekeberg, S. E. (1989) The evaluation of an integrated approach to measuring organizational productivity, *Personnel Psychology* 42: 69–115.

Vance, C. M. and Paik, Y. (2006) *Managing a Global Workforce*, New York: M. E. Sharpe.

Index